INSIGHT GUIDES

*The world's largest collection of visual travel guides*

# HOLLAND

Edited by Christopher Catling

Editorial Director: Brian Bell

APA PUBLICATIONS

Part of the Langenscheidt Publishing Group

## INSIGHT GUIDES
# HOLLAND

**CONTACTING THE EDITORS:** Although every effort is made to provide accurate information in this publication, we live in a fast-changing world and would appreciate it if readers would call our attention to any errors or outdated information that may occur by writing to us at Apa Publications,
P.O. Box 7910, London SE1 1WE, England.
Fax: (44) 171-403 0290.
e-mail: insight@apaguide.demon.co.uk.

*First Edition 1991*
*Third Edition 1999*

*Distributed in the United States by*
**Langenscheidt Publishers Inc.**
46–35 54th Road
Maspeth, NY 11378
Fax: (718) 784 0640

*Distributed in the UK & Ireland by*
**GeoCenter International Ltd**
The Viables Centre, Harrow Way
Basingstoke, Hampshire RG22 4BJ
Fax: (44) 1256-817988

*Distributed in Australia & New Zealand by*
**Hema Maps Pty. Ltd**
24 Allgas Street, Slacks Creek 4127
Brisbane, Australia
Tel: (61) 7 3290 0322
Fax: (61) 7 3290 0478

*Worldwide distribution enquiries:*
**APA Publications GmbH & Co. Verlag KG**
(Singapore branch)
38 Joo Koon Road, Singapore 628990
Tel: 65-8651600
Fax: 65-8616438

*Printed in Singapore by*
**Insight Print Services (Pte) Ltd**
38 Joo Koon Road
Singapore 628990
Fax: 65-8616438

# Discovery CHANNEL®

This guidebook combines the interests and enthusiasms of two of the world's best known information providers: Insight Guides, whose range of titles has set the standard for visual travel guides since 1970, and Discovery Channel, the world's premier source of nonfiction television programming.

The editors of Insight Guides provide both practical advice and general understanding about a destination's history, culture, institutions and people. Discovery Channel and its Web site, www.discovery.com, help millions of viewers explore their world from the comfort of their own home and also encourage them to explore it firsthand.

The team of writers and photographers who worked on this book all shared one basic commitment: to reveal the extraordinary diversity of this compact country and to encourage readers to discover Holland's attractions for themselves.

Editor **Christopher Catling** already knew Amsterdam, Rotterdam and The Hague when he took on the task, having reported on them from a business traveller's angle for *The Economist City Travel Guide to Europe*. His own appreciation of the riches that lie beyond these three cities grew as he travelled through Holland, briefing authors and photographers.

One of the first writers he recruited was **Derek Blyth**, whose *American Express Pocket Guide to Amsterdam* had first inspired Catling to visit Holland. Blyth has also written acclaimed books on Maastricht, Flemish Cities and Berlin.

Fellow writer **Lisa Gerard-Sharp** had lived in Brussels for three years, but says she found Flemish culture more dynamic than that of the French-speaking Belgians – so it was a natural progression for her to use Flanders as a springboard for an exploration of the southern provinces, and later the rest of the country. Her contributions to this guide draw on her fascination with the contrasts between urban and provincial life and between the values of the Protestant north and the Catholic south. Gerard-Sharp is a magazine editor,

*Catling*

*Blyth*

*Gerard-Sharp*

*Harper*

*Gray*

McDonald

broadcaster, book reviewer, travel writer and budding fiction writer.

**Tim Harper** is an American journalist whose articles on European business and politics have appeared in the *International Herald Tribune*, *Time*, the *Washington Post* and the *Chicago Tribune*, amongst other leading US newspapers. His contributions to this book draw on his professional and personal interests. On the professional front, he has reported on Dutch social experiments – everything from housing policy to aid for prostitutes, drug addiction to euthanasia. His pieces on the northern provinces of Groningen and Friesland are based on memories of family holidays exploring waterways and islands by antique schooner.

**Michael Gray** first visited Holland on a round-the-world trip from his native Minnesota and has been back many times since as a reporter for US newspapers. As a journalist, he finds that the Dutch are a joy to work with, straightforward and very quotable. For this guide, he has written about the physical formation of the land now known as The Netherlands, including the controversy that surrounds further land reclamation. He has also investigated one of the country's major sources of income – the production of bulbs, plants and cut flowers.

**Joan Corcoran-Lonis** is known to readers of London's *Daily Telegraph* as the paper's Hague-based reporter, writing under the byline Joan Clements. She came to the country to start an English-language magazine and stayed. In this book, she writes about some of the less well-known provinces, on the traumatic events of World War II and the related battlefields and war graves.

**George McDonald** is a Brussels-based journalist who lived in Amsterdam as deputy editor of the KLM in-flight magazine, *Holland Herald*, before becoming editor of Sabena's in-flight magazine, *Sphere*. Brussels is not far away from the Dutch province of Zeeland, which McDonald visits whenever he needs a breath of fresh air to remind him of his native Scotland and which he writes about here.

**Yvonne Newman** got to know Holland through an art history degree. As she visited the country's museums and galleries, she was captivated by the richness and splendours of the 17th-century Golden Age. Newman, who lectures in communications skills, contributed the features on art and architecture and on food, and compiled much of the Travel Tips section.

This guide contains examples of the work of numerous photographers, each of whom brings to its pages a sense of place and of the character of the Dutch people.

A major contributor, **Eddy Posthuma de Boer**, lives and exhibits his work in his native Amsterdam. He specialises in travel photography, contributing to the KLM and Sabena in-flight magazines. **Paul van Riel** began his photographic career covering jazz events in Holland for daily newspapers and music magazines, and has since had great success covering fashion shows around the world. **Dirk Buwalda**, who began his career as an editorial photographer working in London and New York, says he is fascinated by extremes and enjoys taking pictures in countries where people have to pit their wits against a harsh environment. **George Wright**, a freelance photographer living in Dorset, England, works internationally for magazine and book publishers. He particularly admires Amsterdam for its vitality and unconventional attitude to life.

Other photographs have come from regular Apa contributors: **Christine Osborne**, who both writes and takes photographs for her own books; **Lyle Lawson**, who runs her own travel firm taking amateur photographers to unusual locations, as well as finding time to contribute to many Insight Guides as author, editor and photographer; and **Bodo Bondzio**, a Cologne-based photographer who specialises in capturing people on film.

This edition of *Insight Guide: Holland* was updated by travel writer **Joan Gannij**, who lives and works in Amsterdam, and copy-edited by **Jane Ladle**.

# CONTENTS

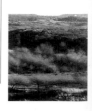

## Maps

# THE DUTCH

For travellers who revel in meeting people and absorbing different cultures, the Netherlands is a land for learning. Beyond the usual tourist refrains – "Oh, look at that. Isn't it beautiful?" – visitors to the Netherlands marvel at the achievement of building a nation on lands reclaimed from the sea, at the diversity of Dutch culture and the contrast between the modern cities of Rotterdam and Eindhoven, ancient towns like Haarlem and Delft and the wild landscapes of the islands and the north.

The Dutch are self-effacing, and often start sentences with: "We're only a small nation…" But make no mistake, the Netherlands has a long and varied history, and the Dutch are proud of it. Few other countries, let alone such a small one, can claim a period comparable to the 17th-century Golden Age when Holland and its allied provinces dominated European culture and commerce. Along the way, the Dutch created many of the concepts of modern humanism, including freedom of religion and freedom of the press, concepts that remain the ideals for modern democratic society.

On top of everything else, the Dutch have made their country one of the most accommodating in the world for foreign visitors, not least in providing the best duty-free airport shopping in Europe and an excellent national train system. Almost everyone speaks English, usually fluently, along with several other languages. Accommodation – from camp sites to hotels – is abundant in every price range. Dutch cities and towns seem deliberately designed with the idea of giving pleasure. The lager is cold, the pea soup and casseroles hot.

The Dutch themselves are an enigmatic people, full of apparent contradictions that they either reconcile with a shrug or not at all. Beyond what seems to be exterior gruffness, most Dutch are cordial, frank-speaking people. Many are willing to talk about themselves, their country, your country and the rest of the world – from wizened old farmers to slick young creative types, from devoutly tidy country folk to hip-talking dopers in the red light districts.

Just when most visitors think they have finally figured out the Netherlands, they go to another part of the country and are forced to recalculate their equations. In all its forms, from the crowded urban west ("Randstad") to the farms of the north and the wilds of the islands, everything about the Netherlands and the Dutch does eventually make sense if you are willing to look and listen long enough.

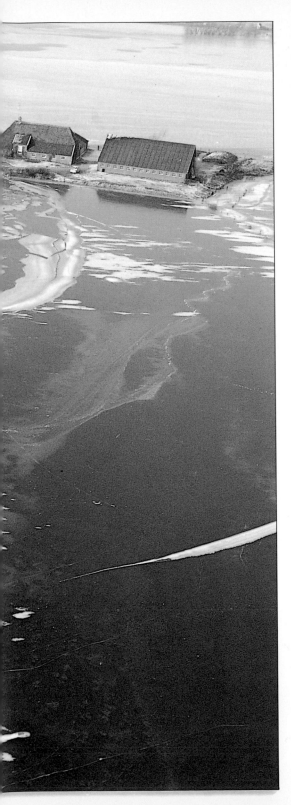

## RECLAIMED FROM THE SEA

The pagan settlers who first colonised the western shores of the present-day Netherlands must have eked out a wretched existence even by Dark Age standards. If they escaped starvation or drowning, both as a result of frequent floods, the marauding Vikings used them to pack their slave holds.

A millennium earlier, inland inhabitants of the dunes and bogs survived through marginal farming and livestock rearing. The tribal warfare that followed the collapse of the Roman Empire forced many to move seaward for a more peaceful existence.

Pushed to what are now the provinces of Groningen and Friesland, in the north of the Netherlands, these people had to find a way to live with the tides. They could not stop the water, so the only choice was to raise the land. Mounds were constructed, anchored by long stakes driven into the mud flats. Seaweed and tidal debris was used to fill in around the stakes, which were then covered with layers of muddy clay soil. Huts were built on top of the hillocks and the finished product, many of which are still visible today, were called *terpen*.

**New lands:** Until the early 11th century AD, the amount of farmable land in the Netherlands was little more than half of its current area. Over the centuries, dykes, canals, polders, windmills and ultimately monstrous tidal barriers have been used to reclaim thousands of square miles. Without them the waves would be lapping at Utrecht and half the country – 7,000 sq. miles (18,000 sq. km) and more than 60 percent of its population – would either be underwater or subject to frequent flooding.

Inhabitants of the Netherlands began building small dykes (embankments) to protect their homes, farms and cattle about AD 700. As the competition for farmland intensified, marshes and swampy lakes were surrounded by dykes and canals and drained. In these simpler times, drainage was often a simple matter of opening a canal sluice gate at low tide and letting the water flow out into the river or sea.

**Dykes:** The first major sea dyke was not

**Left,** Flooding of the River IJssel, near Doesburg.

constructed in the Netherlands until 1320. Then, the residents of Schardam, northwest of Amsterdam, built an embankment across the Beemster basin to prevent the Zuiderzee (today the IJsselmeer) from flooding their lands. Again in 1380, in the same region, local farmers built a dyke to separate the Purmer lake from the Zuiderzee at Monnickendam. This, and other similar dykes, were necessary, because the soft, marshy land sank below sea level once it was drained. The seawater effectively swallowed the freshwater lake and the large bog that lay northeast of Amsterdam, turning the entire area into a shallow, southern bay for the North Sea.

the drying process, prevent the growth of persistent weeds and help extract the salt from the soil.

**Conversion:** The drying process takes several years, and in primitive times was rarely a complete success. Today, once this five-year process is complete, roads, water, electricity and other infrastructural services have to be provided. During this period the government controls the agricultural conversion process before turning the land over to selected farmers a few years later.

Land reclamation work gathered pace during the 14th and 15th centuries, when many towns, like Amsterdam, were beginning to grow. Despite their expertise as engineers,

**Polder:** By dyking low-lying areas, polders were created. The word *polder* comes from the old Germanic word *pol*, meaning the stakes that were used to hold together the dykes, dams and mounds. Now the term is used to describe reclaimed land.

Even with 20th-century drainage and pumping methods, land reclamation methods have changed little in six centuries. After the construction of dykes and drainage canals, the resulting land that emerges after a year or so is still a swampy morass. Many more shallow run-off ditches have to be dug, today using specially designed machines. The land is then seeded with grasses, to help

the Dutch still faced an uphill battle against the forces of nature. Worse still, some people were digging the land out from under their feet at the same time that Herculean efforts were being made to reclaim other parts. There not being many trees in such a watery landscape, peat was the most common form of fuel and peat extraction left many areas a sterile, sandy desert.

Despite great effort, flooding was never completely controlled. The dykes and canals merely provided breathing space between the seasonal high tides, and were frequently breached by the surge of the angry sea. Nevertheless, they provided some protection, and a measure of how important they were to the community at this time can be glimpsed from the cruel and unusual penalty for damaging a dyke. The guilty party would have his right hand amputated and then be banished from the village.

**Disasters:** Until the 1950s, flood tides continued to have a devastating effect. Records as far back as 1287 indicate that great floods have occurred practically every century since. In 1404, an estimated 50,000 people drowned from the floods. Seventeen years later the St Elizabeth's Day flood was even worse. The most destructive flood ever recorded, in terms of loss of life and high water, was the All Hallow's Eve flood of 1570. Granite blocks

there is no truth to the apocryphal tale about the boy who saved all of Holland by sticking his finger in a leaky dyke, even though there is a symbolic statue of him at Spaarndam. There was, however, a captain who saw a dyke near Rotterdam about to be breached during the severe storm of 1953. At great risk to himself, and the ruin of his boat, he steered the vessel into the waters rushing over the dam. At the precise moment, he turned his vessel sideways so that the waters swept him broadside on to the dam, where his ship perfectly plugged the fast-growing gap.

Permanent and substantial land reclamation did not finally emerge in the Netherlands until the late 16th century with the

protecting dykes were tossed aside like driftwood and entire houses swept out to sea. The worst flood in the 20th century was in 1953, when more than 1,800 people drowned and nearly 100,000 people were left homeless in southwestern Holland. The flood level measured 12½ ft (3.8 metres) at the Hook of Holland; estimates place the 1570 flood at over 16½ ft (5 metres).

Such disastrous inundations have created a rich folklore of stories involving heroic deeds committed against all the odds. Sadly,

conversion of the windmill into a windpump. Like the thousands of windmills around the world, the ones in Holland were originally used for milling grain. Only after centuries of use was it realised that wind power could be used to drive a scoop-wheel, fitted with buckets, capable of moving the amounts of water necessary for draining the polders in the Zuiderzee basin.

The great leap forward came with the invention of a windmill whose top could be rotated along an upper track. Until that time the sail cant was fixed and water pumping was sporadic, depending on the direction of the wind. Now the sail could be rotated to face the wind and water could be scooped out constantly and more efficiently. Around 1620, using a series of some 20 windmills, the polders at Beemster, Purmer and Wormer, first created three centuries earlier, were finally drained well enough to allow arable farming.

**Drainage:** Mills, then and now, worked by scooping water from the drainage ditch and emptying it into a larger canal several feet higher up. To be effective on the large polders, windmills had to be used in series, each one raising the drainage water to a higher level. Every polder, whether it was constructed in 1590 or 1990, has a network of drainage ditches that flow into progressively

themselves and soon earned large profits for the owners.

Around 1700 another disaster threatened Holland, potentially as devastating as any flood. The wooden dykes became infested with an aquatic termite known as shipworm. As soon as residents repaired the dykes with new piles and planking the new pieces were immediately infected. Foreign newspapers solemnly forecast the doom of Amsterdam. Begged, borrowed and imported stone was the initial solution and gradually new materials, including metal, concrete and even plastic, were developed for dyke building.

Land reclamation efforts ceased during the early 18th century, when the Netherlands

wider and deeper canals, and ultimately into the ring canal that surrounds the polder. From there the water can be drained into the sea or into a freshwater reservoir. Many such reservoirs can be found around Amsterdam where they are used for recreation and for irrigation in times of drought.

Realising the potential for land reclamation, and greater earnings, windmills proved to be a popular investment with many Dutch landlords. More land meant more tenants and these same tenant farmers were obliged, under what were called "Soke rights", to grind the grain they grew using the landowner's mill. Thus the mills very rapidly paid for

was continuously at war with England and France, and work did not begin again in earnest until the mid-1850s when steam, and later diesel engines, were used to power the pumps. Today only about 1,000 windmills still exist, many as private homes or museums. A handful are still in working order.

The first major area to be reclaimed using the steam-powered pumps was the vast Haarlemmermeer, beginning in 1852. The rehabilitation of this huge swamp, to the west of Amsterdam, created new road and rail connections and more farmland. Today, Schiphol airport and all its surrounding high-tech, printing and distribution businesses are located on the former marsh, 13 ft (4.5 metres) below sea level.

**Sea access:** The North Sea Canal, dug in 1876, was another significant engineering feat that reinvigorated Amsterdam and the country as a whole. Never anything more than an oversized mud flat, the Zuiderzee was already too shallow for large ships by the mid-18th century. With the completion of the canal, deep-draught ships could enter Amsterdam harbour once again, and the canal locks have been enlarged several times since then. The drainage capacity of the canal, which runs west from Amsterdam straight to the North Sea, also allowed for more large polders to be drained behind the

**Zuiderzee Dam:** This monumental project began with the draining of the 50,000-acre (20,000-hectare) Wieringermeer polder and the construction of the Afsluitdijk. This 20-mile (32-km) long, 300-ft (90-metre) wide dyke runs across the Zuiderzee, effectively cutting off the tidal basin from the sea. It was completed in 1932, and the old sea, now a freshwater lake, has been known as the IJsselmeer ever since.

This unique project took many years to complete. An artificial island and harbour, built from concrete caissons and dredgings, was created at the halfway point so that the construction, involving some 500 boats and more than 80 tugboats, could begin from

shoreline dunes. Even Amsterdam Centraal Station, finished in 1899, is built on a series of artificial islands located in the old harbour at the mouth of the Amstel River.

Plans for protecting Amsterdam further, by enclosing and draining parts of the Zuiderzee, had been around ever since an engineer named Hendrik Stevin first proposed a scheme in 1667. Others flirted with the notion in subsequent centuries, but work did not actually begin until after the devastating flood of 1916.

**Left,** canal building in the 1930s. **Right,** modern dyke construction in progress.

both directions at once. Huge willow "mattresses" were laid down first so that subsequent layers of stone and pilings would not sink into the sea bed.

At first building in the shallow water progressed smoothly enough. But as the gap between the two arms of the dyke grew narrower, the apparently calm tidal pond began to cut a deep channel into the sea bed as the water rushed to escape through the increasingly smaller opening. By the time the gap had narrowed to 45 ft (14 metres), the engineers began to have serious doubts about the project's feasibility.

In the end, they were forced to complete

the final section in a matter of hours, racing against time, the incoming tide and an approaching storm. A barrier of sorts was quickly built about 45 ft (14 metres) from the opening to slow the rushing water. This enabled willow mattresses and stones to be positioned properly in order to complete the dyke. Now, at the central point of the barrier, large sluice gates and locks permit the passage of ships and marine life, especially the young migratory eels.

**Flevoland province:** Once this first low-maintenance dyke was finished, more than 700 sq. miles (1,800 km) of polders were developed, some of them completed only in the 1980s. Two of the largest are the

tidal flats and flood-prone estuaries where the Rhine (Rijn), Maas, IJssel, Waal and Scheldt (Schelde) rivers empty into the North Sea. The project also makes possible a reliable network of road and rail links between Amsterdam, Rotterdam and The Hague to the north, and to Brussels and all points south.

When the project was begun, few could have imagined the scale of the problems that would be encountered. Artificial islands had to be built; rivers diverted or dammed. The project dwarfed all previous attempts at flood control. For example, a short stretch of dam at Haringvliet proved to need 65 massive pilings, as much as 175 ft (53 metres) deep.

Noordoostpolder and the new province of Flevoland, located just east of Amsterdam. The new town of Lelystad, Flevoland's provincial capital, is named after the engineer I.C. Lely who designed the whole Zuiderzee reclamation project back at the beginning of the 20th century.

**Compromise:** After the devastating storm of 1953, which flooded 460,000 acres (185,000 hectares) in the southwest Netherlands, the government embarked on another massive scheme: the Delta Plan took 32 years and 12 billion guilders (£4 billion/ US$6.5 billion) to complete. This massive tidal barrier seals off 430 miles (700 km) of

The steel sluice gates are 40 ft (12 metres) high and wide, and weigh 535 tons (543 tonnes). Huge engines are required to open and close them.

Environmental concerns became a serious and unforeseen stumbling block, particularly in the large estuary between Noord-Beveland and Schouwen-Duiveland where a solid dam had been planned. Fishermen, reinforced by the formidable Dutch environmental lobby, warned against the resulting loss of commercial oyster, mussel and lobster beds and the consequences of swamping miles of ecologically rich salt marshes. After an eight-year delay, the government finally reached agreement on a smaller, movable barrier with emergency gates that would permit a degree of tidal flow. The marshes shrunk in extent from 40,000 acres (16,200 hectares) to a mere 1,500 (600) but the submerged mudflats, crucial for birds and fish, were only reduced by one-third in the area.

One potential super project remains on the drawing board for the 21st century – to provide further protection for the IJsselmeer and its many polder farms and communities, not to mention Amsterdam. The government hopes to link up the Frisian Islands in the northeastern tip of the country by means of a series of dykes. Engineers reported that it was only by sheer luck that the Afsluitdijk

recreational and general opposition groups has managed to persuade the government to put off the project rather than risk damaging the extremely fragile ecology of this protected area.

**No more polder:** Further reclamation in the IJsselmeer, under a scheme known as the Markerwaard project, has also been halted; loud opposition to the destruction of this popular sailing reservoir has been heeded. Government planners were also uncertain what effect the creation of new polders would have on existing ones; the water table has to be maintained or the enclosed farmland may sink. In Amsterdam, if the water table falls, the wooden foundation pilings, on which the

across the IJsselmeer did not collapse during the 1953 flood.

This project would cut off the Waddenzee (the waters that separate the Frisian Islands from the mainland) from the North Sea, creating recreational freshwater reservoirs and, more importantly, preventing further saltwater infiltration into scarce ground water and polderised farmland. For now, however, this project is being kept on permanent hold. A strong coalition of environmental,

**Left**, construction of the Oosterschelde Storm-Surge Barrier. **Right**, visitors to the Delta Expo, in Zeeland, study a model of the Delta Works.

city's older buildings stand, will become exposed and eventually rot.

Lobbyists have begun to ask whether new land is now needed at all. Why does the country go to such lengths and expense to create new polder when simple flood protection might be enough? The basic answer is that there is no serious alternative. In the past decade some oil reserves have been discovered offshore, but overall the Netherlands has precious little in the way of natural resources to exploit. This small country – the most densely populated in Europe – has no choice except to make an increased use of all the land available for agriculture.

JAARLYKSE OMMEGANK DER LEPROOZEN. OP

OPPERTIES MAANDAC OPGEHOUDE int JAAR 160

# DECISIVE DATES

**circa 150 BC:** The Romans establish a fort at Noulogmagus (Nijmegen) and continue to use the baths at Maastricht for their recreation.

**69 AD:** The Batavi tribe rebels against Roman rule, their efforts fail to shift the might of Empire, but they remain a thorn in the legionnaires' flesh.

**4th century AD:** Maastricht's St Servaas is the first bishop in the country.

**circa 700:** Following the Frankish King Pepin II's defeat of the Frisian Radboud, Utrecht becomes a bishopric under the English monk Willibrord, establishing itself as a power centre.

**12th century AD:** First communities of herring fishermen settle on the banks of the Amstel.

**circa 1220:** The first Dam, or sluice, is built to hold back the tidal waters of the Zuiderzee.

**1275:** Floris V, Count of Holland, grants the people of "Amestelledamme" freedom from tolls on their goods passing through the county; the first documentary record of Amsterdam.

**1300:** The Bishop of Utrecht grants Amsterdam official city status.

**1350:** Amsterdam becomes the export centre for local beers and an entrepôt for Baltic grain.

**1452:** Fire destroys much of Amsterdam's timber-and-thatch buildings. New laws ordain that new buildings shall be built of brick and tile.

**1519:** Spain's Charles V is crowned Holy Roman Emperor. Amsterdam, as a result of war, treaties and marriage alliances, is part of the Spanish Empire and nominally Catholic. Amsterdam remains tolerant of Protestant minorities.

**1535:** Anabaptists invade the Town Hall to proclaim the Second Coming. The occupiers are executed and strict Catholicism is reimposed.

**1566:** The Iconoclasm (*Beeldenstorm*). Calvinists protesting at the lack of religious freedom storm many of Amsterdam's churches. As a result they are given a church of their own.

**1567:** Philip II of Spain sends the tyrannical Duke of Alva to restore Catholic control. Many Protestants are executed and others flee to England.

**1568:** The low countries revolt against Spanish rule, launching the 80 years' war.

**1572:** The Dutch Revolt against Spanish rule begins in earnest, led by William of Orange.

**1574:** Relief of Leiden by Dutch troops following a 131-day siege by the Spanish. William of Orange rewards the tenacious Leidenaars by giving them a university, the oldest in the Netherlands.

**1576:** Amsterdam, loyal to Philip II, is besieged by Prince William's troops.

**1578:** Amsterdam capitulates to Prince William. Protestant exiles return to the city. Calvinists take over all the churches and the reins of government in a peaceful revolution known as the Alteration (*Alteratie*).

**1579:** The seven northern provinces of the Netherlands sign the Treaty of Utrecht providing for mutual assistance in the event of attack but otherwise allowing for self-determination. The southern provinces remain under Spanish Catholic control and Protestant refugees from Antwerp, Amsterdam's main trade rival, seek asylum in Amsterdam, laying the foundations for the city's Golden Age.

**1595–97:** Dutch ships sail east via the Cape of Good Hope and reach the Indonesian archipelago.

**1602:** The Dutch East Indies Company is set up to co-ordinate trade between the northern provinces and the lands east of the Cape.

**1609:** The Bank of Amsterdam is formed, placing the city at the forefront of European finance. Hendrik Staets draws up the plan for Amsterdam's Grachtengordel, the three concentric canals ringing the city (work starts in 1613).

**1618–19:** At the Synod of Dordrecht held in Dordrecht, hardline Calvinists reject the more moderate notions of the Remonstrant movement and Catholicism is outlawed, although a blind eye is turned to clandestine worship.

**1621:** The Dutch West Indies Company is founded with a monopoly on trade with the Americas and West Africa.

**1626:** Peter Minuit "purchases" the island of Manhattan and founds the colony of New Amsterdam (taken by the English and renamed New York in 1664).

**1632:** The Atheneum Illustre, forerunner of Amsterdam University, is founded.

**1642:** Rembrandt paints *The Night Watch*.

**1648:** Under the Treaty of Münster the seven

northern provinces are recognised as an independent republic. Work begins on Amsterdam's new Town Hall.

**1650:** Amsterdam's population of 220,000, makes it the largest city of the new republic.

**1652:** The first of numerous wars with the English for maritime supremacy.

**1685:** Huguenot refugees flood into Amsterdam after the Revocation of the Edict of Nantes, reversing their rights to freedom of worship.

**1688:** William III of Holland is crowned as King of the United Kingdom, having married the English princess Mary Stuart. William's wars against the French do much to strain the economy of the Netherlands and the Republic begins to decline as a trading nation.

**1697:** Peter the Great visits Amsterdam and the Zaanstreek to study shipbuilding.

**1702:** William III dies without heir. The northern provinces suffer further inroads to their trade when the Austrian Emperor Charles VI sets up a rival East Indies Company based in Ostend.

**1744:** France invades the southern provinces.

**1747:** William IV is elected hereditary head of state of the seven northern provinces ("the United Provinces"), now unified under one leader.

**1751–88:** The United Provinces are torn by civil strife between conservative supporters of the House of Orange and liberal reformers, called Patriots, demanding greater democracy.

**1795:** France invades the north and, in alliance with the Patriots, sets up a National Assembly. The United Provinces are renamed the Batavian Republic after the Batavi tribe that rebelled against Roman rule in AD 69.

**1808:** Napoleon reverses the constitutional reforms and establishes his brother, Louis Napoleon, as King of the Netherlands, with Amsterdam as its capital.

**1813:** After the defeat of Napoleon, William VI is welcomed back from exile.

**1814:** William VI is crowned King of the Netherlands. The Austrians give up their claims to the southern provinces and north and south are united under one monarch.

**1831:** After years of unrest against rule from The Hague, the southern provinces achieve independence and are renamed the Kingdom of Belgium.

**1845:** Riots in Amsterdam calling for democratic reform lead to the establishment of a constitutional committee under J.R. Thorbecke.

**1848:** The new Dutch constitution comes into force, providing for a directly elected parliament.

**1870–76:** A period of rapid developments that lead to the emergence of socialist principles of government; improvements are made in education and public health, the Dutch railway system is established and the new North Sea Canal revives Amsterdam's position as a port.

**1914–20:** The Netherlands remain neutral during World War I, but food shortages lead to strikes, riots and support for the Dutch Communist Party.

**1928:** Amsterdam hosts the Olympic Games.

**1930s:** During the Great Depression, thousands of unemployed work on job creation schemes, including the construction of the Amsterdamse Bos recreation park.

**1940:** Germany, ignoring the Netherlands' neutrality, invades on 10 May.

**1942:** Anne Frank and family go into hiding.

**1945:** After a bitter winter, Amsterdam is finally liberated.

**1949:** Indonesia wins its independence, the first of the former Dutch colonies to do so.

**1963:** Amsterdam's population reaches its peak (868,000). Numerous organised squats are set up in response to housing shortages.

**1965:** The Provos, dedicated to shaking Dutch complacency, win seats on the city council.

**1966:** Protestors disrupt the wedding of Princess Beatrix and Claus von Amsberg.

**1975:** Protest in Amsterdam reaches a peak as police battle with demonstrators over plans to demolish areas of Nieuwmarkt to build the new metro system and the Opera/Town Hall complex.

**1986:** Despite strong opposition, the Muziektheater and Stadhuis complex is completed.

**1989:** The government is brought down because its proposed anti-vehicle laws are not considered tough enough. New laws are aimed at eventually making Amsterdam traffic-free.

**1990:** Van Gogh Centenary exhibition.

**1992:** The proposed far-reaching Maastricht Treaty rocks the European Union, but is finally ratified by all member states in 1993.

**1998:** The Gay Games are held in Amsterdam, attracting thousands of visitors. ∎

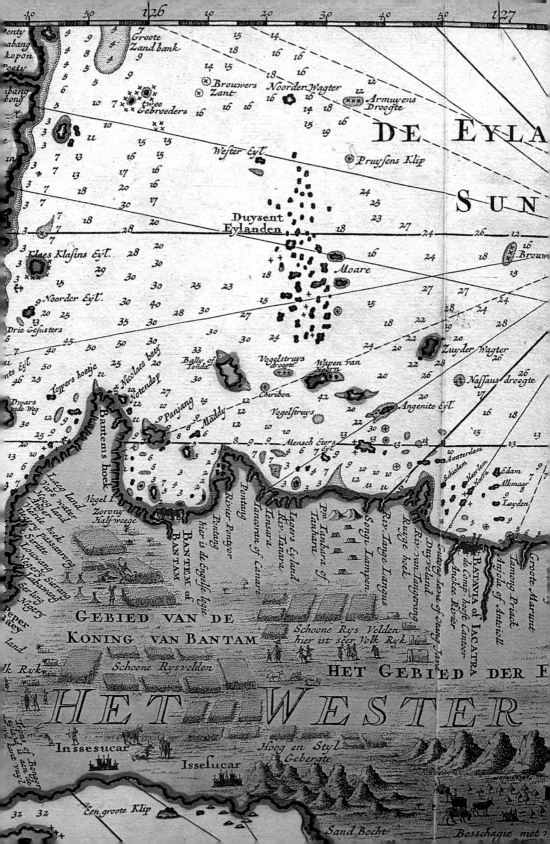

One of the best ways to gauge the impact of the Dutch Empire is to walk into an antique map store virtually anywhere in the world. Ask to see any Dutch-made world maps from the 17th century, and then watch the proprietor's eyes light up at the prospect of dealing with a connoisseur.

For much of the 17th century, when Dutch ships and banks ruled the commercial world, the maps made in Amsterdam were regarded as the best, both for their accuracy (more Dutch ships went more places and brought back more reliable geographic information than anyone else's) and for their beauty. The Dutch cartographers, artists, engravers and printers of the 17th century were to mapmaking what the Dutch Masters were to 17th-century painting – perhaps the greatest collection of talent ever working at one time in any one country. Consequently, many modern-day map collectors and dealers believe that Dutch maps of the Golden Age have never been surpassed for their overall quality. So, when visiting the antique map shop, anyone who isn't planning to spend a fortune on an authentic Blaeu or Jansson map should dampen the proprietor's enthusiasm by adding, "I'm just looking."

**Art flourishes:** The growth of the empire, and the prosperity that it brought to the Netherlands, spawned an extraordinary period of artistic and cultural production. The Golden Age of the Netherlands, noteworthy by any nation's standards, was especially remarkable in that it occurred in a small, sodden country of stubborn people. Many believe the Golden Age of the Netherlands is unparalleled in world history. "There is perhaps no other example of a complete and highly original civilisation springing up in so short a time in so small a territory," one modern historian has written.

The rise of the Dutch Empire was not due solely to the ambition or acumen of the merchant middle class that provided its driving force. Those important qualities were certainly there in abundance in the late 16th century, for the Dutch had already developed a thriving Baltic-based commodities trade in salt, herring, wine, bricks, cereal, wood, iron and copper. Equal in importance to the Dutch merchant-trader's desire to get rich was an external event that triggered their determination to succeed – namely, the 80 years of conflict with Spain that began with a Dutch revolt in 1568.

The conflict with Spain began with the

anti-heresy campaign of the Spanish king, Philip II, who saw it as his duty to wipe out the Protestant movement. Calvinism had rapidly taken root in the northern part of the Netherlands. When Philip outlawed Calvinism, the northern provinces rebelled under the leadership of William the Silent, whom the Dutch regard as the father of their country. The decades of subsequent strife with Spain were the result of religious differences, but there were underlying economic factors. Spain not only wanted to control religion, but also to restrain the Dutch economy; the Dutch reacted in typical hardheaded fashion. They outlawed Catholicism

**Preceding pages:** 18th-century Amsterdam, A. van Nieulandt; sailor's tombstone, Wadden Island; Amsterdam Town Hall, J. A. Beerstraten. **Left, Golden Age map of the Dutch East Indies (Indonesia). Right,** *Man Writing a Letter,* G. Metsu.

and did all they could to expand their economy, including setting up in competition with Spain for trade across the globe.

The 1579 Treaty of Utrecht created the United Provinces, which provided the foundation for the modern Netherlands through the alliance of seven northern provinces – as opposed to the southern provinces, which had remained subject to Spain and eventually became Belgium and Luxembourg. More significantly for the development of the Dutch Empire, the treaty gave the United Provinces effective shipping control of the lower Rhine, and allowed Amsterdam to eclipse its chief rival, Antwerp, as the principal commercial centre of the region.

new routes, establishing new colonies and plundering other countries' trade.

**Financial innovations:** At home, the Dutch became the bankers of Europe, the 17th-century version of the 20th-century Swiss. The Bank of Amsterdam was formed in 1609, and the Amsterdam Stock Exchange followed in 1611. The favourable Dutch interest rates, the establishment of reliable foreign currency exchanges and the willingness of Dutch bankers to loan money not only attracted investors and financiers from across Europe, but also spurred on the ventures of Dutch entrepreneurs.

Born out of religious repression, the United Provinces offered freedom of conscience for

The Dutch sailors and merchants of the late 16th century were skilled, but they were also lucky – lucky that their enemies and competitors were also being distracted by other wars and skirmishes. The English destruction of the Spanish Armada in 1588 is an example. The Dutch were emboldened by the knowledge that many of the cannons that might have challenged them on the other side of the world were now rusting in galleons that lay at the bottom of Plymouth Sound. As Spain's entanglements with England and France continued, more and more Dutch ships undertook ambitious voyages with little fear of reprisal, and set about opening up

all citizens. This meant that Protestants, Jews and other religious refugees poured in from France, Spain, Portugal and other countries. Anyone could emigrate to the United Provinces for the price of eight guilders, the equivalent of about a year's pay for a Dutch sailor. The entry fee was often waived for refugees who showed they had a valuable skill or craft. In addition, the United Provinces boasted a free press – a rarity in those days – that attracted many writers, thinkers and academics. The result was an infusion of many of the best and the brightest of Europe into the United Provinces.

There were some constraints. Speaking

Yiddish was illegal and Catholicism was formally banned, though the authorities allowed Catholics to worship as long as they didn't hold public services. The result was dozens of small private "churches" throughout the provinces, often hidden in secret rooms that were sometimes built into homes and warehouses. A good surviving example can be seen at the Amstelkring Museum, in Amsterdam, a refurbished 17th-century merchant's home that came to be known as "Our Lord in the Attic" because of its Catholic church in the roof. Later, the existence of so many hidden rooms enabled numerous Jews to hide from the Nazis in Dutch homes.

**Merchants and patrons:** The arts and crafts

inspired the beginning of the national pottery industry based in Delft.

Today, the Golden Age is perhaps best remembered for the paintings of Dutch Masters such as Vermeer, Frans Hals and, of course, Rembrandt – an artist, whose work has probably enjoyed a longer period of sustained popularity than any other painter. Quite unlike any other period of great artistic production in Europe, however, the big-name Dutch Masters were surrounded by many so-called "Little Masters", whose paintings are still in demand.

**Inflationary hedge:** The material prosperity of the United Provinces meant that, for the first time in history, ordinary citizens could

flourished in the Netherlands in the 17th century, notably architecture, sculpture, furniture making, silver working and the production of porcelain. Trade provided both the wealth that enabled many Dutch citizens to patronise the arts and the artistic stimulus for new designs. In the early 1600s a Dutch merchant ship returned from an exploratory voyage to China. The ship docked with a hold full of late Ming Dynasty porcelain; the porcelain proved to be so popular that it

**Left**, Battle of Gibraltar, Hendrick Cornelisz Vroom. **Right**, De Veerpont 1653, Salomon J. van Ruysdael.

afford the finer things in life, such as silver salt shakers and original paintings that they themselves had commissioned. Certainly there was a practical side to the Dutch devotion of the arts and crafts: with the economy expanding as rapidly as the empire, quality ceramics and paintings by well-known artists were a sound investment – a Golden Age hedge against inflation.

It must also be said, however, that the Dutch did enjoy art for art's sake – and it was a new, non-classical kind of art. The Dutch School launched realism in painting. Instead of merely being part of the background, landscapes and seascapes became the central subject matter. Individuals and families posed, and were painted, as themselves instead of in the guise of Biblical or mythological figures. Merchants commissioned paintings of their ships, and farmers of their prize cows – the scene often completed by an artistically tidy cowpat on the ground. Realism extended to street scenes and facial expressions that captured a moment or an emotion of everyday life. A modern critic sums it up: "The Dutch described their life and their environment, their country and their city sights so thoroughly that their paintings provide a nearly complete pictorial record of their culture. However, it was more than mere reportage. A sensitive feeling for the

in all spheres of life, not just in art, and attracted an exceptional number of skilled, ambitious citizens to the northern Netherlands who were able to use their talent and determination to improve their lot in life. Unlike many other European cities, it was possible to move from class to class. Members of the middle, and even of the lower, classes could become clergymen, artists, craftsmen, traders and merchants. They could get rich, and have an influence in provincial affairs.

**Parties and politics:** Many joined civic guards, shooting clubs, debating societies or professional guilds – dyers, chairmakers, painters, architects, engravers – that turned

painterly view of everyday life and nature not infrequently raised their production to the level of great art."

Visitors to the Netherlands during the Golden Age routinely remarked on how everyone, from the blacksmith to the baker to the burgher, seemed to have original art, often personally commissioned, hanging prominently both at home and in the shop. The demand led to the creation of the first true market for art. Instead of being tied to patrons, artists could work in an openly competitive arena, accepting commissions and selling their work to the highest bidder.

Openness and market competition existed

into predominantly social organisations. They staged extravagant week-long celebratory feasts and sat for group paintings, some of which are now regarded as masterpieces. The best known such painting is Rembrandt's *The Night Watch*, commissioned in 1642 by Banning Cocq, who was born a poor German and arrived in Amsterdam as a street beggar but rose to make a fortune in business, marrying into a wealthy Dutch family and becoming head of one of the most prestigious civil guard companies.

Amsterdam, which dominated the province of Holland, the richest and most important of the seven, is itself one of the most striking legacies of the Golden Age. In 1607, when the present Singel canal was little more than a ditch running around the 15th-century city walls, the municipal council approved the plan for three new canals: the Herengracht, Keizersgracht and Prinsengracht. Fine houses, built to strict requirements, were constructed along the main canals, with shops along the interlinking side canals. The Jordaan was added in 1612 as a self-contained community for artists and craftsmen.

**Noble scheme:** The plan of central Amsterdam, completed in the late 17th century, remains one of the most successful examples of forward-looking town planning and zoning in history. One modern critic notes: "It is

cially in warm weather. During the summer, the wealthy fled their *grachtenhuizen* for country houses, perhaps only a few miles away but far enough from the canals that looked grand but stank horribly.

The Amsterdam municipal council used the money raised by selling canal-front housing plots to finance the new central city canal system. It was originally believed that only the wealthy would be able to buy and build on the three main residential canals, but Amsterdam's prosperity was such that many middle-class merchants were able to build *grachtenhuizen*, too.

Some of the earliest modern zoning laws limited the dimensions of the canal houses,

not often that a town has been enlarged so sensitively as to increase its characteristic beauty. Its great claim is in the noble dimensions of the canals, in the wonderfully successful relation between the breadth of the water and of the quays on either side, and the height of the buildings."

There was, however, one serious problem with the new design of Amsterdam. No provision had been made for the flushing out of the canals, so the smell was often bad, especially

including their height and depth, which meant that most conformed to what modern critics have called "architectural good manners." Comfortable, solid and not consciously artistic, the main differences that served to distinguish one house from another lay in the style of the gable or the disposition of windows in the facade.

Smaller ships sailed right up the canals, and goods were winched straight off the decks into the attic-storehouses on the fourth floor. Consequently, even the fine big houses often had their views obscured by the masts of the ships docked in front. For a glimpse of how the Golden Age merchant lived, you can

**Left**, view of Amsterdam – wall plaque on Oude Schans, Amsterdam. **Right**, Amsterdam in 1640 showing first stage of canal construction.

# SAILORS' TALK

Although the Dutch language is similar to German, it can sound a strange and alien language. Not for nothing was the term "double Dutch" coined in the 18th century to describe someone whose speech was incoherent or impenetrable.

Even words that visitors think they know turn out to be very different when spoken by a native. Gouda, the town and the world-famous cheese, is pronounced something like "chowda" – the *ch* sound being hard and gutteral, as in the Scottish pronunciation of loch.

Vincent van Gogh, known to English speakers as Van Goff, and to Americans as Van Go, is an almost unpronounceable Van Choch in his native tongue. Again, the *ch* sounds as if the speaker were clearing his throat – perhaps it is the phlegmatic effects of living with cold, damp air rising from the watery polder landscape that has resulted in such a gutteral consonant.

On the other hand, written Dutch can be deceptively easy. Sue Limb weaves real Dutch words into her entertaining autobiography, *Love Forty*, as in this conversation: *"Uur klogs aar bei de bakdor,"* called his wife as he went. *"Ij moovd dem uit ov de utilijtij-roem bekos ov de stink." "Ja, dat wwas de pijg-schijt vrom de manuur-heep. Sorrij."*

Many Dutch words have been assimilated into the English language – most of them earthy and verging on the unprintable. Robert McCrum, author of *The Story of English*, catalogues *fokkinge, kunte* and *krappe* as words that we euphemistically call Anglo-Saxon but which are, in fact, Low Dutch. Poppycock, which has become an acceptable expletive, also derives from the Dutch *pappekak* (literally, soft dung). Sailors from the Low Countries probably introduced these words to England and the Americas, along with purely nautical terms like *smuggler* (from smuckeln) and *keelhaul* (from kielhalen).

Dutch territorial influence in North America ceased when British settlers seized Nieuw Amsterdam and renamed it New York. But the Dutch linguistic contribution to the American language lingers on in place names like Harlem and Brooklyn (originally called Haarlem and Breukelyn).

Contemporary American contains many words derived from Dutch. To quote McCrum, "If you have a *waffle* for brunch, or *coleslaw* with your dinner, or a *cookie* with your coffee, you are using Dutch American. If you ride through the *landscape* in a *caboose* or on a *sleigh*, if you find your *boss* or neighbour *snooping* and accuse him of being a *spook*, you are also using words that come to America from the Netherlands."

Those who visit the Netherlands today and discover the people to be hospitable and generous may be surprised to learn that they were once considered a byword for thrift or downright miseriness. The *Oxford English Dictionary* lists scores of words and phrases that carry a pejorative meaning – going Dutch (expecting your guests to share the cost of meal), Dutch barn (a cheap one without walls), Dutch bargain (one that is not), Dutch courage (drink-induced) and Dutch leaf (cheap imitation gold), to name but a few.

The Dutch have produced few wordsmiths who can compare with the undisputed genius of the nation's painters. The one Dutch poet who has achieved a degree of fame beyond the boundaries of the Netherlands is Joost van den Vondel, who was actually born in Cologne but fled with his Anabaptist parents to the haven of Amsterdam in the late 16th century.

Some pessimists are concerned for the very survival of the language. Already English (or American) is the language of first choice for young people living in the cities. English is the language of pop, video and satellite TV. The Netherlands is one of the world's biggest markets for English-language publications. Historically, Dutch has absorbed many foreign words and yet remained a distinctive tongue, despite Oliver Goldsmith's dismissive comment (of 1759) that the Dutch were "destitute of what may be properly called a language of their own." The pressures are now such that, without a determined effort to keep the language alive, Dutch could die, leaving a legacy of only a handful of (English) four-letter words. ∎

visit the Willet-Holthuysen Museum, a refurbished canal house at Herengracht No. 605. Originally built as a wealthy family's gift to a pampered eight-year-old son, the museum features furniture, glass, silver and ceramics of the Golden Age.

**Rembrandt's home:** Many of the neighbouring houses on the Herengracht show how the merchants, though constrained by strict building requirements and zoning laws, quietly tried to outdo each other with fancy gables and flourished facades. Other examples of the way that comfortable Dutch lived in 17th-century Amsterdam can be seen at Rembrandt's former house, Jodenbreestraat Nos 4–6, which has a good collection of the

but productive Caribbean islands, Manhattan Island, African outposts that provided the slaves for the Caribbean sugar plantations, parts of Ceylon (now Sri Lanka), South Africa and Tasmania, and – as the true jewel of the realm – most of the Southeast Asian islands (Java, Bali, Sumatra, Celebes (Sulawesi), the Moluccas, Timor, Western New Guinea) that make up present-day Indonesia, now the world's fifth most populous country.

Little of the Dutch Empire remains. Much of it was lost even during the Golden Age. As traders, the Dutch were among the best; as colonists, among the worst. More interested in trade than migration, they exploited the

artist's drawings and rooms furnished in the style of the period. The Golden Age also produced some notable architecture, particularly the Town Hall, now the Royal Palace, on Dam square in Amsterdam and the Mauritshuis in The Hague, both designed by Jacob van Campen, a Haarlem-born painter and architect. At the height of the empire, Dutch holdings encompassed parts of Brazil, Dutch Guyana (now Surinam) on the northeast coast of South America, a fistful of tiny

**Left**, wall plaque in Friesland. **Right**, Dam square and the new town hall, Amsterdam, 1673, G. A. Berckheyde.

people and resources of their colonies, and returned home with their wealth instead of putting down the roots that made other European empires more permanent.

**New York:** The end of the Thirty Years' War, in 1648, allowed England, Spain and France to turn their attention to the marauding Dutch. Colonies that had been stolen from the Spanish and Portuguese were taken back again. Neglect by the States General, the United Provinces' ruling body, as much as English aggression, was to blame for the loss, in 1664, of Nieuw Amsterdam, which was renamed New York.

Other factors in the Netherlands added to

the decline of the Empire. The Zuiderzee was silting up, making it difficult for ships to reach the Amsterdam docks, let alone the canal-front homes and warehouses. This did not matter to many descendants of the original merchants, traders and bankers who had been responsible for building the Empire. The new generations seemed more interested in spending than in making money, leading one Dutch historian to suggest that the 17th century should have been called the Age of Wood and Steel because of the commodity trading and shipbuilding, and the 18th century should be called the Golden Age because of all the gold the Dutch locked away in their strongboxes instead of investing in new ventures.

**Colonial independence:** The Netherlands rapidly declined into second-nation status, though it did not formally grant independence to Indonesia until 1949, after Sukarno-led rebels showed they were willing to fight and die for their cause. The last major colony to gain independence was Surinam in 1975.

There is a curious historical footnote to the decline of the Dutch Empire and the fading of the Golden Age. During the late 17th century and well into the 18th century – the period known as the *Pruikentijd*, or "age of wigs" – everything and anything French became all the rage and French was spoken instead of Dutch in the finer salons.

This Francophilia was not even dimmed when France conquered the Netherlands in the late 18th century. French rule was maintained until Napoleon abdicated in 1815, after which the Netherlands gradually evolved into the constitutional monarchy that exists today.

If anyone does find a shop or museum displaying Dutch maps, the decline of the Golden Age is easy to see. By the turn of the 18th century, many Dutch maps were little more than plagiarised copies of the French and English maps that were then leading the way. Indeed, despite contrary evidence, many Dutch cartographers copying earlier maps continued to show California as an island up to the 18th century. Not until 1704, when the French government formally declared California part of the American mainland, did Dutch mapmakers fall into line. The Golden Age was indeed over.

<u>Right</u>, Huize Doorn museum.

# AMSTERDAM: A HISTORICAL PORTRAIT

"The pungent salt smell, the northern, maritime keynotes of seagull and herring, the pointed brick buildings, tall and narrow like herons, with their mosaic of parti-coloured shutters, eaves, sills, that give the landscapes their stiff, heraldic look."

Nicolas Freeling, the Dutch crime-writer, presents this romantic view of the city in his novel, *A Long Silence*. By contrast, historian Simon Schama smells the underbelly of the beast. "In high summer, Amsterdam smells of frying oil, shag tobacco and unwashed beer glasses. In narrow streets, these vapours stand in the air like an aromatic heat mist." Personal reactions to this city vary, but Amsterdam itself seems solidly unchanging. A traveller can arrive by air in any one of half a dozen European cities without knowing immediately in which particular one he is: such doubts would not be possible in Amsterdam. If Romein Verschoor, the historian, is right, then Amsterdam's uniqueness lies in its ingenious and elegant use of space.

Late-medieval Amsterdam developed within the narrow alleys of the 'binnenstad', the fortified inner city crushed between Oudezijds and Nieuwezijds Voorburgwal. But the city's definitive look owes more to the 17th-century development of the patrician *grachtengordel*, the concentric canals which fan the cramped city with air, elegance and space. But in Amsterdam, space itself is illusory, a conjuring trick performed by the city fathers. In reality, with the exception of the Dam, there are no large squares, wide boulevards or distant perspectives. As historian Simon Schama says: "In Amsterdam, alleys attract, avenues repel. The Kalverstraat's din and cheerful vulgarity are the authentic Dutch response to the alienating breadth of a boulevard."

Equally illusory is the sense of homogeneity suggested by the concentric canals. Do not be fooled by the mesmeric effect of a succession of hump-backed bridges or the apparent duplication of classical facades on Herengracht. On second

glance, you may see that the gable stones, colours or sculptural details vary enormously. Neighbourhoods, too, have maintained their individuality, from the raffish waterfront district to the bohemian yet understated Jordaan, melancholy Jodenbuurt (Jewish quarter), the gentrified Museum District, schizophrenic Oude Zijds (Old Side), or sleazy red light Wallen (literally quays). The most appealing districts are, almost by definition, those with peculiar geography and the most chequered history.

A patriotic 18th-century city burgomaster once presented his guests with a banquet celebrating the "courses" of the city's history. Hors d'oeuvres of red herring and cheese (representing early trade commodities) were followed by heavy puddings and roasts (the apogee of the Golden Age) and, for dessert, French wines and delicacies (representing decadence). The guests' reactions to this exercise in patriotic nostalgia are not recorded. Today the final course would be a hearty Indonesian *rijsttaffel*.

By the 13th century a flourishing community had built a dam across the Amstel River and settled on the land around the marshy mouth. Named Amestelledamme, the medieval town prospered as a commodities market, helped by an influx of Flemish weavers and Jewish merchants. Ships unloaded precious wood, wool, salt and spices on Dam square and sailed away with fine cloth, furnishings and grain. As the town expanded, the 14th-century city walls, built along Oudezijds and Nieuwezijds Voorburgwal, gradually outlived their usefulness and began to place constraints on Amsterdam's growth. In 1452, after a series of disastrous fires, the City Council decreed that all houses should henceforth be built of slate and stone rather than of wood.

Amsterdam prospered quietly under Burgundian and Habsburg domination but was politically marginalised until the end of the 16th century. The turning point in Amsterdam's fortunes came in 1578 when the city changed sides and supported the Dutch Calvinist, William of Orange, against Philip II and the Spanish Catholics. Known as the "Alteration", this event made Amsterdam a natural home for Huguenot refugees and Flemish Protestants. After the declaration of the United Provinces in 1581, religious tolerance fostered the creation of "clandestine" Catholic churches such as the Amstelkring on Oudezijds Voorburgwal. Although Catholic worship was officially illegal, the authorities turned a blind eye on discreet observance.

Dutch maritime superiority and the success of the merchant fleet helped usher in the Republic's Golden Age. For Amsterdam, this meant unrivalled prosperity as a banking centre and the hub of the burgeoning Dutch Empire. During the 17th century, Amsterdam perfected its *burgerlijk* culture, an aspiration to the highest civic and moral values rather than a mere embodiment of bourgeois taste. The Republic saw itself as "an island of plenty in a sea of want."

Needless to say, Amsterdam's wealthy merchant class and ruling City Regents saw no reason not to profit materially, as well as spiritually, from this cornucopia of riches. Their ambivalent morality is our gain, however. In 1613, the ruling class embarked on an ambitious foray into town planning with the building of the city's three greatest canals, the Herengracht, the Keizersgracht and the Prinsengracht. These crescent-shaped canals (*grachtengordel*) were soon adorned with magnificent gabled warehouses and patrician town houses.

The 18th century saw Amsterdam's gradual economic decline, coinciding with a conservative reaction against the perceived excesses of the previous century. The decline was only reversed when the creation of the Noordzeekanaal (North Sea Canal) in 1876 engendered a shadow "Golden Age", along with an architectural revival and population growth. The wealthy built neo classical mansions while the poor made do with good low-cost housing schemes in the De Pijp and Old South districts.

As a result of enlightened Dutch social policies, Amsterdam embarked on new low-cost housing schemes between the wars. The Jordaan was already well established as a working-class district but the city's housing shortage was alleviated by the creation of garden suburbs in Amsterdam's New South. Designed by architects of the Amsterdam School, these quirky yet utilitarian estates are characterised by multi-coloured bricks, bulging facades and bizarre windows.

More recently, the city has bucked the Dutch trend towards *cityvorming*, the clinical town planning ethos that has blighted Rotterdam, The Hague and Utrecht. By contrast, conservation and anti-development measures are generally favoured by Amsterdam's left-wing City Council and supported by the city's predominantly young population. Even so, cherished landmarks have been demolished. In the 1970s, Nieuwmarkt and a section of the Jodenbuurt were sacrificed to make way for a metro system. As for the completion of the new Muziektheater and Stadhuis (City Hall) complex on Waterlooplein in 1987, the controversy lingers on.

The former socialist Mayor, Ed van Thijn, was not averse to demolishing the occasional historic site to build a de luxe hotel, but the results can be positive. The presence of a grand new hotel on Zeedijk, for instance, has helped discourage trade with passing prostitutes and drug dealers.

Resistance to *cityvorming* is particularly strong in Amsterdam's most characteristic and close-knit neighbourhoods. The Nieuwmarkt, Jordaan, Western Islands and De Pijp districts are not about to be redesigned in a bland new international style. The Nieuwmarkt's cultural identity is not cast in stone: the buildings have been altered frequently since the 16th century but the neighbourhood's resilience and mercantile spirit remain intact. The district has traditionally welcomed refugees, from 17th-century Jews to today's Chinese, Indonesian and Surinamese immigrants. Contrary to popular belief, more Immigrants are Involved in the restaurant business than in the higher profile vice trades.

Elsewhere, Amsterdam's best-loved district, the Jordaan, is immune to outside pressure. Its rebellious identity was forged in early industrial disputes and this closely packed quarter has been home to Huguenots, craftsmen, almshouse-dwellers, hippies, students and yuppies. This strangely harmonious community lives in a charming network of narrow streets which, tucked in between the grander canals, is little changed despite its gentrification. In essence, then, strong neighbourhood identities provide the key to Amsterdam's fiercely guarded architectural integrity. ∎

## ARTISTS AND ARCHITECTS

The 17th-century Golden Age was a time of excellence in politics and economics as well as in the arts. The Dutch Republic ruled the seas and was one of the most powerful countries in Europe. The Treaty of Westphalia (also known as the Treaty of Münster), concluded with Spain in 1648, merely sealed the formal independence that the seven northern provinces of the Netherlands had won almost a century earlier.

Painting exhibited a distinctive national character and many artists took their subjects from their own experiences and surroundings, though generally they confined themselves to a single type of subject, such as portraiture, still lifes, landscapes or scenes from everyday life.

**Materials:** Many 17th-century Dutch and Flemish painters improved on the techniques used by the Early Netherlandish artists of the 15th and 16th centuries, painting on skillfully cut thin oak panels which rarely warp or crack. Besides wood, other materials such as copper were used, though canvas predominated as it was better for large paintings, allowing a freer and bolder style, even if the weave occasionally showed through. The different surfaces and their preparation had an important influence on the techniques and styles of the Golden Age artists.

Wooden panels with a white chalk ground gave a smoothness that was conducive to minute detail and the meticulous finish that led Gerard Dou (1613–75) to found the important school of genre painting at Leiden known as the *Fijnschilders*. Dou painted *Young Mother* (now in the Mauritshuis, The Hague) "so finely as hardly to be distinguish'd from enamail."

Restored Dutch paintings look clean and crisp, even when dark colours were used. This is possibly because they were covered, according to Hoogstraten, with a "varnish consisting of turpentine, spirit, or turpentine and pulverised mastic dissolved" which could be easily removed by restorers.

Certain colours were more difficult or

**Preceding pages: Amsterdam past and present – the Munttoren (1751) by J. ten Compe, and Zuiderkerk. Left, images of Van Gogh.**

expensive to obtain, particularly blue and green, and were therefore used sparingly and to dramatic effect. The natural ultramarine (lapis lazuli) was the most expensive and azurite, a blue copper carbonate mineral, very scarce. Poor-quality artificial azurite, indigo for underpainting and smalt (ground-up blue cobalt glass) were often used instead. Green was obtained from a mixture of blue and a lead-tin oxide or vegetable-dye yellow. The yellow has often faded, leaving some Dutch paintings of this era with blue foliage and grass in woods and fields.

The Rijksmuseum in Amsterdam has fine examples of most of the painters of that splendid era, and all the works mentioned

was initially very sober, as the works of Pieter Claes (1597/8–1661) and Willem Heda (1594–1680) demonstrate. Their work is characterised by the rendering of a combination of objects carefully chosen for their symbolism. Gold and silver cups and fragile glasses and jugs often feature, serving as a warning against excess and a reminder of the transience of life – a favourite theme.

As the century progressed, the Eighty Years' War came to an end, prosperity increased and Calvanism turned away from depictions of religious themes. More elaborate fruit bowls and flower vases, more splendid gold and silver cups and rich tapestries appear in portraits and sumptuous still lifes,

here are in that museum, unless otherwise noted. Though Rembrandt is today regarded as the most outstanding 17th-century painter, Frans van Mieris and Adriaen van der Werff were considered the greatest painters of the day by their contemporaries. Many others, such as Cesar van Everdingen, Honthorst and Brugghen, were equally talented and highly regarded in their day. Unlike the prolific painters Hals, Steen and Ruisdael, whose work is on public view, their paintings have either been destroyed or are held in private collections and the artists more or less forgotten.

The still-life painting of the Golden Age

such as those by Willem Kalf (1619–93) and Abraham van Beyeren (1620/1–90).

**Institutional patronage:** It was also customary to paint group portraits of the regents and regentesses of institutions, *hofjes* (almshouses for the elderly), orphanages and hospitals. Frans Hals (1581/5–1666) was a masterly portrait painter who captured the essence of his models as shown in his famous *Merry Drinker*. The Frans Hals Museum, in a 17th-century (men's) almshouse in Haarlem, where he lived, exhibits most of his group portraits, which are also known as Corporation Pieces.

Rembrandt van Rijn (1606–69) is undoubtedly one of the world's greatest artists. He can certainly be called the painter of humanity, since he always emphasised the human element, not only in his portraits, but also in his Biblical and history paintings. Until 1631, he worked in Leiden, his birthplace. The first paintings of his early period, such as *The Musical Company* and *Tobias Accusing Anna of Stealing the Kid*, are very colourful. Later on, Rembrandt's preference for strong contrasts between light and shade becomes apparent, as in his *Old Woman Reading* and *Jeremiah Lamenting the Destruction of Jerusalem*.

Rembrandt left Leiden in 1631 to move to Amsterdam, where he worked until his death

in the Arquebusiers' Guildhall. Rembrandt has depicted the moment when the captain gives his lieutenant the order for the guards to march out.

A large painting in the same room from St George's Guildhall, by Bartholomeus van der Helst, shows the banquet at which the Amsterdam civic guard celebrated the signing of the Treaty of Münster in 1648.

**Dutch landscapes:** It is understandable that at a time when the country was fighting for its independence, painters would choose that land, their own environment, as a subject for their pictures. A good example of this genre is the large *Winter Landscape with Ice-Skaters* by Hendrick Avercamp (1585–1634).

in 1667. There he abandoned the meticulous style of his Leiden period for a broader manner, in which light and shadow merge into each other and his greys and browns have a deep warm glow.

A world-famous work of his Amsterdam period, now in the Rijksmuseum, is *The Company of Captain Frans Banning Cocq and Lieutenant Willem van Ruytenburch*, given the title *The Night Watch* in the 19th century – a large painting, which he completed in 1642, that was originally installed

Other good examples are Jan van Goyen's (1596–1656) majestic *Landscape with Two Oaks* and Esaias van de Velde's (c. 1591–1630) sombre *Cattle Ferry*.

Landscape painting reached its peak in the 17th century in the work of Jacob van Ruisdael (1628/9–82). In *The Windmill at Wijk bij Duurstede* and his grand *View of Haarlem* he presented the impressive expanse of the flat Dutch countryside under huge cloudy skies. Other landscape painters worth looking out for are Adriaen van de Velde (1636–72), Aert van der Neer (1603/4–77) and Paulus Potter (1625–54) who painted animals in extensive landscapes. The painters'

**Left**, the Syndics of the Cloth Hall, Rembrandt.
**Right**, Winter Scene, H. Avercamp.

concentration on their own surroundings also gave rise to church interiors as a speciality. Pieter Saenredam's (1597–1665) impressive *Interior of St Mary's Church at Utrecht* is a fine example.

**Genre painting:** Dutch scenes from daily life were divided by subject matter into groups: what we know as "merry company" scenes (*gheselschapjes*), outdoor scenes (*buitenpartij*) and brothel scenes (*bordeeltjen*), most of them containing a hidden moral. These subjects are characteristic of Dutch genre painting, yet there is no word in either 17th-century or contemporary Dutch that directly corresponds to the present-day English sense of the word "genre".

company" paintings showed elegantly dressed and cosmopolitan young men and women eating, drinking, playing music and embracing in taverns or in landscape settings; Dirck Hals, the lesser known younger brother of Frans, was a great exponent of these "merry company" scenes until the 1630s. His contemporary, Jan Miense Molenaer (1609/10–1668), painted children, often in theatrical settings, symbolising freedom from care. The witty and perceptive Jan Steen (1626–79) also depicts the behaviour of children in, for example, the typically Dutch *Feast of St Nicholas* and that of adults at a fair or an inn. Adriaen van Ostade (1610–85), from Haarlem, specialised mainly in

Dutch genre painting originated in the 16th century with Patenir and his Flemish followers, the greatest of whom was Pieter Brueghel the Elder who developed landscape into a subject of its own, rather than using it merely as a background to religious, mythological or historical scenes. Brueghel left Antwerp during the Spanish occupation and moved to Amsterdam, where his work gave impetus to the development of new forms of Dutch painting.

Although Brueghel's paintings retained a moralistic tone, he depicted scenes from peasant life, *kermisses* (fairs and carnivals) and weddings. By contrast, other early "merry

scenes from peasant life.

**Symbolic meaning:** The public well knew how to "read" these paintings: a map indicated the absence of the head of the household, gone travelling overseas; a dog in inns and brothels pointed to gluttony and licentiousness; a cat and a mouse reinforced the sense of the uncertainty of human existence, a painting within a painting often pointed out a moral or a warning.

Amsterdam was a vigorous centre of genre painting in the first three decades of the 17th century, particularly barrack-room scenes and tavern interiors with soldiers drinking, fighting and womanising. It is curious that

Amsterdam merchants should have chosen to hang scenes of brawling soldiery on their walls. Perhaps they wanted a contrast to their relatively peaceful lives (little fighting ever took place in Amsterdam) – or perhaps they enjoyed these pictures for the same reasons that people like to watch the portrayal of violence on television today.

The talented Willem Duyster (c. 1599–1635) specialised in these active, yet delicately painted, scenes and Gerard ter Borch (1617–81), considered by some to be as great as Rembrandt, began his career as a painter of barrack-room scenes. His later refined art, of which his *Gallant Conversation* and *Seated Girl* are remarkable paintings, represents a

distinct departure and stands in a class of its own.

It goes without saying that painters in Holland – a country wrested from the sea – found water a natural subject for their pictures. Willem van de Velde the Younger (1633–1707), of *The Cannon Shot*, is the best known Dutch marine painter, but Jan van de Capelle (1626–79) was by no means his inferior.

Light plays a crucial part in the work of the

Delft Master Johannes Vermeer (1632–75), and, because he is sparing in his use of shadow, he achieves a great translucency of colour. Despite their small size, his paintings belong among the most monumental works in Dutch art. His output was not large: only 30 works by him are known. Four are in the Rijksmuseum – *The Kitchen Maid*, *Woman reading a Letter*, *The Love Letter* and *The Little Street*.

Painters often chose a townscape or a single street as a subject, as did Gerrit Berckheyde (1636–98) and Jan van der Heyden (1637–1712). The domestic interiors of Pieter de Hooch (1628–c. 1683) were similar to those of Vermeer, though less serious and less strong in form. *Woman with a Child in a Pantry* and *Courtyard Behind a House* are among his best works.

**Applied art:** The explosion of artistic talent in the 17th century is truly remarkable yet the popularity of painting in the Golden Age did not obscure other forms of achievement – architecture, sculpture, silver, porcelain and furniture – which demonstrated a high standard of individual craftsmanship. Beautiful objects then being created were integrated into the houses of the wealthy. Chairs, tables and cabinets, even bird cages and doll's houses, were displayed as works of art.

Delft is now known for the blue and white painted pottery which Italian potters introduced to the region, although early production centred on Antwerp. In the 17th century the descendants of these potters, now Protestant refugees, moved from Antwerp into the northern provinces where they made Rotterdam and Haarlem their main centres. Not long after, the city of Delft began producing its characteristic tin-glazed tiles, plates and panels, painted with blue decoration copied from Chinese wares imported by the East Indies Company. By the mid-17th century, Delft jars, vases and bowls, and even door portals and lintels, were everywhere, ornamented with landscapes, portraits and Biblical or genre scenes.

During the 17th century large quantities of silver were also made – not only in cities such as Amsterdam and Rotterdam but also in the smaller towns where traditional forms were kept. One such was the characteristic marriage casket or *knottekistje* made in Friesland; it was shaped like the knotted handkerchief containing money which a fiancé usually presented to his betrothed.

From the first decade of the 17th century silver drinking horns used on ceremonial occasions, as well as vessels, basins, urns and salt cellars, began to be decorated with a new ear-shaped form. This "auricular" design – created by Paulus van Vianen of Utrecht – was developed by his brother Adam and his nephew Christian into flowing patterns of sea creatures and molluscs.

Mid-17th century silverware was also embossed with a profusion of flowers, often including the newly imported and highly prized tulip. Adam and Paulus both excelled in the production of representational scenes. The German painter Sandrart said of Paulus rather than applying it superficially. His masterpiece is the mausoleum of William the Silent, Prince of Orange, built on the site of the former high altar of the New Church in Delft (1614–21). The bronze figure of William the Silent is surrounded by tall obelisks, linking it to the High Gothic interior of the New Church. Two of his most impressive and characteristic buildings that survive in Amsterdam are the Zuiderkerk (1603) and the Westerkerk (1620).

The architect Jacob van Campen designed the Mauritshuis and the Huis ten Bosch in The Hague and the New Church at Haarlem in his French-influenced style, but his major project of the century was the construction of

that "with the hammer alone he could make whole pictures… with animals and landscapes, all perfect in their decoration, design and elegance."

**Brick and stone:** Innovation in architecture and sculpture was largely due to the influence of one stonemason employed by the city of Amsterdam – Hendrik de Keyser. He developed his own characteristic style, freeing Dutch sculpture from its former rigidity and symbolic quality, which resulted in a softer, anatomic style full of movement.

Later becoming an architect, he related the interior spaces of buildings to the exteriors, integrating the ornament to the structure a new Town Hall for Amsterdam. This imposing building (now Koninklijk [Royal] Paleis) was built on a massive scale and is one of the few classical buildings in the Netherlands. Solid and rational, it seems the ultimate expression of the values of the Golden Age. It was built when the Netherlands was at the height of its powers. Like the nation, the building has suffered a sad decline: converted to a palace by Louis Napoleon it now stands grimy and closed to the public for much of the year.

<u>Above</u>, symbols of life's transience – *Still Life*, P. Claesz. <u>Right</u>, Mata Hari.

# FAMOUS AND INFAMOUS

For a small country, the Dutch have produced more than their share of famous – and infamous – people. Perhaps the most widely known Dutchmen today are the artists of the Golden Age: Rembrandt, Frans Hals and Jan Vermeer. Their fame – and certainly their prices at auction – have been surpassed in recent years by Vincent van Gogh (1853–90), the often-mad master of many styles who only sold one painting during his lifetime. Modern art in the Netherlands began with Piet Mondriaan (1872–1944), and, of living Dutch painters, Willem de Kooning is perhaps the best known, though he moved to the United States early in his career.

Dutch scientific contributions came from Christiaan Huygens (1629–95), inventor of the pendulum clock, and his contemporary, Anthonie van Leeuwenhoek (1632–1725), a Delft microscope manufacturer who made the first meaningful studies of microscopic organisms. René Descartes, the 17th-century philosopher and mathematician, was born in France but lived and worked in Holland for 20 years.

Similarly, Linnaeus, the man responsible for the classification of plants into families and species, was educated in his native Sweden, but published his most important botanical works after moving to

Leiden in 1735. Thomas à Kempis (1380–1471), the Augustinian scholar and author, spent most of his life in a monastery near Zwolle working on "Imitatio Christi" and other tracts. In legal circles, Grotius, or Hugo de Groot (1583–1645), of Delft is generally regarded as the founder of international law, in particular that aspect relating to the conduct of wars.

In the late 17th century, one of Europe's dominant political figures was William III of Orange, a brilliant military strategist who fought off repeated challenges to the independence of the Netherlands. He married Mary, the Duchess of York. In 1688, after a revolution deposed her father James II, William and Mary took the English throne, subdued northern Ireland and inadvertently laid the groundwork for sectarian tension between Irish Catholics and the Protestant "Orangemen".

Many Dutch names survive in the former colony that is now New York, but two of the most prominent are a pair of colonial governors: first Peter Minuit (1580–1638), who "bought" Manhattan Island from the American Indians, and then Pieter Stuyvesant (1592–1672), who made a valiant but futile effort to win more autonomy for the New Netherlands from Amsterdam before the colony was finally lost to the English in 1664.

Some of the best-known Dutch are not widely identified as being Dutch at all. An example is Rotterdam native Desiderius Erasmus (1467–1536), the "Dutch Voltaire," the "Prince of Humanists." Another is Baruch de Spinoza (1632–77), whose parents fled the persecution of Jews in their native Portugal to resettle in Amsterdam. Spinoza's pantheistic philosophical works pioneered the scientific approach to studying religion and the Bible.

Mata Hari, born Margaretha Geertruida Zelle in Leeuwarden, Friesland, in 1876, is another vague figure. Her career has been interpretated in many ways, but it is known that she became a popular turn-of-the-century dancer, and was shot by the French in 1917, accused of being a spy.

Anne Frank died in March 1945 in a German concentration camp, but there is little doubt that her teenage diary, recounting her family's experiences in hiding from the Nazi occupiers, will remain one of the most read and most moving books ever written.

Perhaps the name most readily identifiable as Dutch around the world today Is Hans Brinker of silver-skate fame. Of course, he is an invention of American fiction. Much more real in the modern sporting world are two Dutchmen who were arguably the best soccer players in the world at the height of their respective careers: Johan Cruyff, the "Flying Dutchman", in the early 1970s, and Ruud Gullit, he of the exploding dreadlocked headers, in the late 1980s. Finally, in late 20th-century popular music, there is the rock band Golden Earring, still performing, recording and touring 25 years after they formed, and in classical music Bernard Haitink, the Covent Garden conductor regarded as one of the best in the world. ∎

The horror of World War II began, for the Dutch, in the early hours of a beautiful morning – Friday, 10 May 1940. As dawn broke over the flat, peaceful Frans Hals landscape, the first Junker JU 52 transport planes flew in from the east; at the same time troops, including a crack SS division, swarmed over the German-Dutch frontier, dispelling any lingering hopes that the Netherlands could remain neutral – a bastion of peace in the hell which was slowly engulfing Europe. Later on that same morning, the German Ambassador to The Hague, Count Von Zech Von Burckersroda, wept as he handed over the official declaration of war to the Dutch Foreign Minister.

Hitler had pencilled in a one-day schedule for the complete occupation of the Netherlands, one of the important stages of his master plan to overrun first Europe and then the world. There was a slight hitch; the Dutch Davids, confronted with the Teutonic Goliath, actually dared to fight back. The Dutch armed forces were hastily trained and poorly equipped, many of them still trying to get used to their army boots and almost all of them were pacifists at heart, with no enthusiasm for the gore of war – yet they kept their country out of German hands for five days – four more than Hitler had calculated.

The Führer had his master plan for overrunning the Netherlands and Belgium. He planned to launch his main offensive on Britain from Dutch/Belgian bases, after he had subdued the population, occupied France and taken care of "the Jewish problem." He never quite managed to subdue the Dutch, but unfortunately he succeeded only too well with some parts of his plan.

Before the final capitulation, extra time was bought by the combined Dutch forces of 350,000 men, time enough to enable Princess Juliana, accompanied by Prince Bernhard and their two children, to escape to Canada, and for Queen Wilhelmina, together with her cabinet, to reach Britain.

Dutch losses during those first days of

**Preceding pages**: Liberation, Dam square, Amsterdam. **Left**, War-time rations. **Right**, the bombardment of Rotterdam.

confrontation hardly mean much when set against the backdrop of the millions of Allied forces who lost their lives defending democracy during the battle with the Nazis. But the five-day skirmish took its toll, leaving 2,200 soldiers and 2,159 civilians dead, and 2,700 wounded.

It is difficult to calculate the numbers of Germans who died; many lost their lives when the Dutch blew up vital bridges, while others were shot down in the JU-52s. Official records, however, show 1,600 Germans

were taken prisoner. For 1,200 of them, the combat years were short – they were shipped to Britain just before the capitulation of the Netherlands.

**Before the war:** During the developments that took place in Germany throughout the 1930s, which eventually brought Hitler to power and devastation to Europe, the Dutch had hoped that, so long as they did not catch their neighbour's eye, like the playground bully, he would go away, or at least leave them alone.

The Dutch had their own problems to contend with. The same economic shock waves which reached Germany from America in 1929 had also reached the Low Country. The Wall Street crash had just as devastating an effect on the Dutch guilder as it had on sterling and the German mark. But the Dutch thought that stoicism in the face of adversity would win the day. The Prime Minister ordered belt-tightening and curbed spending in order to keep the guilder strong.

Neighbouring Britain had devalued sterling, but the guilder held while unemployment soared. People concentrated on having a good time to avoid the economic issues and they blocked their ears to the echoes of Hitler's ranting and to the sound of marching jackboots drawing uncomfortably close across the frontier.

a Nazi witch-hunt against Prince Bernhard, who let it be known he would have no truck with the Nazis. In fact, three years after his wedding he would be found on the roof of Soestdijk Palace, defiantly machine-gunning low-flying German planes.

The Dutch, who had previously avoided disturbing the enemy at the gate, finally showed their feelings on the day the royal engagement was announced. Some Germans living in the Netherlands flew the swastika. In The Hague, seat of government and home of the country's reticent and well-behaved army of civil servants, the public tore down the hated and feared insignia.

The German press blamed Prince Bernhard

**Royal wedding:** First came the World Jamboree Celebrations, then the marriage of shy young Princess Juliana to the German Prince Bernhard. The 24-year-old Princess had met the young German Prince in 1935. He had been invited to lunch with the Royal Family at their Austrian ski resort, and, while Queen Wilhelmina did most of the talking, the two were falling in love. "She struck me," he said later, "as immensely lovable with a touching innocence."

Her innocence and euphoria could not have lasted very long. Soon the young couple were confronted with Dutch reservations about the Prince's nationality, together with

for the insult and started a campaign against him. The German government withdrew the passports of nationals who had been invited to attend the wedding. The Dutch government opened talks and a compromise was reached. The German government would advise nationals living in the Netherlands not to display the swastika. The Dutch in turn agreed that the German national anthem and the "Horst Wessel" song could be sung at the gala wedding evening. During the singing, some German guests gave the Hitler salute. Dutch and other guests responded by singing *Rule Britannia*. It was a tense evening.

The 1930s also saw the emergence of

Dutch fascism. Though not many in number, the members of the Dutch Nazi movement played a prominent part in betraying members of the Dutch Resistance and rounding up Jews for the death camps. The leader of the Dutch NSB (National Socialist Movement), the party whose members liked to strut around in black shirts and call themselves Nazis, was a short, vain man called Anton Mussert. He was a great admirer of Mussolini and set himself up as the voice of order and of that solidarity which would unite the Dutch Aryan race and get rid of the enemy (i.e. the Jews or any other undesirable foreigners), bringing the country back to prosperity.

three German soldiers waving a white flag picked their way through the smoke-filled city streets of Rotterdam towards the headquarters of the leader of the Dutch troops, Colonel Pieter Scharroo. They came to deliver an ultimatum.

After finally smashing Waalhaven airport, where eight Fokker G-Is managed to take out two enemy bombers, the Germans met with fiercer opposition in Rotterdam itself. The city had a defence force of a mere 1,400 Dutch soldiers with only 24 light and nine heavy machine guns between them. Fuelled by desperation, anger and much courage, these men fought the German infantry division, which had landed on the river Maas in

Mussert hoped for power once the Germans occupied the Netherlands. He liked to quote Mussolini: "The people are like a woman, they will go with the strongest." He never tired of telling people that the Italian dictator was, "like Hitler and I, not very tall." Three small men and a great deal of carnage. Mussert faced a Dutch firing squad on 7 May 1946. He had not grown much in the interim and never achieved the position of power for which he yearned.

**Rotterdam burns:** At 10.30 on the morning of 14 May 1940, four days after the invasion,

**Left**, trench warfare. **Right**, Rotterdam burns.

sea planes and was now heading for the port and city. Rotterdam port was one of the German's main targets and it was taking too long to conquer.

General Schmidt, commander of the German troops at Rotterdam, Moerdijk and Dordrecht, sent Colonel Scharroo a terse message. The city was to be surrendered to his troops or face a heavy infantry attack starting at 1pm on the same day, to be followed precisely 20 minutes later by heavy bombardment from the air. Colonel Scharroo was given two hours to think it over.

Neither Scharroo, nor the city's mayor, needed two hours. Their minds were made up: there was to be no surrender. A quick call was made to a senior Dutch officer, General Winkelman. He contacted the Queen's commissioner and Colonel Scharroo was ordered to send a message to General Schmidt stating that any ultimatum must be officially signed, giving the signatory's identity and rank. Meanwhile, General Schmidt sent a message back to Germany saying that the bombardment was to be delayed while negotiations took place.

**Anticipation:** It was 12 noon and Rotterdammers, taking advantage of the lull in the fighting, were shopping for food. There was general relief that the shooting had stopped. Trams were running, children were seen on the streets. In Germany the first group of heavily loaded bombers were already moving down the air strip at Bremen and Westphalen on their way to their target – Rotterdam.

Eight hundred Rotterdammers had 90 minutes left to live; the time it would take to fly from Bremen and Westphalen on a clear day, and 14 May was another clear spring day. General Schmidt wrote out his latest ultimatum and signed it. The answer was to be in his hands by 4.20 p.m.

The Dutch messenger, a Captain Backer, accompanied by two German soldiers, set off again with a white flag. They may have exchanged remarks; certainly they looked up when they heard a deep sonorous sound in the air coming from the south and the east. The German planes had arrived. The bomber command had been told that if red flares were set off Rotterdam was to be spared. The red flares went up. The Rotterdammers had been given a reprieve.

**Death from the air:** The first group of planes broke formation and flew off, their bombs still in their holds. The second wave of planes, however, remained on course. Their bombs were dropped on thousands of screaming, panicking people who had never really believed the Germans would actually do this. It was 1.30 p.m. and many children were back at their school desks.

The Germans sent a message to the Dutch general headquarters in The Hague. Utrecht was to be next, a beautiful city of many thousand inhabitants. All the other Dutch cities would in turn be bombed. General Winkelman reluctantly decided to give in.

A message of surrender was sent to the German headquarters at the Hotel des Indes in The Hague, the lovely old building where Pavlova died and Mata Hari used to meet her consorts. Word was sent to Dutch troops to destroy their weapons. They did not actually start to do so until the next day, Wednesday, 15 May. They just could not believe the battle was lost and that their country was now in German hands.

Queen Wilhelmina believed the news. She was staying in London, at Buckingham Palace, and was about to sit down to supper with King George VI when details reached her. That night, 125 Amsterdam Jews committed suicide.

Ten weeks later Rotterdam was still smouldering and the damage was recorded at 800

dead (burnt and/or crushed), 24,000 houses destroyed, 80,000 people homeless, 2,500 shops destroyed together with 1,200 factories, 500 cafés, 70 schools, 21 churches, 20 banks, 12 cinemas and two theatres. The Germans had truly arrived.

**The war years:** Four years of misery had begun for the Netherlands. Each day brought its new deprivations and degradations: shortage of food, lack of freedom, curfews, media censorship and death. There were sudden *razzias* (round-ups) during which thousands of men were herded off to work in forced labour camps; long cold winters with no fuel; and, for the country's Jewish population, absolute and unadulterated terror. But the Dutch, like many others in occupied Europe, never gave up hope.

September 1944 was a cruel month which marked two particularly black dates. The first was *Dolle Dinsdag*, "Mad Tuesday", on 5 September. The German army had suffered devastating defeats in northern France and was forced to withdraw to the German frontier through the Netherlands. The Dutch thought freedom was at hand. Panic broke out among collaborators, who joined the retreating Germans. Station platforms were thronged with desperate people who had worked with the occupiers. Hundreds left their luggage on station platforms in their

Arnhem were very still. A horrible realisation began to dawn on the population. The British were not coming and the Germans were not going. They were just recovering, regrouping and preparing to fight another battle, one of the most important of World War II, during which more Allied troops would die than in the Normandy landings.

But the people of Arnhem didn't know this. Nor did the Germans. The event would go down in history as the Battle of Arnhem, or Operation Market Garden.

The operation left 17,000 Allied soldiers, British, American and Polish, killed, wounded or missing. The Dutch toll was 10,000 casualties, most of them civilians and

rush to get on trains heading East.

**False hope:** Dutch people thronged the streets in Arnhem and surrounding villages, jeering the departing troops and the flotilla of traitors scurrying along behind. People started to wave anything they could find coloured orange – the Dutch Royal Family's colour – and rumours were rife: Rotterdam had already been liberated, the Queen was returning, the British were coming.

Just as suddenly as the flow of troops started, it stopped. The next day the streets of

**Left** and **right**, refugees flee the war-torn cities by whatever means they can.

either victims of the campaign itself or of the terrible "hunger winter" which followed.

**Plan to end the war in Europe:** The abortive Allied attack, which took place on 17 September 1944, was meant to open up a Dutch corridor through which troops and tanks would sprint, making their way across the Rhine and into the heart of Germany. The daring and brilliant plan was devised by Britain's Field-Marshall Montgomery, and, had it succeeded, would have brought the war to an end within a few weeks.

It failed, with devastating results. The war dragged on. Thousands of Dutch in the industrial areas around Amsterdam, The Hague and Rotterdam were cut off from food supplies and died of hunger, while, in the death camps of Central Europe, hundreds of thousands of Jews died, as the Nazis, aware of the imminent arrival of the Allies, tried to destroy evidence of what would be called the Holocaust.

Many books have been written on Operation Market Garden, all offering theories to explain why the plan failed. Was it miscalculation? A breakdown in communications? Overconfidence, or the weather conditions? A combination of all these is probably the answer. Recriminations were thrown about, with every side blaming the other.

Cornelis Ryan, author of *A Bridge Too*

In an interview, given at the launch of his book, *A Bridge Too Far*, he said of Montgomery: "He was a vain, arrogant man. Ambitious as hell, popular with his men, a great publicist and highly intelligent, but Montgomery can never be forgiven for one act. This man knew the Second SS Panzer Corps was in the Arnhem area yet still he sent his airborne troops in on top of them, and, for that matter, so did Eisenhower. They both overruled the Dutch intelligence reports."

The Market Garden plan was breathtaking in its brilliant simplicity and historically it reflects the same dreadful blunders and extreme heroism that was seen at Balaclava. The Allied Airborne Operation involved fly-

*Far*, which painstakingly records every detail of the battle, once interviewed General Eisenhower, one of the main leaders involved. Eisenhower, who insisted that the interview should not be published until after his death, described Montgomery variously as "a psychopath" and "egocentric" and "a man trying to prove that he was somebody."

Ryan had also interviewed Montgomery and he was unimpressed. The Irishman, former war correspondent for London's *Daily Telegraph*, *Time* reporter, and author of *The Longest Day*, was himself "difficult" and admitted he did not suffer fools at all. But he did not think Montgomery a fool.

ing in men, artillery and equipment. There were to be 5,000 fighters, bombers, transports and more than 2,500 gliders. On the ground, the massed tank columns of the British Second Army were to be poised along the Dutch/Belgium border.

According to the operational plan, five major bridges and other minor crossings were to be seized, opening up a long narrow corridor, with Arnhem the last gateway to the final goal, the Rhine, and Germany's heartland. The Third Reich would be toppled, bringing an end to the war in 1944.

During the last conference at Montgomery's headquarters, one British officer,

# OPERATION MANNA

The bitterest months of the Occupation began for the Dutch after the failure of Arnhem; life under the desperate and revengeful enemy was to prove horrific. Several thousand Dutch men, women and children died as a result of German reprisals, many killed in retaliation for kidnappings carried out by the Resistance. But the most atrocious figure was the 15,000 who died needlessly, from hunger, in the last year of the war.

By October 1944, the war's front line was running through the Netherlands; the northern part of the country was still in German hands and cut off from food supplies. Food was failing to get through because of rail strikes, and the waterway routes were blocked by Germans in retaliation for the strikes.

The cities were the worst hit: The Hague, Rotterdam and Amsterdam. But in country towns, too, people were suffering. Most heart-rending of all were the children, many of whom dropped dead from exhaustion on the streets. To compound the misery, it was a bitterly cold winter, and fuel had run out. People cut down trees in the cities' parks for firewood; the wooden blocks between the train rails disappeared overnight.

Pathetic streams of people made their way out of the cities to the countryside, pushing wheel-barrows laden with personal possessions to barter for food. They often returned empty-handed. By midwinter the death rate was high.

In December 1944, Minister Gerbrandy, head of the Dutch government in London, wrote to General Eisenhower: "The Dutch government cannot accept that eventual liberators will be liberating dead bodies." The letter pressed for an offensive to begin to free the northern parts of the Netherlands.

But on the day Mr Gerbrandy wrote his letter the Germans started their own desperate offensive in the Ardennes. Every available German soldier was needed for battle, so, to release them from internal duties in Holland, Dutchmen were despatched in their thousands to labour camps in Germany. At the start of the *razzias*, or round-ups, the families

of those men who left voluntarily were promised extra food.

In January 1945, the death rate in Amsterdam was 500 a week; as there was no wood for the luxury of a coffin, most bodies were buried in paper or rolled in a sheet. At the end of January, a Swedish ship managed to sail into Delftshaven near Rotterdam laden with food supplies. Afterwards one woman wrote: "It was like a holiday; today I was able to give the children bread – spread with margarine." It was to be the last food supply from outside the country for some time.

That spring, the first weak sun shone on some very pathetic faces: some were green-tinged from eating too many tulip bulbs; infectious diseases, including typhoid and diptheria, were rampant. Then, on 25 April, posters appeared promising relief from the months of relentless misery. The Allies were to start air-drops of food.

This risky exercise was called Operation Manna. On 29 April the skies above the north of Holland were suddenly filled with the deep sound of low-flying Lancaster bombers; this time when their shutters opened it was to release crates of food rather than bombs. Pilots and crews risked their lives as they manoeuvred their heavy aircraft as low as 200 ft (60 metres) above the dropping areas. People filled the streets waving to the planes; many were crying and waving sheets, shirts, anything that would flap in the wind.

Some of the crews emptied their own pockets, throwing out chocolate and cigarettes. When the second wave of planes came, people had messages ready. Sheets were spread out reading "God Bless You" or, in some cases, "Cigarettes here please."

From the first of May, American B-17s, the "flying fortresses", joined the exercise. Many Dutch still remember "Operation Manna" as the final dramatic sign that the misery was over. "It was a wonderful sight, the great billowing parachutes, crates of food attached. It was 'Manna from Heaven' for us, the survivors," said one Dutch woman who, at the age of five, tasted her first chocolate bar thrown from the cockpit of a Lancaster. "I've never tasted anything as good since, and I still have the wrapping." ∎

Lt-General Frederick ("Boy") Browning, Deputy Commander of the First Allied Airborne Army, made the memorable remark: "I think we may be going a bridge too far." He was tragically proved right. When the paratroopers arrived, the Germans, who were not supposed to be in the area in such strength, were waiting to meet them. The elite Second SS Panzer Corps had been quartered near Arnhem in the quiet, green area near Oosterbeek to rest and recuperate from recent combat.

When the siege of Arnhem bridge began, the Allied Airborne Division was cut off from help along the corridor: they fought bravely and desperately, but most of them

were slaughtered. Dutch families around the area opened their doors and their hearts to the wounded and dying. Many acts of individual heroism that day are recorded for history. But the saddest reminder of the battle must be the rows of simple white crosses in Oosterbeek War Graves Cemetery.

**Freedom:** Finally, on 5 May 1945, the Germans capitulated and the Netherlands was liberated. The official document was signed in Wageningen. A jubilant Prince Bernhard was present, together with General Blaskorvitz, Commander of the German troops in the Netherlands, and the Canadian General Faulkes.

There were scenes of ecstatic joy in Amsterdam, The Hague, Delft and Rotterdam; most of the southern parts of the country had already been liberated before the winter. But there was a marked difference in the appearance of the cheering crowds to those, say, of Paris. The faces of many were grey and hollow; some could hardly stand on their pathetically thin legs. Children were weak and had to be held. Many were suffering from tuberculosis. After the Allied attack around Arnhem, the Germans had deliberately slowed down vital transport carrying food to the industrial areas of the Netherlands. Food and fuel supplies ran out during the winter. Many people were so desperate that they ate tulip bulbs. Thousands died before the spring finally came, bringing the long-awaited liberation.

On the evening of Liberation Day ugly scenes took place as terrified women and girls who had "fraternised" with German soldiers were rounded up and had their heads shaven. Dutch Nazis, and other collaborators who had not already fled, were arrested as the euphoria led to an explosion of bitter anger amongst the recently liberated. But the Dutch are a reticent race. There were no public lynchings. A total of 154 death sentences were passed and only 42 were actually carried out. Practical as ever, the Dutch set most of the collaborators to work rebuilding damaged roads and buildings, especially at the Port of Rotterdam.

As the country slowly started to heal, a list was made of the ravages caused by the war; hundreds of thousands were dead or missing, and the war bill for damaged property soared to billions of guilders. The list of destruction included 70,000 houses, 8,360 farms, 10,000 factories and 200 churches.

There was a special figure for the Jewish population. In 1940, 140,000 Jews lived in the Netherlands – mostly in Amsterdam. At the end of the war much less than a third of that number remained alive. Of those that survived, most had lost everything – family, home, friends and possessions. Then the struggle to understand it all and learn from the lessons began.

**Preceding pages: still from *A Bridge Too Far*, food parcels dropped during Operation Manna. Left, Margraten War Cemetery, Limburg. Right, Liberation Day, Dam Square, Amsterdam.**

Many elements of Dutch society, like the Dutch themselves, are a study in contradictions. The Netherlands is a nation devoted to tidiness and a strong sense of order, yet its capital is known for pavements slippery with dog droppings, for graffiti-scarred walls and dishevelled drug addicts. The Dutch hate taking orders and gleefully jeer the self-important, yet they revere their monarchy. It is a nation founded on religious tolerance, yet features a powerful religious lobby. The people fiercely guard their privacy, yet leave their living-room curtains open all evening.

The Dutch rarely try to explain; to them, the contradictions are simply part of being Dutch. Like their sense of humour: the Dutch revel in hearing or telling a good joke, yet they also admit they are a stolid, dull people ("but not as dull as the Belgians," they quickly point out).

The emergence of the Netherlands as a nation can be traced back to the late-16th century. The whole of the Netherlands was then under Spanish rule, but already divided by religion. The southern provinces (modern Belgium and Luxembourg) were staunchly Catholic and accepted Spanish sovereignty, unlike the Dutch in the northern provinces who rebelled against Philip II's efforts to impose Catholicism on them and to stamp out the Calvinist movement.

The northern, Protestant-dominated region came to be known as the United Provinces after the seven member provinces signed the Treaty of Utrecht in 1579. From that time onwards, the United Provinces acted as a separate nation, though not one recognised by the Spanish. The alliance, which left each of the seven provinces with considerable independence, served as a model for the federalism that evolved in later nations, including the United States.

Then, as now, the Dutch hated being told what to do, whether by a foreign king or by one of their own dukes. As a result, the seven provinces were run in much the same manner as the medieval city-states of Europe. Each

province made its own laws and the other states had little or no say in a province's internal affairs. The only real influence of the States General, the assembly to which each province sent representatives to discuss issues of common importance, came in military affairs and occasionally in drawing up economic policy when that was considered an integral part of military strategy. The United Provinces rarely recognised a national leader, except in dire necessity, such as during times of war.

**Wealth creation:** There was another critical element in the way the United Provinces were run. Instead of allegiance to a king or prince or a set of ruling families, power rested with the commercial classes – the merchants, traders and bankers who created the wealth. And they did create wealth. The 17th century, despite continuing conflict with Spain, has become known as the Golden Age of the Netherlands; in that century the Dutch carved out a trading empire around the world and used their prosperity at home to create an era of achievement in fields as disparate as art, architecture and town planning.

Many believe that the Golden Age would

**Preceding pages: IJsselmeer fishermen. Left, Kurhaus hotel and casino, Scheveningen. Right, bridal flourish.**

have had no lustre if the United Provinces had not been founded on the principle of freedom of conscience. In one of the earliest examples of Dutch contrariness, Calvinism was the official religion and Catholicism was formally outlawed, but from its very beginning the United Provinces allowed anyone to practise any religion they wished, Catholics included, as long as they did not do so publicly.

This religious freedom, along with the then-rare freedom of the press, drew refugees to the United Provinces from all over Europe – many of them the richest, brightest, most ambitious and best-skilled in their own countries. Later, as the empire grew, many

**Roots of the welfare state:** Some commentators believe that the Netherlands transformed itself into a modern welfare state in the 1960s, but the roots go much deeper. Virtually every city and town has surviving examples of the *hofjes*, the small quaint houses, often set around secluded garden squares, that were built by religious organisations and family trusts for the poor and elderly. In Amsterdam, a popular example is the Begijnhof, a square just off the Kalverstraat pedestrian shopping area. Just as the unemployed, disabled and aged of the late 20th century find succour in the Dutch welfare state, the poor and hungry of the 16th and 17th centuries were provided with food and

natives of the Dutch colonies, particularly from what is now Indonesia, came to resettle in the Netherlands, often through intermarriage with the Dutch or working for Dutch companies. Consequently, the Netherlands has always had a cosmopolitan flair, mixing people and languages and races and religions – and everyone had a more or less equal chance of exploiting their own talents. One legacy of the Golden Age is that almost anyone could become a member of the clergy, an artist or a rich entrepreneur. Although not a completely classless society, most Dutch people belong to one large and dominant middle class.

fuel by various public and charitable organisations. Overall, about two-thirds of today's Dutch gross national product is redistributed by the government.

**Social structure:** For centuries, Dutch society was built on *zuilen*, or "columns" representing different components of the population. The members of each grouping kept to themselves but nonetheless did their share in holding up the overall ideals of the nation. The two main columns, naturally, consisted of the Protestants and the Catholics. They not only had their own churches, but also their own schools, civic organisations and political parties. Parts of some towns would be Catholic and other parts would be Protestant, and some whole villages were completely one or the other.

Since World War II, the distinctions have faded. Some historians give Hitler the credit, pointing out that the Nazi occupation forced Dutch who had never mingled – Calvinists and Catholics, city dwellers and villagers, northerners and southerners – to work together. Today, the *zuilen* are still there, but they are ineffective, there are perhaps more of them, and the Dutch find themselves members of more than one column. Perhaps the biggest change has taken place in religious attitudes. Regular church attendance has fallen dramatically, and polls indicate that

Catholic, became the leading Dutch politician of the late 20th century, with a series of Christian Democrat election victories that gave him repeated terms as Prime Minister. When protesters marched on Pope John Paul II chanting "Kill the Pope!" during a 1985 visit to the Netherlands, Lubbers was reluctant to criticise those who took part in the demonstration. "We do not believe in holy men," he told one interviewer. "The Pope came here as a man higher than others. That is not the Dutch way."

**Calvinist legacy:** Yet the Calvinists remain influential, using their powerful lobby to restrict aspects of everyday Dutch life such as drinking laws and shop opening hours.

many Dutch now class themselves as agnostics or atheists. A significant number of Dutch only set foot in a church for one of the non-religious talks, concerts or art exhibitions that seem to take place regularly in almost every church.

**Party politics:** In politics, the Protestant and Catholic parties merged in the 1960s, creating the Christian Democratic Appeal (CDA), which became the dominant centrist party.

Significantly, in this mostly Protestant country, the charismatic Ruud Lubbers, a

**Left**, Catholic church service. **Right**, carnival in the Catholic province of Limburg.

Dutch television features some of the most biting satire in the world, poking fun at all aspects of the so-called Establishment – except God and religion, that is, which still remain largely taboo.

The role of religion and the powerful Calvinist lobby may be at least partly responsible for the continuing contradictions – some might say they are hypocrisy, others just typical Dutch pragmatism – that continue to exist between Netherlands' law and day-to-day practice. To visitors, prostitution and drug use are obvious examples. Dealing in drugs is illegal, though you would not know it from the way that Dutch policemen stroll past marijuana cafés, and brothels were only legalised in mid-1990, though they have been flourishing in many Dutch cities for centuries.

**Contradictions:** A less well-known example is euthanasia – technically illegal but widely practised by doctors with the tacit approval of the authorities. Prostitution, soft drugs and euthanasia remain illegal because any attempts to change the legal status quo would be strongly opposed by the powerful Calvinist lobby. But such practices go on openly because the Dutch people, with their legendary tolerance and live-and-let-live attitude, don't really care whether they're illegal or not. The café owners and prostitutes are even

of the Netherlands can be viewed as a contributing factor in some of the country's most progressive programmes, including a long-term National Environment Plan, which calls for water, air and soil pollution to be reduced by up to 90 percent before the year 2010 – a goal that would consume up to 3.5 percent of the gross national product.

It is a programme and a cost that few other countries would dare undertake, but as one financial analyst concluded: "Gripped by Calvinistic guilt over lapsed stewardship of the earth, the Dutch are convinced that their country is the sink of Europe. They point out that it is a small, densely populated land, a third of which is covered with water, and

invited to become members of the local Chamber of Commerce.

This remarkable ability to look the other way can sometimes embarrass the Dutch. In recent years, for example, the Netherlands has been forced by pressure from other countries to act against its child pornography industry, which was supplying most of the rest of the world with explicit magazines and videotapes of youngsters in acts of sex and violence involving adults, other children and animals. "People, normal people, did not realise how nasty or extensive this stuff is," one Member of Parliament admitted.

At the same time, the Calvinist traditions

close to what they regard as pollution-spewing Britain and western Germany." No doubt the Calvinist traditions also have played a role in the leadership the Dutch have assumed in the world peace movement since it began in the Netherlands at the end of the 19th century.

**Order and respectability:** The Dutch liberal attitudes – perhaps "libertarian" would be a better word, though critics might prefer "libertine" – are one of the country's biggest contradictions. Despite the history of religious intolerance, the Dutch willingness to let anyone do anything that doesn't hurt other people seems at odds with other basic elements of the Dutch character. They are a people in many ways obsessed with respectability, with a strong sense of order. Some believe this is one reason the Dutch traditionally keep their curtains open; they want their neighbours to know that their homes are neat and clean, and that they have no reason to hide anything untoward that might be going on inside.

Some of the Dutch people's most interesting, and indeed most appealing, traits have emerged from this particular contradiction between tolerance and the need for respectability. A good example is the way a Dutch family on holiday will gather up everyone from grandparents to teens to small children,

the woman has no intention of ever meeting the man again, she admits that she, too, enjoys the slightly naughty, forbidden aspect of their telephone relationship. "He makes me laugh," she says, and in the Netherlands that can cover a multitude of sins, whether real or imagined.

**Women at work:** Dutch feminism presents a number of other contradictions. At first glance, women in the Netherlands appear to be among the most broad-minded and outspoken anywhere in the world. Is there any other society where so many women roll their own cigarettes? Yet, until quite recently, relatively few Dutch women worked, compared with other industrialised Western

and head for the nearest brown café so that dad doesn't have to go and drink beer by himself. Another example is the prominent journalist, a husband and father, from The Hague. For years he has been telephoning a woman from Friesland whom he met on a business trip. He always invites her to meet him for a tryst, and after her routine refusal he settles for telling her the latest dirty jokes. He makes these calls only from hotel rooms when he's travelling on business. And while

**Dutch contradictions. <u>Left</u>, porn cinema in Amsterdam. <u>Right</u>, traditional folk dancing in Friesland.**

countries. Formerly, Dutch women worked only until they got married and then they became housewives. Then they worked until they got pregnant. However, today increasing numbers of women go out to work, although a majority wait until their children are at school.

One interesting demographic sidelight of the Netherlands is that the majority of children are born at home, rather than in hospital. Several weeks before the scheduled birth, a midwife inspects the home to make sure the parents (or parent) are ready. Midwives generally supervise the birth. On the day after the birth, the government sends a young woman to the home. For the next eight days, from 7am to 6pm she acts as a mother's help: cleaning up, taking care of the other children, shopping, making meals, receiving visitors, and so on.

**Attitudes to royalty:** The Dutch may occasionally joke about their monarchy, but in fact the royal family is extremely popular. In typical Dutch fashion, they live in much less ostentation than, say, the British royals, and treat the accident of birth as a lifelong job that the fates have assigned to them. In Britain, abdication would probably be viewed as an earthshaking event equivalent to a national crisis; in the Netherlands abdication is routine. The last two queens have "retired"

**Under constant scrutiny:** The Dutch like their royalty down to earth – and will ridicule any pretensions to *kapsones*, or "self-importance". They are also less forgiving of royal foibles than some other nations. In the 1970s, Prince Bernhard, Queen Juliana's husband, was implicated in the Lockheed bribe scandal and was forced to withdraw from the world of business. Some think it may have hastened his wife's abdication, in 1980, in favour of her daughter, Queen Beatrix.

In 1986, Crown Prince Willem Alexander increased his popularity by completing Friesland's rigorous 11-cities ice-skating race under an assumed name, but he was also criticised in Parliament for appearing to align

in great dignity to let their younger heirs carry on, and it is likely that Queen Beatrix will do the same for Crown Prince Willem Alexander.

One of the reasons the Dutch royals are so popular is that they behave just like a modern family and the Dutch people can therefore relate closely to their problems. For example, Prince Claus, husband of Queen Beatrix, has been widely praised for his courage in discussing publicly his battles, over a number of years, with depression. "We like him for it. By discussing it, he's helped lots of other people with the same problems," one Dutch academic said.

himself with commercial interests by wearing a Marlboro ski-jacket and Playboy jogging trousers for the race.

**Family life:** The Dutch are very orientated towards family life and visitors from other countries often remark on the healthy, friendly relationship that exists between Dutch parents and their children. The common emphasis, if there is one, seems to be on avoiding the sort of conflicts that can create a permanent rift. One Dutch mother says she did not try to discourage her two daughters from teenage sex; instead, she accepted the inevitable and advised them on different methods of birth control.

When the daughters dabbled in marijuana, the mother didn't harangue them; she had smoked pot herself, and the burnt-out junkies on the streets carried a stronger anti-drug message to the girls than any of her warnings would have. When one daughter went through a punk phase, the mother didn't criticise her; instead, she agreed that it was ridiculous for people to be afraid of torn clothing and green hair. When the other daughter had her bicycle stolen three times in one year, the mother didn't ask for an explanation when a fourth bike was stolen and the daughter came home with a similar one a few days later. "I suppose she stole it," the mother said, "but who can blame her?"

room, but the Dutch do not feel the need to hide the way they live. At the same time they attach importance to the concept of *gezellig*, or "cosiness, conviviality," as represented by the *schemerlampen*, the soft-shaded "twilight lamps" still found in many Dutch homes. There's even a word in Dutch for sitting up late and watching the fire die down.

The Dutch also have a reputation for hardheaded shrewdness in business (in the 17th and 18th centuries they sold weapons to, and even underwrote the ship insurance of, their enemies). Yet quality of life is not equated with prosperity, and the gap between the highest and lowest incomes is much less than in most other developed nations.

**Golden Age values:** Dutch home life encompasses several values that seem to date back to the Golden Age. The television age has changed traditional trends, but it is still not unusual for a Dutch family to turn off the box and spend an evening together making conversation or playing music.

Still important is the concept of *deftig*, which doesn't translate directly but can be described as "dignity, respectability, stateliness." Visitors express surprise that most Dutch homes have no curtains in the front

Left, cheese porter in Alkmaar. Right, musseleating festival at Yerseke, in Zeeland.

The Dutch may at first may seem standoffish or even gruff. In fact, they love to go out to eat in large, noisy groups, following the Dutch adage, "Pleasure shared is pleasure doubled." The Dutch generally like to make friends and look for any excuse to chat: over coffee in the morning, tea in the afternoon and beer or *jenever* (gin) after that. A Dutch person who is dining alone in a restaurant is unlikely to be offended at an invitation to join someone else who is also seated alone. As a result, there is often ample opportunity for the visitor with the appetite – or the thirst – to learn first-hand about Dutch society and its many contradictions.

# MONARCHY ON A BICYCLE

The Dutch are not monarchists at heart but republicans who come close to thinking that everyone should be his or her own sovereign." If sociologist William Shetter is correct, it is even harder to fathom the appeal of the monarchy to Dutch citizens. Queen Beatrix herself is the most improbable of modern monarchs: this high-spirited, apple-cheeked queen wore a polo-necked pullover for the commemorative photograph of her investiture and is happiest cycling around the Dutch countryside.

The appeal of the House of Orange is linked to its role as a unifying force during the struggles for independence.

The Oranje-Nassau dynasty dates back to medieval times when the German Count of Nassau was granted estates in the Low Countries. However, the dynasty only came of age in the late 16th century when William of Orange, later known as William the Silent, inherited these estates, along with the southern French principality of Orange.

Since then, the moral specialness of the colour orange has pervaded Dutch life, stamping the constitutional monarchy with the Orange seal of approval. But apart from symbolic unity and the Orange name, William only left his heirs 12 guilders. Luckily, the fortunes of the House of Orange have grown considerably in modern times. A shrewd dynastic marriage in 1816 brought a Romanov dowry to the House of Orange and the fortune has accumulated ever since. The family motto is not for nothing *Je Maintiendrai*, maintaining, apart from wealth and power, an anti-militaristic stance, particularly respected during World War II.

In 1940, the royal family ensured its enduring popularity and the loyalty of its citizens by choosing exile in London rather than co-operation with the Dutch puppet government. During the Occupation wearing orange was considered an act of provocation by the Germans but on Liberation Day, the country was a sea of orange banners. Today, the royal colour is displayed on all ceremonial occasions, from Koninginnedag, Princess Juliana's official birthday (on 30 April) to Prinsjesdag, the Queen's ceremonial opening of Parliament (on the third Tuesday of September).

World War II was, however, only the first of a series of crises to assail the modern monarchy. Each successive crisis has proved a litmus test of Dutch sensibilities. In 1966, amidst general social unrest and post-war tensions with Germany, Princess Beatrix married a low-ranking German diplomat, Claus von Amsberg, previously a member of the Hitler Youth and the Wehrmacht. The wedding, held in republican Amsterdam, was the occasion for smoke bombs, tear gas and virulent demonstrations.

A decade later, Queen Juliana's consort, Prince Bernhard, was found guilty of being "open to favours" and of accepting over a million dollars from Lockheed in conjunction with lucrative defence contracts. Even so, Dutch tolerance and esteem for the royal family meant that a constitutional crisis was avoided. The Prime Minister himself accepted responsibility for the Prince's misconduct. Bernhard withdrew from public life, but is still remembered fondly by the nation. Even at the time, the press remained sympathetic to his plight, and quoted the former Queen Wilhelmina's remarks about royal pressures and the need to bend the bars of "the cage of royalty."

In 1980 the Dutch tradition of dissent broke forth with the investiture of Queen Beatrix in Amsterdam. The city was in the throes of a housing crisis, highlighted by the expenditure of 84 million guilders on the royal residence in The Hague. The popular slogan was *Geen woning, geen kroning* (No home, no coronation).

The royals were warned that in Amsterdam the civic ceremony could be viewed as political posturing or as the heavy hand of the Establishment but Beatrix bravely chose to be a scapegoat for anti-authoritarian feeling. The protests, described in such novels as Dirk Kooiman's *The Narratives of a Lost Day*, involved the squatting of 200 buildings in 27 cities and subsequent rioting as the police moved in.

The royal role is enshrined in the Dutch Constitution as promoting "the development of the international legal order." Also defined as "above politics", the monarch is the only fixed factor in a fast-changing political scene based on proportionality and plurality. However, the monarchy can be abolished at any time by an Act of Parliament and, according to the flexible terms of the Constitution, is given plenty of rope to hang itself by. Before the monarchy the country was ruled by an urban patriciate and rule by its modern equivalent, an urban meritocracy, is not out of the question. The Dutch are no blind loyalists and should the Orange dynasty die out, would not hesitate to proclaim a republic the following day.

The monarchy plays a key role in the formation of new governments, acting as a neutral negotiator rather than as a power-broker. In addition to its negotiating and ceremonial functions, the monarch presides over the Council of State, an advisory body on all draft legislation and international agreements. A presidential role is also part of the royal job description: the monarch liaises with provincial governors, ambassadors abroad and foreign leaders. The royal family is enmeshed in a democratic system of checks and balances, co-operation and compromise, but realises that its survival depends on consensus alone.

Yet, despite the brand loyalty towards the House of Orange, much credit is due to the individual influence of recent monarchs. In Queen Wilhelmina's 50-year-long reign (1898–1948), moral leadership was the keynote, albeit from an old-fashioned, autocratic stance. As a child her daughter, Juliana, was forced to sit on a golden throne while her playmates romped at her feet. However, on central issues such as religion, the Queen gave a lead. In accordance with royal custom, Wilhelmina was a member of the Reformed Movement and, as a pious Calvinist, encouraged the Church to resist the secularisation sweeping Dutch society.

In true Dutch fashion, Queen Juliana rebelled against her mother's imperiousness and put an end to the lingering 19th-century mystique of monarchy. During her reign (1948–80), Juliana proved to be a natural communicator with the common touch. Critics accused her of eccentricity, particularly after she employed a faith healer to support Maria Christina, her youngest daughter, in her fight against blindness. Greet Hofmans, the faith healer, came to be seen as a Rasputin in the House of Orange and was eventually sacked.

Irene, another of the four daughters, went on to cause her mother anguish by falling in love with a pretender to the Spanish throne, converting to Catholicism and renouncing her rights of succession. Not that any of this dented Irene's popularity in the public's eyes. As writer Adam Hopkins says, despite Irene's marital breakdown and her relationship with a TV personality, "people would say of her admiringly that she had twice the dress sense of the whole of the House of Orange put together."

The youngest daughter, now known as Christina, married a Cuban-born social worker, while Beatrix often said that if she hadn't been Queen, she too would have been a social worker. Even though marriage to a German was not a popular move, Beatrix soon endeared herself to the public by her egalitarianism, conscientiousness and low public profile.

The second richest woman in Europe, Beatrix is worth just under US$5 billion, has a tax-free income, a vast art collection and holdings in Royal Dutch Shell, KLM Royal Airlines and ABN-AMRO Bank. Yet her wealth is not resented since, in keeping with normal Dutch behaviour, she shows great social restraint, bordering on parsimony. Conspicuous consumption is out: the royal family resists ostentatious limousines and will drink cheap Luxemburger sparkling wine rather than fine French Champagne.

Likewise, Beatrix is careful not to inflate her role in the public's eye. While on a state visit abroad, the former Prime Minister Lubbers was criticised at home for self-aggrandisement; the Queen is careful not to make the same mistake. But in return for toeing the line, the royal family expects to be accorded a degree of privacy envied by members of other European royal families.

Today's House of Orange offers the nation peaceful continuity, symbolic unity, moral leadership and, in a country of faceless governments, an identifiable brand name. Above all, under Queen Beatrix, the Orange dynasty tastes of smooth, sweet professionalism. In fact, when pushed to define her job, Beatrix predictably replied that: "The Kingdom is something to be marketed, just like oranges." ∎

*The Netherlands is not where I want to
    live,
you always have to keep your urges in
    check
for the sake of good neighbours,
who peer eagerly through every crack.
You always have to be striving for
    something, thinking of the well-be-
    ing of your fellow man.
Only on the sly may you give offence.*

In his famous poem *In Nederland*, J.
Slauerhoff presents the typical metropolitan
view of provincial life. Such disparaging
sentiments are probably endorsed by many
would-be sophisticates in Amsterdam or
Rotterdam. The poet's criticism is not necessarily wrong but clearly the view of a privi-
leged outsider from *Randstad* Holland.

The *Randstad*, often translated as Rim-
City Holland or the Western Conurbation, is
the crescent-shaped area embracing Amsterdam, Utrecht, Dordrecht, Rotterdam, The
Hague, Leiden and Haarlem. Although the
*Randstad* is not a geographical region and
has no official status, the term encompasses
the Netherlands' most powerful urban centres in the provinces of North and South
Holland and Utrecht. This wealthy conurbation is the political, commercial and communications centre of the country; everywhere
else tends to be dismissed as "the provinces".

This *Randstad* bias only emerged with the
mighty Dutch Republic in the 17th century.
Before then, the distinction was between
town and country: an inhabitant's sense of
identity was bound up in the municipality;
and, unlike today, the southern cities were
more powerful than those in the west. Towns
relegated to provincial obscurity today were
then in the ascendancy. In the south, Middelburg, Maastricht and the old Flemish
towns were important dukedoms, trading or
religious centres. Nijmegen, in the heart of
the country, was an important member of the
medieval Hanseatic League while Gronin-

gen and Leeuwarden, in the north, were
prosperous merchant cities trading in spices,
tobacco and cloth.

With the creation of the Dutch Empire,
metropolitan Amsterdam and South Holland
province acquired a disproportionate weight
that it has never shed. Despite modern government's attempts at decentralisation, the
*Randstad* reigns supreme economically.
However, unlike the provinces, the *Randstad* is vulnerable to encroaching internationalism. The small-town flavour of the

region is endangered by silicon flatlands,
dormitory suburbs, chain hotels, cosmopolitan culture and fast food values. Paraphras-
ing the poet Hendrik Marsman:

*Thinking of Holland
I see broad bands of highways
cutting unchecked
through endless stoneland...
gas pumps, garages
demolished cities
factories and fences
in rigid expanse.*

This pessimistic view ignores the concentration of cultural riches in the *Randstad*,
from Rembrandts to Delftware, gables to

Van Goghs, international ballet to experimental jazz. The provinces can rarely compete on this scale. Even so, in looking at the glittering shop window of the *Randstad*, it is only too easy to miss the more old-fashioned goods in the stockroom. Despite the surface gloss of metropolitan culture, the provinces offer a truer picture of traditional Dutch culture and values.

There is, then, a strong case for seeing the Netherlands as two separate nations: the *Randstad* and the rest. Painted in broad brushstrokes, the distinction is between metropolitan modernity and provincial authenticity. Compared with the hectic metropolis, the southern and eastern provinces and the islands are more traditional, insular and agricultural, Hendrik Marsman's original poem continues:

*and sunken away*
*in the measureless spaces*
*the farms lie scattered*
*over the land,*
*tree clusters, villages,*
*blunt stumps of towers,*
*churches and elms*
*in one great expanse.*

Stepping outside the *Randstad* enables one to peer through the curtains of small-town Holland. Starting in the north of the country, on the remote Wadden Islands, one might encounter Texel boat-repairers, conservationists or fishermen. In summer, there may be sightings of enthusiasts practising the odd sport of *wadlopen*, "mud-walking" across the tidal mudflats of the Wadden Sea. In rural Friesland, dairy farmers can be spotted chatting outside huge pyramid-shaped farmhouses. Their obscure language, *Fries*, bears some relation to both English and German. In the capital of Groningen, the neighbouring province, university students can be seen gossiping in trendy chrome decorated cafés.

To the west, in Flevoland province, Urk is a poignant reminder of the price traditional fishing villages have had to pay for the damming of the old Zuiderzee (now called the IJsselmeer). Since the building of the Afsluitdijk and the ban on trawling in the IJsselmeer, local fishermen have had to go further afield for their catch. Recent European Community quotas have made life even more difficult yet the majority of fishermen continue to keep faith with Urk. Old values,

perhaps best exemplified by the wearing of traditional costumes, have been sustained.

Just east, in Overijssel province, the lake district based on the water-locked village of Giethoorn has been developed as a boating centre. Giethoorn's relative openness to outsiders contrasts with the tight-lipped insularity of the farming communities located in the region south of the lakes. Staphorst, for instance, has a strict church-going community whose members discourage the use of cars on Sunday and reject many aspects of modern life. South of Staphorst's sky-blue houses and neat farms lies the cheerful market town of Zwolle, yet another colour in the provincial patchwork quilt.

The eastern part of the province, known as Twente, is another casualty of *Randstad* economics. The old textile towns have declined pitifully, deprived of new investment and cut off from the commercial mainstream. West of Overijssel, the inhabitants of Flevoland could also be viewed as *Randstad* victims. The new polder landscape was intended to provide housing and green space for the adjoining metropolis. Instead, they have provided a home for reluctant white and blue-collar commuters who would rather live elsewhere. Emmeloord, on the Northeast polder, is really not much more than an overgrown housing estate.

Just west of Flevoland, North Holland embraces the *Randstad* with happier results. Despite bordering the metropolis, the cluster of former fishing villages has a clear sense of its identity. Volendam, for instance, has exploited its picturesque past as a modern-day tourist trap while Marken remains a traditional fishing village to all appearances – only without the fish.

South of the former Zuiderzee, most of Utrecht province falls into the urban *Randstad* but lesser-known Gelderland is a snapshot of suburban Holland. Apeldoorn advertises itself as "the biggest garden city in the Netherlands" but is, more accurately, a collection of gentrified garden suburbs. The

its surrounding heathland and peat bogs are recognisable as the same that appear in numerous of the painter's early landscapes. Although both provinces are dotted with unspoilt villages, the region offers evidence that international business can succeed outside the metropolis: Eindhoven, for instance, is home to the giant Philips electrical company. As for Limburg, the relocation of government departments to the province has transformed the former coal-mining town of Heerlen. Zeeland, the province just south of the *Randstad*, has elements of both northern and southern provinces. Proximity to old Flanders has given the region more exuberance than its northern neighbours while the

slightly snobbish inhabitants, often wealthy pensioners or old colonial families, suggest the last vestiges of empire, rather like a countrified Den Haag (The Hague).

South of Gelderland lie Noord-Brabant and Limburg, the Catholic, southern provinces which differ from the north in religion, temperament and economic success. Breda and Bergen op Zoom are a hearty commercial towns with a lively carnival and a Burgundian flavour. As for the Brabant countryside, Van Gogh's village of Nuenen and

**Left**, rural retirement. **Right**, IJsselmeer eel auction.

watery isolation has helped preserve intact its Protestant mores and traditions. Contradictory Zeeland is home to costumed farmers' wives in Middelburg, struggling fishermen on the coast and prosperous yacht-owners at scenic Veere.

Though there is no archetypal provincial town or village, it is possible to talk of "successful" and "unsuccessful" places, defined on the basis of quality of life and local satisfaction. Location does not appear to be a key factor: Amersfoort, 's Hertogenbosch, Maastricht and Groningen are all popular cities yet have little in common apart from their size. The same contentment is expressed in small historic towns such as Hoorn (North Holland), Heusden (Noord-Brabant) and Sneek (Friesland). Satisfied residents point to steady, local jobs, an attractive environment, good housing and, above all, to a sense of community.

A look at a few unsuccessful provincial towns in Flevoland proves more enlightening. Lelystad was built in the 1960s as a dormitory town for Amsterdam and Utrecht and as a recreation centre for city-dwellers. Lelystad followed what was then known as "the mathematics of space", the obsessively geometrical lines of the *De Stijl* architecture. The result, a characterless cluster of flat roofs, concrete and glass boxes and perfunc-

of drawers, intended to create the feeling of an old Dutch *buurt* (neighbourhood). Despite their good intentions, Almere has become an impersonal characterless suburb, largely due to its proximity to Amsterdam.

Disaffection with these new towns helps explain opposition to the Markerwaard polder project, which was eventually put aside. In addition, the more prejudiced provincials fear that the new polders will be used to house ethnic minorities, the unemployed and other "undesirables". Dutch planners now realise that provincials prefer vernacular architecture to mono-functional creations. In this vein, in the last few years there has been an interesting and ambitious development

tory tree-lined walkways, did not appeal to eclectic Dutch taste. Despite repeated financial incentives to move there, the town remains an unpopular architectural experiment.

Even so, given the rate at which the metropolitan population is growing and the existing pressure on inner-city housing, Lelystad needs to accommodate 100,000 people by 2000. Current residents complain that there is nothing to do in this anonymous new town planted in the middle of a sea of rape fields.

The architects of Almere, built on the edge of the *Randstad* in the 1970s, attempted to counter the anonymity of high-rise blocks with a construction resembling an open chest

on the Oosterlijke Islands just east of the Amsterdam Maritime Museum, called the "New East". The Java, Borneo and KNSM islands have unique architecture which offers residents a waterfront view just a few minutes by bike or ferryboat from the city centre. Over the next years, an area called Ijburg further southeast will also contribute to solving the housing problem.

In particular, the Dutch reject tower blocks: over 70 percent of the population lives in

**Above**, Amsterdam houseboat; **Right**, farmhouse interior at the Netherlands Open-Air Museum, Arnhem.

# DUTCH INTERIORS

In the Golden Age, Dutch canal-side mansions were very different from Venetian *palazzi*: the grandest Dutch rooms were always on the ground floor while the depth of the building was always greater than its breadth. Inside a gabled mansion in Amsterdam, Delft or Leiden lay a cornucopia of treasures. Marble fireplaces would be surrounded by Delftware tiles; the heavily embossed sideboards and cabinets indicated the burghers' taste for exuberant Flemish Mannerist design. Oriental porcelain, Venetian glassware and mirrors shone brightly despite the clergy's denunciation of such "devilish vanity".

Superficially, the modern Dutch home would appear to be a complete break with the past. Despite the love of order, there are occasional sentimental lapses into houses of cloying sweetness and Hänsel and Gretel tweeness. An immaculate front garden is often complemented by well-trained hanging baskets, matching window boxes and topped, perhaps, by a mail-box masquerading as a bird-house or dolls' house. The house itself is open to inspection. Through open or half-open frilly lace curtains, the domestic scene reveals yet more plants and even a collection of porcelain pigs on the knick-knack shelf. The provincial Dutch home often draws a fine line between sweetness and kitsch – before accidentally crossing it.

Closer examination, however, reveals shades of 17th-century values and tastes in the solid furniture, soft lighting and cut flowers, not to mention the orderliness, cleanliness and propriety. Sir William Temple, the British ambassador to the Netherlands during the Republic, was puzzled to find that spitting at banquets was frowned upon. Thomas Nugent, a 17th-century traveller, agreed, reporting that the Dutch were "perfect slaves to cleanliness... for the streets are paved with brick and as clean as any chamber floor." There is still a low shame threshold as far as cleanliness is concerned: until about 10 years ago, doorsteps were often scrubbed daily.

As for interior design, furniture is generally solid, imposing and, although shunning flamboyance, contains intricate details. Wardrobes embossed with Oriental porcelain and Delftware may be a relic of the past but traditional corner cabinets remain, often containing small Delftware collections. In the provinces, engraved Zeeland chests and ornate panelled Frisian wardrobes are not uncommon. Frisian clocks with heavy brass fittings have been treasured since Christiaan Huygens' invention of the pendulum in the 17th century. In the Wadden Islands and around the old Zuiderzee ports there is still enthusiasm for lacquered furniture, a taste acquired by sailors who voyaged to the Far East in the times of Empire.

Flowers are essential to the Dutch concept of homeliness. In provincial homes you will find a far greater variety and profusion of pot plants and cut flowers than in the restrained *Randstad*. All guests, however, are expected to offer flowers, rather than wine, to their host or hostess. Contrary to expectation the most popular flowers are not tulips but roses and chrysanthemums. "Say it with flowers" could have been a slogan coined by a Dutch copywriter.

The Dutch are natural magpies so just as every town has its own ethnographic museum, so every household has its traveller who has brought back foreign *objets d'art*, old prints or tacky souvenirs. Genteel Dutch taste occasionally stoops, if not to flying ducks, at least to horseshoes and, on the walls, a collection of rustic tools or Delftware animals. The soft lighting, which is reminiscent of Rembrandt's *chiaroscuro* paintings, creates the desired snugness. Candles are commonly used at home but they have cosy rather than romantic connotations.

Jacob Cats, the 17th-century moralist, likened the ideal woman to "a bright lamp, a golden chandelier", a very Dutch image of the woman as the moral beacon in the home. A virtuous housewife was also compared with a tortoise (the symbol of *zedigheid* or morality). The assumption was that by carrying a mobile home on her back, homely virtue was always with her. Still today the home is seen as her preserve and the font of peace, virtue and prosperity. ∎

one-family houses and rejects the architectural credo of the *De Stijl* movements: "No more masterpieces for the individual... but mass production and standardisation with a view to providing decent housing for the masses." The rural ideal is recreated in the Netherlands Open-Air Museum in Arnhem, where traditional farmsteads from Friesland, Drenthe and South Holland transplanted complete with woodland settings. In the real countryside, the residents favour neat, barn-like farms which are adorned with mottoes or decorative gables.

Any comparison between the *Randstad* and the provinces must take account of the importance of the land to the provinces. The

Brabant and Limburg. The farm buildings are equally individualistic.

Grand T-shaped farms are common in Gelderland and Overijssel while Noord-Brabant favours farms with long, low facades and Flemish barns. Limburg boasts delightful white half-timbered farmhouses and fortified farms built around a central courtyard. Friesland has the most eccentric farms, ranging in style from long barns to pyramid-shaped or granary-style ones, raised above the surrounding land on *terpen* (artificial mounds).

All Dutch farmhouses exude an air of security and dependability, the epitome of Dutch rural values. Old farms in Flevoland

Netherlands is 12 percent rural and 38 percent urbanised rural; the rest, including most of the *Randstad*, is urban. Farming is the one occupation that the provinces have in common. The fact that the Netherlands is the world's third largest producer of agricultural produce is, with the exception of bulb growing, largely thanks to provincial efforts.

Although specialisation is increasing, most farms are still family-run and passed on from generation to generation. The type of farming varies from region to region. Apart from horticulture on the polderland, there is cattle and dairy farming in Friesland, fruit farming in Gelderland and mixed farming in Noord-

often have mottoes adorning the facade. One typical motto, *Werklust* (joy in work), makes an important point: this is serious hard-working countryside. Elsewhere in the provinces, bourgeois new garden suburbs are popular, as are well-restored traditional gabled town houses. Because of the high cost of land, houses tend to be small, emphasising a love of miniaturisation and neatness.

**No ostentation:** Certainly there are differences in social status between a modest fisherman's cottage in the Biesbos marshes and a grand villa on the wooded outskirts of The Hague but extremes of visible affluence are rarer in the Netherlands than elsewhere. This was even the case in Amsterdam's 17th-century architecture: to our modern eye, the gabled working-class houses in the Jordaan are scarcely less impressive than the prosperous merchants' houses that line both sides of the Herengracht.

The provinces have long been a shrine to family values and a strong case can be made for saying that, since the 17th century at least, the Dutch have worshipped a domestic culture rather than a bourgeois one. As historian Simon Schama says: "The predominant perception among Dutch people is that for all their international orientation and progressiveness, there is still something of the mentality of the village or the small town: one's

image is important, an eye must always be kept on what the neighbours are doing, what the neighbours think, and anything that breaks out of the comfortable small-scale pattern is to be treated with suspicion."

The Dutch are besotted with children and most festivals accord children the central place. Many children's games were invented in the Netherlands and Pieter Brueghel's *Children's Games* depicts an extraordinary assortment of hoops, barrels, sticks, balls and climbing frames. Seventeenth-century

**Left**, Netherlands Open-Air Museum, Arnhem.
**Right**, first of the new year's lambs.

paintings present contrasting views of childhood. Jan Steen's *Family Scene* depicts a merry drunken scene in which the children behave just like their parents and have to fit in with the chaos while Pieter de Hooch's moral fables present an idealised view of family life. Docile children go fishing, play or help their mothers peel apples and stack the linen cupboard.

Today's children tend to be slightly spoilt materially yet, in return, are expected to be extremely polite, obedient and respectful. Critics of the provincial upbringing claim that too much emphasis is placed upon being *normaal*, which means conforming to parental expectations. In fact, a common expression is "Act normally and you're conspicuous enough," indicating the level of modesty and reticence expected.

It is not a coincidence that the most important national festival, *Sinterklaas* (St Nicholas), encapsulates a Dutch childhood. On 5 December the streets are full of shoppers buying last-minute presents for the feast of St Nicholas, the Dutch Christmas. St Nicholas, the patron saint of merchant sailors and children, traditionally arrives from Spain with his Moorish assistant, *Zwarte Piet* (Black Pete). Although the duo are impersonated by a father and uncle, the children's sense of awe is not dispelled when the mysterious guests say a few appropriate words about the children's behaviour.

Each present is signed by *Sinterklaas* and must be accompanied by a rhyming poem that characterises the recipient. The reading of the rhymes is a time when Dutch reticence and conformity are put aside. It is a chance to praise or scold children for their recent behaviour, manners or school record. The importance of the festival can be seen by the fact that it is the one holiday still invariably celebrated by those Dutch who have long since settled abroad.

Psychologists characterise the Dutch as an introverted family culture, one in which the well being of the family is paramount and the home is a fortress against the world. Most provincial housewives believe that cherishing the home is a virtue and an honour which outweighs the benefit of a second wage. As a result of this attitude, fewer women in the Netherlands go out to work than in any other European Community country.

Dutch feminists present a different story,

pointing out that the Dutch government was the last to sign an EC directive granting equal pay and rights to women. Moreover, the Dutch social services originally assigned benefits solely on a family basis. Feminists complain that even today social legislation discriminates against women and favours men. Although these criticisms are well founded, there is no conspiracy to keep women at home; the belief in the home as the cornerstone of Dutch life is a view genuinely upheld by most provincial women.

The role of the virtuous housewife is enshrined in Dutch art and standards of orderliness and cleanliness are high in real life. There are still set days to perform certain household chores. Mealtimes also have fixed rituals, including the 11am coffee break, the early evening meal and the greeting of *Eet smakelijk* (enjoy your meal).

In addition to acting the role of the perfect housewife and mother, the ambitious Dutch woman aspires to be a reasonable wife. But whether she lives up to the 17th-century definition of an ideal wife is debatable: "the spirit of Sarah, the virtue of Ruth and the humility of Abigail."

As befits the methodical humanity of the Dutch caretaker state, sick or elderly members of the family are well-cared for. Sheltered workshops are provided for the mentally handicapped while the elderly receive the largest state pension in Europe. Their economic power means that they are rarely a burden on the family and can spoil grandchildren with presents if they wish.

Provincial family life is essentially low key, comforting, conservative and conformist. The domestic cocoon is easily mocked but seldom pierced by outsiders. In fact, a predilection for cosy domesticity is often cited as the fundamental flaw in Dutch literature. Lyric poetry and fiction make all too few forays into the darker recesses of the soul. At the feast of St Nicholas, a budding Dutch Dostoyevsky would probably have been roundly criticised for his anti-social behaviour and encouraged to write fairy stories instead. Visitors who restrict their travels to Amsterdam could be excused for thinking that the Dutch spend their leisure time at the National Ballet, fringe theatres and discotheques. This is, however, a misleading picture of provincial culture. In a small village in Friesland, entertainment may be lim-

ited to singing in a local choir, television, skating or duck-hunting. As Simon Schama says: "If there is one Dutch culture, there are many rooms in it."

A clearer picture of provincial culture is presented by Heerlen, an unexceptional commercial town in Limburg. On a typical day, an amateur group will be performing a play in local dialect, various brass bands will be rehearsing for the Carnival and an experimental ballet will be on at the *Stadschouwburg*. For those in need of a simple night out, there are bowling clubs, multiplex cinemas, pancake houses and rustic-style bars. There, the beer is passed across the *teek*, the local word for bar counter, and regulars smoke,

drink, socialise or just read the evening newspaper. As Heerlen tourist office correctly claims, "the civil servant from The Hague feels just as much at home as the farmer selling eggs from the neighbouring village of Kerkrade."

Provincial culture is essentially populist and, in this, is heir to the hearty alehouse scenes painted by Jan Steen. Seventeenth-century burghers used to claim that: "the first little glass is for health, the second for a toast, the third for a nightcap and the next can only be for pleasure." Smoking, then as now, remains a popular pastime. Ludovico Guiccardini, a 16th-century visitor, called it "abominable but necessary" to ward off the chilly vapours from the swamps and dykes. Gambling also remains popular in the provinces. A visit to one of Heerlen's casinos on a busy night shows that the old Dutch dictum still holds good: "I invest, you speculate, they gamble."

Outside the *Randstad*, the survival of regional dialects, costumes, folkloric festivals and traditional sports indicates the diversity and depth of provincial culture. Even though there are few remote areas in the Netherlands, regional accents are proudly retained. Dialects are spoken in the Veluwe, Groningen, Drenthe and Gelderland. Frankish is spoken on the German border while dialects

of *Vlaams* (Flemish) survive in the provinces of Brabant and Limburg.

Guessing where someone comes from is a popular provincial game. In the case of Friesland, however, there is little room for doubt. The province has its own difficult language, quite distinct from Dutch, and, as the Frisian expression claims, "Bûter, brea en griene tsiis is goed Ingelsk en ek goed Frysk." *(Butter, bread and green cheese - it sounds the same in English and in Fries).*

**Dressing up. Left, traditional male attire among IJsselmeer fishing communities. Right, Alkmaar street performer.**

Regional costumes are yet another sign of the consciousness of local roots. Costumes are most common on the shores of the IJsselmeer, in Overijssel and on the islands of Zeeland. However, even within the *Randstad*, costumes have not died out completely. In Scheveningen, formerly a small fishing village near The Hague but now a popular holiday resort, matronly fishwives still wear their black costumes unselfconsciously; by contrast, young locals refer to their elders with embarrassment as "the black stockings."

In touristy Volendam, men pose for pictures in baggy trousers and women wear black striped or pleated skirts. In neighbouring Marken, once an island, the costumes are entirely different and worn more naturally. Women's dress includes bonnets, long-sleeved shirts, cotton waistcoats and embroidered bodices while men wear a red sash and a blue smock over their baggy black trousers.

Traditional sports and regional festivals continue to draw enthusiasts. Many activities such as skating, walking, fishing and sailing arose naturally from the landscape. In Friesland, duck-trapping, with dogs or decoys, was once known as "poor people's hunting" but is now open to all. In Middelburg (Zeeland), *krulbollen*, a curious form of bowling, is still played in summer. Friesland boasts the greatest variety of quaint sports, including *fierljeppen*, pole-vaulting over a canal, and *skûtjesilen*, races in flat-bottomed sailing boats. Even within the *Randstad*, several traditional pursuits remain. Every year, in the North Sea near Scheveningen, a five-day pole-sitting marathon takes place: the winner is the last person left sitting on the pole.

Ordinary sports are popular throughout the provinces but the emphasis is always upon group involvement. Soccer *(voetbal)*, the country's biggest spectator sport, is worshipped throughout the Netherlands. Cycling is naturally a common leisure pursuit, particularly on the polderland or in the Gelderland national parks. Walking events, such as the famous four-day Nijmegen marathon, are highly organised but community spirit is more important than competition. Golf, tennis, sailing and boating are increasingly democratic sports, with little snobbery attached to yachting.

Given the importance of domestic values,

leisure is often family-oriented or home-based. Gardening is so popular that even families without gardens cultivate allotments on the outskirts of town. Music is a deeply felt pleasure: even the smallest community has a music group or choir with its own banner, motto and public performances. Seventeenth-century genre paintings by Molenaer or Martens-Sorgh show leisured couples playing the virginal, lute or piano. Today, one is more likely to hear church choirs, woodwind groups and, in the southern provinces, brass bands. Even on a daily basis, the streets of many provincial Dutch towns (and even those of Amsterdam) are filled with music, ranging from muzak to

The Elfstedentocht (11-cities race) is a marathon skating competition over the lakes and waterways of Friesland. The race begins in Leeuwarden and covers 200 kilometres and 10 other cities before ending in national exhaustion, watched on television by virtually the whole population. There are usually about 300 serious competitors but over 18,000 skaters also try to complete the gruelling eight-hour course. The ritual begins and ends in darkness and skaters endure black canals, bitter winds, frozen polders and deep snow-drifts.

The competition is only held in severe winters but the infrequency of the race alone cannot explain its fierce mystical hold over

Flemish carillons and street organs.

Folklore fairs, cheese markets, herring festivals and southern carnivals have survived all over the provinces. In the time of the Republic, the *Middenstand* ("the bourgeoisie") had a taste for public displays and today's festivities are little different. Culturally, the provinces would seem to prove Huizinga right when he said: "Whether we fly high or low, we Dutchmen are all bourgeois – lawyer and poet, baron and labourer alike." If what he meant by "bourgeois" was a comfortable, conformist, unadventurous culture, then there is one ritual that elevates Dutch culture to higher ground.

the nation. One explanation for its cathartic effect is that it reminds the Dutch that theirs is not simply a plodding middle-class culture. At heart they aspire to an heroic flood culture that has forged its identity from ancient struggles against ice and water.

Although this may seem a romantic or charitable interpretation, the attachment to the provincial landscape suggests a similar intensity. A deep appreciation of Dutch landscape unites painters as various as Brueghel, Hieronymous Bosch, Ruysdael and, in more recent times, Mesdag and the Dutch Post-Impressionists. The love of landscape is best expressed in Ruysdael's moody paintings:

he places the horizon so low that cities and human life appear submerged in the cloudy skies.

This attachment to the landscape is at once proud and sentimental, as shown in Aad Nuis' poem *Abroad*:

*Holland is a field of grass, a sandy road,*
*a little yard with two chickens*
*I pack it around on my back,*
*It foams like the sea in my ear.*

On the face of it, the love of landscape is hard to fathom since nature dealt the Dutch an indifferent hand. The puritanical Dutch reply that through God-given grace they have redesigned the watery landscape. If so, having valiantly fought to retain the polders

against countless floods, the Dutch may have a right to feel proprietorial about their achievement. Feeling part of an heroic flood culture undoubtedly has an effect on the Dutch moral landscape.

The Dutch are a relentlessly moral people, in their aspirations at least. As Simon Schama puts it, "To be Dutch still means coming to terms with the moral ambiguities of materialism in their own idiosyncratic but inescapable way: through the daily living of it, in

**Left**, the Elfstedentocht (11-cities skating competition). **Right**, costume of the Marken islanders.

Sunday sermons on nuclear weapons and Monday rites of scrubbing the sidewalk." The 17th-century battle to put "honour before gold" continues, as does the struggle between puritanism and sensuousness. Newer, but equally important, moral dilemmas seek out the balance between individuality and conformity, tolerance and righteousness, merit and grace.

There are, however, significant differences between the moral values of the *Randstad* and the provinces. In practice, the *Randstad* weights the balance in favour of tolerance and individuality rather than conformity. Metropolitan intellectuals have even coined the term *Hollanditis* to describe the "Dutch disease" of excessive liberality. In The Hague and Amsterdam new *aktie* protest groups emerge daily to challenge the authorities on the housing crisis, environmental issues or unemployment. The provinces are far less confrontational.

The world view in the *Randstad* is also coloured by scepticism or cynicism, expressed in the Dutch concept of "relativising". This attitude involves casting an ironic eye over each situation to put it into perspective. The self-deprecating quality of being *ludiek* (playful) also helps deflate those in danger of earnest literal-mindedness. By contrast, the provinces view situations with classic Dutch earnestness and exactitude.

The provinces think of themselves as holding the moral high ground, usually supported by their religious faith and old-fashioned domestic virtues. The cornerstone is the belief in *deftigheid*, which, translated as dignity or decorum, masks the provincial yearning for respectability. The younger generation, however, even in the provinces, often equates the term with excessive civility, stiffness and even hypocrisy.

For the older generation, *deftigheid* can take the form of an obsession with propriety and good manners. One popular book of etiquette, *Now what's the right way to do it?*, provides invaluable advice. Nuggets include: "Well-bred people gesture as little as possible and, if they do so, ensure that it is done gracefully and harmoniously." Likewise, "Greeting someone with a big hug isn't done." Certainly, provincials attach great importance to manners. There are set times when coffee should be served to guests. When coming into a room, the newcomer must shake hands with everyone and introduce himself formally. In business letters, men and women often use only their initials to protect their privacy.

Such propriety and reserve can expose the provincial to the charge of mindless conformity but luckily individuals have ways of escaping this straitjacket. The tyranny of conformity is often broken by an outburst of bluntness. Writer Adam Hopkins recounts a typical incident in which a woman, with no slight intended, apologised for not greeting someone with the words: "I'm sorry I didn't recognise you but you're not the kind of person I would normally remember."

*Nivellering*, the trend towards equality,

**Sex and sanctity:** The Dutch are often accused of having the good life but of not knowing how to enjoy it. Certainly, the old battle between puritanism and sensuousness still rages in the provinces. The *Randstad* does not have a monopoly on liberal attitudes towards sex, as a visit to the small village of Baarle-Nassau indicates. Most of the 6,000-strong population are Catholics and worship with Father Dekkers at the Church of Our Lady. Virtually next door is the Funhouse, a sex shop *"gespecialiseerd in porno-video tapes, Amerikaanse magazines."*

The Dutch claim that the shop is aimed at the repressed Belgians in the adjoining village of Baarle-Hertog. A greater sign of

has helped blur class barriers, particularly in the larger cities. However, in the north of the country and on the islands, the social hierarchy is noticeably more rigid. In Friesland, Overijssel and Zeeland, for instance, social cachet still belongs to the bigger farmers, landowners and wealthy shopkeepers.

As if to counteract differences in wealth and status, there is little display of affluence or conspicuous achievement. Cheap champagne may be served in important receptions; a director of Philips lives in a house little better than his colleagues; in Groningen, an ABN-AMRO bank manager may drive the same make of car as his clerks.

tolerance lies in the shop opening times: all the Dutch shops are allowed to open late to keep up with their Belgian rivals. The struggle between godliness and greed is tricky but as a trading people, the provincials are no oasis of goodness in a sea of greed.

As far as illicit sex is concerned, the provinces prefer to blame *Randstad* decadence: "raffish" is a common provincial cliché used to describe Amsterdam. Yet, according to Dutch crime writer Nicolas Freeling, "the Dutch have a belief that sex has made them less provincial somehow – but few attitudes are more provincial than the anxious striving to be modern and progressive."

While partially true, the comment fails to explain why a search for a balance between sensuality and self-righteousness has occupied provincial minds (and bodies) since the 17th century. According to Simon Schama, "Orthodox marital sexuality was regarded as 'chaste', a kind of prolonged virginity" but illicit sex was frowned upon. Advocates of sensuality could take comfort from such paintings as Jan Steen's *Girl with Oysters*, an accepted visual euphemism for sexual availability. Lapsed puritans, however, could indulge in self-mortification by gazing at a 17th-century *Vanitas* still life.

Contemporary attitudes to sexuality are hard to fathom but the Catholic south is

*A wife that honours neighbours close*
*But seldom outdoors doth go*
*A wife that never grunts with food*
*Or goes into a pouting mood.*

Provincials are far from being jolly Burgundians in their overall attitude to life. Who else but a Dutch academic, Ruut Veenhoven, could write a book entitled *Is Happiness Bad For You?* On the vexed question of happiness, the modern artist Lucebert († 1994) should have the last word: "The Dutch are terribly heavy-handed about things. Of course, this has always been so… [we] take such a tormented path through life."

Most moral paradoxes come from the provincial attitude to religion. As the Dutch

undoubtedly even more liberal than the Protestant north in this respect. If the Amsterdam prostitutes' collective is to be believed, double standards prevail because provincial married men tend to be among their regular clients. According to Dutch feminists, Jacob Cats' 17th-century recipe for marital bliss is only too prevalent today:

*For wife, I'd wish a middling mate*
*Not too high born nor low estate*
*No slut at home no doll outdoors*

**Urban and rural contrasts. Left, Amsterdam's red light district. Right, horse market in the province of Drenthe.**

theologian J. van Laarhoven says, "Nowhere are there so many theologians – sure of possessing the truth – as in this country of churches and conventions, of peaceful believers and stern debaters, of practical tolerance and impractical pedantry." The provincial Dutch are tied to their religious landscape as a matter of course: religion is a key pillar in the traditional Dutch scheme of compartmentalising society. Known as *verzuiling*, this practice of dividing society into denominational groups was once widespread but has loosened its hold over the major cities and the younger generation.

Religion and *verzuiling* still pervade the

provinces, however, influencing the family's choice of school, newspaper, leisure pursuits, political party, hospital and pension scheme. It is still common for, say, a young Catholic teacher living in Noord-Brabant to be educated at a denominational college, join a Catholic brass band or chess club, listen to a Catholic radio station, read a Catholic newspaper, and go on a holiday organised by a local Catholic club.

By the same token, it is quite common for a Protestant member of the Reformed Church (*Hervormde Kerk*) or Orthodox Reformed Church (*Gereformeerde Kerk*) to follow a completely separate yet parallel path. A farmer from Zwolle in Overijssel might typi-

services of the Catholic Church have much more ritual and Catholics favour melodic hymns over more sombre psalms.

Although the two main Protestant parties are in the process of merging, the distinction between them is still important in the provinces. Approximately 32 percent of Dutch people are Calvinists; of this number 22 percent are Reformed and 10 percent Orthodox Reformed.

In the countryside the smaller, stricter Orthodox Reformed Church has greater power. It is traditionally more cohesive, conservative and working class than its big sister. By contrast, the Reformed Church is perceived as being more liberal on social

cally subscribe to a Protestant weekly, shop at a Protestant grocery store, be innoculated at a Protestant hospital, meet his future wife at a church dance and end his days in a Protestant old people's home.

Given the importance of these religious distinctions, people are skilled at reading each other's affiliations by scanning all visible clues. Catholics, for instance, distinguish themselves from Protestants by wearing their wedding ring on the third finger of the left hand instead of on their right hand. Naturally, the church services vary considerably in style and content. Compared with the sober tone of Protestant services, the

issues but more vulnerable to the modern trend towards secularisation. While Protestants dominate the northern provinces, the Catholics are in the majority in Noord-Brabant and Limburg and form a narrow majority nationally (38 percent). In the Catholic world, the Dutch are amongst the most liberal, in favour of contraception, women priests and Third World issues. Such views bring it into frequent conflict with Rome and a public protest during the Pope's last visit proclaimed: "The church, once built on a rock, is slowly sinking into the marshy soil of the provincial Netherlands."

Given the Church's high profile in the

media, trade unions, schools and social life, it is hardly surprising that Ruud Lubbers' Christian Democratic Party held sway in the 1980s and early-1990s. Interestingly enough, 70 percent of Dutch schools are still divided along religious lines despite the fact that 40 percent of all citizens are non-believers. The standard explanation is that academic standards are so high that no one wishes to change a winning formula.

In Amsterdam and other major cities, churches are being turned into exhibition centres but a Dutch Sunday is still sacrosanct. Although there are no Sunday newspapers, Sunday trading laws have recently been amended to allow larger stores to stay

open. Thus the former tranquillity of cities like Amsterdam on Sunday has been destroyed by hordes of visitors from the suburbs as well as tourists. Yet a Sunday visit to any rural community presents a scene little changed for centuries. In Staphorst and Rouveen, for instance, costumed farmers and their families walk to church in silent files. An old Dutch expression says: "Where blood can't run, it will creep" and religion has certainly crept into all corners of provincial society.

**Left**, a provincial interior, Marken. **Right**, Netherlands Open-Air Museum, Arnhem.

In the provinces, religion and morality can be as oppressive as an old-fashioned and tight-fitting Staphorst bodice. Dutch poets have often voiced uncomplimentary views on provincial values. Slauerhoff concluded *In Nederland* with a scathing attack:

> *The Netherlands is not where I want to live...*
> *I would grow into thicket and turn rigid*
> *Everything is too calm for me, too proper...*
> *And though the defenceless are tormented*
> *Never is one of those coarse peasant heads lopped off*
> *People never dance on the slack rope*
> *And never, no never, is there a lovely crime of passion.*

Although there still is some truth in this , particularly in the northern provinces, one is tempted to reply that if the poet had lived in a crime-ridden inner city slum, he might well prefer the tranquillity of provincial life.

In *Abroad*, Aad Nuis, a modern poet, presents a more ambivalent, hence more accurate, portrait of provincial life. The domestic imagery is typical of Dutch poetry yet also proof of the homely tenor of life:

> *Holland is an old house without a roof*
> *It has been occupied so long and so earnestly*
> *that nobody misses it, that roof, and the clock*
> *ticks, it's usually Sunday afternoon there.*

Attachment to place, family, God, domestic virtues and a restrictive moral code are not uniquely provincial. Most Dutch people would subscribe to a watered-down version of these traditional domestic values. However, in the *Randstad*, the blurring of social classes and an increasingly liberal and secular outlook have wrought changes in traditional values. Even so, the urban moral landscape differs more in emphasis than in essence: the *Randstad* dweller tends to present an international face to the world but you can be sure that he displays a provincial heart when he is at home.

If you are invited into a Dutch home, you may notice the cut flowers, the family Bible, the old piano, the home-made *appeltaart*, the expensive handmade toys – all clues to the fact that few nations are more domesticated than the Dutch. In this respect, then, little – except for a lapse in good taste – has changed since de Hooch executed his paintings of family life in the Golden Age.

Rare is a Dutch house or apartment that doesn't have flowers on the table or a window box in constant bloom. In rural areas, a house isn't a home without a garden. Only the Japanese buy more flowers than the Dutch. In the Netherlands, people spend an average of 150 guilders a year (£54/US$80) on cut flowers alone.

Bouquets appear for any occasion, often complete with their own mythology and hidden meaning depending on flower type, colour and presentation. A bouquet of less than 10 flowers is always a social blunder in Holland. And yellow tulips, for example, are the specified flower on birthdays that occur on 21 May. Legend has it that on this day yellow flowers also signal unrequited love. If presented upside down, however, this forlorn situation can be remedied.

Today the specially cultivated flowers, bulbs, fruits and vegetables that comprise Dutch horticulture bring in 10 billion guilders a year (£3.6 billion/US$5.6 billion) as an export. Horticulture accounts for nearly 25 percent of the revenue from all Dutch agriculture exports. With this boost, the Netherlands is the third largest agricultural exporter in the world after the United States and France, with most of its production going to European Union nations.

The Netherlands, and, in particular, the Westland area between Amsterdam and Rotterdam, exports more cut flowers than the rest of the world combined (70 percent global market share). In potted plants, the market domination is the same but the competition is tighter among neighbours. The Dutch sell 51 percent of the world's pot-plants; Denmark is next with 18 percent, followed by Belgium with 14 percent.

**Acres of glass:** In the Netherlands, more than 23,000 acres (9,200 hectares) are under glass in modern greenhouse production. About half is devoted to flowers and plants, the rest to hydroponic fruits and vegetables. The Dutch were quick to take advantage of

**Preceding pages: Keukenhof gardens in spring. Left, Keukenhof at the height of the bulb season. Right, preparing for the flower show at Eelde, Drenthe province.**

this 20th-century method of growing tropical or seasonal produce year-round. It works without soil by anchoring the plants in porous gravel and flooding them frequently with highly enriched, inorganic nutrients. Dutch hydroponically grown tomatoes, cucumbers, aubergines, lettuces and strawberries end up in grocery stores worldwide.

Over 60 percent of available land in Holland – 5 million acres (2 million hectares) – is used for agriculture. The specific activity is dictated by soil type. The abundance of

sandy soil means that over 60 percent of the land is used as pasture for feeding livestock to support the enormous Dutch dairy industry. Another 35 percent is rich enough for arable farming. Outdoor production of flowers and house plants occupies the rest: about 5,000 acres (2,000 hectares). With so much space for livestock, it is not surprising that the Netherlands has more pigs than people. The nation's 50,000 livestock and poultry farmers keep more than 14 million pigs, 5 million cattle and 90 million chickens.

**Manure problem:** Also not surprisingly, this small, densely populated country, with a very high water table, has a monumental manure problem. These animals produce more than 90 million tonnes of waste annually, about twice as much as is needed for fertiliser. Unfortunately, all of it has been going back on to the ground. The result is diminishing soil fertility, nitrate poisoning of the groundwater and even acid rain as a result of gases given off by the manure.

For the moment the government has restricted the wholesale spreading of manure, set herd limits and established "manure banks" for farmers to deposit their excess while scientists search for alternative uses for the unavoidable by-product.

**Origins:** As far back as the late 1500s, Dutch gardeners and botanists were setting European standards for horticulture and the design of stately gardens. As Dutch merchant vessels began to sail the world's oceans in search of tradeable goods, they often brought back new species and varieties of plants never seen before in the Netherlands or northern Europe.

The Dutch reputation for horticulture spread internationally, and, in particular, to England, as the result of the work of a Flemish botanist called Carolus Clusius (or L'Ecluse in French). From the 1570s, he was advising gardeners all over Europe on the care, cultivation and more scientific aspects of gardening and flower care, with special attention to the newly imported tulip. In 1587, Dutch enthusiasm for flowers combined with their appreciation of scientific study to found one of the first European institutes for botanical study in Leiden. Clusius was its second director and went on to lead the institute into the successful propagation of many new plant varieties, including tulips, crocuses and irises, thereby laying the foundation for the Dutch horticulture industry that we see today.

During this period, and for centuries to come, Dutch and French garden styles set the standard for the rest of Europe. This was especially true for the English where, during and after the Civil War, Royalists and Catholic sympathisers favoured French garden style, while Parliamentarians and Protestants leaned toward the Dutch style.

In Britain, the reign of the Dutch Protestant King William of Orange and his wife Mary (1688–1702) also had a large influence on English and European garden styles. Their royal gardener, a Dutchman named Bentinck,

designed one of the best surviving examples of a Dutch-style enclosed garden: the magnificent Hampton Court at Richmond-on-Thames.

Dutch gardens (ironically called English gardens in the Netherlands) were typically enclosed by a wall and divided internally by hedges. Brilliant and colourful floral patterns, topiary designs, tightly ordered and decoratively trimmed trees and ornamental hedges have always been considered typical Dutch features.

**Tulips:** The roots of Dutch horticulture and garden influence can equally be traced back to the import and development of the tulip, the Netherlands' most famous flower. The

tulip originated in the Caucasus and spread as far as present-day China. In the wild, the flower grows along a corridor on either side of the 40th Parallel. Explorers were sending back new varieties from this area until the start of World War II.

The first recorded instance of the tulip being successfully cultivated for garden use was in Turkey. By the 18th century, Turkish growers had registered more than 1,500 different tulip varieties and were the undisputed masters of tulip growing in the world. Strict standards for shape and colour were maintained and Constantinople was the only place where Turks could legally sell their bulbs.

For several Turkish sultans, the flower held a position of courtly honour, and festivals involving at least 500,000 tulips were annual events.

**Symbol of wealth:** Tulips came to Europe in the middle of the 16th century through trade and diplomatic channels, which is how Clusius obtained his first bulbs. With the growth of the East Indies Company, trade and prosperity increased in the Amsterdam area. The bulbs travelled easily and the rare and colourful flowers became a natural way for the increasingly wealthy merchants and *nouveaux riches* to flaunt their wealth. A garden full of expensive tulips was a sure sign of prestige and social standing.

During this period and long after, the most valued tulip had petals that were known as "feathered" for their broken or striated colour patterns. For centuries no one could determine what made the unusual and beautiful petals. Botanists were especially confounded because the patterns of one generation of bulbs would produce seedlings whose flowers often did not resemble their parental generation at all. Only much later did scientists discover that the breakage in colouring was due to insect-borne viruses attacking the

**Left**, posing at Keukenhof. **Right**, tulip and spider, Balthasar Assteyn.

bulbs. Experts also say that the tulips of this period did not resemble the familiar shape we know today. Paintings of the time depict them with larger, often ragged heads with more petals, less graceful leaves and overall a less streamlined look.

Because of the unpredictability from one crop to the next and the rising demands, rabid speculation on bulb prices took hold in the 1630s. The craze became known as "tulipomania" or "the wind trade" by Dutch florists, satirists and historians alike because nothing in the market reflected any true value of the bulbs; hence, trading the wind.

**Speculation:** As wealth trickled down to the middle classes the speculative frenzy in the bulb trade increased. Family fortunes were made and eventually wiped out in the bidding fever that gripped Amsterdam and the western Netherlands. At one point, one white flamed Semper Augustus bulb reportedly sold for at least 10,000 guilders (£3,600/US$5,600). Churches echoed with sermons on the evils of bulb gambling and politicians tried to prohibit it, no doubt fuelling prices even more.

Eventually, prices returned to more reasonable levels, and other bulb and corm flowers, such as daffodils, lilies, crocuses, irises and hyacinths, dahlias and gladioli, became popular, though none rivalled the tulip. Glass greenhouses, which began to multiply rapidly at the turn of the 20th century, changed the nature of the industry. In due course the rose displaced the tulip as the best-selling flower, a trend that continues to this day, with the tulip relegated to fourth on the sales charts, behind roses, chrysanthemums and carnations.

Growers in the Netherlands now produce more than 9 billion bulbs annually, two-thirds of them grown for export. Export bulbs are split into two markets: dry sales and the forcing market. Dry sales are simply propagated bulbs harvested from the fields. For the forcing market, bulbs are sold to greenhouses for year-round cultivation to produce cut flowers.

Hundreds of different species of flowers are daily sold at auction in the Netherlands. The vast majority – 90 percent of all bulbs and flowers and 85 percent of other fruits and vegetables – are sold through the unique Dutch "clock" auction system. Under this system, the pointer turns round a large dial indicating the price of a lot. Prices start high and decrease as the pointer turns. Bidders can stop the clock at the price they are willing to pay. Across the country 41 separate auctions use this system for selling flowers, fruit and vegetables, including the world's largest, located at Aalsmeer, near Schiphol airport, which is also open to visitors.

In the old days, buyers used to gather in the growers' fields to inspect the crop in the ground before the bidding would start. Today these so-called "green" auctions have become exceedingly rare. With the technical precision and predictability of greenhouse growing, produce and bulbs are now "sold forward," meaning that the bulbs are still in

a set number of weeks depending on the plant. Then the process starts all over again, with the best samples used for breeding, and the rest sold. These plants have not seen a rainy day for dozens of generations and black dirt, to them, is ancient history.

Growers prefer test-tube methods because they increase productivity and speed up the search for new colours, qualities and varieties. Methods are now so well developed that 1 million seedlings a year can be produced from a single plant. This method also guarantees that the plants are disease-free, which opens up new export markets, such as Australia and New Zealand, both of which have strict import regulations.

the ground or the produce still on the vine at the time of purchase. At the auctions now, brokers acting for buyers and sellers do all the bidding, while thousands of packers and shipping agents wrestle with millions of flowers in other parts of the auction.

**New techniques:** Most plants are still cultivated vegetatively, by sowing or striking off young buds from the more mature and strongest plants. But tissue culture and meri-stem culture are used increasingly as methods of ensuring quick, identical and disease-free flowers. Under a microscope, laboratory technicians cut tiny stems from young plants. The cuttings are then grown in test tubes for

With the rising cost of natural gas needed to heat the greenhouses and of electricity to run every other automated, and computer-controlled, climatological aspect, growers are now hunting for plant strains that can be grown without the consumption of so much heat and light. Many Dutch laboratories are also working hard to produce infertile plants so that competitors cannot profit from their research and produce new generations of flowers nearly identical to the seedlings they purchased. One can only imagine what these vegetative eunuchs might be called.

**Left and right, Aalsmeer flower auction.**

# BLOSSOMS AND BULBS

The first truly commercial cut-flower farm was established almost 200 years ago in Aalsmeer when local growers switched from producing strawberries to the cultivation of flowers. Today the nation's centre for floriculture remains embedded in much the same place, although West Friesland is becoming a major contender.

The bulb district or *de bollenstreek* is generally the corridor between the dunes and the dairy farms west of Amsterdam, extending south as far as Rotterdam. The compact, easily traversed area is also known as the Westland. The major bulb-growing fields, greenhouses, gardens, research laboratories, auction centres and bulb distributors are all located in this region.

Spring is the best time to get the double-barrelled fragrant and visual effect. The miles of tulip fields are generally in bloom during the last week in April. From North Holland, all the way down the dunes, the paths and roads are crammed with cars, bicycles and pedestrians come to view the blossoms. Whether from a distance or up close, the fields are a mass of alternating tracts of yellow, reds, oranges and pinks. And then it starts all over again a few miles away.

Hordes of people are drawn to this annual sight because it is so short-lived and the acres of colour are so spectacular. The tulip blossoms are out for only seven to 10 days before they are mechanically mown down and, with callous efficiency, piled by the canalside.

The bulbs are only allowed to flower because the grower needs to be sure the plants in his field are the proper tint and free from disease or mutation. The longer the plant is allowed to support the blossom, the more nutrients it draws off the bulb, resulting in a weaker plant that will produce fewer side bulbs in future years, and the aim of the game is to encourage the parent bulbs to produce bulblets for growing on and subsequent sale.

The best way to see the fields, weather permitting, is on bicycle. Rental is easy in the Nether-

lands and the paths through the bulb fields are extremely popular and well-marked. Go during the week if possible, to avoid the weekend scrum. The Dutch tourist office has set up a route from Alkmaar in northern Holland south to The Hague which is about 70 miles long (112 km) and divided into two portions. Another popular route is the 38-mile (60-km) stretch between Leiden and Haarlem. Maps are available locally along with peak viewing information.

The accurately self-described "greatest flower show on earth" takes place every spring at the Keukenhof in Lisse just south of Haarlem. The 70-acre (28-hectare) site features numerous canals, 10 miles (16 km) of paths, indoor and outdoor exhibitions and three cafeterias, which have to cope with over 900,000 visitors during the nine weeks of the bulb season, when the ground erupts with the buds of over 7 million tulips and other flowers.

The site of an old castle, the land at Keukenhof was leased by the owner, Count van Lynden, to a group of bulb growers who turned it into a permanent showcase for the floral industry in 1949. The grounds are only open from late March to the last week in May. Crocuses bloom first, then tulips around mid to late-April, followed by daffodils, narcissi and hyacinths.

Just a few minutes south of Amsterdam by train is Aalsmeer, home of the first Dutch flower auction, established in 1911. It is also the largest flower auction in the world in both volume and size – 50,000 deals daily are crammed on to a 75-acre (30-hectare) site.

The unique Dutch "clock" auction is the major method of selling nearly every sort of produce in the country. The brokers in the gallery are seated at desks equipped with electronic bidding buttons connected to the price clock.

The clock starts at "noon", which represents the highest prices, and sweeps downward. Buyers can stop the clock when it reaches the price they are prepared to pay. The highest bidder gets the first choice from the produce in that lot and his bid is recorded and posted. Then the auction quickly continues until the whole of the lot is sold. Only with this rapid method is it possible to move as much merchandise as they do here. ∎

Traditionally the Dutch eat plain, wholesome food; several different types of bread, a wide choice of vegetables, various meats – veal, beef, pork and lamb, poultry and game – fish and seafood, milk and dairy products and fruit.

The southern provinces are well known for Burgundian pleasures of the table, while the whole country now goes in for every exotic food fad that comes along. Most national cuisines can be enjoyed in the larger cities – everything from Kurdish to Thai, to French and Ethiopian. Even the smallest villages will have a Chinese-Indonesian takeaway and, increasingly, Surinamese (a spicy mixture of Creole and Indian) is becoming popular for low-budget dining.

In the 17th century the Dutch, inspired by their East Indies Company, began to cultivate as many exotic fruits as they could induce to grow. In 1636 the great still-life artist Jan Davidsz de Heem even chose to live in Antwerp (now in Belgium) because, Sandrart recorded, "there one could have rare fruits of all kinds, large plums, peaches, cherries, oranges, lemons, grapes, and others, in finer condition and state of ripeness to draw from life."

**Winter fuel:** Severe winter weather and travel by foot, on skates or by boat necessitated large, hearty meals rich in fats and carbohydrates to provide energy and keep in body heat. Life is now more amenable so vast meals are a thing of the past and thick pea soups and mashed vegetable dishes omit the extra fat for the weight-conscious. The most traditional winter dish, and still popular among the older generation, is *boerenkool - stamppot met worst* (cabbage mashed with potatoes and served with smoked sausage *rookworst*). There is a Dutch saying that *boerenkool* ("farmer's cabbage", which we know as kale) is best when taken from the ground after the first frost. But young people tend to prefer McDonald's.

Other specialities include ham and asparagus (in May and June), smoked eel, beans

**Preceding pages:** oyster barons of Yerseke, Zeeland. **Right**, traditional method of consuming herrings.

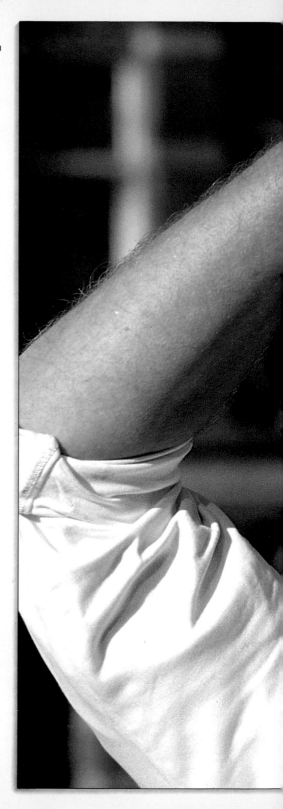

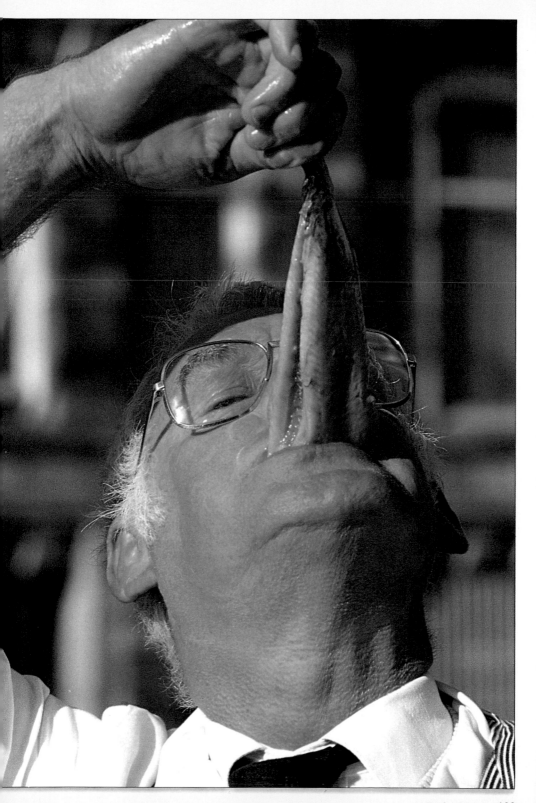

and bacon, special puddings with whipped cream, pancakes and the famous herring. Herrings are eaten as a snack, raw or salted, with plenty of chopped onion, either picked up by the tail and dropped whole into the mouth, or, more often, eaten with a fork from a small plate. Herring stalls are a feature of Dutch life, especially in May when everyone wants to try the mild *nieuwe haring* – the first herring of the season.

The Dutch are thrifty and consequently do not waste time in lengthy preparation of food or in the use of fuel for cooking; they prepare what is easily available for the least effort.

Many people drink beer, especially *pils*, a light beer, though the national drink is *jenever*

Nicholas. This mulled wine is used for a Dutch toast – *Gezondheid* (Your health!) or *Proost*.

Coffee is usually served with a special thick condensed milk. Hot chocolate is mostly a winter drink and when people go skating, private stands are set up on the ice, with large urns on stoves, selling the warming liquid all day to the skaters.

The bread basket on a breakfast table holds a varied selection of bread – from insipid, pre-cut white to heavy, black rye, and perhaps wholewheat, raisin and seed bread. A spiced cake, *ontbijtkoek* or *peperkoek*, often eaten just with butter, varies according to each province. Some towns have their own

or Dutch gin, made from distilled malt wine with juniper berries.

At about 5pm people drop into their local café for a *borrel*: a small glass of either the colourless *jonge* (young) *jenever*, less creamy than the *oude* (old), which has a pale yellow colour and a noticeably heavier, more perfumed flavour.

The Dutch are famous for their liqueurs and fruit brandies, although these are now losing popularity to imported drinks, such as Campari. Beer, mineral water and wine are drunk with meals. A favourite New Year drink called *Bisschopswijn* ("Bishop's Wine") may have been named after St

special recipes for *peperkoek* which are closely guarded by local bakers. In larger towns croissants are overtaking the *broodje* (bread roll) as a snack food, and are sold filled with combinations of cheese, ham, liver, shrimp, smoked eel, steak tartare, salad or herring.

Pastries are light and inventive. On St Nicholas' Eve (5 December) chocolate letters of the alphabet are made to be given to friends and family. The *boterletter*, made from old-fashioned puff pastry and almond paste filling served hot, is still a traditional part of the festivities. For a Christmas wreath (*kerstkrans*) the Dutch shape the *boterletter* into a ring instead of a letter. It is then spread with icing and decorated with candied cherries, orange and lemon peel and a red bow.

The Dutch are becoming increasingly vegetarian – an easy way of life in a country so rich in vegetable and fruit farms. Potatoes, kale and *zuurkool* (*saur kraut*) are winter staples. There is an abundance of asparagus in the late spring, and fennel and various green and white beans, peas, courgettes, eggplant, artichokes, carrots, onions, spinach and many salad foods are all produced in quantity by the hothouse horticulturalists of the Netherlands.

At the other extreme, the Netherlands is the only country in Europe where it is legal

son covered with mashed potatoes made into a pie and topped with sliced apples and breadcrumbs. It is served with red cabbage.

In all country areas free-range poultry is plentiful – many families rear their own chickens, guinea-fowl, turkeys, ducks and geese. In restaurants fowl is often accompanied by apple sauce or *stoofpeertjes* ("little stewing pears" cooked in red wine and cinnamon), or redcurrant sauce.

Oysters and mussels are on sale from mid-September to the end of April depending on the weather – if it is too hot the season is delayed. Lobster, shrimp, scallops, trout and crab are also on most good menus and fresh salmon is often smoked just before serving,

to shoot wild boar all the year round. The main hunting areas lie in the province of Limburg, particularly the woods between Maastricht and Venlo. However, restaurant customers are used to a distinct game season in the cold months and there is no demand for wild boar in the summer. Quail, partridge, pheasant, hare and rabbit are all popular and frequently encountered winter dishes, mostly cooked in beer, wine or cognac.

A traditional game recipe is *Jachtschotel* ("Hunter's Dish"), made from stewed veni-

**Left**, a herring stall in Albert Cuypmarkt, Amsterdam. **Right**, smoked eels, Volendam.

giving it a much lighter taste.

**Sweeteners:** Desserts in restaurants might well be the traditional Dutch *flensjes* (thin pancakes) but given a fancy French name – such as crêpes Suzette or crêpes Bresilliennes, the latter filled with vanilla ice cream coated with a warm sauce made from half chocolate and half coffee. Ordinary pancakes are usually served with maple syrup or *stroop*, a type of treacle similar to Golden Syrup. At home the dessert is likely to consist of a delicious and filling bread pudding made from slices of stale bread, eggs and dried fruit. *Vla* is also a popular country dessert, similar to custard. You will seldom find it in restaurants but shops and supermarkets sell many different kinds of *vla* flavoured with vanilla, chocolate or fruits.

The Dutch are also fond of sweets and biscuits. *Stroopwafel* consists of two thin wafers sandwiched by syrup, best eaten when warm and served with afternoon tea. Spiced cookies, *speculaas*, often windmill-shaped, are sold in packets or by weight and eaten with coffee. In the past they were made on *koekplanken* ("cookie planks"), moulds hollowed out into the shapes of windmills, mermaids, elephants or whatever; today, genuine *koekplanken* are sold in antique shops and modern copies are made as souvenirs and widely available.

opened to flood the surrounding land; faced with the prospect of drowning, the invaders retreated.

When a Leiden boy climbed up to explore the deserted ramparts he found a big black iron pot left by the Spanish containing a stew of beef and vegetables. The people of Leiden make their own commemorative *hutspot* with *klapstuk* (boneless beef short ribs), carrots, potatoes and onions.

In Zeeland, fish and seafood predominates, especially mussels, oysters, sole and turbot. Many local restaurants are built on stilts at the water's edge. There are also many glass-fronted restaurants where you can sit and enjoy the outlook over the beach.

**Regional foods:** Each province has its own food specialities: in Maastricht, in Limburg province, the local dish is a stew resembling Hungarian goulash. Raw vegetable salads served with sausages are also popular. Their local pastry (*vlaai*) is either filled with seasonal fruits (ranging from apricots abd cherries to apples or plums) topped with a lattice pattern or filled with rice and cream.

The people of Leiden, eat *hutspot* on 3 October to commemorate the town's liberation from the Spanish in 1574. Leiden had been under siege for several months and the townspeople were starving until Prince William of Orange ordered the sluices to be

In the polder lands in the northern part of the country, and also in the new province of Flevoland, country dwellers keep their own cattle, pigs and hens. These people are reknowned for their hard work, and on the whole they eat more meat than city dwellers. A family of six might, on average, eat more than 4 lb (2 kg) of meat every day, whereas in Amsterdam a similar family may only have a smaller amount of meat twice or three times a week.

Because of Holland's colonial legacy, Indonesian food is extremely popular and has become integrated into the Dutch way of life. The best Indonesian restaurants, though, are in the larger cities such as The Hague, Amsterdam and Rotterdam.

Some have adapted traditional regional cooking to create hybrid dishes, more suited to Dutch taste. Thus *saté* often consists of grilled steak on small bamboo skewers, or other meats such as veal and lamb instead of the more traditional pork or chicken saté served with peanut sauce or fish served with limes.

Another dish which is served hot with peanut sauce poured over it is *gado gado* – a salad, too often a mixture of green and white cooked beans, carrots, potatoes, onion and spinach decorated with hard-boiled eggs instead of more exotic and more authentic combinations of avocado, bean sprouts and prawn crackers.

nanas), and *atjar ketimoen* (cucumber sticks marinated in vinegar).

To follow, *spekkoek* is an Indonesian sponge cake layered with spices; alternatives include a spicy fruit salad of sweet and sour fruits, or banana fried in light batter with a honey sauce.

**Eating out:** Restaurant food can be expensive, though a relatively inexpensive Tourist Menu is offered by more than 400 restaurants in Holland, all of which display the sign of a white fork on a blue background. The Tourist Menu consists of an entrée, a main dish and a dessert. The price of this meal is the same everywhere, though the menu is always different. In most restaurants there is

**Oriental banquet:** The Indonesian rice table, *rijsttaffel*, has anything from 16 to 30 dishes based around rice. Good restaurants never serve the same choice twice so each visit is a new experience. A selection of dishes might include *sambal telor* (egg in fiery red sauce), *sambal oedang* (shrimps in a red sauce), *babi pangang* (pieces of roast suckling pig in a mild spicy sauce), *pisang goreng* (fried bananas).

**Left**, traditional butcher, Groningen province. **Right**, baked with pride – festival pies in Limburg province.

a children's menu (*kindermenu*) offering what has proved to be the Dutch child's favourite food – grilled chicken, chips and apple sauce – plus other familiar favourites such as meat rissoles.

You can recognise a typical Dutch restaurant by the emblem *Neêrlands Dis!* accompanied by a red, white and blue soup terrine. More than 300 excellent restaurants bear this sign. It means that a wide choice of original Dutch and/or regional specialities can be found on the menu, which varies with the season. And when the waiter says "*Smakelijk eten*", he is not being rude; he is telling you to enjoy your meal.

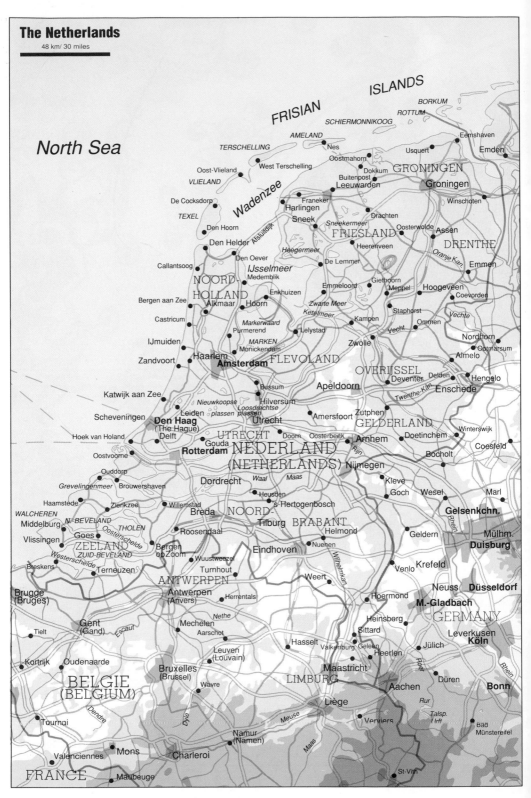

# The Netherlands

48 km/ 30 miles

FRISIAN ISLANDS

BORKUM

ROTTUM

SCHIERMONNIKOOG

AMELAND

North Sea

TERSCHELLING
Nes
Oostmahorn
Eemshaven
Usquert
Emden

West Terschelling
Dokkum
Buitenpost
GRONINGEN

Oost-Vlieland
Franeker
Leeuwarden
Groningen

VLIELAND
Harlingen
Winschoten

De Cocksdorp
Sneek
Drachten

TEXEL
FRIESLAND
Oosterwolde
Assen

Den Hoorn
Heerenveen
DRENTHE

Den Helder
Aflsuitdijk
De Lemmer

Den Oever
Oranje Kan.
Emmen

Callantsoog
IJsselmeer
Medemblik
Emmeloord
Giethoorn
Hoogeveen
Coevorden

NOORD-
HOLLAND
Enkhuizen
Meppel

Bergen aan Zee
Alkmaar
Hoorn
Zwarte Meer
Staphorst
Vechte

Castricum
Ketelmeer
Vecht
Ommen
Nordhorn

Markerwaard
Purmerend
Lelystad
Kampen
Ootmarsum

IJmuiden
MARKEN
Zwolle
Almelo

Zandvoort
Monickendam
FLEVOLAND
OVERIJSSEL
Delden
Hengelo

Haarlem
Bussum
Deventer
Enschede

Amsterdam
Apeldoorn
Twenthe-Kan.

Katwijk aan Zee
Nieuwkoopse
plassen
Hilversum
Loosdrechtse
plassen
Amersfoort
Zutphen
GELDERLAND
Winterswijk

Scheveningen
Leiden
Utrecht

Den Haag
(The Hague)
Delft
UTRECHT
Doorn
Oosterbeek
Arnhem
Doetinchem
Coesfeld

Hoek van Holand
Gouda
NEDERLAND
Bocholt

Oostvoorne
Rotterdam
(NETHERLANDS)
Nijmegen

Ouddorp
Dordrecht
Waal
Maas
Kleve
Goch
Wesel
Marl

Grevelingenmeer
Brouwershaven
Heusden
's-Hertogenbosch

Haamstede
Zierikzee
Willemstad
Breda
NOORD-
Gelsenkchn.

WALCHEREN
N.-BEVELAND
Roosendaal
Tilburg
BRABANT
Geldern
Mülhm.

Middelburg
THOLEN
Helmond
Duisburg

Vlissingen
Goes
ZEELAND
Bergen
op Zoom
Eindhoven
Nuenen
Venlo
Krefeld

Breskens
ZUID-BEVELAND
Wuustweezel
Weert
Neuss
Düsseldorf

Terneuzen
Turnhout
Roermond
M.-Gladbach

ANTWERPEN
Heinsberg
GERMANY

Brugge
(Bruges)
Antwerpen
(Anvers)
Herrentals
Sittard
Leverkusen

Gent
(Gand)
Nethe
Mechelen
Aarschot
Hasselt
Valkenburg
Geleen
Jülich
Köln

Tielt
Leuven
(Louvain)
Heerlen
Roer

Kortrijk
Oudenaarde
Bruxelles
(Brussel)
Wavre
Maastricht
Düren
Bonn

BELGIE
(BELGIUM)
LIMBURG
Aachen
Rhein

Liège
Rur
Talsp.
Urft
Bad
Münstereifel

Tournai
Verviers
St-Vith

Valenciennes
Mons
Namur
(Namen)
Maas

FRANCE
Maubeuge
Charleroi

120

# PLACES

The Netherlands is a small country, approximately 160 miles (255 km) north to south and 112 miles (180 km) east to west. English speakers habitually refer to the country as "Holland". The Dutch know the country as the Kingdom of the Netherlands. Strictly, Holland refers only to the two provinces of Noord (North) and Zuid (South) Holland. Most of the best-known cities of the Netherlands are located in these two provinces, including the administrative capital, The Hague ('s-Gravenhage, or Den Haag, in Dutch), Rotterdam, Amsterdam, Delft, Leiden, Gouda and Haarlem.

This densely populated region seems, from the train, one unbroken conurbation. The distances separating these cities and towns is small, and the Dutch call the region the *Randstad*; this means ring-town but a better, if less literal translation, is "the big village".

The rest of the Netherlands comprises 10 provinces: Zeeland, Utrecht, Noord-Brabant, Limburg, Gelderland, Flevoland (created in the 20th century from reclaimed land and declared a province only in 1986), Overijssel, Drenthe, Groningen and Friesland.

The landscape and character of these more rural provinces is surprisingly varied and conforms little to the cliché-ridden image of flat, monotonous polder. Zeeland is a region of islands, peninsulas, sandy coastline and bird-filled marshes. The southern provinces of Noord-Brabant and Limburg have a distinctly Catholic culture, a more flamboyant, Gothic-inspired architecture and wooded hills.

Further north, the great rivers (Rhine, Meuse and Waal) cut through the heath and woodland landscape of the central provinces, while Gelderland and Overijssel form a region of meadowlands, orchards and streams, known as the *Achterhoek* (back corner).

In Drenthe the wilder landscape is dotted with megaliths, marking the giant communal graves of prehistoric settlers, and, as the province merges into Groningen, with man-made hillocks rising from the peat levels, further evidence of early settlement. Finally Friesland, with its thatched barns and farmhouses, gives way to the shallow Waddenzee and a chain of unspoiled islands.

Exploring this varied country is made easier by the network of tourist information centres (known by the initials vvv), which are found in virtually every town. As well as handling bookings for accommodation and entertainments, they are an excellent source of free maps and general information.

<u>Preceding pages</u>: the windmills of Kinderdijk; Amsterdam's Oude Kerk; traditional Friesland pottery.

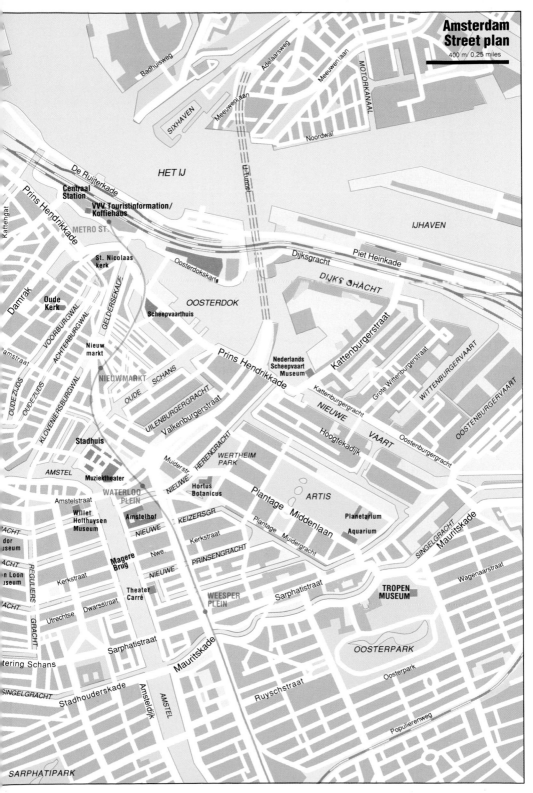

**Amsterdam Street plan**

400 m/ 0.25 miles

Badhuisweg

Adelaarsweg

Meeuwenlaan

MOTORKANAAL

SIXHAVEN

Meeuwenlaan

Meeuwenlaan

Noordwal

De Ruijterkade

HET IJ

IJt-Tunnel

Centraal Station

VVV Touristinformation/ Koffiehaus

Prins Hendrikkade

IJHAVEN

METRO ST.

St. Nicolaas kerk

Dijksgracht

Piet Heinkade

Kattengat

Oosterdokskade

DIJKS GHACHT

Damrak

Oude Kerk

VOORBURGWAL

ACHTERBURGWAL

GELDERSEKADE

Nieuw markt

OOSTERDOK

Scheepvaarthuis

Kattenburgerstraat

Grote Wittenburgerstraat

WITTENBURGERVAART

amstraat

OUDEZIJDS

OUDEZIJDS

KLOVENIERSBURGWAL

NIEUWMARKT

OUDE

SCHANS

UILENBURGERGRACHT

Prins Hendrikkade

Nederlands Scheepvaart Museum

Kattenburgergracht

NIEUWE

VAART

Oostenburgergracht

OOSTENBURGERVAART

Valkenburgerstraat

Hoogtekadijk

Stadhuis

AMSTEL

Muziektheater

Amstelstraat

WATERLOO PLEIN

Muiderstr.

NIEUWE

HERENGRACHT

WERTHEIM PARK

Hortus Botanicus

Plantage

Middenlaan

ARTIS

Planetarium

Aquarium

SINGELGRACHT

Mauritskade

ACHT

dor

useum

Willet Holthuysen Museum

Amstelhof

KEIZERSGR.

NIEUWE

Kerkstraat

Plantage

Muidergracht

REGULIERS

n Loon

useum

Kerkstraat

Magere Brug

Nwe.

PRINSENGRACHT

NIEUWE

Wagenaarstraat

ACHT

GRACHT

Utrechtse

Dwarsstraat

Theater Carré

WEESPER PLEIN

Sarphatistraat

TROPEN MUSEUM

tering Schans

Sarphatistraat

Mauritskade

OOSTERPARK

SINGELGRACHT

Stadhouderskade

Amsteldijk

AMSTEL

Ruyschstraat

Oosterpark

Populierenweg

SARPHATIPARK

123

# AMSTERDAM

For most visitors, an encounter with Amsterdam begins among the organ-grinders, hippies, tumblers and tired travellers on Stationsplein, in front of **Centraal Station**. This is a disconcerting yet appropriate beginning, in keeping with the district's voracious appetite for novelty, trade and travel.

Since 1855, however, the city has been severed from the sea by the Centraal Station and now looks inward for its identity. Built on an artificial island in Het IJ, the city's old inner harbour, the station gives little sense of its watery origins until you cross Prins Hendrikkade towards **Damrak**. Only then are you aware of the redundant stretch of water (on the left) that was once the cutting edge of the Dutch Empire, its quaysides and warehouses disgorging goods on their way from the East Indies to Germany and the Baltic.

**Starting point:** Now, like the city, visitors turn their backs on the sea and rush down busy Damrak. If Centraal Station is Amsterdam's perpetually gaping mouth, Damrak and its offshoots are the city's distinctly unhealthy lungs. This tawdry thoroughfare, bordered by smoky cafés, tacky souvenir shops and bobbing canal boats, pumps traffic south to the heart of Amsterdam. Ignoring the "change" shops on the right, focus instead on the **Beurs van Berlage**, the former Stock Exchange, on the left. The Dutch have always been a nation of gamblers and when, in the 17th century they would lay a wager on anything from the sex of a baby to the profits from the tulip harvest, much of this speculation centred around the Beurs.

The origins of the Beurs lie in informal dealings in neighbouring Warmoesstraat but in 1608 a Stock Exchange was created on the Rokin and, at the turn of the century, a new Beurs replaced it on Damrak. The greatest Dutch poet, Vondel, railed against the first Exchange as a "bringer of misery; sunlight never penetrates thy building." Today, however, travel writer Michael

Leitch rightly calls the new Exchange, an eclectic Dutch Modernist building, "a kind of updated Ridderzaal or Hall of Knights" (the reference is to the medieval Ridderzaal, now the seat of Dutch government, in The Hague).

**Tulipomania:** Slip into the spacious main hall of the Beurs and admire the plain ironwork, narrow arcades and the Romanesque and neo-Renaissance motifs. Designed by renowned architect H.P. Berlage, and now a refined cultural centre where concerts and exhibitions are held throughout the year, this building is far removed from the chaos of the original Stock Exchange. In 1636, tulip mania was widespread and bulbs, imported from Turkey and traded on the exchange, were considered more exotic than emeralds, Arab stallions, Ming vases and other less precious commodities. Aristocrats snapped up flowers in rare colours, but even ordinary burghers traded in red or yellow tulips. This widespread preference for flowers over jewels is seen as proof of the essential bourgeois nature of Dutch culture.

**Preceding pages:** Damrak. **Left,** Zuiderkerk. **Right,** locally brewed brown beer.

It is wise to continue along Damrak into Dam square rather than to turn into **Nieuwendijk**, a snaking street of vulgar shops running parallel to Damrak. The **Dam**, the city's only unencumbered square, was for long a public and political forum, thanks to the presence of the **Royal Palace**, once the Town Hall (Stadhuis), and a space large enough for medieval executions, Republican processions and 1980s demonstrations against cruise missiles.

Although now sliced by shuttling trams, the Dam has kept some of its public character but today its political role is marginal. The sombre palace, built between 1648 and 1655 by Jacob van Campen, is used by the Queen only two or three times a year.

**Proud symbol:** At its inception, however, the former Stadhuis was a celebration of Dutch independence and renewed peace. Poet Constantijn Huygens praised it as "the world's Eighth Wonder/ With so much stone raised high and so much timber under," a reference to its creation on 13,659 wooden piles.

The Stadhuis's symbolic importance to 17th-century Amsterdam is emphasised by the innumerable paintings of the building that hang on the walls of the Historical Museum. To modern eyes, however, its glories are vastly overrated: the City Regents foolishly rejected Rembrandt's mural sketches in favour of acres of marble, vacuous paintings and spurious allegory. The addition of Empire furniture during the French Occupation has only completed the impression of style over content. If Amsterdammers remain fond of the building, it is an indication of their preference for monumental grandeur over Dutch vernacular architecture.

Also on the Dam is the **Dutch National Monument**, a sign of Dutch taste for strident statues. This obelisk is a war memorial containing urns of earth from each of the Netherlands' 11 provinces (the monument predates the creation of the 12th province of Flevoland) and from Indonesia. The sculptures of naked war victims bear the message "Never again". Vivid memories and marks of

**Nieuwe Kerk, Dam square.**

World War II are ever present in Amsterdam, from the excellent Resistance and Jewish Historical Museums (*see page 149*) to the Anne Frank House (*see page 139*).

Providing stiff opposition to the Royal Palace is the **Nieuwe Kerk**, new in name only. Built in 1400, after a series of fires the New Church received grand 17th-century additions to its late Gothic structure. Then, however, it was forbidden a tower because the Regents feared competition with the Town Hall. Today, the church's fine interior and importance as a social centre have helped it emerge from the Town Hall's shadow. Even so, the proliferation of temporary art exhibitions often makes it difficult to see the 17th-century organ, choir rail and pulpit or to admire the marble mausoleum of Admiral de Ruyter. Since 1815, Dutch kings and queens have been invested here, most recently Queen Beatrix in 1980.

**Interlude:** Tacked on to the church are several miniscule shops and a quaint café. However, for the more genuine article, try *De Drie Fleschjes* in Gravenstraat, a 17th-century tasting house tucked behind the church. Known as *proeflokalen*, such atmospheric bars originally allowed customers to sample *jenever* (Dutch gin), but now serve an extraordinary range of spirits and cocktails. *Wijnand Fockink*, innocent despite its name, was the most famous, but closed in 1990 after failing to compete with the rash of brown cafés and designer bars. On parting, the owner proudly declared: "At least I always considered myself to be a host, not a mere publican."

Thus restored, cross the Dam and walk down commercial **Kalverstraat**. Escape the unappealing clothes shops by turning into a lopsided gateway adorned with the triple-cross arms of Amsterdam. On second glance, notice the figures of chubby children dressed in red and black uniforms, a reminder that the gate once led to the **City Orphanage**. Founded in 1578 on the site of St Lucy's, a former convent, the orphanage was a tribute to the enlightened rule

**Street art or blot on the landscape?**

of the city fathers. The orphanage board had a seat on the City Council because "the rich need the poor for the quiet of their souls." On reaching adulthood, successful orphans were supposed to show their gratitude by becoming donors to the orphanage. The majority of orphan entrepreneurs, however, had already been recruited as lowly errand boys by local fishwives.

The orphanage was moved out in 1960 and the site was transformed into the far-reaching **Amsterdams Historisch Museum**. Before entering the museum itself, however, prolong the sense of solitude by entering the adjoining **Begijnhof**, Amsterdam's finest almshouse court and one of the city's most spiritual enclaves. In the 15th century this religious quarter was literally an island and although the insalubrious Beguinensloot moats were filled in in 1865, the Begijnhof remains a place apart. First mentioned in 1389, the almshouses became home to the sisters of St Lucy, a Franciscan order, which replaced the once popular lay *beguine* way of life for women. *Beguines* chose to lead a partial form of convent life, including the vow of chastity. The last *beguine* died in 1971 but the almshouse remains to this day as a grace and favour retirement home for "unmarried women of good repute."

**Timber house:** The Begijnhof, reached through a number of inner courtyards, comprises a series of brick and stone gabled houses built between the 14th and 17th centuries. *Het Houten Huys*, No. 34, was built in 1460, making it the oldest surviving dwelling in Amsterdam and one of only two remaining wooden houses. Fire regulations introduced by the city fathers forbade the building of wooden houses so later houses were built in brick and stone.

Amsterdammers are fondest of the Begijnhof in spring when the lawn is a carpet of daffodils and crocuses. No. 26, one of the grandest houses, was the home of Sister Antoine, the last *beguine*, and has been preserved as she left it. Inside the house, the present residents move about deferentially.

**Amsterdams Historisch Museum.**

In the middle of the square is a small, unostentatious church given to the city's English and Scottish Presbyterians over 300 years ago. On the outside wall is a tribute to the Pilgrim Fathers, who set out from Delfshaven, in Rotterdam, bound for the "New World" in 1620. Opposite the church is one of the city's many clandestine Catholic chapels, a darkly Italianate church which still smells of hot wax and serious prayers. The spiritual atmosphere of the Begijnhof hushes even the most confirmed atheist.

From here, walk back through the courtyards of the former orphanage and visit the **Historical Museum**. Stopping for a drink in the rather cavernous, adjoining restaurant is quite acceptable given that the original residents, the nuns at St Lucy's convent, brewed and marketed their own beer.

**Informative collection:** Inside the Historical Museum itself, the trail through Amsterdam's history is imaginatively presented, running both chronologically and thematically. Apart from Anthoniszoon's bird's-eye view painting of the city, there are few individual masterpieces. The strength of the collection lies in its accurate portrayal of social history through paintings, furniture and cleverly juxtaposed artefacts.

Anthoniszoon's painting (Room 4), created in 1538, is the first known map of Amsterdam. In the picture, the semicircular shaped city, bisected by the dammed Amstel and the two central canals, lies open to a sea of tall ships and playful dolphins.

In the same room is a detailed cross-section of 16th-century Warmoesstraat, revealing the residents' occupations as boat-builders, soap-makers, coopers, shoe-makers and money-lenders. Room 6 presents the power behind the scenes, the Regents, members of the select merchant caste who ruled the city during the Golden Age. A glassed-in gallery contains mannered portraits of the Civic Guards, employed from the 14th century onwards to protect the citizens of Amsterdam.

In Rooms 13 and 14 the focus shifts to

**Taking it easy.**

the home: domestic art and manners amongst the prosperous burgher class whose birthright included grandfather clocks, silverware, still lifes and flowers. After this peep behind the front door, Room 15 presents the mercantile bustle of the outside world. Paintings depict the confidence and precision of the city during the Golden Age: gateways are transformed into decorative arches; the world's first fire brigade is formed; traffic is controlled and coaches are refused entry into the city after sunset.

Room 16 represents the Velvet Revolution, an 18th-century popular uprising that signalled the dimming of the Golden Age. The exhibition skips rather lightly over the final death throes of the Golden Age and the city's decline.

The final rooms, however, present a lively audio-visual display of city life between and during both World Wars. Here, as in the Resistance Museum, the presentation of Dutch "anti-democratic movements" deals frankly with the existence of Dutch Fascist sympathisers and with the later Jewish deportations.

**Contrasting moods:** After such a punishing schedule, light relief can take many forms. Any street east will lead to the beginning of the red light district along Oudezijds Achterburgwal. Alternatively, find the doorway between the houses numbered 37 and 38 in the Begijnhof and follow the passageway to **Spui**, the lively university quarter and home to numerous brown cafés. *Café Hoppe* (Spui 18) is perhaps the city's most celebrated brown café, frequented by artists and writers, with an initimate, slightly louche atmosphere matching the proverbial nicotine-stained walls. Opposite is *Café Swart*, outside which bankers and men in suits stand with their beers in warm weather. For elegance and great people-watching, try *Luxembourg* (Spui 22–24), but to escape the crowds there is only *De Stoep* (Singel 415).

If you have the energy for extended café crawling or nightclubbing, follow Kalverstraat south to **Rembrandtsplein**, the most frenetic part of town. En route, call in at the **Tuschinski Cinema** in

A fairground organ arrives in Leidseplein.

Reguliersbreestraat and admire its splendid art deco interior. Alas, its expansion into a multiplex threatens its original charm. If dinner in a more stylish district appeals, cross the Singel and follow Leidsestraat to **Leidseplein**. Insofar as any square can be singled out as quintessentially Dutch, this one can, particularly in winter when the tourists are fewer, the ice rink is busy and the aroma of hot chestnuts hangs on the air.

Simon Schama's words could easily apply to the Leidseplein: "Dutch culture was the property of all sorts and social conditions. An Avercamp landscape with gentlefolk skating alongside rustics and sober bourgeois is an idyll but not so far from the truth."

**Oude Zijde (Old Side):** Affectionately known as "Mokum" (the Yiddish word for "place"), the historic heart of Amsterdam contains the Old Church and the Amstelkring, a "clandestine" church on Oudezijds Voorburgwal. The red light district crowds around the north end of the latter canal. The area also harbours more subtle attractions, including the Weigh House, the East Indies House and countless medieval gables.

After the space of the Dam and Damrak, turning into cramped, dingy **Warmoesstraat** is a shock. In medieval times, this narrow street (running parallel with, and to the east of, Damrak) was once the centre of the fabric and furnishing trades. The shops stocked Nuremburg porcelain, Lyons silk and Spanish taffeta as well as Delftware and Haarlem linen. Fallen on harder times, the narrowest shopping street in town now relies on cafés and restaurants, but practises a smattering of traditional trades.

**Geels**, at No. 67, is a long-established coffee and tea merchant's, whose owner, Piet Geels, will tell you that the first Dutchman to drink a bowl of coffee was the daring Professor Clusius in 1596. At No. 58 is **Het Karbeel**, a cheese shop and café which has been trading since medieval times, while at No. 163 is a silversmith's workshop.

Despite these pockets of respectability, Warmoesstraat glows, if not hot, at least a warmish pink. At the *Condomerie Het Gulden Vlies* (The Golden Fleece), a post-AIDS boom means that the shop sells nothing but condoms, including joke ones that explode on use. From here, any alley east leads to the heart of the **red light district** in Oudezijds Achterburgwal and Zeedijk.

**The Old Church:** Although Oude Zijds has been blighted by the sex industry, the district's dilapidated condition should not blind visitors to the architectural treasures hidden behind the uninviting facades. At the Damrak end of Warmoesstraat, for instance, the Wijde Kerksteeg alley leads to the **Oude Kerk** (Old Church), the oldest building in Amsterdam and the original church of the Amestelledamme fishing community. Despite a number of fires, the church's 13th-century tower remains, along with a chapel added in the 15th century.

Before the "Alteration" in 1578, many of the windows and paintings were destroyed by Protestant iconoclasts, but enough treasures remain to make this the best preserved of Amsterdam's churches. In the 17th century, the Oude

**Unfortunately, dogs can't read.**

Kerk was the city's first experiment in transforming churches into community centres, a secular tendency which is most marked in today's Nieuwe Kerk. By contrast, the Oude Kerk continues to attract a congregation, even if many of those who attend services are partly drawn by the excellent organ recitals.

Inside this freezing cold church, the dusty medieval misericords, heavy grey flagstones, half-erased family crests and faded murals give the interior a forsaken feel. This contrasts with many other Dutch churches, which tend to be clinical and over-restored.

Here there is much to admire, from the ornate organ to the wooden vaulted ceiling and cherubic statues. Some of the stained-glass windows, a vivid kaleidoscope of reds, blues and purples, date from the 16th century but others are modern replicas. The best time to see the church is during the winter months, when the light is low and shining through the coloured glass.

If you happen to meet the sexton, he may proudly inform you that his church alone has kept its authentic medieval atmosphere. Comments on the number of ominously drawn red curtains in the vicinity of the church are likely to provoke a wave of resentment from him, however. "Don't forget that many ordinary working people live in this area. The women come from elsewhere and are not welcome."

**Hidden church:** Lucky visitors may hear the 15th-century bells before crossing the smelly Oudekerksbrug to the right bank of the Oudezijds Voorburgwal. Turn left and follow the canal a little way north, then cross the Leidsesluis bridge back to the left bank.

Beside the bridge is the **Amstelkring**, one of Amsterdam's most charming and least explored museums. Also known as *Ons' Lieve Heer op Solder* (Our Lord in the Attic), this unremarkable canal house conceals the finest of the city's "clandestine" churches. It was used by Catholics from 1650 until 1795, when the French rulers gave Catholics back the right to worship openly. Jan Hartman, a Catholic sympathiser, linked the top

**Houseboat style.**

floor of three gabled houses to form two galleries with space for up to 400 worshippers. The lower part of the house, however, remains a perfect and unchanged example of a 17th-century merchant's home.

A small sitting room leads up a flight of rickety stairs to "de Saal", a formal 17th-century parlour decorated with a marble floor, an ornate walnut chimneypiece and heavily varnished paintings. On the wall, a 1633 Pieter de Hooch domestic portrait confirms the authenticity of the scene. The painting of a family playing music echoes the sounds all around you, from the ticking clocks to the bells chiming outside. Overlooking the canal is the front dining room, a sunny space with a grand 16th-century laquered cabinet.

Upstairs, a chaplain's tiny room nestles on the landing, but right under the eaves lies the large church itself, a tiered gallery formed by opening up the three attics. The size of the lower gallery, not to mention the creaking floor, makes the secrecy of the services rather notional.

Apart from the sweet Maria Chapel, decorated with fresh flowers and 18th-century paintings, the charm lies in odd details such as the revolving mahogany pulpit, ready to be hidden at a moment's notice. From the upper gallery, views over the rooftops embrace the sombre St Nicolaaskerk and the garish promises of *Club 17 Live Show*: the attractions of the Old Side in a nutshell.

**Seediness and gentility:** From here there is a choice of routes. The faint-hearted can avoid the brashness of the red light area by walking south down Oudezijds Voorburgwal towards **Rokin**. Known in the 16th century as the Velvet Canal, because of its prosperous air, refined traces still remain in the unusual gable stones of houses lining the canal. From Rokin, the red light area can be viewed from the safety of a candle-lit boat cruise.

The fearless can cross to the right bank of the Oudezijds Voorburgwal and brave the junkies or heroin dealers on the **Damstraat** in order to see some more of the city's architectural gems as the Zeedijk. At No. 2 is a well-restored

**Banquet, Indonesian style (rijsttafel).**

gabled house, the second of the city's remaining wooden houses. This whole area is a place where you should be careful to keep a close watch on purses and cameras, but don't let it spoil the experience.

The Zeedijk ends in **Nieuwmarkt**, an abrasive but interesting area housing China town and some prize-winning social housing but historically bordered the Jodenbuurt (Jewish quarter). During World War II, Jews were penned in here to await deportation to transit camps.

Have a look at the imposing **Waag** (weighing house) on the square. In its time, this medieval gatehouse has been a civic weighing house, a guild house for both the militia and the surgeons and the predecessor of today's Jewish Historical Museum. An *eetcafé* now operates on the ground floor.

**Ruling élite:** Nieuwmarkt can also be reached by a more salubrious route via **Koestraat**. In passing, notice the optimistic carvings of Faith, Hope and Charity on Nos. 7 to 11, and the wine-mer-chants' guild house at No. 10. Koestraat ends in Kloveniersburgwal and the 17th-century mansion (No. 29) known as the **Trippenhuis**.

The military insignia on the facade indicate that this was once the home of the Trip family of armament manufacturers. The Trips were powerful members of the "Magnificat", the ruling clique of families who governed the city during the Golden Age.

Opposite, at No. 26, is the so-called smallest house in Amsterdam, once owned by the Trip family's coachman. From here, you can turn left into Nieuwmarkt or follow the canal to the right until you come to the imposing red-brick building by the next bridge. This was the headquarters of **The East Indies Company** and, as such, frequently received deliveries of precious commodities, such as spices, coffee, ebony and mahogany.

Further down Kloveniersburgwal, a small alley lined with bookstalls, Oudemanhuispoort, passes through former almshouses to the photogenic **Huis op**

East Indies Company headquarters.

de Grachten (House on the Canals). On the right is the **Agnietenkapel**, the cradle of the Amsterdam University while, almost opposite, is an historic pawn shop known as **Ome Jan** (Uncle Jan). For some four centuries this "municipal bank for movable property", as it was euphemistically known, was a testament to the powers of the Lombardic money-lenders. Above the entrance is what many would regard as an appropriate Dutch inscription, which translates as: "Hast thou money still, then pass by the door. Hast thou the latter, but lack the former, enter here."

Poor Joost van Vondel, the poet, ended his days here as a doorman, and "from the tomb of usury… forgot what honour means." After such an adventurous and dishonourable walk, you would do well to withdraw to the safety and comfort of the brown cafés in the neighbouring **Spui** district.

**The Jordaan:** This area to the west of Dam square is a tight grid of narrow streets bounded by Brouwersgracht, Prinsengracht, Rozengracht and Lijn-baansgracht. **Jordaan North**, the area above Westerstraat, is a maze of small alleys, quiet restaurants and thriving workshops and retains many of its working-class roots. The North has many "true" Jordaaners, independent-minded students, crafts and trades people born and bred in the quarter.

**Jordaan South**, situated below Westerstraat, is more gentrified, with highly individualistic shops on the larger canals and a variety of renowned brown cafés. The Jordaan is now popular with intellectuals and media folk. In a sense, specific routes through the Jordaan are unnecessary in that these appealing canals and geometric alleys entice strollers to abandon fixed plans and fall into the nearest brown café, trendy craft shop or secluded *hofje* (almshouse court). Apart from the Westerkerk and the Anne Frank House, technically on the edge of the Jordaan, there are few historical set pieces; gentle wandering is the order of the day.

With its bouquet of streets named after flowers and plants, the Jordaan

**Distinctive decoration may help deter the thieves.**

probably acquired its name from the French word *jardin* (garden). This French connection has been present since Huguenot refugees settled here in 1685, but the Jordaan's history dates back to the preceding century. Then, the overcrowded city was bounded by the Singel canal and the Jordaan, outside the city walls, was a district inhabited by immigrants and the lower classes.

Many of the early residents were employed to dig Amsterdam's great concentric canal system in 1607. Since it was a mere suburb, the Jordaan was outside the city's jurisdiction and therefore prey to property speculators, resulting in diverse architectural styles and standards.

By the 19th century, the Jordaan housed the city's industrial working class and was a hotbed of political activism. With 83,000 people living in this cramped district, protests and strikes were frequent, provoking the Netherlands' first asphalt road programme – the original cobbles had been thrown at Queen Wilhelmina during an official visit in the 1930s. In the 1970s, the district was given a major face-lift and began to attract professionals as well as arty and "alternative" Amsterdammers.

**Outdoor life:** Starting from the hectic Leidseplein, head into central Amsterdam along Leidsestraat and turn left at Prinsengracht. Soon you will cross **Leidsegracht** and (five streets beyond, on the left) you will reach **Looiersgracht**. At the first sign of sun, locals bring their chairs out into the street or sit sunning themselves on balconies. The low-key *Café de Chaos* on Looiersgracht is typical of the city's laid-back atmosphere.

Just north of Looiersgracht, **Elandsgracht** is best known for its idiosyncratic indoor market (the Looier), a mass of stalls selling anything from 1950s memorabilia to handmade pottery or silver statuettes. **Lauriergracht**, the next real canal north, has attractive gabled houses towards the eastern end, but where it meets the seedier **Lijnbaansgracht**, at the opposite end, African music blares from tatty-looking bars well decorated with "no dealing" signs.

**Leidsegracht gables.**

138

Continue along Prinsengracht and across the hectic Rozengracht, you'll see the **Westerkerk** (West Church). The small canals and streets radiating from the Westerkerk are distinctly chic and occasionally over-restored. Even so, the neighbourhood remains eclectic, and the sights around here range from the elegant Christophe restaurant to the minimalist architects' studios or the second-hand bookshops..

The **Westerkerk**, renovated in 1990, is the city's finest church, a masterpiece in Dutch Renaissance style by the talented father and son, Hendrick and Pieter de Keyser. The soaring spire, the highest in the city, is crowned by a glinting yellow and blue Imperial crown, a reminder of former Habsburg rule. The view from the tower stretches to the Rijksmuseum in the south, to the harbour in the north. Anne Frank, who lived in a house bordering the Prinsengracht, described Westerkerk's carillon chimes in her diary, but the old chimes have now given way to folk melodies, mechanically changed each year. Com-

**Anne Frank.**

pared with the Oude Kerk, the Westerkerk's interior is slightly disappointing. However, its popularity with tourists is secured by the fact that Rembrandt's grave was discovered here during excavations.

**Monument to the persecuted:** Beside the Westerkerk is the **Homo-Monument**, a sleek flight of marble stairs leading into the canal although you have to be looking to spot it. This new memorial commemorates homosexuals who died in the Nazi camps, or suffered persecution at other periods in the past.

For a vision of life in Amsterdam during the Occupation, visit the **Anne Frank Huis** at Prinsengracht 263. From 1942 to 1944, the Frank family hid in a secret attic annexe and were sustained by helpers who provided them with food bought on the black market.

In 1944, German police raided the home and deported the family, first to the transit camp at Westerbork, and then to Auschwitz and Bergen-Belsen. The Anne Frank Huis is always crowded though the exhibition inside is not very

Dit is een foto, zoals ik me zou wensen, altijd zo te zijn. Dan had ik nog wel een kans om naar Holywood te komen.

Anne Frank.
10 Oct. 1942

(translation)
"This is a photo as I would wish myself to look all the time. Then I would maybe have a chance to come to Hollywood."
Anne Frank, 10 Oct. 1942

extensive. However, the renovated adjacent building will from September 1999 have a larger exhibition space, bookstore and café. The front room of the annex has returned to its original appearance as when it was the office of Otto Frank, Anne's father.

To restore your sense of balance cross Prinsengracht and retreat to the Jordaan proper. Beyond Egelantiersgracht turn left and look for the 17th-century almshouse court in Eerste Egelantiers Dwarsstraat. Known as the **Claes Claesz. Anslo Hofje**, these beautifully restored houses offer fine examples of step, spout and neck gables. On neighbouring Egelantiersgracht is the *Café 't Smalle*, a cosy brown café.

Smoking and drinking have been part of the Jordaan's charm since the 17th century. The description of the stereotypical Dutchman at the time, quoted by Simon Schama, could well apply to a dying breed of Jordaaner: "Barrel-shaped in girth, sozzled with gin, he is often seen lighting the next pipe with the smouldering embers of the last."

**Quiet courtyards:** If hidden almshouses appeal, the Jordaan district is the right place to be. From Claes Claesz. Anslo, a short walk northwards along the **Prinsengracht** takes you to **Zon's Hofje** at Nos. 157–171 and the **Van Bienen Hofje** at Nos. 89–133. Stemming from the early Dutch Republic's belief in the virtue of personal charity, such almshouses nowadays represent the institutionalised form, but nevertheless manage to retain a tangible spirituality.

The leafy Zon's Hofje, now occupied by deserving students and the elderly, was built in a mixture of periods and styles. Cooking smells mingle with the freshness of newly watered plants, while above is the incongruous sight of fighting doves and falling feathers. The Van Bienen Hofje, built in 1804, is much grander. Brick houses overlook a peaceful inner courtyard and an attractive fountain. The courtyard is dotted with stern public warnings to keep silent and donate a guilder to the general fund, a reminder that intruders should be discreet – and charitable.

From here, a short walk across Prinsengracht leads to the **Noordermarkt** and Hendrick de Keyser's last great church, the Noorderkerk. En route, visitors may be detained by cafés and stylish shops along the Prinsenstraat. Approaching the Noorderkerk, the atmosphere becomes more laid-back Jordaan than upmarket chic.

On Saturday morning and Monday, this friendly square is home to a market. The latter market is devoted to fashionable junk and ecologically correct produce. It attracts a lively crowd of shoppers, street musicians and curious tourists, and should not be missed. In summer, several festivals are held here, featuring marching bands and baton twirling competitions. The dignified **Noorderkerk** (North Church) stands aloof from the chaos. Like the Westerkerk, this church is owned by the state and renovations have at last been completed following a fund-raising initiative; the official reopening was honoured by Queen Beatrix. Organ concerts are now held throughout the year. The building itself is notable for its

Groenland Pakhuizen (Greenland Warehouses) Nos. 40–44 Keizersgracht, which were once used to store whale oil.

subdued atmosphere and the stark statue outside.

In keeping with such a radical area, this statue of chained figures is a monument to the *Jordaanoproer 1934*, the Jordaan unemployment riots during the Depression years. "The strongest chains are those of unity," is the moving inscription. Jordaaners still commemorate the uprising every year with poems, posters and floral tributes. On the church itself is a memorial to another significant event in local history. A sign commemorates the 400 local Jews who were deported as a reprisal for the killing of a single Dutch Nazi-sympathiser during a street battle.

From the Noorderkerk, myriad escapes lead to the measured, bourgeois calm of **Prinsengracht**; the elegant clusters of typical facades range from grey to ice-cream pink. Guessing the meaning of the gable stones provides an interesting game: Jesus and the fishes gives way to the three wise men, two turtle doves and finally to St Paul blowing a trumpet.

**The Noorderkerk, 1644, A. Beerstraten.**

From the Prinsengracht, all choices are open. Walking east leads to **Keizersgracht** and **Herengracht**, the grander *grachtengordel* canals. Alternatively, continuing north along the Prinsengracht leads to an entirely different cityscape: the **maritime quarter** beginning in Brouwersgracht and Haarlemmerstraat is unquestionably one of Amsterdam's most picturesque canals. The Haarlemmerstraat is a long street filled with small shops and restaurants..

But for those who love bohemian Jordaan, the decision is made: a hearty *eetcafé* in Jordaan North (perhaps near Westerstraat); an elegant restaurant near the Westerkerk; or a late-night blues bar on Lijnbaansgracht (choose between *Maloe-Meloe* and *De Kroeg*).

Certainly it is inexcusable to leave the Jordaan before discovering a final brown café. On **Lindengracht**, *De Kat in de Wijngaert* offers classical or blues music and beer in a mirrored bar. For a rougher clientele, the owners of *De Doffer* on Runstraat promise that "In the Jordaan, we serve tramps as well as

lawyers." Here you can, as the Amsterdammers say, "consume your days in smoke." But as Jacob Cats, the famous poet, used to say, "My kitchen is my pipe; my pouch a well-stocked larder; smoking is my drink. What need I then of wine?"

**The grachtengordel:** Each of Amsterdam's three main canals is approximately 2 miles (3 km) long, so it may not be an attractive proposition to walk the entire length of each one, although many enjoy the scenic stretch. As with the Jordaan, you can select small sections or to follow your instincts. Since the waterways are not far apart, and are linked by side streets, it is easy to switch between canals.

The *grachtengordel* canal network was created in the early 17th century in order to cater to a wealthier and expanding population. As these grand houses became ready, the merchant class gradually moved from the insalubrious Oude Zijds to the relative opulence of these new canals. The City Council imposed strict regulations to preserve the tone of the neighbourhoods: barrel-making was forbidden because of the noise; brewing was forbidden because of the bad smell; and sugar refining was out of the question as it posed a severe fire hazard. But trade was not excluded altogether: these steep-roofed houses were also intended to double as warehouses, with storage space in the attics and basements.

Taxes were levied according to the size of the frontage, a system which often encouraged ostentation and vulgarity. The maximum permissable width was 30 ft (10 metres) but the depth could extend to 190 ft (60 metres). The facades were decorated with heraldic motifs or other religious or self-promotional devices. Typical designs feature coats of arms, trade signs, mythological animals, cherubs or Biblical scenes.

**Gable styles:** However, if these canal houses remain special today it is largely for their decorative gables. The old-fashioned pointed or spout gable was gradually replaced by the simpler step gable, while in the 1630s the gracious neck gable became fashionable and re- **Singel canal.**

mained so until the mid-17th century. From about 1660 onwards, the flowing bell gable was popular but, in grander houses, was superseded by the Italian style, with a straight or triangular cornice. By the end of the Golden Age, the most ostentatious patrician houses had broad pedimented facades decorated in neoclassical style with garlands or extravagant sculptures.

Inside, the grandest 17th-century houses had a warehouse in the basement, lavish reception rooms on the ground floor and, above, a dining room and banqueting room. Inventories from the time describe Persian silk furnishings, Turkish rugs, Japanese lacquerware, Venetian or ebony-framed mirrors as well as oil paintings or alabaster statues in most rooms. All in all, the greatest houses outshone even the Venetian *palazzi* – in a Republic which claimed to put virtue before gold!

Although not the grandest of interiors, the **Willet-Holthuysen Museum** on Herengracht 605 and the **Van Loon Museum** at Keizersgracht 672 are the best remaining examples of a burgher's stylish household in the 17th and 18th centuries.

Walks along the three concentric canals reveal significant differences in style. **Prinsengracht** (the Prince's Canal) is perhaps the humblest of the three, with a greater number of warehouses. **Keizersgracht** (the Emperor's Canal) is the most approachable and varied waterway, especially the stretch of renovated gables near No. 324.

To Amsterdammers, however, **Herengracht** (the Gentlemen's Canal) is the undoubted star. The stretch between **Brouwersgracht** and **Raadhuisstraat** has a number of fine warehouses as well as the Bartolotti mansion (Nos 170–172), a Renaissance cascade of decoration. The east bank, from Huidenstraat to Leidsestraat, provides the greatest variety of gables spanning Renaissance and classical styles.

But the **Golden Bend** section, between Leidsestraat and Vijzelstraat, is the one that Amsterdammers most admire. An outsider might find this stretch

**Seventeeth-century bell gables.**

a vain exercise in grandeur, in which a sumptuous copy of a classical Loire chateau, for instance, is allowed to dwarf its adjoining Renaissance gables. Most of these mansions are now austere hotels, offices and banks. Even so, there is much to enjoy in the quirky sculptural details or gables decorated with dolphins or mermaids. The Amsterdammers have kindly lined the route with benches from which to admire the view; so, if you question their choice, do so quietly, in the privacy of a brown café.

**The Museum District:** For art lovers, the real centre of Amsterdam is Museumplein, situated to the south west of the canal circle's "Golden Bend", in an area known as the Old South. Within a small space are the world's best collections of Rembrandts, Vermeers and Van Goghs, to mention but three masters. For relaxation, there is the Vondelpark, a popular, watery park with lively music festivals in summer. Avid shoppers may prefer a stroll along P.C. Hooftstraat, the chicest designer street in town, or along Spiegelgracht, the city's antiques shopping centre.

The **Stedelijk Museum** specialises in modern art, from the mid-19th century to contemporary times. The foreign highlights include works by Chagall, Braque and the German Expressionists as well as many new names from the USA and UK. For a Dutch flavour, however, Mondriaan and Karel Appel are outstanding, although the Mondriaan collection in The Hague is more comprehensive than this collection and the focus on Appel, Constant and Corneille, members of the celebrated COBRA movement, has been shifted to the new COBRAMuseum in Amstelveen. Take tram 5 to the end of the line and visit the modern building filled with the work of these experimental painters who proved to be ahead of their times by breaking away from constructions of traditional art.

The **Van Gogh Museum**, next door to the Stedelijk, has recovered from the world-wide interest in Van Gogh in 1990, the centenary of his death, only to begin an extensive renovation which will be completed in June 1999 as part of an expansion of the Museumplein into a landscaped park (end of 1999). After 25 years of hosting almost a million visitors a year, the museum will aquire a new wing for exhibitions designed by Kisho Kurokawa.

The permanent collection, at once chronological and thematic, is, like Van Gogh's art, eminently approachable. The main focus is on Van Gogh's development, from his dark landscapes painted in the Dutch provinces of Noord-Brabant and Drenthe to his light-strewn Parisian Impressionist phase and then to the climax of his life's work in the visionary Mediterranean atmosphere at Arles.

**Packed with treasures:** Compared with the simplicity of the previous museum, the **Rijksmuseum** needs more guidance. The Van Gogh Museum, representing the artistic development of a maverick genius, is self-explanatory and not specific to Amsterdam's cultural past. The Rijksmuseum, however, is a vast, unwieldy collection which draws much of its inspiration from the city itself.

The Rijksmuseum.

Arm yourself with the Rijksmuseum's clear floor plan and concentrate on the Dutch Masters unless you wish to follow one of the Museum's thematic walks, such as "still life" or "paintings as narrative". Time permitting, there is also the *Dutch History* collection which has been renovated recently, a vast sweep from the Middle Ages to 1945, and *Painting: 18th–19th Century*, a glance at Dutch Impressionism and the schools of Amsterdam and The Hague. The main course, however, has to be the 17th-century Golden Age.

The greatest paintings are on the top floor and masterpieces are signalled by dutiful crowds of bored schoolchildren listening to their teachers. Luckily, in the scramble to see *The Nightwatch*, the great works of Frans Hals, Jan Steen, Pieter de Hooch, Jacob van Ruisdael and Vermeer can also be enjoyed in relative peace, as can the works of 15th-and 16th-century painters such as the Master of Alkmaar (Room 202).

Jan Steen (Rooms 216–219) is a genre painter whose work humorously cap-tures the lower orders at play. Steen's *The Morning Toilet* is full of sexual innuendo while in *The Merry Family*, even the baby looks drunk. Adriaen van Ostade (Room 218) also has a nice line in revellers. Pieter de Hooch (Room 221) is the undoubted master of Dutch interiors, usually with a door left open to shed a homely light on the scene. But his paintings also offer moral comfort, even if, as in *Maternal Duties*, it is only a mother consoling her child after a punishment. There are also four master-pieces by Vermeer here.

As far as 17th-century painting is concerned, even the lesser Masters deserve to captivate. Van de Valkaert (Rooms 206 and 208), for instance, is one of many to see beyond the sobriety of the black-clad burghers, militia or City Regents; the sombre cloth or stance is used to direct one's eye to the expres-siveness of the faces. Even so, with the exception of Rembrandt, Dutch paint-ers tend to rehearse the same litany of facial expressions, from circumspect to careworn, complacent to vain, virtuous

**Everyone comes to see *The Night Watch*.**

to lascivious. Morality is never far away in 17th-century Dutch painting.

Many painters, however, looked to place rather than to people for spiritual and emotional values. Portraiture was, after all, the most conservative of genres: if it failed to please the sitter, the painter had no future. Pieter Saenredam's cool church interiors are deeply truthful while Vermeer's street scenes (Rooms 207 and 210) are luminous, vibrant and absorbing. The brooding Dutch landscape is exposed by Jacob van Ruisdael (Rooms 217 and 218); his variants on lowering sky, boat, mill and man have rarely been bettered. The Dutch seascapes are almost as atmospheric but tend to be overladen with too much battle narrative for modern taste.

Naturally, Rembrandt's *The Nightwatch* dominates the Gallery of Honour but, after admiring the scope and scale of the group composition, return to the more intimate portraits. His 1629 *chiaroscuro* self-portrait is deeply expressive, as are his portraits of Maria Trip, his son, his mother, and his wife, Saskia.

**Jodenbuurt (old Jewish quarter):** Admirers of Rembrandt's work might like to visit the remains of Amsterdam's Jewish quarter, where the artist lived for much of his life. The Jodenbuurt (sometimes called Jodenhoek) stretches east of the waterfront area and the Dam. Even though the quarter has been sadly neglected and, in recent years, partly demolished, the indomitable Jewish spirit seeps through the ruins.

From the Centraal Station, an intriguing walk leads southeast to Rembrandt's House and the Jewish Historical Museum on Jonas Daniël Meijerplein. The quickest route is via sleazy Zeedijk but a safer approach would be to take Tram 9 or the metro to Nieuwmarkt. If arriving by metro, look at the demolition ball on display inside the station, a reminder of the wanton destruction of this area and a typically Dutch indulgence in self-mortification.

**Jewish migrants:** By the 17th century, up to 10 percent of Amsterdammers were Sephardic Jews from Spain and Portugal who, although relatively pros-

Jodenbuurt under the Occupation.

perous and well-integrated, were not allowed to join trade guilds. They worked in the cloth, tobacco, sugar or bookselling industries. From 1620 waves of poorer Ashkenazic Jews from Poland and Germany settled in the eastern section of town and, unable to speak Dutch, turned to menial ghetto jobs around St Antoniesbreestraat. Still, in polyglot Amsterdam, it was possible to be at once an insider and an outsider. Poet Andrew Marvell recorded this religious melting pot in the 17th century: "Hence Amsterdam, Turk-Christian-Pagan-Jew/Staple of sects and mint of schism, grew."

By 1900, 95 percent of the residents in this area were Jewish and played a visible role in Dutch society until World War II. However, between 1940 and 1945, the area became a sealed ghetto (the *Joodse Wijk*) and over 70,000 Jews, 90 percent of the Jewish population, met their deaths in Auschwitz, Sobibor or Bergen-Belsen. There are now about 25,000 Jews in Amsterdam, formerly known as the "Jerusalem of the West".

**St Antoniesbreestraat** is now a shadow of its colourful self. Even so, amongst the shoddy modern buildings peer several original gables and even a Jewish bakery. Although it is still a working-class area, the many new residents include an international "alternative" crowd, often congregating in the trendy *Tisfris* café.

At No. 69 is the **De Pinto House**, once owned by a wealthy Portuguese merchant but now a public library. After admiring the decorative scrollwork around the windows, glance inside at the elaborate painted ceiling.

**Urban renewal:** Just over the road is one of Hendrick de Keyser's famous gateways, surmounted by a skull and crossbones. It leads to another de Keyser masterpiece, the **Zuiderkerk** (South Church), sadly marooned in a sea of concrete tenements. The elegant spire valiantly tries to rise above the ugliness but a sense of desolation hangs stubbornly in the air. Even though the church is currently a "centre for urban renewal", it will forever be associated with Jewish misery. In 1945 it was turned into a temporary morgue for Jews killed in Nazi raids.

By contrast, neighbouring **Oude Hoogstraat**, with its older houses, fabric shops and controversial *Stopera* café, is a more ordinary reminder of the Jewish presence.

St Antoniesbreestraat crosses the **Oude Schans** by means of a windswept bridge. On the near side is a quaint lock-keeper's house and a cluster of gabled houses; on the far side, the rambling BIMhuis, Amsterdam's premier jazz club, brings life to the canal at weekends. To the right of the bridge, the edges of Waterlooplein market spill over the quayside.

Jodenbreestraat takes over from St Antoniesbreestraat but the only vestige of its 17th-century self is the **Rembrandt House Museum**. The painter lived here from 1639 to 1660, until bankruptcy forced him to move. The recently restored mansion contains over 250 of his drawings and etchings, including a portrait of Jan Six, one of Rembrandt's patrons. In painting his patron as a re-

*Zuiderkerk and the redeveloped Jewish quarter.*

fined art lover instead of the ostentatious merchant that he was, Rembrandt won a permanent place in the magnificent Six Collection (now closed).

Note that in late 1999 and 2000 there will be two major Rembrandt exhibitions, on the Rembrandt House and on Rembrandt as a collector, featuring paintings the artist acquired from his colleagues. In addition, the Mauritshuis in The Hague will hold an exhibition of his self-portraits.

The best works in the Rembrandt House are the low-life portraits of beggars, barrel-organ players and a rat-catcher. Even though these trades have moved elsewhere, Rembrandt's physiognomies are recognisable in the faces of present-day residents. Admission also includes a visit to the Holland Experience (17 Waterlooplein), a 25-minute multimedia trip through the Netherlands.

**Diamonds and dockers:** From here, make a brief sortie into **Uilenburg**, formerly a maze of back alleys and sweat shops. The building on the right was the Boas diamond-polishing works, a ma-

jor source of employment for the Jews in the 19th century. Jodenbreestraat peters out in chaotic Mr Visserplein but it is worth negotiating the traffic hazards to see Mari Andriessen's posturing statue of a docker. *De Dokwerker* commemorates the round-up of 425 Jews in February 1941. The event provoked a general strike, led by the dockworkers, in which outraged Amsterdammers expressed solidarity with their fellow citizens using the slogan: "Keep your dirty hands off our rotten Jews". The short-lived strike was short-lived was a unique protest against Nazi inhumanity in Occupied Europe.

On the far side of the traffic island is the **Portuguese Synagogue** which, in the 1670s, was the largest synagogue in the world. Originally a "clandestine" synagogue, it had the same status as the "secret" Catholic churches. To see the authentic 17th-century interior, do not be deterred by a locked door: persistent knocking brings results.

On Jonas Daniël Meijerplein, just opposite the synagogue, is the **Jewish** Oude Schans.

**Historical Museum**, housed in a complex of four former Ashkenazic synagogues. Beginning in the domed New Synagogue, the exhibition traces the spread of Judaism in the Netherlands from its humble beginnings to the years of prestige in the 18th century, and to the decimation of the community during the Holocaust.

Highlights include an 18th-century Ark, the ritual baths and War memorabilia. (Unfortunately, although there is a leaflet in English, exhibits are only labelled in Dutch.) If it does not seem too irreverent amidst a record of so much suffering, call in at the Kosher Café before leaving.

By St Antoniesbreestraat is a statue of a turtle which represents Time, and its loss, for the Jewish community. Towards the Botanical Gardens (Hortus Botanicus) and **Plantage Middenlaan**, a prosperous 19th-century Jewish neighbourhood, doorways are occasionally adorned with pelicans. According to Jewish (and Christian) legend, the pelican will, in adversity, feed its starving young with its own blood. More positively, let your eye run over the Portuguese names that still speak of Jewish blood in the quarter: the Coelho, Quendo and d'Oliveira families have all returned to the nest.

If you wish to dwell further on the past, visit the nearby *Verzetsmuseum* (**Dutch Resistance Museum**) in its new location for a vivid reconstruction of the war years, from the *onderduikers* to black-marketeering. In the same neighbourhood are two Jewish memorials which should be visited. One is **Hollandsche Schouwburg**, a former Jewish theatre which during the war became the assembly point from which the unsuspecting Jews were transported to concentration camps. The other, at nearby Wertheim Park across from the Botanical Gardens, is an Auschwitz memorial sculpture. Best of all, read Marga Minco's *The Glass Bridge*, an account of Dutch Jewish women who survived the war by assuming false identities but then had to live in the past to make their Gentile present bearable.

**Below, Rembrandt's House. Right, the Jewish Historical Museum.**

# SEX, DRUGS AND VIOLENCE

If Nicolas Freeling's detective novels accurately reflect Dutch life, then Amsterdam is a crime-ridden city. Police motor launches chase drugs smugglers down the central canals; the most innocent-looking gabled houses are vice dens; and a canal is the usual final destination for a drugs baron or for clients who fail to pay for sexual favours. In reality, these are just a few pieces of the criminal jigsaw.

Curiously, smaller Dutch cities tend to have relatively higher crime rates than Amsterdam. It is merely that Amsterdam's perceived "crimes" of drugs and prostitution are both more visible and more sensational than elsewhere. When asked about their notorious drugs problem, Amsterdammers shrug and say that it is no worse than in any other major city, only more public.

Since the city's relatively successful battle against hard drugs, this half-hearted defence is almost true. Zeedijk, the city's original sea dam, used to be a major heroin-dealing district until the police dammed the flow in the late 1980s. Dealers are still prominent on certain corners in the Zeedijk area, but it is now forbidden to loiter in groups and the police are empowered to arrest suspected dealers for questioning. The Council has also set up a "Guardian Angels" force, the Stadswacht, as a way of helping to combat crime in central Amsterdam. Critics, however, complain that released suspects are sometimes back on the streets again within hours.

Although hard drugs are illegal, soft drugs are treated more leniently. Cannabis, for instance, has been legal since the 1960s and 28 grammes of the drug is allowed for individual use. However, dealing is not officially permitted and since 1988 the authorities have imposed tougher penalties on traffickers. "Smoking" cafés, where soft drugs are used, are now banned from displaying the tell-tale cannabis leaf symbol.

However, the names of cafés, not to mention the aromas, often provide clues: *Maloe-Meloe*, *Just a Puff* and *Extase* continue to puff away peacefully. To avoid any misunderstanding, cafés often display "No dealing" or "No smoking" notices in English. An innocuous survivor from the 1960s is the Cannabis Museum (Oudezijds Achterburgwal 148) which retains a wealth of documentation on the drug but has lost its central exhibits in police raids.

Despite the efforts of the police, and assertions by the authorities to the contrary, Amsterdam remains a place where drugs are readily available. After midnight, the bridges off Warmoesstraat attract junkies and dealers while Zwarte Handsteeg (Black Hand Alley) is as ominous as the name suggests. Do not mistake any lack of sensationalism for an absence of danger: Thai Skunk and Ketama Gold are sold in the Station area; the occasional desperate addict lurks in wait along the dingier streets leading to the Amstel. For visitors, common sense should prevail: resist "space cake" in coffeeshops; avoid eye contact in sinister alleys; and beware of admiring medieval gables on the central canals after midnight.

Yet there is no need to be alarmist about drug-related issues. The Dutch have long conducted a delicate balancing act between individual freedom and the collective well being, between permissiveness and orderliness.

The majority of Dutch soft-drugs users are tolerated even by strict Calvinists, provided that they do not infringe on the rights of others. As the writer Michael Leitch says: "It all depends on tolerance or respect for individual privacy. The individual is still allotted a certain space, an area of tolerance, in which to move freely – provided he or she does not go too far."

The same tolerance has always applied to sex in the city, much to the delight of surprised foreigners. John Ray, a visitor to the Dutch Republic, commented: "The women are more delighted with lasciviousness and obscene talk than either the English or French." Modern visitors are no less prurient when mentally unwrapping the charms of the red light district.

Known as the *walletjes*, the red light district is a sex supermarket offering every variant on pornography and prostitution. Rembrandtsplein and Thorbeckeplein, just south of the red light district, provide a foretaste of things to come. Peep shows and pick-up clubs, boisterous gay bars and saucy striptease shows give way to sex without the frills in brash Oudezijds Achterburgwal, just around the corner.

There are about 25,000 female prostitutes in Amsterdam but most first-time visitors are drawn inexorably to the titillating prospect of the girls in the goldfish bowls. The window girls unconvincingly promise transports in leather or lace. Tired-looking Filipinos sit on padded red window seats and, between clients, desultorily flip through pages of film magazines. Apart from the girls' semi-nudity and a blankness about the eyes, there is little sense of their profession, not even any simulated eroticism. In padded chambers nearby, pale, overweight Dutch housewives look uncomfortable in their bondage gear. If business is slack, the women hiss or click their tongues at passing men. Only the drawn red curtains above suggest any sense of urgency.

Female onlookers are given a glassy-eyed stare from the women inside the goldfish bowls. Although solitary women may be intimidated by the district at any hour, night is not necessarily the most dangerous time. Moods to avoid are the early morning desperation of passing junkies and the early afternoon edginess of pimps waiting for the evening's business to begin. The northern end of Spui and Geldersekade are just far enough from the tourist crowds to exude a quiet sense of menace.

In between the *kamer te huur* (rooms to hire) signs are sex shops boasting "Marilyn Monroe special discount" and "100 percent hard porno." However, even some of the bars offering orgasm cocktails do so tongue in cheek. Many are friendly neighbourhood bars catering to shopkeepers and students as well as to working girls.

Amsterdam prostitutes are currently up in arms over new government legislation to regulate the sex industry. There has been pressure for tighter control since the 1970s when the authorities feared that profits from prostitution were fuelling the drug-smuggling trade. Prostitution itself had long been legal but earning money from the prostitution of others had not. Ordinary households also added their voices to the protests, complaining that the presence of prostitutes encouraged street brawls and hooliganism.

In 1990, therefore, the government responded by legalising brothels. The legislation largely restricted prostitution to non-residential areas, although the distinction is blurred in Amsterdam. The law favours a licensing system of government-approved brothels, each with standard facilities and bedrooms of a standard size. According to one prostitute: "It makes it far too clinical – like little hutches. We should be allowed the freedom to work when and how we want."

Behind the prostitutes' concern lies a deeper fear that their immoral earnings will be taxed. De Rode Draad (The Red Thread), the prostitutes' unofficial union, functions in some ways as a go-between for the "working" women and local government agencies, informing the women of their rights and the law.

But the city does not merely cater for the conventional tastes of a married male executive. Amsterdam is second only to San Francisco in its social acceptance of homosexuality. Although homosexuals were persecuted in the 1730s, they gradually became a visible force in Dutch society, to the extent that gay debating societies emerged in Amsterdam while "entertainment and sex" markets were regularly held at the end of the Rokin.

Aids has not led to widespread homophobia but rather to more efficient health programmes and increased solidarity within the gay community. Today, the city has a number of recognisable gay districts, all dotted with gay hotels, clubs and bars. The friendliest district is centred on Kerkstraat and Reguliersdwarsstraat, but elsewhere the city offers everything from sing-along bars on Rembrandtsplein to sinister cellars on the central canals. Women's Amsterdam is equally liberal, with women-only bars and disco nights and women-oriented sex boutiques such as Female and Partners on Spuisstraat.

Given Amsterdam's general permissiveness, it is hardly surprising that the city is the major contributor to a national sex industry estimated to be worth more than £400 million a year. But the sex industry remains aimed almost exclusively at males, with services ranging through the whole gamut from top-class call-girl agencies to the cheap heroin hookers who haunt the waterfront behind Centraal Station. ∎

# A NIGHT OUT

"The café is my church" goes the local chant, a tribute to the conviviality of café life. An intimate bar takes precedence over a sophisticated night at the opera or ballet, not that these options are mutually exclusive. An Amsterdam night is renowned for its variety and longevity: what may start simply as an after-work drink in a *proeflokaal* (tasting house) can end hours later on the dance floor of a converted warehouse on the far side of town.

An evening often begins with a *borreltje* (small glass) of spirits in somewhere cosy like De Drie Fleschjes (Gravenstraat 18) or Papaneiland (Prinsengracht 2). Clients must be prepared to follow custom by leaning over the bar, hands clasped behind their backs, to slurp down the first glass of spirits. An early closing time (around 8 p.m.) at De Drie Fleschjes postpones inebriation for a further few hours.

If the taste for juniper-scented or blackcurrant-flavoured gin has taken hold, then 1,400 bars are there for further alcoholic experimentation. The only difficult choice is between a *bruine kroeg* (brown café) or a designer bar. The most famous brown café is Hoppe (Spui 20), not just because it sells more draught beer than any other bar. The smoke-stained interior is decorated with old paintings and threadbare Persian rugs, but the view is obscured by the crowds of local university students businessmen in suits who have made Hoppe their home – and can be seen drinking outside in a crowd during warm weather.

Next door is Hoppe's spiritual opposite, Luxembourg (Spui 22), a chic "white" café popular with yuppies and marketing executives. The absence of music, clutter and colour encourages the owners to call it "the brown café of the nineties." (It is also very smoky.)

Amsterdammers combat excessive drinking by eating, usually well before 9pm. Long-term residents complain that Amsterdam's cuisine is more limited than in most European capitals, but visitors are spoilt for choice. Amongst the 750 restau-rants, exotic Indonesian fare, particularly the *rijsttafel*, is a tasty variant on the sweet and sour theme, best accompanied by white wine or beer. Many such restaurants are centred on the hectic Leidseplein, but if you are looking for a quieter, more authentic experience there is Speciaal (Nieuwe Leliestraat 142), with inexpensive spicy side dishes served in a soothing setting of Indonesian raffia-work and prints.

As far as upmarket dining is concerned, Amsterdam is under the spell of French cuisine but, with its customary flair, has created a filling French-Dutch hybrid. This culinary partnership is celebrated in 't Swarte Schaep (Korte Leidsedwarsstraat 24), an elegant restaurant decorated like a burnished ship's cabin. Elsewhere, the culinary high ground is captured by exquisite fish restaurants such as Lucius (Spuistraat 247) and D'Theeboom, a French-style bistro in a restored warehouse (10 Singel).

If planning an excursion into high culture, Amsterdammers often call in at the Café Americain (Leidseplein 28) to luxuriate in art nouveau splendour. From here, the next-door Stadsschouwburg (Leidseplein 26) is a convenient choice for operetta or a play in English. This is also the primary venue for Dutch classical (and often ponderous) theatre. Dine at the adjoining Café Cox, before or after the performance.

Just a short walk or tram ride south of here, Amsterdam's major concert hall, the Concertgebouw (Van Baerlestraat 98), is home to one of the world's most respected orchestras as well as the Amsterdam Baroque Orchestra and the Orchestra of the 18th century.

Back towards the centre is the huge Muziektheater (Waterlooplein 22), the city's most controversial, and very costly, modern monument. Luckily, much has been forgiven because of the world-wide reputation of the resident Netherlands National Ballet and Opera companies. But, despite the presence of showpiece concert halls, many music lovers prefer a more subdued setting, including, perhaps, a concert in the Beurs van Berlage (Stock Exchange, Damrak) or a church organ recital in the mysterious Oude Kerk (Old Church) or the tranquil Engelse Kerk (English Church, Begijnhof).

Amsterdam is equally proud of its reputation for exciting pop and rock music, with a strong preference for the latest, most offbeat sounds. Although there is no major rock venue, the Melkweg entertainment complex (Lijnbaansgracht 234) is still the most talked-about location. Its origins lie in the laid-back 1960s but today it attracts both erstwhile hippies and would-be yuppies to its blend of African bands, "alternative" discos and the occasional opportunity to see The Nits, Amsterdam's most famous rock band. Sixties love-ins may be long since over but in the Melkweg that was just yesterday.

The Melkweg and its rival Paradiso (Weteringschans 6) are barely awake before 10pm so there is time before the main gig to savour the neighbourhood nightlife at its most exuberant. Try a drink at the Bamboo Bar (66 Lange Leidsedwarsstraat), a cosmopolitan haunt that acts as host to quite an eclectic range of live music, from soul and funk to country and western or jazz and blues.

If this is not your scene you can head east towards Rembrandtplein for gay clubs, bondage shows, dancing on tables and endless thigh-slapping fun. En route, admire the striking art deco interior of the Cinema Tuschinski (Reguliersbreestraat 26), which, alas, is in the process of undergoing expansion into a multiplex.

Crowds in the streets around Rembrandtplein are game for anything, especially late at night when the disco crowd and piano bar clientele are taking to the streets and making merry. Do beware of walking along deserted streets off the busy Leidseplein and Rembrandtplein late at night because tourists have lately been robbed. You have been warned.

Style-conscious Amsterdammers turn their backs on such pedestrian neighbourhoods in favour of bohemian bars and *eetcafés*, often situated in the red light district or between the canals. The hallmark of these architect-designed bars is a slickness encapsulated by the white marble interiors and architect-designed clients. Frascati (Nes 59, behind Rokin) draws theatre-lovers, cabaret artistes and designers to nibble late-night snacks, discuss the latest exhibition and posture in a spacious, mirrored interior.

A few streets further, La Strada (Nieuwezijds Voorburgwal), inspired by Fellini's film, proudly calls itself an Art Café. Apart from live music on Saturdays, there are regular art exhibitions, experimental plays and video shows.

As the evening wears on, the jazz clubs warm up, not an easy feat considering the coldness of the warehouse locations. The newly restored BIMhuis (Oude Schans 73) is the city's major jazz and blues venue but near Leidseplein there are also some small clubs including Café Alto (115 Korte Leidsedwaarsstraat), which has jam sessions during the week, and Bourbon St. (6 Leidsedwaarsstraat).

The newest musical strand in the Amsterdam scene is Latin American music. In the summer, the Latin Club (Oudezijds Voorburgwal 254) is the place for a steamy salsa session.

After midnight, Amsterdam's discotheques begin to wake up. Escape (Rembrandtplein 10) attracts droves of Amsterdammers of all ages and persuasions, while the Odeon (Singel 460) aspires to yuppified elegance in a gabled town house. The Arena youth hotel complex also has a popular disco (s' Gravesandsstraat 51). The Roxy (Singel 465), located in an atmospheric *fin-de-siècle* cinema, is perhaps the most exclusive disco, and offers theme nights.

Jordaan's notorious "singing" brown cafés offer an equally frantic end to an evening, albeit in low-life style. Sentimental versions of French *chansons* echo around Nol's (Westerstraat 109) and Twee Zwaantjes (Prinsengracht 114). As customers collapse into their Heinekens, the night is seen out with hearty bonhomie and raucous singalongs. Watch out – this option is definitely not for those with a business appointment the following morning.

For real night owls, there are late bars which stay open until 5am, including some that serve food into the night. Try Café de Koophandel (49 Bloemgracht) or P 96, unsurprisingly at 96 Prinsengracht.

But, despite the best of intentions, a typical night on the town all too often ends in an alcoholic stupor. As the bartender claims in true Amsterdammer logic: "The second beer only has an effect after you've downed the fourth." ∎

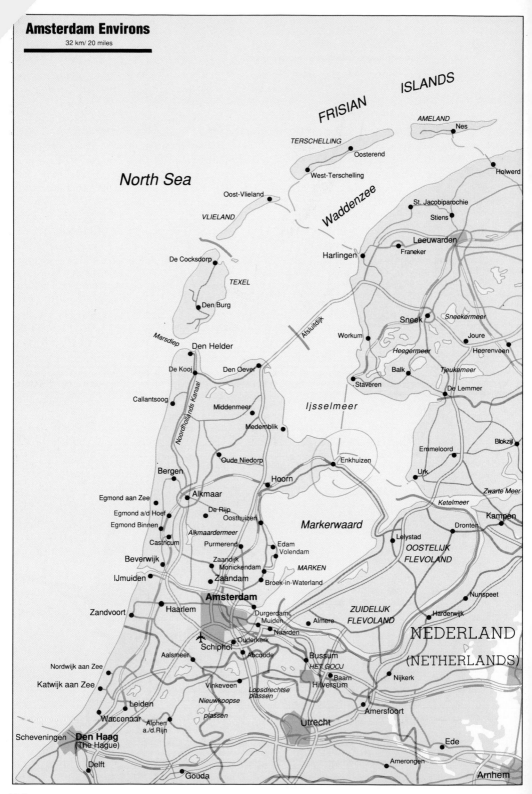

# Amsterdam Environs

32 km/ 20 miles

ISLANDS

FRISIAN

AMELAND
Nes

TERSCHELLING
Oosterend
West-Terschelling

Holwerd

## North Sea

Oost-Vlieland

Waddenzee

St. Jacobiparochie
Stiens

VLIELAND

Harlingen
Franeker
Leeuwarden

De Cocksdorp

TEXEL

Den Burg

Sneek
Sneekermeer
Joure
Workum
Heegermeer
Heerenveen

Marsdiep
Den Helder

Aflsuitdijk

Balk
Tjeukemeer
De Kooij
Den Oever
Staveren
De Lemmer

Callantsoog

IJsselmeer

Noordhollands Kanaal

Middenmeer

Medemblik

Blokzijl
Emmeloord

Bergen
Oude Niedorp
Enkhuizen
Urk

Egmond aan Zee
Hoorn
Zwarte Meer

Alkmaar
Ketelmeer
Kampen

Egmond a/d Hoef
De Rijp
Oosthuizen
Markerwaard
Dronten

Egmond Binnen
Alkmaardermeer
Lelystad

Castricum
Purmerend
Edam
Volendam
OOSTELIJK
FLEVOLAND

Beverwijk
Zaandijk
Monickendam
MARKEN

IJmuiden
Zaandam
Broek-in-Waterland

Nunspeet

Amsterdam
Harderwijk

Zandvoort
Haarlem
Durgerdam
Muiden
Almere
ZUIDELIJK
FLEVOLAND

NEDERLAND

Schiphol
Ouderkerk
Naarden

(NETHERLANDS)

Aalsmeer
Abcoude
Bussum
Nijkerk

Nordwijk aan Zee
HET GOOJ
Baarn
Hilversum

Katwijk aan Zee
Vinkeveen
Loosdrechtse
plassen

Leiden
Nieuwkoopse
Amersfoort

Wassenaar
plassen

Scheveningen
Alphen
a./d.Rijn
Utrecht

Den Haag
(The Hague)
Ede

Delft

Gouda
Amerongen
Arnhem

156

# AMSTERDAM ENVIRONS

This section covers the rest of the province of Noord-Holland, bounded to the east by the IJsselmeer, to the south by the provinces of Utrecht and Zuid-Holland, and to the west by the North Sea. Haarlem (population 152,500) is the provincial capital. It is an attractive old Dutch town on the edge of the Kennemer Dunes, with a famous collection of paintings by Frans Hals. Further north is Alkmaar (population 83,800), a pleasant market town. The towns along the river Zaan, known collectively as the Zaanstreek, lie only a few miles northwest of Amsterdam.

The flat landscape of Noord-Holland is familiar from paintings by Dutch Masters such as Ruisdael. Large areas in this province consist of reclaimed polder lying below sea level. **Schiphol** airport, 8 miles (13 km) southeast of Amsterdam, lies 15 ft (4.5 metres) below sea level on a former lake, the Haarlemmermeer, where a great sea battle took place against the Spanish during the Dutch Revolt. Three huge pumping houses were built in the 19th century to drain the lake. These distinctive neo-Gothic industrial buildings still stand; a museum which charts the Dutch struggle against the sea is housed in the former pumping house **De Cruquius**, in Heemstede, a suburb of Haarlem.

The most rewarding areas for walking or cycling in the Amsterdam environs are the dunes along the west coast and the woods of Het Gooi. Bulb fields extend along much of the eastern fringe of the dunes. The main flower and plant auction takes place in a vast complex at **Aalsmeer**, 12 miles (19 km) southwest of Amsterdam. Another curious auction, the Broeker Veiling, is held in the village of **Langendijk**, near Alkmaar, where boats laden with vegetables are navigated through the auction sheds.

**Haarlem** is an interesting historic town on the winding river Spaarne, and it has clung to its antique character more than any other town in the *Randstad* – the great conurbation, also known as the big village, that spreads south to Rotterdam and embraces Leiden and Utrecht, Delft, Gouda and Amsterdam as well as Haarlem itself. Though only 15 minutes by train from Amsterdam, Haarlem still seems very much under the sway of sober 17th-century virtues. It has an abundance of antique dealers in the brick-paved lanes to the south of Grote Markt, and many curious old shop interiors, such as the violin seller's at Schagchelstraat 16, the comic strip store at Jacobijnestraat 8, and the cheese shop at Nieuwe Groenmarkt 39.

H. de Vries' bookshop at Jacobijnestraat 3 has a Dutch Renaissance interior, reminiscent of paintings by Pieter de Hooch. Also on this street at number 22 is Galerie Année which exhibits contemporary paintings, sculpture, ceramics and glass. But perhaps the most curious shop in Haarlem is the chemist A.J. van der Pigge at Gierstraat 3, where you can buy herbal teas or *drop* (liquorice), in a dark, wooden interior crowded with ancient apothecary jars.

Haarlem was the birthplace of many

famous Dutch artists, including Geertgen tot Sint Jans (who lived in a monastery in the St Jansstraat) and the landscape painters Salomon van Ruysdael and his nephew Jacob van Ruisdael (so spelled). Jacob painted the dramatic *View of Haarlem* seen from the dunes at Overveen, now in the Mauritshuis in The Hague.

**Renowned artist:** But the most famous artist of Haarlem was Frans Hals. Probably born in Antwerp, Hals spent most of his life in Haarlem, where he specialised in group portraits of military guilds and governors and governesses of charitable institutions. Eight of these extraordinary works, which inspired the French Impressionists and Van Gogh, are now hanging in the town's Frans Hals Museum.

The best place to begin a walking tour of Haarlem is the **railway station**, a handsome art nouveau building of polished wood and tile pictures dating from 1908. Now head down Jansweg and turn left into Korte Jansstraat to reach the **Bakenessergracht**, named after a

Gothic church whose delicate 16th-century spire overlooks the canal. Groenebuurt (a lane to the right) brings you to the former Begijnhof quarter, of which all that survives is the church, a curious edifice with several houses built within the nave.

Continuing along Bakenessergracht brings you to the broad River Spaarne. Standing on the waterfront nearby is the **Teylers Museum**, the oldest museum in the Netherlands. This magnificent relic of the Dutch Enlightenment has been preserved in its original state.

The museum was founded in 1778 by Pieter Teyler van der Hulst, a prosperous silk merchant who amassed a large collection of fossils and scientific instruments. The round entrance hall of the museum, with its marble statues and bas reliefs depicting the sciences, has all the grandeur of a country house.

More splendid still is the Oval Hall, a two-storey neoclassical hall built in 1779, with glass cabinets filled with antique scientific instruments, and bizarre pyramid-shaped display cabinets

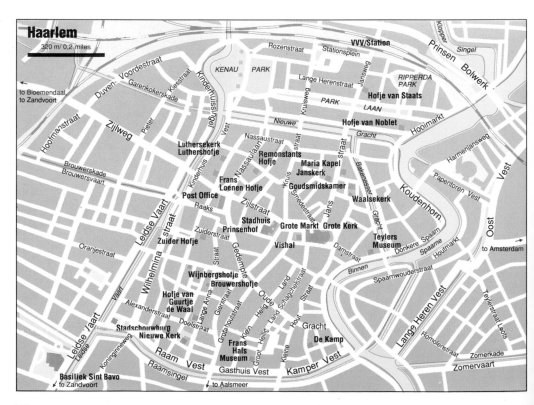

for minerals. The museum also has an important collection of Dutch and Flemish prints, and 19th-century Romantic paintings displayed in a gallery lit only by daylight.

Damstraat leads from the Spaarne to the **St Bavokerk** (Grote Kerk). This enormous Gothic Church was a favourite subject of 17th-century artists such as Pieter Saenredam and Gerrit Berckheyde. It dates mainly from the 15th century, though the ornate bell-tower above the crossing is a 16th-century embellishment.

The church is a marvellous jumble of roofs and gables, with several low buildings attached, such as the Vishal (once a fish market, now used for art exhibitions) on the north side, and several tiny 17th-century houses (rented out by the church authorities to raise revenue) along the south wall.

The entrance to the church is through one of these little shuttered houses, which adds to the dramatic impact of the vast nave. Though the church seems rather empty, it contains many fascinating features, including some curious medieval misericords, and several decorated graves of shoemakers in the ambulatory.

St Bavokerk is particularly renowned for its 18th-century Muller organ, which brought Mozart (aged 10), Händel and Liszt to this town.

The **Grote Markt**, Haarlem's main square, still looks very much as it did in the 17th-century townscapes of Gerrit Berckheyde in the Frans Hals Museum. The **Vleeshal** (meat hall) on the south side was designed in 1602 by Lieven de Key in a crowded Dutch Mannerist style, with a giant oxen head to indicate the building's function. Opposite, exhibiting the more restrained classicism typical of the mid-17th century, is the **Hoofdwacht**, a guard house.

The **Stadhuis** (city hall) on the west side, standing on the site of a banqueting hall of the Counts of Holland, is an attractive mixture of buildings dating to the medieval and Renaissance periods.

The old town is dotted with some 18 *hofjes* (almshouse courts) founded by

**Haarlem's art deco railway station.**

wealthy burghers, mostly situated in the quiet streets to the west of Grote Markt, though there are three stately 18th-century almshouses on the east side of town (including a *hofje* on the Spaarne founded by Pieter Teyler in 1787).

The other main reason to visit Haarlem is the **Frans Hals Museum**, which is easily reached from the church down Warmoesstraat (notice the curious patterned pavements of brick), Schagchelstraat and Groot Heilig Land. The museum occupies a Dutch Renaissance building designed by Lieven de Key in 1608 as a hospice for old men, but two years later converted to an orphanage. It contains several attractive period rooms and a detailed dolls' house, but its principal treasure is the collection of eight group portraits by Frans Hals.

Three paintings show members of the Guild of St George, and two depict the members of the Guild of St Adrian – whose guild house (the Kloveniersdoelen) is still standing in Gasthuisstraat. These military guilds seem to have been more interested in banqueting than in exercising, and Hals' portraits marvellously capture the slightly tipsy guild members, with their distinctive pointed beards and flowing orange and pale blue silk sashes.

The other group portraits are extremely sombre by comparison. One shows the governors of St Elizabeth's Hospital and the other two are rather embittered portraits of the governors and governesses of the old men's home, painted when Hals, aged over 80, was himself an inmate.

To the south of the old town is a large wood, the **Haarlemmer Hout**, all that remains of an ancient forest that once extended from Haarlem to The Hague, where the Counts of Holland were fond of hunting.

Standing on the old waterway to Leiden, to the west of the town, is the **Basiliek St Bavo**, a bizarre 19th-century church of considerable architectural impact (best appreciated from Koorstraat).

An extensive area of bulb fields extends along the eastern edge of the dunes

The Teylers Museum, Haarlem.

160

from Haarlem to Leiden. These intensely cultivated fields are mainly situated on the polder created when the Haarlemmermeer was drained. This new land is extremely fertile, and provides enormous yields of tulips, daffodils and chrysanthemums. A visit to the busy Aalsmeer Flower Auction, near Schiphol airport, provides a marvellous glimpse of this efficient Dutch industry.

**Cheese capital:** The town of **Edam**, 14 miles (22 km) northeast of Amsterdam, is a cheerful, interesting little place with attractive canals crossed by narrow wooden bridges. Like many towns of the region known as Waterland, Edam was once an important whaling town, as the quay named Groenland recalls. In the 17th century it was an important port with large shipyards situated on the waterway to the east of the town.

Edam is now world famous for its round cheeses, which are produced by farms on the fertile Beemster and Purmer polders. Edam cheeses, wrapped in a protective skin of red wax for export, can still be bought in the 16th-century **Waag** (weigh house) on Waagplein.

The main attraction in the town is the curious **Edams Museum**. This occupies a late Gothic house with a curious floating cellar that rocks to and fro as you walk across it. Opinions differ as to the purpose of the cellar; the romantic theory is that it was built by a retired captain to remind him of the sea, while a more prosaic explanation is that it was built this way to keep the cellar dry in times of flooding.

The museum proudly displays the portraits of three eccentric local characters: Jan Claeszoon Clees, who was extremely fat; Trijntje Cornelisdochter Kever, who was very tall; and Pieter Dirkszoon Langebaard, who (as his name suggests) had an extremely long beard. "Long Beard" toured the country displaying his beard to raise money for the local **Weeshuis** (orphanage), which is still standing on Kerkstraat.

The museum faces an unusual square; **Damplein** is built in the form of a long arched bridge to allow ships to pass beneath. South of here stands the soli-

St Bavokerk (the Grote Kerk), Haarlem, 1668. (Painting by Berckheyde)

tary tower of a 15th-century church, with a beautiful 16th-century carillon of bells from Mechelen. Further south, you come to Edam's most attractive canal, the **Schepenmakersdijk** (shipbuilders' dyke), with curious tea houses on the water's edge on one side.

**Alkmaar** is a modest inland town 25 miles (40 km) north of Amsterdam whose one moment of glory came in 1573 when it successfully withstood a Spanish siege, prompting the quip "from Alkmaar to victory." It is now a busy market town where a "traditional" cheese market is staged on Friday mornings during the tourist season.

The yellow-skinned cheeses are piled on to wooden sledges by porters in traditional garb, before being taken to the **Waaggebouw**, a 14th-century chapel which was converted to a weigh house in the 16th century by the addition of a Renaissance gable and a jaunty bell tower. It now contains a small museum of cheese-making techniques. To explore Alkmaar on foot, take Stationstraat from the station, then follow the moat to the right, which brings you to a bridge leading to the **Grote Kerk**. This imposing 15th-century church was built of mellow Brabant limestone by the Keldermans family of Mechelen. The 17th-century organ was designed by Jacob van Campen, the architect of the Amsterdam town hall. Heading into town along Langestraat, you come to the **Stadhuis** (Townhall). The east wing and tower were built in late-Gothic style in the 1510s; the west wing was added in 1694 in baroque style. North of here is the **Stedelijk (Municipal) Museum Alkmaar**, which has a local collection of guild group portraits, antique toys, tiles and paintings. Situated in the attractive Renaissance guild house of the archers, it is worth a visit solely to see the panoramic view of the *Siege of Alkmaar*, painted by an unknown Master in the 16th century, and including touches of typical Netherlandish humour such as a drunken soldier and a couple making love as the battle rages.

Heading east from here, you will eventually come upon the **Waagplein**, scene

**Alkmaar cheese porter.**

162

of the Friday cheese market. Further east, the canal Verdronken Oord leads to the Noord-Hollands Kanaal, which has an animated maritime atmosphere. The curious **Accijnstoren** was built in 1622 to collect tolls on local shipping. In a delicate operation in 1924 the tower was moved by some 13 ft (4 metres), using a system of rollers, thereby (but only temporarily) improving traffic flow.

A more elegant quarter lies to the south of the Waagplein. The simple baroque-style **Wildemanshofje** on Oude Gracht was founded in 1714 for 24 elderly women. The statue of a wild man above the entrance is a curious play on the name of the founder, a certain Gerrit Wildeman. A thin ribbon of landscaped park runs along the town moat south of here, making a pleasant route back to the station.

The industrial towns of Zaandam, Koog aan de Zaan and Zaandijk are strung out along both banks of the Zaan River, forming the conurbation of **Zaanstreek**. In 1592 a windmill-powered sawmill was invented in the Zaan region, leading to the development of a large timber industry which supplied nearby shipyards.

Other windmills were built along the river banks to supply power for oil-mills, paint-mills, flour-mills and mustard-mills (which produced the celebrated Zaanse mustard). By the 18th century there were more than 1,000 windmills slowly turning in the breeze in this region.

**A visit from the Czar:** In 1697 Czar Peter the Great travelled incognito to Zaandam to visit the famous shipyards on the river Zaan. A tiny wooden house is preserved in Zaandam, the **Czaar-Pieterhuisje**, where he stayed with Gerrit Kist, a local smith he knew from St Petersburg.

The building developed an alarming tilt and is now propped up by a 19th-century frame. Occasionally large groups of Russian sailors descend upon Zaandam to see the small wooden bed into which the Czar used to squeeze his 7-ft (2.1-metre) frame.

**Zaandijk**, a few miles north, has the

*Zaanstad, working flour mill.*

sole surviving example of a complete street built in the old Zaan district style, with a small museum, the **Zaanlandse Oudheidkamer**, in an 18th-century merchant's home. The adjacent river was once the region's main thoroughfare.

The abundance of timber in the Zaan region led to a distinctive local style of green wooden houses decorated with pointed or bell-shaped gables. In the 1950s many of the surviving houses and windmills in Zaan style were relocated to an open-air museum, the **Zaanse Schans**, situated on the river bank opposite Zaandijk. A working windmill here produces local mustard, and a clogmaker demonstrates his craft. The new **Zaans Museum** houses the locally themed collections formerly at the Zaans Historisch Museum.

To the east of Amsterdam is the restored **Muiden Castle**, situated where the River Vecht enters the IJsselmeer. This attractive brick castle was built in 1285 by Count Floris V of Holland, the founder of many Dutch towns. Floris V was murdered here 11 years later by a group of nobles enraged by his policy of encouraging urban development. In the 17th century the poet and historian P. C. Hooft occupied the castle in his capacity as bailiff of Gooiland, and it became the meeting place for the illustrious *Muiderkring* (Muiden Circle) group of poets and writers; members included jurist Hugo Grotius, diplomat and poet Constantijn Huygens, and the prolific Amsterdam poet Joost van den Vondel.

A boat leaves from behind Amsterdam's Centraal Station May–September (Rederij Naco landing 7, tel: 626 2466) on excursions to Muiden as well as to the Fort Pampus Island fortification. In Muiden, the Rederij Toman ferryboat landing is next to the castle.

**Remembering a massacre:** Further east along the IJsselmeer coast is the historic town of **Naarden**. In 1572 the Spanish army under Don Frederick of Toledo murdered almost all the inhabitants. The massacre is commemorated by a 17th-century stone tablet on a building at Turfpoortstraat 7. The town fortifications were demolished by the Spanish and Naarden became a virtual ghost town.

More advanced defences were erected in the 17th century. These fortifications still completely encircle the town and are fascinating to explore. They are explained in the **Vestingmuseum**, which is located within a bastion connected to underground passages and casemates, themselves now home to a complex of up-market restaurants and interior design stores called the Arsenaal.

Naarden is also associated with Comenius, a 17th-century philosopher and pedagogue who fled here from Moravia (now part of the Czech Republic) in 1621. The **Comeniusmuseum** contains a small exhibition on him.

The woods of **Het Gooi**, south of Naarden, attracted wealthy Amsterdam merchants in the 17th century. Dutch Impressionist Anton Mauve lived in Laren and painted the Gooiland countryside.

**Hilversum**, the main town of the area, is the home of Dutch national radio and TV. Its town hall was designed by W.M. Dudok in 1931. The town also has the Pinetum Blijdenstein and a botanic garden (Costerustuin).

Below, Zaanse Schans windmill. Right, typical duneland scenery at Kennermer Duinen.

# NATURE RESERVES

areful planning has preserved several areas of traditional Dutch landscape around Amsterdam. Beyond Amsterdam-Noord lies Waterland, an area of red pyramidal farmhouse roofs poking above clumps of trees, and reed-fringed lakes populated by ragged herons and rare waders. Many of the village names in this area end in *dam*, indicating the importance of water management in this soggy region.

Once you have crossed the IJ by the ferry that leaves from behind Amsterdam's Centraal Station, you follow the ancient dyke route along the IJsselmeer coast, which is lined with brightly painted wooden houses imitating the gabled houses of Amsterdam.

Durgerdam is the most attractive of these elongated villages, perched boldly above the dyke to enjoy a splendid view of the IJsselmeer, which on breezy Sundays is dotted with traditional brown-sailed boats. The village of Uitdam nestles more cautiously in the lee of the sea dyke on a narrow thread of land between the dyke and a lake.

The spires of the inland villages can be seen from afar. The squat church tower of Ransdorp is a distinctive feature of Waterland, and appears in a sketch by Rembrandt.

Broek-in-Waterland, which lies inland, often featured in travellers' anecdotes because of the obsessive cleanliness of its inhabitants, who could sometimes be spotted scrubbing the walls of houses and even tree trunks, apparently to maintain the high level of cleanliness on which the town's cheese manufacture depended.

This village of canals and stately houses still has a prim and precious air, though the frenzied graffiti in the concrete underpass linking the two parts of Broek suggests that an undercurrent of dissent exists here just as it does in Amsterdam.

Het Twiske is a recently landscaped park between Oostzaan and Landsmeer, with lakes for windsurfing, cycle paths, woods and picnic areas. To reach it from Amsterdam, take the IJ ferry and follow the Noord-Hollands Kanaal out of the city, then turn off down the road to Landsmeer.

The Amstel and its tributaries to the south of Amsterdam offer a different Dutch landscape. A quiet road ideal for cycling follows the meandering river, past stately 18th-century country houses, to the village of Ouderkerk.

A Jewish cemetery (you must ask permission at Kerkstraat 7 before entering) was founded in Ouderkerk in 1614 for the Portuguese Jews of Amsterdam. This romantic spot, with its tombs inscribed in Hebrew and Portuguese, attracted several 17th-century Dutch artists. Beyond Ouderkerk, the river Bullewijk meanders through peaceful fields, though the high-rise suburbs of Amsterdam are rather too close for comfort.

The reed-lined river Holendrecht takes you to Abcoude, an attractive town at the confluence of three rivers. Here, the Amstel flows southwards into Utrecht province, while the Gein – a popular subject with Amsterdam Impressionist painters – flows northwards, to link with the Amsterdam-Rijnkanaal, which then leads back to the port of Amsterdam.

The dunes extending along the west coast of Noord-Holland offer a quite different Dutch landscape. The North Holland Dunes Nature Reserve is particularly attractive for cycling. (Bicycles can be hired at Castricum railway station, 30 minutes from Amsterdam; maps and tickets giving access to the nature reserve are sold at the adjacent vvv tourist office.)

The undulating dune landscape is totally devoid of vegetation and looks almost lunar. Yet the land just behind the dunes is thickly wooded, giving way to extensive bulb fields.

Several cycle routes converge on Bloemberg, the highest point in the dunes. But the most popular destination by far is Johanna's Hof, a large pancake house in the woods, complete with a small zoo.

Het Gooi, an area of woods to the east of Amsterdam, has been a popular country retreat for Amsterdam's prosperous merchants and ship captains since the 17th century. Hiring a bicycle at Hilversum railway station, you can head north to the Bussummerheide, an area of heath and woodlands, or south through the woods to the village of Lage Vuursche, renowned for its pancake houses and its miniature golf course. ∎

# THE HAGUE AND ENVIRONS

The Hague and the neighbouring cities of Leiden and Delft lie in the prosperous northern part of Zuid-Holland province. Each of these old Dutch cities has played a crucial role in the history of the Netherlands and the development of Dutch painting, and, not surprisingly, they have some of the best museums and art galleries in the country.

**The Hague** (Den Haag in Dutch) is different from most Dutch cities in that it does not owe its existence to trade or the sea; its principal activities are government and administration. The town grew up around a hunting lodge of the Counts of Holland, which gave The Hague its curious Old Dutch name of 's Gravenhage (the Count's hedge).

The town first became important in 1586 when the States General of the new Dutch Republic met here, and The Hague gradually assumed the role of political capital, even though officially it was not even a town, since it had no city walls or medieval privileges. The main attraction of this "village" was that it offered a neutral meeting ground for representatives of the seven northern provinces, who each jealously guarded their independence.

Attractive streets and squares were laid out around the old castle in the 17th century, including the Plein and the Korte Vijverberg, which were designed by the diplomat and poet Constantijn Huygens. Further improvements were made in the 18th century along the Lange Vijverberg and Lange Voorhout.

The gracious style of the 18th century reached its highest expression in the former Royal Library at Lange Voorhout 34, begun by Daniel Marot in 1734 with wings added in 1761 by Pieter de Swart. By the 19th century The Hague had become a fashionable literary and artistic centre, while the nearby village of Scheveningen was one of the most elegant resorts on the North Sea.

In recent years The Hague has largely lost much of its allure, due to the disappearance of many of its canals and the unchecked development of roads and office blocks. Fortunately, the extensive woods where the Counts of Holland hunted have been preserved, and the windswept dunes where the Impressionists of The Hague School painted are as wild as ever. The Hague authorities are now attempting to improve the inner city by such projects as the new concert hall on Spui (Anton Philipszaal), which has become the home-base of the progressive Nederlands Dans Theater.

**Seat of the Dutch government:** The most attractive area of the city lies around the old castle of the Counts of Holland. A gateway on Buitenhof leads into the **Binnenhof**, the former courtyard of the Count's castle. The building that looks like a chapel in the middle of the courtyard is the **Riederzaal**, a 13th-century hall built by Count Floris V.

Heavily restored in the 19th century, the building has come to symbolise the Dutch Parliament, though it is now only used on ceremonial occasions. A new building has been designed for the Sec-

ond Chamber with a glass facade on Hofsingel to provide the public with a glimpse of the government in action.

A gateway behind the Ridderzaal leads to the **Mauritshuis**, which rises out of the water like a Venetian palace. This was the former home of Count Johan Maurits, an enlightened governor who ruled over Brazil on behalf of the Dutch West Indies Company. Built in 1633–44 by Pieter Post from plans by Jacob van Campen, the classical building perfectly embodies the Dutch principles of reason and balance. In a letter to Johan Maurits, Constantijn Huygens praised "the beautiful, very beautiful, and most beautiful building."

Maurits' house was once famed for its "cabinets of curiosities," rooms filled with exotica brought back by Dutch trading ships. In the 19th century the Koninklijk Kabinet van Schilderijen (Royal Picture Cabinet) was moved here to create one of the most beautiful small picture galleries in the world. More like a private house than a museum, the Mauritshuis has a choice collection of Flemish, Dutch and German Old Masters. The works are hung in a series of handsome period rooms, ranging from grand gilded salons to intimate wood-panelled chambers.

**Works by Rembrandt:** The ground floor is mainly devoted to Flemish paintings, including the *Descent from the Cross* by Rogier van der Weyden and the *Portrait of a Man* by Hans Memling, although Warhol's portrait of Queen Beatrix is there too. The rooms on the first floor contain some of the finest works of the Dutch Golden Age, including Rembrandt's first major commission, *The Anatomy Lesson of Dr Tulp*, executed in 1632. The figure of *Susanna*, painted in 1637, was probably modelled on his wife Saskia. There are also several self-portraits from different periods of Rembrandt's life. In the earliest, dated 1629, he looks almost arrogant, but by the time of the 1669 portrait (painted the year he died), the artist's face has weathered to an expression of infinite sorrow. One of the strangest paintings in the collection is *The Goldfinch*, by Carel

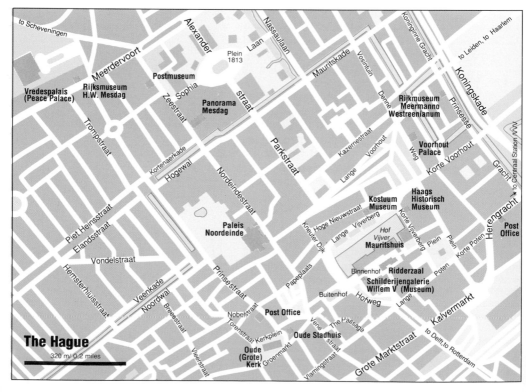

The Hague
320 m / 0.2 miles

Fabritius (one of Rembrandt's many pupils). It is one of the few works by Fabritius to have survived, and was painted in 1654, the year the artist was killed in a gunpowder explosion in Delft at the age of 22

Six years later, Vermeer painted the *View of Delft*, which shows no evidence of the destruction. In 1994 this painting as well as his *Girl with a pearl* were restored. The Mauritshuis also has a striking *View of Haarlem* by Jacob van Ruisdael, and several white church interiors by Pieter Saenredam.

Wandering through the Mauritshuis, you are inevitably struck by the wonderful views of the Hofvijver, all that remains of the castle moat. Several small museums overlook this lake, including the new **Haags Historisch Museum** on the east side. This museum of local history occupies the Sebastiaansdoelen, a Dutch Classical building commissioned by the archers' guild in 1636. In Room 1, which looks out on the Hofvijver, you can see several old paintings of the lake, almost invariably featuring

the distinctive 15th-century octagonal tower still standing alongside the Mauritshuis. You also see the archers' *doelen*, or firing range, that once stood on the east side of the lake. The museum's other main attraction is a dolls' house beautifully furnished in 19th-century style.

After many years of closure, the **Museum Bredius** has reopened in a handsome 18th-century house on the north side of the Hofvijver. Its collection of paintings was formed by Dr Abraham Bredius, a director of the Mauritshuis at the turn of the 19th century, and contains works by both well-known names and unknown artists of the Dutch Golden Age.

A pleasant walk around the lakeside brings you to the **Schilderijengalerie Willem V**, the oldest picture gallery in the Netherlands. Founded in 1774 by Prince William V, this small stately gallery has been restored to its original appearance, and paintings are crammed on the walls in several tiers (as they are in the painting in the Mauritshuis by

**Koninklijke Bibliotheek, The Hague.**

Willem van Haecht of *Alexander the Great Visiting the Studio of Apelles*). The collection of Dutch Old Masters of the 17th and 18th centuries does not compare with the Mauritshuis, but this eccentric gallery is well worth a visit.

**Buitenhof** divides the government quarter from the old town, now an area of pedestrianised shopping streets. **The Passage**, off Buitenhof, is an elegant shopping arcade dating from 1885. Groenmarkt, not far from here, is the centre of the old town. Here stands the **Oude Kerk**, a 15th-century Gothic church with an early 16th-century choir. The **Oude Stadhuis** (Old Town Hall) opposite was built in 1564–65 in spirited Renaissance style, while a large wing was added in the 18th century.

Noordeinde is the most elegant shopping street in The Hague, and has several well-preserved art nouveau shop fronts. It runs past the **Paleis Noordeinde**, a royal residence with impressive stables on Hogewal.

*Trompe-l'oeil* **seascape:** Continuing down Noordeinde and across a canal,
you reach the **Panorama Mesdag**. Inside, you enter a darkened tunnel and ascend a spiral staircase to a mock pavilion, from which you obtain a very lifelike panoramic view of the coast and dunes at Scheveningen.

The panorama was painted in 1881 by the Hague Impressionist Hendrik Willem Mesdag on a circular canvas 400 ft (120 metres) long by 46 ft (14 metres) high. In executing this work, Mesdag was assisted by his wife (who painted the village of Scheveningen), Theo de Bock (delegated to paint the sky), and the Amsterdam Impressionist G.H. Breitner (who added his favourite theme of a group of cavalry officers charging on the beach). The astonishingly realistic effect is obtained by the indirect daylight falling from above, and the artificial foreground strewn with real objects.

Not far from here is the **Rijksmuseum H.W. Mesdag**, occupying a house built in 1887 by the artist. This once neglected museum is now under the same management as the Van Gogh Museum

**The Panorama Mesdag.**

in Amsterdam. It contains Impressionist paintings by Mesdag himself and other members of The Hague School, plus a large collection of dark melancholy works by members of the Barbizon School, including paintings by Corot and Millet which inspired Mesdag.

The **Vredespaleis** (Peace Palace) is just north of here. Built to house the Permanent Court of Arbitration set up after the 1899 Hague conference on the suppression of war, this stately pile was paid for by the Scots millionaire Andrew Carnegie. Completed in 1913, its work failed to prevent the hostilities that led to World War I. The building is now used as the seat of the International Court of Justice, and contains a curious miscellany of objects donated by member states.

**The Netherlands in miniature:** The Scheveningseweg runs north of here to the sea through the vast wooded area of the Scheveningse Bosjes. Situated on the edge of the woods to the east, **Madurodam** is a miniature town (recently renovated and extended) with exact reproductions of historic buildings in the Netherlands. It also has a working port, an extensive railway network and some interesting details reflecting contemporary Dutch life.

The elegant quarter to the west of the woods contains a cluster of interesting museums. The **Haags Gemeentemuseum** houses an excellent collection of modern painting and decorative art in an attractive low brick building overlooking an ornamental pond. This was the last work designed by the founder of Dutch modern architecture, H.P. Berlage, who died a year before its completion in 1935.

Berlage's modern masterpiece provides an appropriate setting for an extensive collection of works by Piet Mondriaan, ranging from early paintings in the style of The Hague School to abstract works composed of blocks of red, yellow and blue. The museum also has a renowned Delftware collection, an exquisite Dutch dolls' house, a large collection of musical instruments and a section devoted to fashion.

**Madurodam.**

The nearby **Museon**, which is built in a style that echoes Berlage's Gemeentemuseum, is a modern science museum with many working models. Also in this area is **Omniversum**, where films are screened on a planetarium dome to achieve a striking realism.

There are several other specialised museums in The Hague, including the **Rijksmuseum Meermanno-Westreenianum**, which contains an important collection of illuminated manuscripts and classical antiquities, and the **Postmuseum** (opposite the Panorama Mesdag).

If you are keen to follow in the footsteps of the Hague Impressionists, the coastal resort of **Scheveningen** is just a short tram ride from the city centre. The trams follow the Scheveningseweg, a broad straight road created to link The Hague to the coast in the 17th century by Constantijn Huygens. Every July the famous North Sea Jazz Festival weekend attracts visitors and top players from around the world.

Like most resorts on the sea, Scheve-ningen is a mixture of faded elegance and brash modernity, in recent years increasingly dominated by ugly high-rise buildings. The most striking buildings are the Kurhaus, a grand 19th-century hotel, and the modern Pier, which has an observation tower, a children's playground and a café.

**Seaside entertainment:** By far its most eccentric attraction is a model of the Nautilus submarine described in Jules Verne's *Twenty Thousand Leagues Under the Sea*. Looking out of the iron portholes of this wonderful 19th-century vessel, you are treated to various quaint and endearing illusions.

**Leiden**, on a branch of the Rhine in the bulb-growing region between The Hague and Haarlem, is a likeable university town full of cafés and book-shops. Leiden University is the oldest and most renowned in the Netherlands. It was founded in 1575 by William of Orange in recognition of the town's heroic resistance to the Spanish. Despite hunger and disease, the towns-people withstood a siege of 131 days.

**Left**, Haags Gemeente-museum; the history of fashion. **Right**, Rembrandt self-portrait, 1629.

# REMBRANDT IN LEIDEN AND AMSTERDAM

R embrandt Harmenszoon van Rijn was the greatest painter of the Dutch Golden Age. He was born in Leiden in 1606, the eighth child of Harmen Gerritszoon van Rijn, a prosperous miller, and Cornelia van Zuytbrouck, a baker's daughter. Rembrandt's father owned a mill on a branch of the Rhine, from which he derived his name. A replica of the windmill has been built on the waterfront just south of the Morspoort in Leiden. Not far from here (across a white wooden drawbridge) is the Weddesteeg, where Rembrandt was born (a plaque marks the site of the house).

Rembrandt was sent to the Latin School, a Renaissance building designed in 1599 by Lieven de Key, and still standing near the Pieterskerk. In 1620 he enrolled as a student at Leiden University, probably to prepare for a career in city government, but soon abandoned his studies in favour of painting. His father sent him to study under Jacob van Swanenburgh, who owned a step-gabled house still to be seen at Langebrug No. 89. After some three years here, Rembrandt moved to Amsterdam, where he spent six months in the studio of Pieter Lastman, a famous painter of classical and historical subjects.

In about 1625 he returned to his home town as a skilled painter. Rembrandt was an ambitious young artist, and when advised by the diplomat Constantijn Huygens, an early admirer of his work, to study in Italy, he replied that he was too busy to travel, and in any case he could see all the Italian work he wanted in Holland. The self-portrait in the Mauritshuis painted in 1629 shows the young Rembrandt as supremely confident and slightly haughty.

In about 1631 Rembrandt settled permanently in Amsterdam. The first work he executed here was the *Portrait of Nicolaes Ruts*, now in the Frick collection in New York. In 1632 he received his first major commission, *The Anatomy Lesson of Dr Tulp*, painted for the Amsterdam guild of surgeons and now displayed in the Mauritshuis Museum in The Hague.

Two years later Rembrandt married Saskia van Uylenburg, the daughter of a prosperous burgomaster of Leeuwarden. He painted Saskia many times, including once as Flora in a marvellous painting in London's National Gallery.

By 1639 Rembrandt was sufficiently wealthy to be able to afford a handsome Renaissance house in the Jewish quarter of Amsterdam (now the Rembrandthuis Museum). But his good fortune did not last; Saskia fell ill and died in 1642, having borne four children, three of whom had died in early childhood, leaving only Titus. A stone simply inscribed "Saskia" in Amsterdam's Oude Kerk marks her grave.

Ironically, this was the period of Rembrandt's greatest triumph, *The Night Watch*, which received its misleading title in the 19th century due to a thick layer of grime (now removed). The work was completed in 1642 for the Amsterdam guild of arquebusiers, and now hangs in the gallery of honour in Amsterdam's Rijksmuseum.

At about this time Rembrandt appointed Geertghe Dircx, a widow, as a nurse for Titus. Living together as a couple, they never married, as this would have deprived Rembrandt of income from Saskia's will. In 1649 they parted after a quarrel, probably sparked off by the arrival in the household of an extremely attractive 23-year-old servant, Hendrikje Stoffels.

Rembrandt's problems increased in 1656 when he was declared bankrupt. He was forced to sell his house and move to a more modest dwelling in the Jordaan. Though beset by personal and financial problems, Rembrandt painted one of his greatest works in 1656 – the now-damaged *Anatomy Lesson of Dr Deyman* hanging in the Amsterdam Rijksmuseum. His work continued to mature, and in 1661 he executed the famous *Syndics of the Drapers' Guild*, also in the Rijksmuseum.

Titus died at the age of 27 in 1668. Eleven months later, in October 1669, Rembrandt died. He was buried in an unmarked pauper's grave in Westerkerk in Amsterdam, and his exact burial place, which had been lost for three centuries, was only rediscovered early in 1990, during restoration of the interior of the church. ∎

They were finally liberated by a drastic measure; the sea dykes were broken, allowing the sea to flood a large area to the south of Leiden, so that Admiral Boisot could sail a fleet of ships up to the city walls. A magnificent tapestry in the Lakenhal Museum depicts this historical episode.

**Cradle of talent:** Many distinguished academics have taught at Leiden University, including Herman Boerhaave, professor of medicine, and Carl Linnaeus, the Swedish botanist. Several notable Dutch artists were also born in the city, including Rembrandt, Lucas van Leyden, Jan van Goyen, Gerrit Dou and Jan Steen.

The **Stedelijk Museum De Lakenhal** provides an interesting introduction to the history of this important Dutch town. The museum occupies a distinguished canal-side building designed in Dutch Classical style in 1640 by Arent van 's Gravesande.

The windmill flanked by cloth and wool above the entrance symbolises the building's original function as a cloth hall. Cloth making, which was introduced to Leiden by Flemish weavers fleeing the Black Death in the 14th century, was the town's main industry up to the 18th century. Five stone tablets on the facade illustrate the stages in cloth making, beginning with spinning and ending with the inspection by the Staalmeesters (syndics, who applied a metal seal to certified Leiden cloth).

A small art gallery in the Lakenhal contains works by 16th and 17th-century Leiden artists. Pride of place is given to Lucas van Leyden's *Triptych of the Last Judgement*, a faltering early Dutch Renaissance work painted in 1526 for the Pieterskerk. There is also an interesting scale model of the chapel of Marienpol Abbey, illustrating the locations of two altarpieces by Cornelis Engebrechtszoon now in the museum.

The Lakenhal has just one painting by Rembrandt, an unremarkable historical work dating from 1626, which is hung for comparison alongside a somewhat better work by Jan Lievens, with whom he probably shared a studio in Leiden.

**The Kurhaus, Scheveningen.**

176

There is also a gloomy painting by Jacob van Swanenburg, Rembrandt's teacher in Leiden. But probably the most alluring work in the collection is the *View of Leiden* painted by Jan van Goyen in 1650 eschewing bright colours in favour of muddy brown tones.

The Lakenhal also has a number of period rooms rescued from old buildings in Leiden, including an 18th-century kitchen and a room in Biedermeier style. The most attractive rooms are in the wings on the first floor. The room in the east wing comes from the brewers' guild house, and is decorated with five murals depicting different steps in the brewing process. The Staalmeesterskamer in the west wing, which is hung with sumptuous gilt leather, was the chamber in which the syndics of the cloth guild used to meet.

The best view of Leiden is from the **Burcht**, a 12th-century castle surmounting an ancient artificial mound built at the convergence of two branches of the Rhine. From the battlements, you can see the two vast churches of Leiden which appear in Van Goyen's painting in the Lakenhal. The nearer of the two, the **Hooglandse Kerk**, has a very curious appearance. Its 16th-century nave was never completed in length or height, and is dwarfed by the 15th-century Flamboyant Gothic choir.

To reach the university area, head down Hartesteeg to the Nieuwe Rijn, then continue along Gangetje. The park you pass stands on the site of several houses destroyed in 1807 when a barge laden with gunpowder exploded. The park contains a statue of Burgomaster Pieter van der Werff, who refused to surrender the city to the Spanish army in the siege of 1574.

**University quarter:** You come then to Rapenburg, a handsome canal enlivened with many university buildings in Dutch Classical style – the finest undoubtedly being the **Bibliotheca Thysiana**, at No. 25, which was built in 1655 by Arent van 's Gravesande. The University began in the former chapel facing the Nonnenbrug. A lane alongside leads to the **Hortus Botanicus**, one of the oldest

**Gables in Leiden.**

botanical gardens in the world. Founded in 1587, it was originally stocked with numerous exotic species brought back from the Dutch East Indies and from the Americas.

Across the Nonnenbrug, an attractive lane leads to the **Pieterskerk**, a 15th-century Gothic church containing the tombs of Leiden academics, including Herman Boerhaave and the Remonstrant theologian Jacobus Arminius.

The university law faculty is situated opposite the church in the Gravensteen, a gloomy former prison of the Counts of Holland. The attractive cobbled lanes around the Pieterskerk contain antiquarian bookshops and pleasant cafés. This quarter also has associations with the Pilgrim Fathers, who spent 12 years in Leiden before setting sail from Delfshaven on the *Speedwell*. John Robinson, the spiritual leader of the English religious community, lived on the south side of the Pieterskerk in the Jan Pesijnshofje. He had hoped eventually to join the Pilgrim Fathers in America, but died in 1625 in Leiden and was buried in the Pieterskerk. A plaque in the nearby Pieterskerk-Choorsteeg commemorates the Pilgrim Press run at No. 17 by William Brewster.

This lane emerges on **Breestraat**, the principal street of Leiden. The long facade of the **Stadhuis** on the right was designed in Dutch Renaissance style by Lieven de Key in 1595. The **Rijnlandshuis** to the left was designed by the same architect one year later for the powerful local water authority. De Key also built the beautiful **Stadstimmerwerf** on Galgewaard, which when floodlit at night is particularly striking.

**Egyptian treasures:** Several outstanding national museums are situated in Leiden, including one of the oldest museums in the Netherlands, the **Rijksmuseum van Oudheden**, founded in 1818. This attractive museum has an extensive collection of archaeological finds from the Netherlands, ancient Greece, Rome and Egypt. The mysterious floodlit Temple of Taffel in the entrance hall was presented by the Egyptian government in gratitude for Dutch

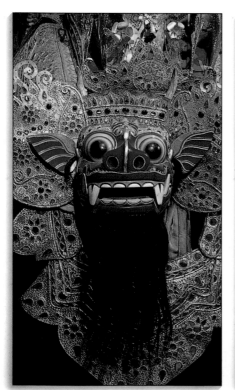

**Left,** Indonesian mask in Leiden's Rijksmuseum voor Volkenkunde. **Below,** Hooglandse Kerk.

aid in rescuing buildings threatened by the Aswan High Dam project.

The national ethnographic collection in the **Rijksmuseum voor Volkenkunde** was founded in 1837. The museum has particularly interesting displays on the Dutch East Indies Company and the countries with which it traded, such as China, Japan and the islands of Indonesia.

Anyone for whom a trip to Holland is not complete without seeing a windmill should visit the **Molenmuseum "De Valk"**. Like the mill owned by Rembrandt's father, this 18th-century working windmill was erected on the site of a bastion. It contains several unusual rooms once occupied by the miller and his family.

**Picturesque town: Delft** is situated on the River Vliet midway between The Hague and Rotterdam. This pleasant old town has changed very little since Vermeer painted the *View of Delft* now in the Mauritshuis in The Hague. Standing on the Hooikade, where Vermeer painted his home town on a threatening summer's day in 1660, you can still recognise many features from the painting, such as the dusky red brick Armamentarium and the slender white spire of the Nieuwe Kerk.

In the Middle Ages, Delft was a typical Netherlandish town of weavers and brewers, with numerous monasteries and convents within its walls. But its tranquil mood was shattered during the Dutch Revolt when William of Orange chose the town as his military headquarters, taking up residence in the Prinsenhof, a former monastery. He was assassinated here in 1584 by Balthasar Gerards, a fanatical Catholic, and is buried in the town's Nieuwe Kerk.

In the 17th century Delft had the dubious distinction of being the main arsenal of the Dutch Republic. In October 1654, the town was devastated by an explosion in the Secreet van Hollandt (a gunpowder store hidden in the garden of a former convent), which destroyed one-third of the houses in the city and killed 200 people. One of the victims was Rembrandt's gifted pupil Carel

**Old and new side by side in Leiden.**

Fabritius, the painter of the beautiful study of the *Goldfinch* in the Mauritshuis in The Hague.

A walk along **Oude Delft**, a narrow leafy canal, takes you past some of the most interesting buildings in the city. The letters VOC on a Renaissance house at Oude Delft No. 39 is a reminder that Delft was once one of the cities that combined to form the Verenigde Oostindische Compagnie, the United Dutch East Indies Company.

The massive brick building rising up from the water opposite is the **Armamentarium**, formerly the arsenal of the provinces of Holland and West Friesland. Its function is symbolised by the bearded figure of Mars, the god of war, perched awkwardly on a lion and a heap of weapons. The **Koninklijk Nederlands Legermuseum** (Royal Dutch Army Museum) now occupies the building.

The bridge at the end of Oude Delft marks the site of a medieval city gate, the Rotterdamse Poort, which appears in the foreground of Vermeer's *View of Delft*. Only one of Delft's eight medieval gates – the Oostpoort, to the east of here – is still standing.

A narrow canal, which begins as Lange Geer but changes its name four times, runs north from here. The curious **Museum Paul Tétar van Elven** on the section of canal called Koornmarkt was the 19th-century home of an artist who attempted to recreate rooms reminiscent of Vermeer paintings.

Vermeer lived on **Markt**, Delft's broad market square. The **Nieuwe Kerk** was begun on the east side of this square in the 14th century on the site of a medieval miracle. The slender spire of the church manages to appear harmonious though it was built in separate stages from the late 14th to the early 16th centuries, and subsequently damaged several times by fire.

**Founder of the Dutch Republic:** The lofty late-Gothic choir, which dates from the 15th century, contains the marble and bronze **Mausoleum of William the Silent**, the founder of the Dutch Republic. Begun by Hendrick de Keyser in 1614

**Delft rooftops.**

180

(long after William's assassination) and completed eight years later by his son Pieter, it is richly decorated with uplifting motifs for the young Dutch Republic; the dog at William's feet symbolises fidelity, and the four female figures represent liberty (holding a hat), justice, religion and courage. The epitaph was composed by the statesman and poet Constantijn Huygens. The tombs of subsequent stadholders and monarchs are in the crypt of the Nieuwe Kerk.

The jurist Hugo Grotius, who was born on the Nieuwe Langedijk in Delft in 1583, is commemorated by an 18th-century memorial. In 1618 Grotius was imprisoned in Slot Loevestein for his support of the Remonstrants, but two years later his resourceful wife helped him to escape in a book trunk (possibly the one that is now displayed in the Prinsenhof Museum in Delft, though the Rijksmuseum in Amsterdam also has a chest which is claimed by some historians to have been the jurist's historic hiding place).

Grotius spent the rest of his life in exile, and died in Rostock in 1645. His most famous work, *De Jure Belli et Pacis*, laid the foundations of modern international law. A plaque was attached to the monument by delegates to the International Peace Conference in The Hague in 1899. In recent years, the writings of Grotius on justifiable warfare have been cited to shed light on the nuclear weapons debate.

The Renaissance **Stadhuis** (city hall), which stands opposite, was built in 1618 by Hendrick de Keyser. It is decorated with ferocious lions' heads, a characteristic feature of buildings of the early Dutch Republic. This square building incorporates the stone tower of a medieval town hall gutted by fire in 1618. Botermarkt, a covered canal, leads to the most fashionable quarter of Delft. The weathered stone house at Oude Delft No. 167, built in the Flamboyant Gothic style of Brabant in 1510, was one of the few houses to survive the great fire of 1536.

**Scene of the crime:** A lane north of here leads to the **Prinsenhof Museum**, which

Hendrick de Keyser's Renaissance Stadhuis, Delft.

contains an excellent collection of topographical paintings of Delft (often illustrating one calamity or another), medieval sculpture, portraits of prominent figures of the Dutch Revolt, Delftware and maps.

The museum occupies a beautiful 15th-century Burgundian Gothic nunnery with ancient tiled floors and leaded windows looking out on leafy gardens. This nunnery was the unlikely setting for the murder of William the Silent in 1584 by the Spanish sympathiser Balthasar Gerards. The bullet holes in the wall of the Moordzaal have been carefully preserved behind glass.

The bell of the **Oude Kerk** opposite sounds a suitably melancholy note. The tower dates from the 14th century and has a pronounced lean. The church was built over the course of the 14th and 15th centuries, and a magnificent Flamboyant Gothic north transept was added in the 16th century by Anthonis Keldermans of Mechelen (though the effect is rather weakened by the absence of a south transept).

**Pepys' approval:** Within the white-washed interior, the **tomb of Admiral Piet Hein** is given pride of place on the site of the main altar. Admiral Maarten Tromp, the hero of some 50 sea battles, is also buried in the Oude Kerk. The memorial is decorated with a marble relief depicting a sea battle – "the smoke the best expressed that ever I saw," Samuel Pepys noted.

Another monument commemorates the Delft scientist Anthonie van Leeuwenhoek, who is credited with inventing the microscope, thus enabling him to observe such organisms as bacteria, red blood corpuscles and spermatozoa for the first time. A modern sculpture symbolising a yeast cell in the park at the end of Oude Delft commemorates Van Leeuwenhoek's discoveries. Perhaps fittingly, the air is now filled with a pungent yeasty smell from a nearby biochemical factory.

In a nearby clump of trees lies the derelict tomb of Karl Wilhelm Naundorff, who claimed he was the son of the executed King Louis XVI of France.

**Below,** old Delftware. **Right,** modern Delft ceramics.

# DELFTWARE

**D**elftware is the name given to a distinctive blue and white tin-glazed pottery produced in Delft and other Dutch cities. The earliest known tin-glazed pottery in the Netherlands was called majolica, after the Mediterranean island of Majorca where it was produced. The Italians were the main majolica producers in the 16th century, using techniques derived from Moorish and Spanish craftsmen. The term *faïence*, which is sometimes applied to Delftware, derives from the Italian town of Faenza, another important centre of majolica production.

In the early 16th century, the Italian potter Guido da Savino moved to Antwerp where he established the first majolica workshop in the Low Countries. Antwerp soon became a major centre of majolica production, exporting tiles throughout northern Europe, and even as far south as Portugal. After the fall of Antwerp in 1585, skilled craftsmen fled from the Spanish terror to Holland or England. The Antwerp majolica workers mainly settled in Dutch towns such as Delft and Haarlem, where they began to produce wall tiles for kitchens and fireplaces. These provided protection against damp and dirt, the two great enemies of the Dutch housewife. Gradually new motifs were introduced to suit Dutch taste, including ships, flowers, animals and children at play.

In the early 17th century trading ships of the voc (United Dutch East Indies Company) returned from the Far East laden with curiosities, including Chinese blue and white porcelain. The popularity of the delicate Chinese porcelain led to a drop in demand for the coarser Dutch majolica. Many pottery workshops went bankrupt at this time, while others responded by producing blue and white pottery modelled on Chinese porcelain, often decorated with Biblical episodes or scenes from Dutch life. In 1645 civil war broke out in China, causing a sharp decline in the supply of imported porcelain and a temporary upswing in demand for local pottery. In the mid-18th century the Dutch pottery industry suffered another major blow when cheap mass-produced English creamware began to flood the market. Firm after firm went bankrupt, and by the mid-19th century "De Porceleyne Fles" (founded in 1653 by David van der Pyet) was the only pottery left in Delft. In 1876 Joost 't Hooft injected new life into the business by reviving the art of hand-painted blue decoration. Adolf Le Comte, a teacher of decorative art in Delft, served as artistic adviser from 1877 to 1921. Traditional designs were reintroduced, and later art nouveau motifs began to appear.

Today many museums in the Netherlands possess large Delftware collections. The Gemeentemuseum in The Hague has one of the finest collections in the world, mostly from the famous Van den Burgh legacy. The Rijksmuseum in Amsterdam also has a splendid collection, including curious tulip vases which were especially popular in Britain and the Netherlands during the reign of William and Mary.

There is an interesting collection of Delftware tiles in Delft's own Rijksmuseum Huis Lambert van Meerten, donated by the architect of the house, Jan Schouten. The collection illustrates the wit of Dutch tile painters. One series depicting children's games includes a tile with two children fighting, and another in which a child is about to kick someone from behind. This museum also has several tile pictures, which were a speciality of Rotterdam's potteries. A large tile painting by Cornelis Bouwmeester hanging above the stairs depicts a furious sea battle. There are also several tile pictures of caged birds, a popular decoration in Dutch kitchens.

The Museum Het Prinsenhof in Leeuwarden also boasts an extensive collection of Dutch and Chinese ceramics, including the world's largest collection of tiles, with examples from Persia, Spain, France and Holland.

The visitors' centre at "De Porceleyne Fles" exhibits numerous vases, plates and tiles and even ceramic architectural details made in Delft. But the most remarkable decoration made at the pottery is the tiled interior of the bodega in the Hotel Port van Cleve, Amsterdam. ∎

# ROTTERDAM AND ENVIRONS

The southern part of Zuid-Holland province is dominated by the port of Rotterdam, which extends for 23 miles (37 km) along both banks of the Nieuwe Maas river, from Rotterdam to Hoek van Holland (the Hook of Holland). The port activities, however, hardly impinge on the city of Rotterdam, which is unexpectedly quiet and attractive.

Dordrecht to the south retains much more the atmosphere of an old Dutch river port, with crumbling brick warehouses and canals lined with barges. The eastern part of this region is still largely rural, with several pleasant small towns, such as Gouda to the northeast of Rotterdam, and Schoonhoven and Nieuwpoort on opposite banks of the river Lek to the east.

**Rotterdam** was largely rebuilt after World War II, when the city centre and the port were devastated by German bombers. The spacious pedestrianised streets of the Lijnbaan quarter, completed in 1953, inspired many similar – though seldom so successful – developments elsewhere. In recent years some imaginative modern buildings have sprung up along the Maas waterfront (signposted Waterstad), and the city has grown livelier with new museums, cafés and restaurants.

The most exciting architecture is found around the **Oude Haven**, the former harbour, now containing a collection of redundant Rhine barges owned by the Maritime Museum. This area was devastated in 1940 and the only medieval building still standing is the **Grote Kerk**, gutted in the war but subsequently restored with great skill.

On a bleak square in front of the church stands a statue of Erasmus, who was born in Rotterdam in 1469. His birth caused a scandal as his father was an unmarried Catholic priest, while his mother was the housekeeper. Although Erasmus left home at the age of six to study in Deventer and later Oxford, he spent most of his life in Rotterdam, and the city's university is named after him.

The bronze statue by Hendrick de Keyser in front of the church dates from 1622.

**Regeneration:** For many years the devastated area around the old harbour remained wasteland, but it was rapidly transformed in the late 1980s by the construction of a huge public library in glass and steel, which gives fantastic views over the port and the modern city as well as its own hanging gardens.

The **Blaakse Bos** nearby is a bizarre cluster of tilted cube houses on tall concrete columns, designed by Piet Blom. A raised pedestrian street lined with shops (Promenade Overblaak) runs beneath the houses to create a modern version of the Ponte Vecchio in Florence. You can visit the **Kijk Kubus** for an impression of life in these strange futuristic houses, where all the furniture has to be adapted to the sloping walls.

The waterfront promenade along Boompjes brings you out on **Leuvehaven**. An Imax cinema facing the waterfront shows feature films on an extra large screen. At the end of Leuvehaven, behind a redundant red lighthouse, is

the **Maritiem Museum Prins Hendrik**, a modern museum devoted to Rotterdam's maritime history. The interior is somewhat like a ship, with long steel gangplanks leading to the upper floors. The café terrace enjoys one of the best views in Rotterdam, looking down the Leuvehaven to the river. The museum also displays exhibits on the quayside, including a reconstructed rope walk.

The **Museumschip De Buffel** is permanently moored here. This 19th-century iron warship is worth visiting for the opulent officers' quarters furnished in the style of a Victorian club. In the middle of the windswept square beside this museum stands the sculpture *De Verwoeste Stad* (The Razed City). Designed by Ossip Zadkine in 1953, it symbolises the destruction of Rotterdam in 1940. A figure contorted with fear holds up his arms to the sky; the large hole in the sculpture represents the destruction of Rotterdam's heart.

Hemmed in by modern office blocks opposite, the **Historisch Museum Schielandshuis** occupies a handsome 17th-century classical building once owned by the Schieland district water board. This small museum has a collection of paintings, period rooms and dolls' houses. The famous Atlas van Stolk, an extensive collection of historic prints and maps, is housed here, and frequently forms the basis for interesting temporary exhibitions.

**Spido Havenrondvaarten** (harbour trips) depart from the quay at the southern end of Leuvehaven, heading downstream to the modern port. They also transport guests across the water to the Hotel New York , occupying the stately twin towers of the former Holland-America Line offices, which retains a 19th-century atmosphere despite contemporary styling. Occupying a pastel neoclassical building further along the waterfront, the **Museum voor Volkenkunde** regularly organises stimulating temporary exhibitions on non-Western cultures and has a very good ethnic restaurant. (It is closed until 2000 when it will reopen expanded to almost double its former size.)

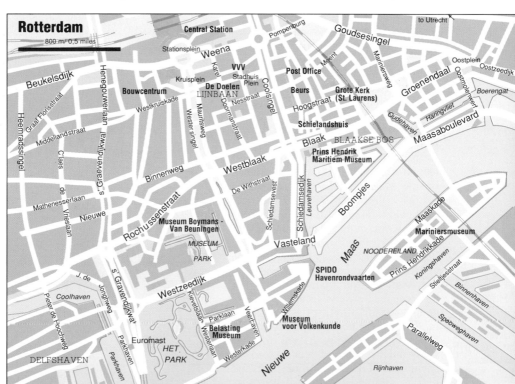

Overlooking the small **Veerhaven** beyond are several 19th-century shipping offices decorated with telling maritime details. Westerkade leads from here along the waterfront to the attractive English-style **park**, with a curious wooden church for Norwegian seamen. The **Euromast** rises above the trees on the west side of the park to a height of 600 ft (185 metres). The observation platform, at 330 ft (100 metres), offers a panoramic view of the city and port. Those with a head for heights can continue to the top of the mast by means of a slowly revolving cabin.

Rotterdam is undergoing enormous changes. With the opening of the Erasmus Bridge in 1998, the city centre was extended further into the harbour area where an ambitious, well-conceived Docklands-style development of shops, cafés and housing was created. With a new tram and metro line, it is easily accessible.

**Pilgrim Fathers:** Downstream lies **Delfshaven**, founded in the 14th century as the port of Delft, but now part of the municipality of Rotterdam. Delfshaven survived the bombardment in 1940, and most of its buildings are now protected monuments. Admiral Piet Hein, who seized the Spanish silver fleet in a daring escapade in 1626, was born here. The port also has associations with the Pilgrim Fathers, who set sail for the New World in 1620 from the Middenkous quay in Delfshaven.

A lofty double-gabled warehouse dating from the 19th century, **De Dubbelde Palmboom**, has been attractively converted into a museum of Rotterdam history. As befits a city that prides itself on toil, the museum is devoted to work in the Rhine delta region, from medieval crafts to modern industrial concerns. The nearby **Zakkendragershuisje**, built in 1653 as the guild house of the grain porters, is now a small museum where pewter manufacture is demonstrated.

Though no specific school of painting is associated with Rotterdam, the city has numerous cultural attractions. The **Museum Boymans-Van Beuningen**, founded in 1847, has one of the

The Rotterdam Maritime Museum.

# THE PORT OF ROTTERDAM

In the late 19th century, Rotterdam eclipsed Amsterdam as the principal port of the Netherlands. The decisive event was the completion in 1890 of the Nieuwe Waterweg between Rotterdam and Hoek van Holland. This provided Rotterdam with a direct link to the North Sea; previously ships were compelled to to navigate a series of notoriously difficult channels. Rotterdam rapidly transformed itself into a dynamic modern port, and the first skyscraper in the Netherlands, the 10-storey Witte Huis, was erected beside the old harbour in 1898.

After suffering heavy bombing in 1940, the port was rebuilt, with massive investment, to meet modern requirements. It is now the world's biggest and busiest port, stretching for 23 miles (37 km) along the waterfront of the Nieuwe Maas. Each year Rotterdam handles 250 million tons of goods, representing about 4 percent of world tonnage shipped by sea. About 85 percent of citrus fruits consumed in Europe are shipped through the port of Rotterdam. More than 50 percent of Europe's tobacco imports and 40 percent of the tea drunk in Britain arrives via Rotterdam.

The port has several natural advantages, the most important of which is its situation on the main branch of the Rhine (the Lek). The Rhine is the world's busiest river, carrying barge transport from as far away as Switzerland, France and Germany and even Central Europe. Rotterdam is also connected to France and southern Belgium by the river Maas (the Meuse in French), and with northern Belgium by the river Schelde.

The Waalhaven, a predecessor to the modern port, was begun in 1907. When completed in 1930, it was the world's largest harbour, and was originally used for loading dry goods such as grain and coal. Much of the Waalhaven is now devoted to container ships, a form of mass transport pioneered by Rotterdam. In 1972 the first container ship between Europe and Japan docked in the Waalhaven. The ships now in use for container transport can measure up to 1,000 ft (300 metres)

in length, with a capacity for transporting some 3,000 containers – which if placed end to end would stretch 11 miles (18 km).

The world's largest container port is the Europe Container Terminal in the Eemhaven, the next harbour downstream. This terminal, with its 14 giant cranes, can easily deal with one million containers annually.

Rotterdam is also the world's most important oil terminal. Petroleum was first stored in Rotterdam in 1888, and a small refinery was built near the city in 1902. Today five major companies – Shell, BP, Esso, Q8 and Gulf – have storage tanks and refineries in the port. The oil installations are located in the Europoort, a deep harbour built in 1958 near the mouth of the Nieuwe Waterweg to cope with the world's largest tankers. The Europoort can handle vessels of up to 280,000 tons with a draught of 75 ft (23 metres), which is one half of the height of the nearby Witte Huis.

The harbour now constitutes about 50 percent of the area of Rotterdam, covering about 150 sq. miles (240 sq. km) of the city. Some 400 cranes and 450 tugs work in the port area. Every year about 32,000 sea-going ships visit Rotterdam harbour, while 180,000 inland barges depart upstream from the port.

The best way to see the port is to take a 75-minute Spido harbour tour from the Willemskade. Each kilometre of the Rhine is numbered, beginning at kilometre 0 on Lake Constance, and reaching 1001 at the Spido quay. At kilometre 1008 the boat turns across the busy shipping lanes and enters the Eemhaven, then heads back upstream to enter the Waalhaven.

Although covering only 5 miles (7 km) out of the 23 miles (37 km) of quays between the city and the North Sea, the boat trip provides a fascinating glimpse of the port activities, as it darts beneath the bows of ships stacked with containers, or passes vessels in dry dock for repair.

A route for cars signed "Rotterdamse Haven Route" has been devised by the ANWB, covering almost 63 miles (100 km) from Rotterdam to the Europoort. Amidst the oil refineries and chemical works in this area, small patches of nature have been preserved for recreation. ∎

best art collections in the Netherlands, even though many of the original paintings donated by Frans Boymans were destroyed in a fire in 1864. A new museum was built in 1935 and extended in 1972. In late 1999, it will begin an ambitious renovation, during which it will be partially closed.

The museum contains a number of well-known Early Flemish paintings, including *The Prodigal Son* by Hieronymus Bosch, and one of the two versions of *The Tower of Babel* by Pieter Brueghel the Elder. The modern collection has canvases by Monet, Van Gogh and Kandinski, and several surrealist works by Magritte and Dali. The department of decorative art has a large collection of majolica, Delftware and glass.

The **Kunsthal** exhibition gallery, which opened in 1993, focuses on contemporary art, occupying a building by well-known architect Rem Koolhaas. The **Nederlands Architecture Institute** also opened in 1993; it offers exhibitions and lectures on architecture.

Most of Rotterdam's private art galleries are situated either in the streets bordering the Boymans-Van Beuningen Museum or in Delfshaven. Attractive cafés and restaurants are more difficult to discover. Conveniently close to the museum, the **Café De Unie** at Mauritsweg No. 35 is a faithful reconstruction of a building designed in 1924 by the Rotterdam architect J.J.P. Oud. Like the Rietveld-Schröder House in Utrecht, it obeys the tenets of the De Stijl movement, using vertical and horizontal lines and blocks of primary colour for decoration. Other attractive cafés line the quayside of the Oude Haven.

The old river port of **Dordrecht**, situated at the confluence of three busy waterways, provides a pleasing contrast to the modernism of Rotterdam. A castle was built here by Count Dirk III in the early 11th century to control vital shipping routes into and out of Holland. The town that grew up around the castle is the oldest in Holland, and was granted a charter by Count Willem I in 1220.

Dordrecht played an important role in the emergence of the Dutch state; in

**Left, Rotterdam Port. Right, Museum Boymans-Van Beuningen.**

1572 this was one of the first towns to side with the Protestant rebels, and later the same year the United Provinces met in the Statenzaal (still standing in a courtyard known as Hof, which once belonged to an Augustinian friary).

Dordrecht was also the scene of the famous Synod , held in 1618–19, at which the hardline Dutch Calvinists rejected the more moderate tenets of the Remonstrants. This led in 1619 to the imprisonment in Slot Loevestein of Hugo Grotius, a leading Remonstrant, and the execution in The Hague of the statesman Johan van Oldenbarnevelt.

The waterfront at Dordrecht is the town's most interesting area, though many of the old warehouses are abandoned and decaying. Some bear the names of German towns or rivers, a reminder that Dordrecht was once a major port for the shipment of German wine.

The best approach to the harbour is down **Wijnstraat** (whose name recalls the wine trade). This is an old street of damp warehouses and curiosity shops, including an interesting antiquarian bookshop crammed with dusty novels in many languages, old records, faded prints, framed paintings and second-hand navigation maps. The overspill stock is stored in old St Emilion crates, suggesting that Dordrecht is still a wine port of some importance.

Turning left at the end of this street, you come upon the **Groothoofds Poort**, a magnificent city gate built in the 17th century on the site of its medieval precursor. The Groothoofds Poort was once the principal entrance to Dordrecht and is designed in a suitably grand Renaissance style, with a large cartouche depicting the Maid of Holland, symbolised by a plumpish woman protected by a wicker fence.

**River junction:** The gate occupies a spectacular site at the confluence of three major waterways. To the right, the Beneden Merwede carries river traffic east to Gorinchem and the river Maas. Straight ahead, the Noord is used by barges travelling north to the Lek and Rotterdam, while to the left, De Dordtse Kil carries shipping bound for Holland's

**Grote Kerk, Dordrecht.**

Diep and Antwerp. An estimated 1,500 barges and ships pass by this spot every day, making it the busiest river junction in Europe. The quayside is now sadly deserted, except occasionally in the summer months when the *Pieter Boele*, a steam tug built in 1893, leaves from here on a round trip through the local waterways.

Turning left along the waterfront, then across the little drawbridge, will bring you to Nieuwe Haven, a picturesque harbour filled with creaking boats and surrounded by the cluttered premises of ships' chandlers.

The **Museum Simon van Gijn** overlooks this harbour. This richly furnished merchant's house was built in 1729. In 1864 it was acquired by the banker and collector Simon van Gijn, who lived here until his death in 1922.

The house is now a museum, but it still feels as if it is inhabited, and its handsome period rooms convey a sense of quiet prosperity and well being. The kitchen, with its tiled walls and gleaming brass pots, dates from the 18th century, while a room on the first floor contains a Renaissance fireplace dating from about 1550. Decorated with curious figures of savages, it once heated the banqueting hall of the guild of arquebusiers (marksmen).

Also of interest is the study on the first floor built by Van Gijn in neo-Renaissance style and intended to evoke the 17th-century interiors of Vermeer.

**Antique Dutch toys:** The Van Gijn collection includes paintings, Flemish tapestries, glass and historical relics. On the first-floor landing is an attractive 17th-century shop sign, which may have been painted by Albert Cuyp for a relative who sold wine. Most visitors are particularly delighted by the large collection of antique Dutch toys displayed in the attic and garden house, including dolls' houses, miniature shops, mechanical models (some still working) and magic lanterns.

The museum also contains a model of Dordrecht in 1544, in which the town looks rather like a ship sailing downstream. From the top of the tower of the

**Trawlerman in Dordrecht harbour.**

**Grote Kerk**, not far from the museum, you can compare the situation today. The Grote Kerk was built in the 15th century by Evert Spoorwater of Antwerp in a subdued Brabant Gothic style. The distinctive squat tower is older; it was begun in 1339, but never completed. The massive size of the first tier indicates that it was intended to support a very lofty edifice, but instead it is surmounted rather oddly by four 17th-century clocks.

The narrow canal by the church called Voorstraatshaven leads into the centre of town. The view of the Stadhuis (old city hall) from the Visbrug is particularly impressive. This 19th-century building spanning the canal rests on the foundations of a 14th-century exchange established by Flemish merchants. An attractive café, *Crimpert Salm*, is just over the Visbrug at Visstraat Nos. 3–7. The café occupies a Renaissance building of 1608 where the guild of fishmongers used to meet.

The **Dordrechts Museum**, situated in a former lunatic asylum, is worth visiting for its collection of paintings by 17th-century Dordrecht artists, including Albert Cuyp, Samuel van Hoogstraten, Nicholas Maes and Ferdinand Bol. The self-portrait by Ferdinand Bol clearly shows the influence of Rembrandt, under whom he studied. Jan van Goyen, though not a native of the town, painted a very alluring *View of Dordrecht* in 1651, seen from the north bank of the Oude Maas. The low horizon and threatening sky characterise 17th-century Dutch landscape painting.

A panoramic view of Dordrecht by Adam Willaerts, which hangs on the main staircase, shows the busy waterfront in 1629. A room of 19th-century works by the Dordrecht-born artist Ary Scheffer is furnished attractively in Victorian style. An interesting painting by a fellow artist portrays Scheffer in his Paris studio working on one of the paintings now also hanging in the Dordrecht collection.

**Meaningful paintings:** The museum also has several 17th-century "vanity paintings", still lifes depicting symbols of

Al fresco banquet, Dordrecht.

194

mortality such as snuffed candles and pipes. This popular Dutch motif of human mortality is echoed on the portal of the nearby Arend Maartenshof, a 17th-century almshouse at Museumstraat No. 56, where a Latin inscription above the entrance reminded its elderly residents that *Vita Vapor* – roughly translated as "life is but a wisp."

**Waffles and cheese: Gouda** is an old river town situated where the river Gouwe enters the Hollandse IJssel. Though its harbour activities have ceased, Gouda remains a lively market town, especially on Thursday mornings from June to September when a traditional cheese market is staged on the Markt. Gouda is famous for its round yellow cheese which the Dutch consume in large quantities, whether as *jong* (a young creamy cheese), *belegen* (matured for four months), *oud* (10 months old), or *extra belegen* (a crumbly old cheese). Thin syrupy waffles known as *Goudse stroopwafels* are also made in the town of Gouda.

The main activity in Gouda revolves around the **Markt**, which for Holland is unusually spacious. In the middle stands the Stadhuis, built in 1450 in a Gothic style reminiscent of Flemish town halls, with numerous statues of Burgundian dukes and duchesses, and lofty step gables sprouting pinnacles. The **Waag** (Weigh House) on the north side of the square is an imposing Dutch Classical building, built in 1668 by Pieter Post. An interesting relief in the tympanum by Bartholomeus Eggers depicts the weighing of Gouda cheeses.

**Stained glass:** Kerkstraat leads from the Markt to a beguiling medieval area of quiet cobbled lanes surrounding the **St Janskerk**. This elongated Gothic church, rebuilt after a fire in 1552, is well worth entering to view the exceptional stained-glass windows, most of which were donated to the church during its reconstruction. The 14 finest windows were designed by the brothers Wouter and Dirck Crabeth in 1555–77, in a transitional style between Gothic and Renaissance art.

The windows were given by a wide

Buying cheese in Gouda.

range of donors, including municipalities, abbeys, guilds, princes and burgomasters. The guilds liked to chose Biblical episodes that were connected in some way with their trade.

In 1565 the guild of fishermen presented the window depicting *Jonah and the Whale* (window 30), while the butchers' guild donated *Baalam and his Ass* (window 31). *The Last Supper* (window 7) was donated by Philip II in 1577, when Gouda was still a Catholic city, while in 1561 William of Orange presented the church with *Christ Driving the Moneylenders out of the Temple* (window 22). By the time this window was executed, William had been branded a Protestant traitor, and hence his figure was omitted from the composition.

Other interesting windows were executed after Gouda fell to the Protestants. Window 25, illustrating the relief of Leiden in 1574, was given by the city of Delft in 1603. In 1596 the city of Haarlem donated window 2, showing the capture of Damietta by Dutch Crusaders, while Dordrecht proudly presented window 3, illustrating its own attractions, the following year. In the 19th century, Jan Schouten of Delft added three very curious windows (numbers 1A, 1B and 1C) made up from old fragments of glass.

A handsome sandstone portal dated 1609 opposite the church leads into the leafy garden of the **Catharina Gasthuis**. This was founded in the 14th century as a hospice for travellers, and was later used as a hospital. Today the complex is used to display objects from the **Stedelijk (Municipal) Museum's** varied collection.

Several rooms are furnished in period style, including a Dutch kitchen, which here has the added attraction of a cooing turtledove in a cage. The collection of paintings is remarkably good for a town of this size, and includes several works by the Gouda-born artist Pieter Pourbus the Old, a deeply tender portrait of a dead child by Bartholomeus van der Helst, a series of civic guard group portraits, and some Impressionist paintings by members of the Barbizon and Hague Schools.

Achter de Kerk leads to a curious brick chapel modelled on the Church of the Holy Sepulchre in Jerusalem. Turning right here down Spieringstraat takes you past the ornate 17th-century portals of the orphanage (on the left) and an almshouse (opposite). Turning right along Minderbroederssteeg, a narrow street with some old warehouses, you reach Oost Haven, a former harbour now bereft of shipping.

On the opposite quay is a 17th-century shop with a Renaissance frontage which once sold tobacco, coffee, tea and snuff. Its name, **De Moriaan** (The Moor), arose from an 18th-century belief that blacks were avid pipe smokers. The beautiful 17th-century interior houses an large collection of clay pipes, the manufacture of which was introduced to Gouda in about 1620 by some English pipe-makers.

The long thin-stemmed pipes, familiar from paintings of crowded inn scenes by Jan Steen and Adriaen Brouwer, had particularly small bowls because of the high price of tobacco at this time.

**Left**, one-man brewing company. **Right**, 16th-century glass in St Janskerk.

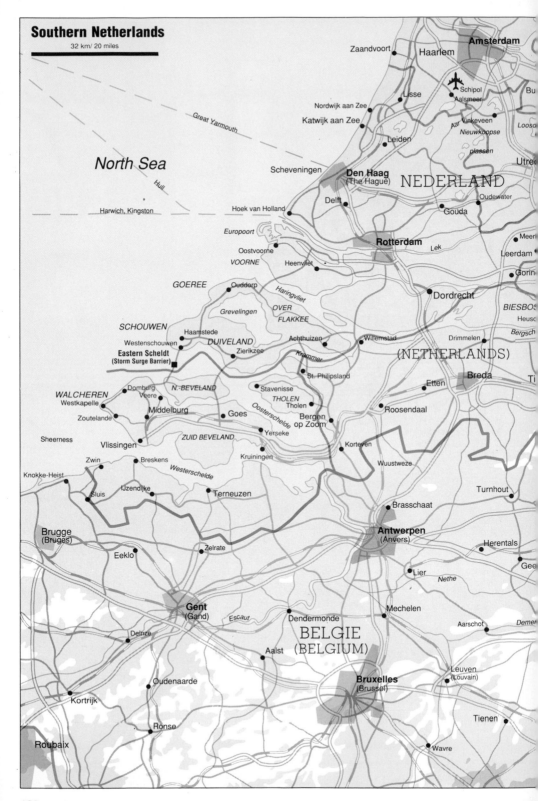

# Southern Netherlands

32 km/ 20 miles

**North Sea**

Great Yarmouth

Hull

Harwich, Kingston

Zaandvoort
Haarlem
**Amsterdam**

Lisse
Schipol
Aalsmeer
Bu

Nordwijk aan Zee
Katwijk aan Zee

Vinkeveen
Aar
Nieuwkoopse
Looso
plassen
Utre

Leiden

Scheveningen

**Den Haag**
(The Hague)
NEDERLAND

Delft
Oudewater

Hoek van Holland
Gouda

Europoort

Oostvoorne
**Rotterdam**
Lek
Meer

VOORNE
Heenvliet
Leerdam

GOEREE
Ouddorp
Haringvliet
Gorin

OVER
FLAKKEE
**Dordrecht**

Grevelingen
BIESBOS

SCHOUWEN
Haamstede
Heuso
Bergsch

Westenschouwen
DUIVELAND
Achthuizen
Willemstad
Drimmelen
(NETHERLAND)

Zierikzee
Krammer

**Eastern Scheldt**
(Storm Surge Barrier)
St. Philipsland
**Breda**
Ti

Etten

Domburg
N. BEVELAND
Stavenisse
Roosendaal

WALCHEREN
Veere
THOLEN
Tholen

Westkapelle
Middelburg
Goes
Bergen
op Zoom

Zoutelande
Oosterschelde
Korteven

Sheerness
ZUID BEVELAND
Yerseke
Wuustweze

Vlissingen
Kruiningen

Zwin
Breskens
Westerschelde
Turnhout

Knokke-Heist
Brasschaat

Sluis
IJzendijke
Terneuzen
**Antwerpen**
(Anvers)
Herentals

**Brugge**
(Bruges)
Zelrate
Lier
Gee

Eeklo
Nethe

Mechelen

**Gent**
(Gand)
Escaut
Dendermonde
Aarschot
Demer

Deinze
BELGIE
(BELGIUM)

Aalst
Leuven
(Louvain)

Oudenaarde
**Bruxelles**
(Brussel)

Kortrijk
Tienen

Ronse

Roubaix
Wavre

Zeeland is well named. The south-westernmost province often seems to be more a part of the North Sea than of the Netherlands, to which it is so fragilely attached. Even in a country where a close and stormy relationship with the sea is the stuff of both legend and everyday life, Zeeland seems a place apart, isolated from the bustling mainstream of Dutch life, slashed by great jagged stretches of water.

In the past, this was even more true. Look at old maps of Zeeland. The further back in time you go, the more the landscape breaks up into a crazy-paving pattern of little islands, all below sea level, shakily protected from the North Sea by dykes and dunes. As the centuries rolled past, these islands were patiently stitched together with characteristic Dutch ingenuity and hard work.

Today, that process is about as complete as it is ever likely to be and Zeeland has emerged from its isolation. Two diametrically opposed factors have accounted for this more than any others: disaster and tourism.

Disaster struck – and not for the first time – in the night of 1 February 1953, when a deadly combination of bad weather conditions sent the North Sea crashing through the protective dykes and across the spirit-level flat landscape beyond. More than 1,800 people lost their lives and an immense amount of destruction was wrought by the tides.

Ironically, the project that was subsequently launched to shut out the North Sea forever – the Delta Plan – has, as a by-product, given Zeeland superb road links along which holidaymakers pour from the rest of Holland and from neighbouring countries.

They discover a land of vast horizons, infiltrated on every side by lakes and sea channels, a water wonderland of beaches and harbour towns. There are few urban centres, but many of the now-sleepy villages once sent their adventurers as

**Left**, oyster boats working the Oosterschelde.

explorers and merchants to the farthest corners of the globe. New Zealand is just one legacy of Zeeland's seafaring traditions.

Tourism, fishing and farming are the main sources of wealth in Zeeland. The first two arise out of the ever-present sea which, if it has threatened much, has also given much in return. The third comes from the superb farmland left behind by centuries of land reclamation. Fields that stretch endlessly under broad skies, market garden centres and orchards ensure that Zeeland will never go hungry.

**The Delta Works:** Begun soon after the 1953 disaster, the series of giant dams and movable barriers that form the Delta Works have become a tourist attraction in their own right. Over a period of 30 years, and at immense cost, the sea inlets that pierced Zeeland's coastline, leaving it almost at the mercy of the North Sea, have been closed off. The coastline has been shortened by 450 miles (700 km), leaving behind a series of sheltered lakes that are now a paradise for water sports and nature lovers.

The scale of some of these engineering works staggers the imagination, and the highways that sit comfortably on top of them whisk the visitor effortlessly from one former island to another. Pride of place goes to the **Eastern Scheldt Storm Surge Barrier**, opened in 1986 after a 10-year construction programme. In bad weather, the Barrier's 65 enormous gates can be slammed shut on the North Sea, while at other times they remain open to preserve the inlet's valuable saltwater shellfish beds and mud flats.

The **Delta Expo**, which tells the story of Zeeland's 2,000-year-long struggle with the sea, is housed in the Barrier's service building on **Neeltje Jans**, an artificial island in the middle of the Eastern Scheldt.

Other works protect threatened areas in Zeeland, with yet more dams to the north in the Delta zone of neighbouring South Holland province. The Delta is so called because it lies where the rivers Rhine, Maas, Waal and Scheldt drain

The Oosterschelde (Eastern Scheldt) Storm Surge Barrier.

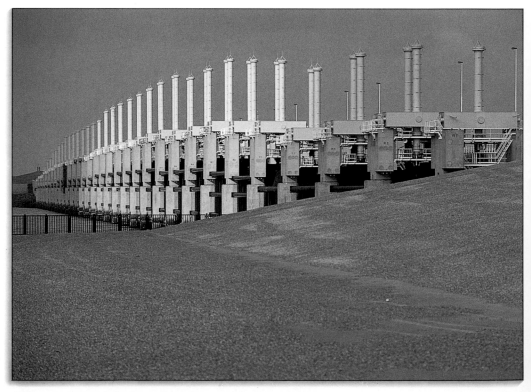

into the North Sea. What were once islands are now linked to each other and the mainland by the Delta Works' giant's causeways of dams and barriers. In addition, all the dykes in the province have been raised and strengthened.

But the sea still presents a threat – even if a much diminished one – and they say that no one in Zeeland sleeps soundly when the North Sea rages beyond the defensive walls.

**Schouwen-Duiveland:** It's as well then that the sea offers compensations – and Zeeland takes advantage of every one of them. Coming into Zeeland by the coastal road from Rotterdam, over the broad back of the Brouwersdam, you arrive at the one-time islands of **Schouwen** and **Duiveland**. On the seafront, some 11 miles (17 km) of magnificent sands are the main attraction, with beach cafés placed at strategic points.

Behind the beach, and the protected area of the sea dyke which is studded with World War II German gun emplacements, are the dunes, 2,750 acres (1,100 hectares) of them. This hilly, sandy terrain, is criss-crossed with a network of paths, and is excellent for walking, bicycling and horse-riding.

Camping sites are tucked out of sight behind the dunes, but between holiday-makers and day-trippers, even this amount of beach can fill up on a sunny summer day.

The beach at **Westenschouwen** offers one of the best views of the Eastern Scheldt Storm Surge Barrier, with its serried rank of giant towers stretching into the distance. An even better view can be had by hitching a lift on a glider from the nearby airfield at Nieuw-Haamstede, and asking the pilot to swing out over the water.

The little towns of Schouwen are mostly residential, but the castles near **Renesse** and **Burgh-Haamstede** are worth a visit.

Further east, the northern coast of Duiveland is a windsurfer's paradise. The now freshwater **Grevelingenmeer** (Grevelingen Lake) provides a huge expanse, ideal for practising. There is fishing too, with boat trips leaving from

**Time passes slowly in Zeeland.**

the harbour villages of **Scharendijke** and **Brouwershaven**.

The farmland interior of Duiveland offers the motorist – but even more so, the cyclist – one of the delights of Zeeland: exploring the many side roads that lead either nowhere in particular, or to one of the tiny villages, identifiable only by their church towers, that hang amidst the haze on the horizon. **Drei-schor** is typical of these Zeeland gems, neat and peaceful, its church dating from 1340 ringed by a canal and a circle of charming houses.

Duiveland also boasts one of Holland's most dignified and elegant towns: **Zierikzee**. It is so nearly perfect, you can easily believe that beauty was the prime requirement of its builders. Approached through unprepossessing modern suburbs, the road into the old town brings you to rows of stately merchants' houses, snug sailors' cottages, cobbled streets and a medieval harbour.

Zierikzee looks like an open-air museum but is a living town, with *gezellige* (cosy and friendly) bars and fine restau-rants. A long inlet, lined with visiting yachts in summer, leads to the Eastern Scheldt, and boat trips leave from here to tour the Storm Surge Barrier.

**Marine sports:** The least developed "island" of Zeeland, **Tholen**, and neighbouring **St Philipsland**, bordering the adjacent province of Noord-Brabant, are mainly agricultural. Their long coastline along the Eastern Scheldt provides plenty of marine sports possibilities while being quieter and closer to the mainland than Zeeland's other centres.

Until recently, a car ferry used to run between the western tip of St Philipsland and Zijpe on Duiveland but, alas, a highway now runs across the Delta Works' dams in the area and the ferry has been retired. It's still on older maps, however, and some visitors find themselves at what is really a dead end – although an attractive one – on the shore. Often they are happy to stay there instead of pressing on further.

Sport fishing is the main tourist draw on Tholen, with boats leaving from the small harbour at **Stavenisse**, and an-

**Left and right, elegant Zierikzee.**

glers taking up position along the shore. A nature reserve near **St Maartensdijk** attracts bird-watchers and ramblers.

**Noord- and Zuid-Beveland:** An island once connected to its neighbours only by ferry, **Noord-Beveland** has now leapt into the high-tech transport age. One road runs from Schouwen-Duiveland atop the Eastern Scheldt Storm Surge Barrier and another over the Zeeland toll bridge (3 miles/5 km long), while two more dam-top roads link the island with its southern companions.

Agriculture, fishing and tourism put the money in the pockets of Noordbevelanders, with the freshwater **Veerse Meer** (Lake Veere) being an exceptional yachting and windsurfing area. The **Schotsman** holiday centre just behind the Veersegat dam recalls nearby Veere's past maritime trading links with Scotland. Like the rest of Zeeland, the coastline of Noord-Beveland is dotted with picturesque little fishing villages, such as **Colijnsplaat**, and yachting harbours like **Kortgene** located on the Veerse Meer.

Off **Yerseke**, on the eastern, landward coast of Zuid-Beveland, lies one of the reasons why a movable barrier was built to protect the Eastern Scheldt rather than a solid dam. The oysters and mussels of Zeeland are a byword for quality, and special deliveries rush the pick of the crop from Yerseke's auction house to expensive shops and elegant restaurant tables across Europe.

In the mussel season, which lasts from September to April, ton after ton of this "black gold" is lifted from offshore beds by a shuttle service of big fishing boats from Yerseke. Restaurants throughout Zeeland brandish their *Zeeuwse Mosselen* signs and a kind of feeding frenzy for this fresh, inexpensive delicacy develops. (The finest are said to be exported to Belgium, where demand is even more fanatical.) In any case, a visit to Yerseke's mussel auction house is a must.

One of Zeeland's few large towns, **Goes**, is located in Zuid-Beveland. Goes adds a modern shopping centre to its typically Zeeland Renaissance-style

**Zierikzee's medieval fortifictions.**

town centre and harbour front. But old-world charm lives on in the **South Beveland Steam Railway**, whose trains puff southwards from Goes through an area of great natural beauty – an original landscape of dykes, lakes and woods.

Zuid-Beveland also carries Zeeland's two most important transport arteries from the mainland: the A58 highway and the province's only regular railway line. Both run to Goes, then on to Middelburg and the busy port of Vlissingen (Flushing), and both can get very crowded at peak times in summer.

From a small airfield near **Arnemuiden**, light aircraft can be hired for a *rondvlucht* (round trip) over Zeeland – an ideal way to view the flat, watery land that characterises the province.

**Walcheren:** If Zeeland is a holiday area *par excellence*, **Walcheren** is the province's star performer. Circled by dunes and beaches, the historic island is a magnet for beach lovers, but even at the busiest times of year there always seems to be a wide stretch of sand that no one else has occupied.

The sea is the most obvious attraction – the North Sea coastline running on to the Western Scheldt estuary, with a constellation of small resort towns sheltering behind the dunes. These include **Domburg**, where people came for centuries to take the curative waters at the grand hotel, and where an artists' colony grew up (Mondriaan and many others came to Domburg to paint); **Westkapelle**, with its giant lighthouse; and **Zoutelande**. Hotels, campsites and bed and breakfast lodgings are plentiful.

From the Western Scheldt shore, a fantastic parade of cargo ships of all sizes can be seen streaming through the narrow (and unfortunately polluted) estuary, coming or going to Antwerp.

On the shore of the Veersemeer is **Veere**, a wonderfully preserved medieval town with a fine Gothic town hall dating from 1470 and a fortified 15th-century harbour tower, now a hotel and restaurant. Nearby **Vrouwenpolder** has a tranquil beach on the Veerse Meer – the North Sea (as always) shut out by one of the Delta Works' series of dams.

**Goes harbour.**

**Middelburg**, the provincial capital, is a small, elegant canal-side city of some 40,000 inhabitants, with a beautifully ornamented town hall – one of Holland's most perfect – on the Markt (Market Square). There is also a fine abbey with a famous tower, Lange Jan, which offers a view that makes the 300-ft (91-metre) climb seem worthwhile.

A bustling town, frequently choked beyond its capacity with peak-time summer traffic, Middelburg remains the hub of Zeeland. Many of its cafés and restaurants merit the prized description *gezellig* (you should eat mussels and *frites* while in Zeeland), and its cobbled streets reward the casual stroller.

The **Miniature Walcheren** park in Middelburg is a classic model world, with the island's main centres and buildings reduced to a bird's-eye view and all accurately represented at 1/20th scale. The miniature houses, churches and public buildings are brilliantly executed. Radio-controlled trains and boats, and Lilliputian carillons add to the awesome sense of realism.

**Vlissingen** (Flushing) is the industrial heart of Zeeland. It is also an important port with a terminal for car ferries connecting with Sheerness in England, and a ferry service across the Western Scheldt. The sea-wall walkway offers a pleasant stroll beside the harbour and another view of the Antwerp-bound cargo ships. A statue of the famed 17th-century Dutch admiral Michiel de Ruyter looks out across the water.

**Zeeuws Vlaanderen:** Just as Zeeland is a place apart from Holland, its southernmost part, on the south coast of the Western Scheldt, bordering Belgium, is different again from the rest of the provinces. Zeeuws Vlaanderen is connected to Zeeland only by car ferry services between Breskens and Vlissingen on the west, and Perkpolder and Kruiningen in the eastern part. Road links are through the Flemish region of Belgium, specifically via Antwerp.

At both its western and eastern extremities, there are nature reserves associated with that inexhaustible Zeeland resource, namely water. In the east is the

**Zeeuws Vlaanderen.**

birdwatcher's paradise of the **Verdronken (Drowned) Land van Saeftinge**, mud flats once reclaimed from the Scheldt and now mostly reclaimed by the river. On the North Sea coast is the **Zwin**, another birdlife sanctuary, which continues across the border into Belgium. The border town of **Sluis** is possibly better known in Belgium than in Holland, because many Belgians hide their "black" money from the taxman in its banks and, after visiting their bank manager call at the town's numerous porn shops and sex clubs.

There are popular beaches around **Cadzand Bad**, from where it is possible to walk through the Zwin to Belgium, and the nearby resort of **Knokke**. Other handsome Belgian cities – Bruges, Ghent and Antwerp – lie within a short distance of the border. The to and fro of visitors makes the border between Belgium and Zeeuws Vlaanderen little more than a formality. Along the canal from Terneuzen to Ghent, the terrain is mostly industrial, although there is another nature zone nearby at **De Braakman**, a former inlet on the Western Scheldt, now dammed off to form a lake.

The neighbouring village of **Philippine** is virtually a place of pilgrimage for mussel fanciers, with some of the best restaurants in this part of Zeeland. As with almost everywhere in Zeeland, fishing is a primary recreation, and seafishing trips can be arranged from **Breskens** and **Terneuzen**.

**Cycling:** There is no better way to experience Zeeland than by bike. It can often happen at the busiest times in summer that traffic is bumper-to-bumper on the main access roads. This gives a misleading impression of a congested province – misleading because, in reality, Zeeland is too big to become congested and the back roads are a mostly undiscovered resource.

By bike you can be far from sweltering traffic jams in minutes, into another world of pretty villages and quiet cafés, little islands of civilisation amidst a vast sea of green fields. Zeeland has no hills so it is perfect for cycling – but watch out for unobstructed winds that can make the going harder. Bicycles can be hired in most towns and from the bigger railway stations. Many cycling routes have been specially prepared by the tourism authorities in Zeeland, and information on these is available from local tourist offices.

**The Delta Route:** For those who do all their touring by car, there is a route through Zeeland suggested by the provincial tourist authority (the ANWB-routes) that combines all aspects of the Zeeland experience – town, country, coast, history and the Delta Works. The province-wide route breaks down into more easily managed segments covering each of the islands and Zeeuws Vlaanderen.

**Windmills:** Zeeland would not be a genuine part of Holland if it did not have at least a handful of windmills, and, sure enough, this traditional sight is to be seen all over the province. Many are still in working condition. Windmills can be found at Zierikzee, Brouwershaven, Arnemuiden, Oostkapelle, Vlissingen, Goes, Colijnsplaat, Cadzand and Sluis, among other places.

**Below, Zeeland's clean beaches. Right, a mussel boat.**

# UTRECHT

The small province of Utrecht owes its existence to the Christian Church. In the early 7th century, this region was ruled by the Franks, recent converts to Christianity. The city of Utrecht grew up around a castle and church built on the site of a Roman fort on the Rhine. In AD 689 King Pepin II consolidated his power here by defeating the Frisian King Radboud at Wijk bij Duurstede.

The Frankish king then set out to convert his lands to Christianity. St Willibrord, a missionary from Northumberland, was appointed the first Bishop of Utrecht. Het Sticht, as the see was called, gradually extended its power, and by the 11th century reached as far north as Groningen. The Bishops of Utrecht played an important political role in the Netherlands up until 1528, when Bishop Hendrik sold his temporal powers to Charles V.

The most striking symbol of the power of the Church in Utrecht province today is the 14th-century tower of the Utrecht Dom (cathedral), which can be seen from as far away as Culemborg. Numerous churches, monasteries and convents have also survived in Utrecht and Amersfoort as evidence of the influence of Het Sticht.

The Bishops of Utrecht erected a number of castles to defend Het Sticht from the Dukes of Gelderland to the east and the Counts of Holland to the north. Many of these castles are still standing along the Rivers Kromme Rijn and Vecht. **Huize Doorn**, built in the 14th century, was, like many of these castles, rebuilt in the 18th century. It is mainly of interest as the residence of the deposed Kaiser Wilhelm II of Germany, who lived here from 1921 until his death in 1941.

Before moving to Huis Doorn, the Kaiser lived (from 1918 to 1920) in **Kasteel Amerongen**. This medieval castle, rebuilt in the 17th century, is one

**Preceding pages**: Kasteel de Haar.**Left**, Oudegracht and the Domtoren, Utrecht.

of the most interesting in Utrecht province, with rich furnishings and curiosities. The Kaiser was not the first exile to live in the province. In 1629 King Frederik V of Bohemia, the Winter King, fled to Rhenen, where a palace was built for him.

The Van Zuylen family occupy a prominent place in the history of Utrecht. Of their many castles in the province, the most interesting is **Kasteel de Haar** to the west of Utrecht. In the 19th century the ruined medieval castle was transformed into an ornate Gothic Revival edifice by P.J.H. Cuypers, architect of the Rijksmuseum in Amsterdam. An entire village was demolished to create the extensive castle gardens. Slot Zuylen is another of the castles that belonged to the Van Zuylen family, situated just north of Utrecht on the river Vecht. The castle is a curious mixture of medieval turrets and 18th-century baroque, designed by the Huguenot refugee Daniël Marot.

**Utrecht** itself is one of the oldest cities in the Netherlands. It stands on a tributary of the Rhine, and was founded in AD 47 as a Roman garrison. A posting to *Trajectum ad Rhenum* (the Ford on the Rhine) must have seemed a bleak prospect to any soldier used to sunnier climes. This frontier was constantly being attacked from the east and the Roman settlement at Utrecht was destroyed five times before it was totally eradicated by Germanic tribes in the 3rd century. All that now remains to show for two centuries of Roman occupation are a few pottery fragments in the Centraal Museum.

**Bishops and missionaries:** In the 7th century Pepin, king of the Franks, made Utrecht a bishopric. The Anglo-Saxon missionary Willibrord, who is commemorated by a statue opposite the Janskerk, built two churches on this strategic site, and set about converting the surrounding area to Christianity.

Utrecht flourished in the 11th century under the protection of the German emperors and Bishop Bernold embarked on an ambitious plan to make Utrecht a great spiritual centre of northern Eu-

**Huize Doorn.**

rope. He drew up a plan to create a cross of four churches, with the Domkerk at the centre. Only two churches, the Janskerk to the north and the Pieterskerk to the east, are still standing from Bernold's great project. However, the position of the other two buildings can easily be identified. The cloister still standing on Mariaplaats belonged to the Mariakerk, the church at the west end of the cross, completed after Bernold's death. A portal on Nieuwegracht leads down a lane to the ruined transept of the Paulusabdij, built at the southmost point of the cross.

Numerous other churches and monasteries were built within the city walls, and the skyline of Utrecht was once a mass of spires. But many of these were toppled by a hurricane that struck the city in 1674. The nave of the Dom also came crashing down that day, and was never rebuilt, leaving a bleak, empty space between the cathedral tower and the transepts.

**Oudegracht**, the oldest canal in the city, is a good starting point for a tour of the old city. This canal was dug in the 14th century below street level to allow for sudden changes in the level of the Rhine. The canal is lined with brick quays and cavernous cellars that extend back to connect with the houses on the street above. Once used to store goods shipped from the Rhine and Flanders, the vaulted cellars are now occupied by student restaurants and bars. In summer, café terraces are crammed into the short stretch of sunlit quayside between the Bakkersbrug and the Stadhuis. Out of season these quays remain silent and derelict, with water dripping mournfully from the mossy drainpipes.

Several medieval town houses still stand on Oudegracht. **Oudaen** (No. 99) is a stern, fortified house built in 1320, when the Netherlands was gripped by an obscure dispute between two rival gangs called the *Hoeken* (Hooks) and *Kabeljauwen* (Cods), rather like the 14th-century quarrel in Verona that ensnared Romeo and Juliet. Recently restored, it now has a magnificent café on the ground floor, and a restaurant above.

**Utrecht baker celebrates the Dutch royal family.**

Opposite there is an even older building called Drakenborch (No. 114), dating from 1280 and restored in 1968.

**Soaring tower:** From the Bakkersbrug you obtain a good view of the **Domtoren** (cathedral tower), one of the architectural marvels of the Gothic age. Built between 1321 and 1383, it rises to an ethereal octagonal lantern 376 ft (112 metres) up. It was for several centuries the tallest spire in the Low Countries, and even today it is impossible to remain unmoved by the elegance and sheer daring of the structure. Imitations of the Domtoren were built in Amersfoort, Delft, Groningen, Maastricht and Breda. Its unmistakable silhouette also appeared in several medieval paintings, such as the Van Eyck altarpiece in Ghent (as can be seen from a reproduction in the Janskerk).

The tower has also had its critics, most notably the monk Geert Groote, founder of the Brotherhood of the Common Life. Groote published a diatribe against the tower at about the same time as the octagonal lantern was being built, warning that it would encourage "vanity, curiosity, boasting and pride." He claimed to have had a recurrent dream involving the collapse of the tower, though the structure seems as firm as ever. It survived the hurricane in 1674 and, more recently, a lifesize space rocket was built against the tower without causing damage. In spring and summer you can climb the Domtoren. Tickets and information are provided at the office on the square.

**Cathedral remains:** By following Oudegracht as it bends southwards, then turning left into Servetstraat, you come to the foot of the tower. A Renaissance gate on the right leads into the secret Bishop's garden, where you obtain a superb view of the soaring tower. The archway beneath the Domtoren once led into the **Domkerk**, the cathedral of Utrecht. A road now runs under the tower, and any traveller examining the Gothic vaulting runs the risk of being hit by a bus. All that remains of the Domkerk, which was begun in 1254, are the choir and transepts on the far side

**Tranquil waterside gazebo.**

of the road. The nave, which had been built with inadequate buttressing, came crashing down during the freak hurricane in 1674.

The **Pieterskerk**, the first church of Bishop Bernold's cross, was the Bishop's favourite church, and he elected to be buried here rather than in the Dom. Completed in 1048, it stands on the Pieterskerkhof, a tranquil square near the Domkerk. It is a rare example in the Netherlands of German Romanesque style. Utrecht was then part of the Holy Roman Empire, and the building materials were shipped here from the Eiffel: grey tuffa walls and red sandstone columns form a striking contrast to the ubiquitous Dutch brick.

Sadly, the storm of 1674 brought down both of the Pieterkerk's spires and caused considerable structural damage. The necessary repairs to the church were funded rather drastically by demolishing the westwork (an important architectural element of Romanesque church design) and selling the stone.

**Curious wager:** Turning right along

Achter St Pieter brings you to an unusual house called **De Krakeling** (the pretzel) at No. 8. It was built in 1663 by Everard Meyster, an eccentric local aristocrat who once laid a bet that he could persuade the people of Amersfoort to haul a nine-ton boulder, the *kei*, into the town. He won his bet and spent the money on a lavish feast of beer and pretzels for the 400 people who dragged the stone into town. The pretzel-shaped bell pull on the front door recalls this curious event.

Keistraat (renamed to commemorate Meyster's triumph) leads to the second of Bishop Bernold's churches, the **Janskerk**. Completed about 1050 in a similar German Romanesque style to the Pieterskerk, it originally had red sandstone columns but these had to be encased in brick when the church showed signs of collapsing.

One of the original columns has subsequently been laid bare in the nave. As with the Pieterskerk, this church has lost its Romanesque westwork, one tower of which fell down in the 14th century, while the other followed on that bleak day in 1674.

**Motto of the Republic:** After the Reformation, the choir – which had been rebuilt in the 16th century in Flamboyant Gothic style – was used to house the university library. In 1660 one of the chapels in the north aisle was converted into a guard house and adorned with a brightly painted coat of arms bearing the motto of the Dutch Republic: *Concordia res parvae crescunt* (Unity makes small things great).

Back on Driftgracht, you can turn off down the elegant Kromme Nieuwegracht, the canal which bends along the former course of the Rhine, to reach Pausdam. This attractive bridge is overlooked by the **Paushuize** (Pope's house), a Flamboyant Gothic building dating from the early 16th century. It was built for Adriaen Floriszoon of Utrecht, who was appointed Pope by Charles V in 1522. Pope Adrian VI, the first and only Dutch pope, immediately made himself highly unpopular in Rome by embarking on a vigorous programme of reform; none of his proposals was implemented before he died in the following year.

**Nieuwegracht**, a deep narrow canal dating from 1393, runs south of here. Like Oudegracht, it has a lower quay lined with cellars, but these have all been abandoned. Nieuwegracht has some attractive examples of Dutch domestic architecture, such as the tiny classical house at No. 37.

**History of Dutch religion:** Several religious orders built monasteries and convents on this canal. A former Carmelite convent is now the **Rijksmuseum Het Catharijneconvent**, a museum devoted to the history of Catholicism and Protestantism in the Netherlands. The collection includes medieval sculpture and paintings, vestments, architectural models and documents from the Reformation. The nearby **Catharijnekerk** occupies a curious place in Dutch ecclesiastical history. Formerly the chapel of the Carmelites, it became the national cathedral of the Dutch Catholics in the 19th century, when the ban on Catholic worship was officially lifted. The jubilant Catholics attempted to improve the chapel by adding a spire modelled on that of Kampen Stadhuis, and decorating the interior in rich neo-Gothic style. This offended the Dutch Protestants, who insisted that it be restored to its pristine whiteness.

**Relics of the railway age:** Across the bridge from the Catharijneconvent museum, Brigittenstraat leads to a park bordering the city moat. When the city walls were demolished in the 19th century, the municipal authorities created a series of landscaped parks around the circumference of Utrecht. For train enthusiasts, the **Spoorwegmuseum (National Railway Museum)** is straight ahead across an ornate iron bridge, situated in a disused 19th-century railway station. The old steam train provides a short ride.

Turn right along the cobbled lane to reach the **Bruntenhof**, a row of whitewashed almshouses founded in 1521 by Frederik Brunt. A Renaissance portal leading to the Governors' Chamber (No. 5) bears a reminder of mortality in the form of an hourglass and skull.

Medieval painting, Rijksmuseum Het Catharijneconvent.

Three more almshouses at the southern end of the old town are worth a glance. Twelve homes known as the **Pallaeskameren**, after their founder Maria van Pallaes, stand on Agnietenstraat. The date of foundation, 1651, and the Pallaes family coat of arms appear on every door lintel. Around the corner in Lange Nieuwstraat, the **Beyerskameren** consist of 16 terraced houses founded by Adriaen Beyer. The foundation date, 1597, is cut in the keyhole casing of the Governors' Chamber (No. 120).

When Maria Duist van Voorhout, Baroness of Renswoude, decided in 1757 that she was going to found an institution to educate poor boys, she spared no expense. The **Fundatie van Renswoude** on Agnietenstraat is a magnificent sandstone rococo building, decorated with the coats of arms of the founder and of the 13 members of the original board of trustees.

The former convent next door now houses the **Centraal Museum**. Though rarely visited, this museum has an excellent collection of local history, furniture, costumes, sculpture and paintings. The paintings are mainly by Utrecht artists, the most notable of whom are Jan van Scorel, who was appointed keeper of the Vatican art treasures by Pope Adrian VI. While in Rome, he assimilated the ideas of the Italian Renaissance, as can be seen in several of his works hanging in the former upper chapel of the convent.

Van Scorel returned to a more traditional style of portraiture in the three long panels depicting members of the Utrecht Chapter of the Jerusalem Brotherhood. The members of this order are carrying palms to signify that they have completed a pilgrimage to Jerusalem; the inscriptions below give the date of the journeys. Van Scorel, who made the pilgrimage in 1521, also appears in one panel. The only woman of the group is referred to merely as "Dirck Evert's daughter."

The museum also has six attractive period rooms on the ground floor illustrating changing interior styles in the

# RADICAL WOMEN OF UTRECHT

Utrecht may seem strait-laced compared with Amsterdam, yet it counts many radical women among its citizens during its long history. In 1529 a certain Zuster (Sister) Bertken made the bold resolution, at the age of only 30, to retreat from the world in a bricked-up cell in the choir of the Buurkerk. At that time, this part of the church was older and considerably lower than the nave, and the church authorities decided they should replace it. They had to wait until 1586, however, when Sister Bertken finally died at the age of 87.

Catharina van Leemputte was a spirited local woman who, in 1577, headed a band of women in an attack on Vredenburg citadel. This Renaissance fortress built by Charles V had become a symbol of Spanish tyranny during the Dutch Revolt. Though the Spanish troops had, in fact, quit Utrecht by 1577, Catharina and her followers set about demolishing the citadel.

As a result of this women's revolt, little remains of Vredenburg except for some fragments of masonry near the tourist office. The name Vredenburg, which means "Castle of Peace", has now been given more deservedly to a modern concert hall on the site (which is unfortunately enveloped by Hoog Catharijne, a large, unsightly indoor shopping complex).

Isabella Agneta van Tuyll van Serooskerken was born in Utrecht in 1740. She came from a powerful local aristocratic family, which owned numerous castles and houses in Utrecht province, including Slot Zuylen on the river Vecht, and a rather sombre town house on Utrecht's Kromme Nieuwegracht. Adopting the pen name of Belle van Zuylen, she published Le Noble, a satirical novella involving a foolish aristocrat who inhabited a crumbling castle clearly modelled on Slot Zuylen. Her conventional father promptly forbade Belle to write any other novels, so she reverted to letter writing.

In 1763 Belle van Zuylen met James Boswell, then a dejected law student in Utrecht. They were both 23 years old at the time, and Boswell imme-

diately fell in love with Belle, who was astonishingly beautiful (as can be seen from the portrait by Maurice-Quentin de la Tour in the Musée d'Art et d'Histoire in Geneva). Eventually Boswell angrily rejected her liberated opinions, yet he remained painfully attracted to her, and they continued to exchange letters up to 1769.

Truus Schröder is a 20th-century rebel. Her burning ambition was to be an architect, but there were no openings for women when she was young. When her husband died in 1923, she decided to build herself a new house, and enlisted the help of the Utrecht architect Gerrit Rietveld. Together they designed a small family house that permanently changed the direction of Dutch architecture.

The Rietveld-Schröder house was tacked on to the end of a row of dull 19th-century houses in a calculated attempt to shock the bourgeoisie of Utrecht. The exterior looks like an abstract painting by Mondriaan, with flat surfaces rendered in red, blue, yellow and various shades of grey. To give the house a truly modern appearance, the external brick walls were concealed under a layer of plaster.

The interior design is equally radical, particularly on the upper floor, which was described as an "attic" to avoid local planning regulations. The most striking feature is the ingenious method by which all the dividing walls can be folded away to create a single room. Rietveld was particularly adept at inventing space-saving solutions, such as a bathroom door that doubles as a slide projector screen and a cupboard in the hall that holds a child's wooden beach cart (designed by Rietveld and now in the Centraal Museum in Utrecht).

This unconventional partnership took a more personal turn when Gerrit Rietveld moved into the house, working in a studio on the ground floor originally intended as a garage.

Up until 1963, the house enjoyed an enviable situation on the southern edge of the city. In 1963 this situation was shattered by the construction of an elevated section of the N222 ring road a few yards from the house. This proved too much for Rietveld, who died the following year – a victim of the modern age which he and Truus Schröder had done so much to help to create. ∎

Netherlands from the Middle Ages to the 18th century. A recreated medieval garden contains various moss-covered fragments rescued from demolished buildings. A path leads through the garden to the **Nicolaaskerk**, a parish church built in 1150. It once boasted two spires, but one was replaced by an octagonal bell tower in 1586 (where a Hemony carillon now plays), and the other was felled by the storm in 1674.

The most pleasant route back to the centre is along the landscaped ramparts. You will pass an abandoned Gothic Revival church, the St Martinuskerk, which overlooks a series of 19th-century workers' terraced houses known as *De 7 steegjes* (the 7 lanes), where patterned brick pavements create the impression of an outdoor carpet. The fact that the huge church is now neglected, while the humble dwellings alongside have been saved from demolition by a vigorous campaign, shows how the Dutch aspire not to grandeur but to *gezelligheid* (snugness).

Heading down Springweg, past a row of 11 almshouses founded in 1583 (Nos. 110–30), you come to the **Mariaplaats**, where a cloister is all that remains of the fourth of Bishop Bernold's churches. Turning right down Zadelstraat, then left into the Buurkerkhof brings you to the **Buurkerk**, the oldest parish church in Utrecht, where one Sister Bertken was walled up for 57 years at her own request, in order to escape the evils of the world. Begun in the 13th century, it was converted into a hall church with five aisles in the 16th century.

The church now houses the delightful **Museum Van Speelklok tot Pierement**, a collection of mechanical musical instruments, ranging from a glass case of twittering birds to several ear-splitting dance hall organs. Guided tours are given by enthusiastic music students from the university, whose job includes playing the piano and singing a lusty Berlin *lied* to the accompaniment of a street organ. The presentation is unforgettable, though one wonders what Sister Bertken would make of this.

On Saturdays, markets take place on

every available square in Utrecht: a plant market occupies the leafy square surrounding the Romanesque Janskerk, a general market is crowded into Vredenburg, and a second-hand market fills the streets around the Jacobikerk. The colourful Saturday flower market, held on the bend of Oudegracht around the Bakkersbrug, reaches a climax in the late afternoon when the stall keepers offer enormous bunches of blooms at bargain prices.

**Medieval attractions: Amersfoort** is a sober provincial town on the river Eem, with small neat houses and simple Gothic chapels. Its traditional industries were brewing, cloth-making and tobacco, and in the Middle Ages it was an important place of pilgrimage. The **Museum Flehite** contains a local history collection, including painful reminders of a camp for deportees built during World War II in the suburbs of Amersfoort. The medieval convent Mariënburg houses since 1994 the first Dutch Culinary Museum. Amersfoort is an old town by Dutch standards, and its first

wall dates from about the 12th century. It was presumably a fairly prosperous place, because a new wall was begun in the 14th century enclosing a much larger area. An unusual medieval feature of the old town is the **Muurhuizen** (wall houses), which stand on the foundations of the inner city wall. The Muurhuizen form an almost complete circle of lanes, which makes a very attractive walk through the old town beginning from the Museum Flehite. The outline of the old wall can still be seen quite clearly in the facade of Groot Tinnenburg at Muurhuizen No. 25. The house called Bollenburg at No. 19 was the boyhood home of Johan van Oldenbarnevelt, the statesman executed in 1619.

When the second wall was demolished in the 19th century, some parks were laid out on the site, as in Utrecht. Several medieval gates are still standing from the second ring, including the unusual **Koppelpoort** near the Museum Flehite, a watergate on the river Eem defended by two towers. Amersfoort's main church, the Onze Lieve Vrouwekerk, was destroyed in the 18th century by an explosion in a gunpowder store situated in the church. All that is left is the tower, a copy of the Domtoren in Utrecht. South of here, on the edge of the old town, is the famous *Amersfoortse kei* (the Amersfoort boulder), a large glacial rock which Everard Meyster persuaded the locals to drag into town in 1622. The gullible folk of Amersfoort immediately became the butt of popular jokes, and so they resolved to bury the boulder. It was not until 1903 that they plucked up the courage to unearth the stone and place it on a pedestal.

Perhaps the best day to visit Amersfoort is a Friday, when a flower market takes place on the Havik quayside. De Hof (where the Bishop of Utrecht once had a residence) has several attractive cafés and is the scene of a lively market on Saturdays.

To the southwest of Utrecht is the pleasant town of **Oudewater**, famous for centuries for its public weigh house, the **Heksenwaag**, where women suspected of witchcraft were brought to be weighed from as far away as Cologne.

**Left, fairground organ, Museum Van Speelklok tot Pierement. Right, surrealistic scenes in Oudewater.**

# NOORD-BRABANT

Noord-Brabant is one of the largest provinces in the Netherlands. The south hugs the Belgian border, the northern limits are bounded by the river Maas (Meuse) and the east adjoins Limburg. Apart from the polderland west of Breda, the rest of the province is above sea level and presents landscapes as varied as woodland, moorland (*De Kempen*) and fenland (*De Peel*).

**Bergen op Zoom**, just north of Antwerp, is an ancient fortress town built to protect the Eastern Scheldt and the rich Flemish cities to the south. Bergen op Zoom is nicknamed "Crab Town" because the inhabitants are said to have crawled out of the clay. Once safely on the shore, the crab-dwellers set about building the most impregnable fortress in the Netherlands. Known as the "Virgin City", Bergen survived sieges by the Spaniards in 1588 and 1627, only to yield to the French in 1747.

**Preceding pages:** autumn leaves. **Left**, Sint Jans-kathedraal, Den Bosch. **Below**, the Markiezenhof, Bergen op Zoom.

Since the great flood of 1953, however, the main enemy has been the sea. After Bergen op Zoom, the Biesbosch and Willemstad were flooded, plans were laid to build a complex system of interlocking waterways. Known as the Delta Works (*see section on Zeeland*), the most impressive section is the barrier around the mouth of the Ooster-schelde (Eastern Scheldt). Plans for a solid dam were rejected because this would have created a stagnant lake and destroyed a unique eco-system.

Instead, in 1986, a movable barrier was placed on the shifting sands and sea, allowing the tides free flow but protecting the land from storms. This masterpiece of geometrical grace is rightly called "the eighth wonder of the world" by the Dutch. Although technically in Zeeland, the barrier is considered town property, a watchful crab guarding Bergen op Zooms's mouth.

**Nautical relics:** The approach to Bergen op Zoom town centre, past ugly low-rise blocks and industrial sprawl, is not encouraging. Even the historic centre has lost its air of impregnability: the fortifications were demolished in the 19th century, leaving only pockets of architectural splendour. But a crab-like exploration reveals grand red-brick warehouses and glinting weathervanes of mermaids and dolphins. If the shabby Butter Market is no longer full of sailors' wives, there are still salty tales at bars like the Africa Coffee Shop.

On the **Grote Markt**, the main square, are further nautical reminders. The 17th-century crest on the Stadhuis says *Mille periculus supersum* (I overcome a thousand perils), referring to fears of flood, fire or lack of faith in the declared Spanish truce. Since the first town hall was destroyed by fire in 1397, the builders of this one lacked confidence in the survival of their handiwork. As Bergen op Zoom expanded, so did the Stadhuis, swallowing up the adjoining English Merchant Centre and a burgher's house.

Also on the Grote Markt is the narrow frontage of **St Gertrude's Church**, a Gothic structure topped by a pepper-pot belltower. Called *Peperbus*, this 18th-century lantern-shape was added after

much of the church was destroyed by fire in 1747.

At night, the pepper-pot tower, gold weathervane and herringbone brick are illuminated. The scene is only marred by the presence of a hamburger joint beside the church. Elsewhere on the square, however, more traditional local delicacies are sold, including asparagus, anchovies and oysters.

Just northwest of the Markt is the **Markiezenhof**, the finest building in Bergen op Zoom. Although similar to the Ridderzaal in The Hague, the tranquil Markiezenhof is truer to the spirit of Flemish Bruges than to any other buildings in the Netherlands. An imposing gateway leads to an illuminated inner courtyard, adorned by a delicate gallery and well. Inside this part of the palace, now restored, is a muddled museum, mixing Flemish tapestries and Louis XV furniture.

In the rear courtyard are tempting aromas from the city's best restaurant, *La Pucelle*, housed in late Gothic splendour. But before sitting down to eat,

visit the **Gevangenpoort**, Bergen's only remaining medieval gateway. Gothic in style but Flemish in spirit, this turreted stone and red-brick gateway leans against sturdy walls, the remains of the early fortifications. Formerly used as the city prison, the Gevangenpoort is now a focus of the pre-Lenten carnival procession.

**Northwards to Willemstad:** From Bergen op Zoom, the N259 leads north across the polders to Willemstad, an historic fortress town on the Hollands Diep. Approaching Willemstad, the wide estuary of the **Hollands Diep** comes into view. Cars on the raised road into the town are dwarfed by the slow-moving barges on the Diep.

Divided by a narrow man-made spit and intricate locks, this misleadingly tranquil section of the Diep leads to the Haringvliet and services Rotterdam's vast Europoort. The sweeping scale of the waterworks is best appreciated from the observation tower at the southern end of the **Haringvlietbrug**.

A narrow bridge leads into the star-

Noord-Brabant harbour.

228

shaped bastions of **Willemstad**, a stronghold bounded by geometric canals, moats and the Diep itself. Once a mere fishing village, albeit celebrated for its huge herring catches,

Willemstad was transformed into a fortress town by its namesake, William the Silent, in 1583. Designed to protect the entrance to the Diep, Willemstad remains the best-kept fortress town in the Netherlands. Harmony in scale is the town's distinguishing visual aspect, its perfect geometry proved by 17th-century prints, topographical maps and aerial photographs.

The compact town is centred on the inner harbour, now converted into a marina full of brightly coloured Dutch, Belgian and German boats. Looking down on these paint-box colours is the **Prinsenhof Mauritshuis**, a severe red-brick building designed in Dutch Renaissance style. Originally a hunting lodge for Prince Maurice, it was later the residence of the provincial governors until its present incarnation as the town hall. On the roof is a mermaid weathervane

which once graced the Markiezenhof at Bergen op Zoom. She now enjoys fine views of the inner harbour, with its watchtower, stocky warehouses, old Arsenal converted into a hotel, wind-surfing school and fish restaurant. Beside the tower, a wooden bridge leads across the bastions, restored after the storms of spring 1990.

A walk to church, past outdoor cafés, clog shops and half-hidden discotheques suggests that Willemstad is only a thin shell concealing a modern bazaar. However, unlike Volendam, the mock fishing village near Amsterdam, tourism here is never allowed to swamp local Dutch life. The neat white houses, duck-filled canals and tiny wooden bridges may make Willemstad look like an unreal, model village, but this is an illusion. In Willemstad, the doorsteps really are washed on Monday and the church filled on Sunday.

The octagonal **church**, surrounded by a shady cemetery, was built in 1607 and is therefore one of the first Protestant churches to be built in the Nether-

**Bell founding and statue casting in Noord-Brabant.**

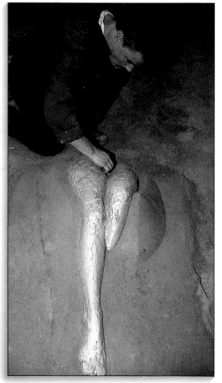

# THE CATHOLIC SOUTH

"The Dutch are half-baked, without fire, melancholy and stale" was the damning judgement of Lepeintre, the 19th-century French traveller to the Calvinistic northern provinces. By contrast, the southern provinces have always revelled in their Burgundian heritage. As the Dutch specialist, William Shetter, puts it: "Residents of the southern provinces may well feel themselves to be religious, bourgeois and dominant, but they do not easily fit the Dutch stereotype of unemotional, reserved or earnest."

Instead, these latter-day Burgundians pride themselves on their warmth and generosity and accuse their northern neighbours of meanness. In fact, niggling miserliness (*krenterigheid*) is the defect that southerners find synonymous with the Dutchness of Holland, along with the smugness known as "Calvinistic fascism".

The northerners are not slow to respond: southerner jokes feature in the cabaret routines of Den Haag and Amsterdam. Southerners are mocked for their soft Flemish accents, liberal Catholicism and suspect morals. Residents of Noord-Brabant and Limburg are teased for their light-hearted holiday mentality yet many northerners choose to spend their own holidays in hilly southern Limburg, the least Dutch region of the Netherlands. The term "southern Lowlands" is something of a misnomer since Noord-Brabant and Limburg form the High Netherlands, a mainly sandy region lying above sea level. Yet behind the stereotypes lies more than a grain of truth, cultivated over the centuries in the southern Lowlands. At the heart of the difference lie the geographical boundaries between north and south: the great rivers forming the most prominent cultural boundary in the Netherlands. The term *beneden de Moerdijk* refers to all the people "below the rivers", the Moerdijk being the the wide river delta south of Rotterdam. The term can also embrace Belgian Flanders, thereby implying a Flemish solidarity which transcends or ignores modern boundaries. The Flemish are often called the only Romance

people to speak a Germanic language and certainly many southern Dutch feel a greater cultural affinity with the Belgian Flemish rather than with "Hollanders", the northern Dutch. The origins of the southern provinces predate Dutch statehood. In the Middle Ages, Flemish culture was the predominant one in the region and, as a result, Noord-Brabant's medieval towns, such as Den Bosch, have more in common with Bruges and Leuven than with Amsterdam or Den Haag.

In the 15th century, ownership by the Dukes of Burgundy ensured the southern provinces continued to look south for their inspiration. From the 16th century the southern provinces were conquered by the Princes Maurits and Frederik Hendrik and, with the 1648 Treaty of Münster, became part of the United Provinces. Dutch Brabant and Limburg were allowed to remain Catholic but were otherwise alienated and excluded from power by the rising Dutch Republic.

In the 17th century the Protestant Dutch Republic was a forward-looking maritime nation. By contrast, the southern provinces, populated by Flemish-speaking Catholics, looked to the rural hinterland and, alienated from the Dutch state, dwelled on past glories. This bias continued until recently: there was no equality of wealth until the late-19th century. The reversal of the cultural brain-drain from south to north only began with the recent electronics-led economic boom.

In the late 19th century, the south developed vigorous manufacturing and coal-mining industries, particularly in Limburg. The rise of Philips, the electronic giant, in Eindhoven helped Noord-Brabant on the road to recovery, and more recently the region has been termed the "silicon flatlands" thanks to its ability to attract hi-tech industries.

The state claims credit for creating modern universities in Eindhoven and Maastricht and for relocating government departments and state industries in once depressed rural regions of Middle Limburg. Certainly this long overdue interest in the south has helped but southerners have a different explanation for their relative prosperity. It lies in the rich Flemish and Burgundian heritage which has produced a cosmopolitan people and an openness to other cultures. ∎

lands. Enclosed by a small moat, it lies at the end of a leafy arbour. From the church, a short walk leads you to the **Oranjemolen**, a cosy 18th-century mill lying against the town ramparts and the old *jachthaven*. Beyond this outer harbour is yet more water, a wide estuary scattered with sluggish barges and the occasional ocean-going cruiser.

From the ramparts, a long walk leads along the old city fortifications and main canals while a shorter walk traces the smaller waterways back to the inner harbour. Behind the inner harbour are more recent fortifications: concrete bunkers from World War II, perched like ant-hills on top of the star-shaped bastions. Nearby is a cemetery to the 134 Belgian prisoners-of-war who died when their ship was mined in 1940.

Tired and hungry visitors tend to stop at the **Arsenal**, rebuilt in 1793 by the French but recently converted into a fish restaurant. The Arsenal is as good a place as any from which to recall the time when Willemstad was the chief fishing port on the Haringvliet. As the foundation of the Dutch fortune, herring was always the patriotic dish and, as historian Simon Schama says, "Fish, bread and ale were traditionally considered 'Fatherlands food'."

**The Biesbosch fenland:** From Willemstad, an inland route leads past the villages of Oudemolen, Klundert, Zevenbergen and Made to Drimmelen; the latter is a good base for exploring the nature reserves of the Biesbosch fenland. The most appealing village is **Klundert**, noted for its free-standing **Stadhuis** designed in Flemish Renaissance style. In the blue-green windows are reflected a well, double staircase and lion statues. Opposite is the renovated **Prinsenhof**, bearing the town's blue and yellow insignia.

Towards Drimmelen, the flat, dreary landscape gives no indication of the ecologically rich wetlands to come. Drimmelen itself is an unremarkable port on the Maas river but is the gateway to the watery wilderness known as the Biesbosch ("reed forest").

The **Biesbosch** owes its uniqueness

to a 15th-century flood. In 1421, on St Elizabeth's Day, a storm broke the dykes on the Waal and the Maas, flooding the polderland. The waters reached Geertruidenberg, Drimmelen and Heusden, turning Dordrecht into an urban island and creating an eerie inland sea. The *St Elizabeth's Day Panel* in the Amsterdam Rijksmuseum depicts submerged gables, floating churches and marooned sheep. Over 70 villages were drowned, along with around 10,000 inhabitants.

Gradually, sludge and sand were deposited from the Maas and Waal rivers and the area became overgrown with rushes, reeds and willows. In 1685 and 1904 parts of the Biesbosch were reclaimed and given over to farming, thatching and basket-weaving. The building of the Haringvlietdam in 1971 further changed the ecological balance of the area. Today, the Biesbos is an ever-changing fenland, part sea and part land, but still home to a rare collection of flora and fauna. As the **Drimmelen nature centre** suggests, there are op-portunities to see what makes the Biesbosch the richest nature reserve in the Netherlands. Once in the wild, look out for hawks and herons, swans and spoonbills, cormorants and kingfishers, as well as wild ducks and geese. While squirrels and bats inhabit the willows, beavers and polecats may be lurking among the marsh marigold and yellow irises. After the windswept Biesbosch, civilisation beckons in the form of Heusden, a charming, quintessentially Dutch town.

**Heusden**, lying on the Maas east of Drimmelen, is an ancient fortified town not dissimilar to Willemstad and Woudrichem. After the signing of the Union of Utrecht in 1579, Heusden declared its allegiance to the Protestant cause and star-shaped bastions were built around the castle and harbour. Within the safety of the walls, an elegant canal-lined town thrived on boat-building, arms dealing and, of course, the herring catch. Heusden remained a Protestant stronghold and garrison town until the successful French invasion in 1795.

*Below, Heusden. Right, carnival costume.*

# CARNIVALS

"The back door is always open." This phrase is a byword for southern generosity and hospitality. Nowhere is this truer than in Bergen op Zoom during carnival. *Kermissen*, a concept embracing most folkloric festivities, is a heart-felt tradition in the southern Lowlands. *Carnaval*, its finest flowering, is as popular in Brabant as in Flemish Belgium. Whereas carnival in Amsterdam is a pale affair, the celebrations in Bergen op Zoom and Den Bosch are famous nationwide.

The tradition of carnival goes back to the 15th century when the southern provinces were ruled by the Dukes of Burgundy. Burgundian rule coincided with the southern Golden Age, a time of opulent town halls, noble mansions and artistic excellence. The region acquired a taste for open-air theatricals, banquets and, above all, riotous carnivals, which remain an integral part of southern Dutch life today.

Seven weeks before Easter the carnival is at its pre-Lent peak, but preparations begin months before. Bergen op Zoom's 700 brass bands practise in neighbouring towns; the witches' costumes are created; the totemic giants are repainted; the carnival cabaret is rehearsed; a new carnival song is composed in local dialect. A Carnival Prince is elected as master of ceremonies, an onerous responsibility involving charity appearances and fund-raising until the following year.

In the three weeks leading up to the carnival, the shops are decorated with folkloric characters while the bands start performing in local bars and children's clubs. At night, singing students, draped in red kerchiefs and net curtains, roam the bars. Masked children torment passers-by with off-key renditions of the carnival song, *Wa d'n Kemedie* (What a comedy). Stray carnival carts career through the narrow streets by Bergen op Zoom's Gevangenpoort.

The traditional Old Wives Ball, held a few days before the grand carnival weekend, is a colourful pub crawl attended by young women (and occasionally men) dressed as old hags, harridans and witches. At midnight, the women and "transvestites" are unmasked and, if female, are kissed by male revellers hovering in the wings.

During the carnival weekend, the restaurants are full of brass bands and, in the case of the proprietors of the Old Dutch, cooking plays second fiddle to performing. The weekend is for adult revellers but Monday is Children's Day, a private occasion when local youngsters wear fancy dress and meet the Carnival Prince in the Grote Markt.

The Prince, or an imposter with a head for heights, greets the children from his eyrie in the Peperbus, the church tower. Dressed as a giant, the Prince dangles huge arms and legs over the side of the tower and challenges children to hunt him through the town. A mad chase leads to a dishevelled Prince, exhausted children and truanting parents ensconced in cosy bars. The following day is almost an anti-climax as far as local people are concerned: the carnival procession, led by giants, floats and the long-suffering Prince, is a stage-managed occasion designed to appeal to the thousands of visitors.

Carnival is above all a celebration of community spirit; those who do not participate are termed spoil-sports or, worse, cold Hollanders.

Unlike the Maastricht carnival, a relatively private affair, the Bergen op Zoom carnival is a peacock's public display. Community spirit can verge on exhibitionism: shrinking violets who cannot face the merry-making depart on hastily organised skiing trips, sulk indoors or visit relatives in New Jersey. At midnight, the celebrations stop and Lenten austerity begins. This ebb and flow of feast and fast spills over into the northern Netherlands but it is most alive here in the south. Jan Steen's *The Fat Kitchen* depicts the Dutch love of carnival in a riotous scene.

But it is left to a southern painter, Bruegel the Elder, in his *Battle of Carnival and Lent*, to suggest the yin and yang of "fat" carnival and "skinny" Lent. In this symbolic confrontation between Church and inn, a merry band of guzzlers is pitted against crippled beggars and Calvinist moralists. The victory would appear to be with the beer barrels, pancakes and giant-tailed fish: a southern vision of the world. ∎

233

Although shelled in 1940, the town has been fully restored to its 16th-century glory and, four centuries later, even the local trades remain little changed.

The liveliest spot in town is the former fish market which, naturally enough, is sandwiched between the butter market and the harbour. Both the **Botermarkt** and the **Vismarkt** are framed by assymetrical gabled houses, many of which have been converted into fish restaurants. At one end of the Vismarkt is an incongruous-looking stone portico. Built in 1591, it looks more like a Roman arch than a custom house (Commiezenhuis), its true function. But once you pass through the arch and on to the wooden landing stage, the hustle and bustle of the Vismarkt is forgotten.

As if behind the looking-glass awaits a circular sheet of water, its surface unbroken but for the reflections of a feathery tree, a miniature bridge, a raised windmill and a neat lock-keeper's house. The Dutchness of this scene lies in its scaled-down perfection and simulated naturalness. Heusden, like an emblematic Dutch town, appears to grow organically out of the landscape. Yet the landscape is itself landscaped: the pool is a basin; the river is a canal; the river banks are ramparts and sea walls. Here, nature is unnatural, down to the over-domesticated ducks.

Nor does the rest of the town disappoint in its Dutchness, from the Gothic **St Catherinakerk** to the functional Stadhuis, gabled houses and 17th-century market halls. As if for confirmation, there is yet another windmill, a tumbledown castle and the provincial governor's house, enclosed by courtyards and gardens. The Woonhuis also represents a very Dutch welcome: built on the site of a medieval arms factory, this ornate 18th-century building remained a family-run armaments business until quite recently.

For a friendlier but equally traditional Dutch farewell, return to one of the fish restaurants which surround the Vismarkt and be comforted that, unlike the landscape, the herrings and hospitality are indubitably real.

**Den Bosch, Stationsplein.**

234

**'s-Hertogenbosch (Den Bosch):** The Dutch officially refer to 's-Hertogenbosch as Den Bosch, pronounced "Den Boss". The full title literally means "the Duke's woods", referring to the fact that the town grew up on the site of a 12th-century hunting lodge owned by Henry I, Duke of Brabant, who gave the town its charter in 1185. Den Bosch flourished as a rich wool town and, after its absorption by Burgundy in 1430, became a noted centre for the arts. Den Bosch was governed by Spain until 1629 when William the Silent's son took the town after a long siege.

After the Kingdom of the Netherlands was proclaimed in 1814, Den Bosch and the rest of Noord-Brabant soon joined, while southern Brabant declared its allegiance to Belgium. This unnatural severing of Flanders has left Den Bosch adrift, only moored to the Netherlands politically and economically. The stronger cultural pull is towards Catholic Flanders and the hearty, catholic tastes that characterised the old Burgundian empire.

In modern Den Bosch, the rustic cuisine, locally brewed beer, noisy carnival and lively cultural scene ensure the survival of Burgundian instincts. The town boasts classical concerts and modern dance, with the North Brabant Orchestra in residence at the Schouwburg casino, near the cathedral. The physical shape of the old city is little changed, remaining a triangle centred on the cathedral and bounded by the Binnendieze, the inner canals.

A visit to Den Bosch opens with the vision of its soaring **Sint Janskathedraal**, both the greatest Gothic church in the Netherlands and the most Flemish of cathedrals. **Parade**, the central square, accords Sint Janskathedraal the space it demands. Enough of the plain Romanesque belltower remains to provide a severe counterpoint to the flight of Gothic fantasy. But unadorned red brick loses out to Flamboyant Gothic at its most exuberant. Since the house of Hieronymus Bosch overlooks the cathedral, one can imagine that the view of richly carved sculptures and surreal symbols

Cattle market, Den Bosch.

must have wormed their way in to the painter's work.

The cathedral was built between 1330 and 1550 but, in keeping with the politics of the Netherlands, switched its allegiance regularly. In 1629, it was seized by the Protestants but was returned to the Catholics in 1810, a change more attuned to the spirit of the cathedral. Entering through the great west door, the first impression is one of space, closely followed by disappointment that the restoration in 1980 has left the cathedral too neat and sparse, Dutch rather than Flemish.

The grandeur of conception is clear in the vaulted ceiling yet the eye is drawn to artistic details. After looking at the magnificent organ, the choir stalls and the carved baptismal fonts, one's gaze falls upon the aisles decorated with statues of calm women staring at stony-faced men. One small chapel off the left aisle contains dramatic Byzantine icons, including a dark-faced Christ against a rich orange background.

In the north transept there are grisaille figures of the Virgin and St John, reputedly by Bosch. This mischievious couple originally decorated the cathedral doors. Even in this minor work, there is a sense of the charge levelled against Bosch in his lifetime: "He had the audacity to paint mankind as he is on the inside."

Eventually declared a heretic, Bosch is still little celebrated in his home town. Most of his works are in Rotterdam's Boymans-Van Beuningen Museum or in the Prado in Madrid, to which Philip II spirited away his favourite Flemish treasures.

Nearby is the flowery, over-restored **Chapel of Our Lady**, where a statue of the Virgin is traditionally associated with miracles. In the adjoining **St Anthony's Chapel** is the cathedral's finest work, the **Altar of the Passion**. This early 16th-century panel-painting depicts the life of Christ through a combination of vivid Flemish painting and purposeful figure carving. Outside, in the bustling Parade cafés, a purposeful crowd drinks under the stern gaze of a statue of Bosch. The painter also supervises the Markt, the site of the town hall and De Moriaan, the Duke of Brabant's fabled hunting lodge. Turning your back on Bosch, walk down **Verwerstraat** and, amongst the attractive gables, notice the 14th-century bakery, still in use, and, at No. 78, a facade decorated with Delft tiles. A small alley, **Oud Bogardenstraatje**, leads over a canal to an enclosed gateway, an over-restored mews and a rear view of the **Noordbrabants Museum**, its gardens dotted with modern sculpture.

This 18th-century patrician building now houses a collection reflecting the province's medieval origins and Burgundian traditions. In addition, the works of Brueghel and Rubens pay tribute to the Flemish Catholic character of the people. Van Gogh's paintings of Brabanter peasants stress the region's rural roots and the painter's attachment to the wooded Meierij area outside town. The popularity of brooding works by Constant Permeke, the Flemish-Belgian Expressionist, underlines the local affinity with Flemish culture, an affection

**Statue of Hieronymus Bosch, eponymous native of Den Bosch.**

which continues to transcend modern political boundaries.

From the Museum, narrow Beurdsestraat leads back to Verwerstraat and a turning left along Peperstraat returns to the cathedral. En route, the Mayor's gilded residence is indicated by a miniature **statue of Atlas**, his back burdened by the (small) cares of office.

At the cathedral, turn right into **Hinthamerstraat**, once home to Bosch. Sadly, the painter's undistinguished gabled house has no architectural flights of fancy and is devoid of winged demons and gluttonous monks. The house grounds the imagination with the reminder that here Bosch led a comfortable burgher's existence, even though his works were collected fanatically by Burgundian and Spanish rulers, including Charles V and Philip II.

But, although he found favour with these monarchs, Bosch the artist was accused of heresy during his lifetime and beyond. Today he is still seen as a solitary genius, belonging to no artistic school. The painter's spirit, if it lives at all in his home town, hovers over the gargoyles on the cathedral or floats into the city's Burgundian restaurants.

Virtually next door to the house of Bosch is the building that houses one of the country's oldest religious societies, the **Swan Brotherhood**, signalled by statues of the medieval stations in life, from lawyer to priest. Bosch himself belonged to this medieval society which, then as now, promoted church music, religious art and Christian good works. In 1629 the Brotherhood opened its doors to Protestants as well as Catholics and has attracted active support from the Dutch royal family ever since. Although the Swan Brotherhood's small collection of antiques, books and statuary is rarely visited by foreigners, the Dutch find comfort in the musty, unchanging displays. The characteristic reverence of Dutch visitors partly explains Bosch's need to rebel.

The rest of Hinthamerstraat is devoted to more earthly pleasures, typified by the quantity of gabled shops and restaurants in the adjoining streets. But

**Heineken brewery, Den Bosch.**

older trade is suggested in Korte Waterstraat, a blind alley leading to the original town ramparts and the **Binnenhaven**, the Inner Harbour. After seeing the murky waters disappear under a decaying warehouse, rejoin Hinthamerstraat and turn left towards the Markt. The **town hall's** classical facade and carillon are worth pausing for, as is the brasserie in the 16th-century cellar. Alternatively, pickled herrings are available from the herring cart outside.

From Den Bosch, a motorway leads directly south to Eindhoven, passing through **De Kempen**, an unspoilt region of woodland, heaths and sand dunes. Unlike the coastal dunes protecting the inland plains, these sands' sole function is to be the green lungs to the industrial triangle of Den Bosch, Tilburg and Eindhoven. The landscape runs through deeply wooded river valleys until the trees peter out amongst the dunes and broom-covered heath.

Until the 19th century this landscape was neglected by inhabitants and visitors. The poet Potgieter poured scorn on the bleak landscape: "Grey is your sky and stormy your beach. Naked are your dunes and flat your fields... Nature created you with a stepmother's hand."

But contemporary visitors appreciate the sandy expanses and the horizons seemingly placed so low that the heath is submerged in the cloudy sky. The views towards Eindhoven are reminiscent of Van Ruysdael's spacious, forlorn landscapes.

**Eindhoven:** Eindhoven needs to be placed in this rural perspective if it is not to be dismissed as a soulless metropolis, or "Philips Town" as people refer to it. The city can afford to be materialistic and monolithic because it has the countryside to keep it sane: De Kempen stretches south and west while the marshy Peel overlaps the Brabant-Limburg border. Now the hi-tech centre of the Netherlands, Eindhoven was a mere village until the arrival of the Philips dynasty at the turn of the century. Although no architectural beauty, Eindhoven has a reputation for its striking modern sculpture, inspired or funded

**Den Bosch.**

by the family firm. Just outside the station is an imposing statue of Dr Anton Philips while, on Emmasingel, the original **Philips building** has been preserved, complete with low-tech chimney and sculpted bust of G. L. Philips. Outside another Philips building, on Mathildelaan, is *Natuursteen*, Fred Carasso's tribute to nature, a dancing, globe-shaped bronze.

By contrast, Mario Negri's statue of an automaton on the central **Piazza** represents the dehumanising nature of city life. As if in confirmation of this thought, it shields a sharply metallic library and clinical shopping centre; the only humour lies in the steel tubing, designed to look like a cross-section of a Philip's component.

Eindhoven's artistic focus is the **Van Abbemuseum**, housing a unique modern art collection with many innovative exhibitions through the year. Set beside landscaped gardens on the river Dommel, the museum was established by Van Abbe, a leading industrialist. Cubist works by Picasso and Braque compete with Surrealist paintings by Chagall and Delvaux, or Expressionist works by Kokoschka, Kandinsky and Permeke. The Dutch De Stijl movement is well represented, as is Mondrian and the COBRA school. Pop Art, Conceptual art and modern German art also feature highly. Apparently, each nationality has its own artistic bent: Dutch visitors come to see foreign works from Miró to Bacon; the British seek out Mondriaan and De Stijl; and the Germans flock to exhibitions of the most recent of contemporary art.

Eindhoven advertises itself as *een stad apart*, "a town with a difference", but sadly this is yet to be reflected in the city's architecture or culture. The closure of the Evoluon, formerly the city's star attraction, did nothing to improve Eindhoven's tourist appeal. The city authorities have promised urban renewal before the end of the decade.

**Van Gogh's Peel:** As if to compensate for modern Eindhoven, the surrounding countryside contains much of historical interest, with Kempen farmhouses and,

**Silicon chips produced by Philips in Eindhoven.**

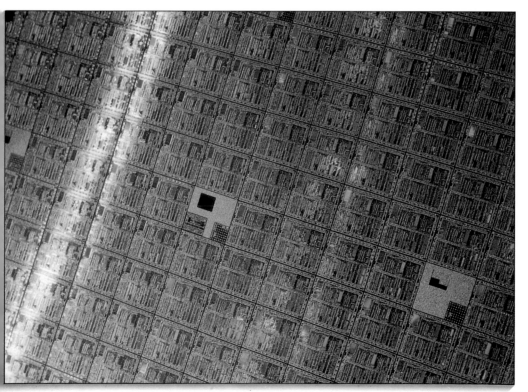

at **Heeze**, a 17th-century castle with period furniture and Gobelin tapestries. One quiet route from Eindhoven leads north east to **Nuenen**, Van Gogh's village. In 1883 Van Gogh came to stay in the family rectory at Nuenen. Returning home was an admission of defeat as a preacher in Belgium and followed a troubled relationship with Gien Hoornik, a prostitute and artist's model in The Hague. In Nuenen Van Gogh made his first studies of peasant life, spending more time in the fields than in his small studio. His sketches of faces and hands were awkward and rough, echoing the timbre of his life.

The culmination of the artist's explorations in Nuenen was the first of his early masterpieces which he called *De Aardappeleters* (The Potato Eaters). Vincent's brother, Theo, was at first shocked by the coarseness of the work but Van Gogh, equating manual labour with honesty, replied that: "These people, eating potatoes in the lamplight, have dug the earth with those very hands they put in the dish."

Nuenen today is very much a shrine to Van Gogh; the rectory, with its green shutters and neat hedgerows, remains frozen in time. A monument honours the painter's memory, as does a permanent exhibition in the **Van Gogh Documentatiecentrum**, near the town hall. **St Clemenskerk**, the solitary, pointed church, is a reminder that the painter's friendship with the verger resulted in the loan of a studio.

In 1885 Vincent's father died so the painter abandoned Nuenen and the Netherlands for Antwerp, Paris and, finally, for the radiant Mediterranean light near Arles.

Just east of Nuenen is Helmond, a characterless town bordering the mysterious **Peel**. This marshland stretches between Helmond and the Limburg border but the most characteristic parts, De Grote Peel and Helena Peel, are peatland nature reserves. (For background information on the area, nature lovers can make a visit to the Natuurstudiecentrum in Asten, located south of Helmond.)

**Van Gogh's**
*The Potato Eaters.*

For centuries this part of Noord-Brabant was deserted or, in the popular imagination, haunted by spirits, lawbreakers and vagabonds. In the 1850s, impoverished peat-cutters moved in to the area, using the old defensive canals to transport the peat. As the peat was removed, bogs and lakes were gradually formed and, in the process, they attracted shrieking black-headed gulls and countless marsh birds. The lakes were not drained and transformed into polders because, unlike the rich clay soils of Holland province, the soil underlying the peat in De Peel is sandy and infertile.

This century, however, large-scale reafforestation has turned parts of De Peel into heath and woodland, with the occasional village built using traditional pile dwellings. Today, the authentic Peel landscape has contracted but not disappeared. East of Eindhoven, **Helena Peel** and **Peel de Veluwe** still lie among bird-filled swamps, open waters hooded by hump-back *knuppel* bridges.

**The bird-filled swamps of De Peel.**

Access to the nature reserve is via Moostdijk near Meijelsedijk. The black-headed gulls are visible between March and July but are most vocal in early spring, when nesting among the reeds. But to many hikers, the rare insects and the views over the bleak fens encrusted with World War II pill boxes are reason enough to visit the area at any time of year.

The poet De Genestet aptly described De Peel on an overcast November day:

> *O land of manure and mist, of dirty*
> *clammy rain*
> *Soggy patch of ground, full of chilly*
> *dews and damp.*
> *Full of bottomless mire and*
> *unwadeable roads,*
> *Full of gout and umbrellas, of tooth-*
> *ache and cramps.*

Despite this somewhat jaundiced, albeit realistic, view of the De Peel landscape, there remains much for the visitor to enjoy, especially if you like walking alone with nature. In fact you may well find that, on a fine day in De Grote Peel, your spirit leaves the bogs to soar with the gulls.

# LIMBURG

The Dutch divide Limburg into three zones. North Limburg includes the area west of the Maas, an expanse of moorland which is sparsely populated despite the presence of Weert and Venray, two confident market towns. Middle Limburg, centred on Roermond, is a flat playground of lakes, rivers and canals. By contrast, the South is hilly enough to merit the epithet "the Dutch Alps", particularly near the Drielandenpunt, at 1,050 ft (321 metres) the highest spot in the Netherlands. Nearby are Maastricht and Valkenburg, where the Dutch seek out caves, castles and classy cuisine.

A new museum on the history of Limburg, **Het Limburgs Museum**, will open in Venlo in 2000. (Contact the VVV, tel: 043 601 7373, for details.)

From De Peel or Helmond in Noord-Brabant, military enthusiasts should drive east towards Venray and the National War and Resistance Museum at

the neighbouring village of **Overloon**. Venray is now the centre of the Dutch market garden region – a term that in 1944 had a special significance.

Operation Market Garden was devised to prevent further German incursions along a corridor from the Belgian border to Nijmegen and Arnhem, via Eindhoven. As a key part of the corridor, known as Hell's Highway, Overloon was subject to sustained German attack. The Allied plan was to cut off German troops in a pincer movement and, by isolating them from supplies, to force an end to the war. At Overloon, as at Arnhem, the plan was foiled. Here, for three weeks in 1944, British and American forces fought the Germans in the only tank battle on Dutch soil.

**War graves and memories:** The battle is often compared with Caen because of the scale of destruction: Overloon was ruined, along with 300 tanks. As to the thousands of casualties, a visit to war cemeteries in the region testifies to American, British, Canadian, German and Polish losses. In the IJsselsteyn cemetery, between Deurne and Venray, are the graves of 30,000 Germans alone. The Overloon museum lies on the original battlefield and was built out of the wreckage. A well-marked route leads past real tanks, planes, cannon, minefields, bombs and anti-tank devices.

After the harrowing pilgrimage to Overloon, visitors can escape to the river Maas (Meuse). Following the river south to Limburg provides plenty of opportunities to leave the motorway and visit riverside castles, to enjoy water sports or just water gazing.

Just off the N271 is **Château Arcen**, a graceful 18th-century mansion set on a series of floating islands interspersed with thematic water gardens. A walk past the moated château leads to the orangerie, an ornamental lake and, as a centrepiece, the vivid rosarium (rose garden). Elsewhere oriental gardens, tropical gardens, terraces, waterfalls and pergolas serve to delight the garden-loving Dutch.

**Roermond**, like Eindhoven, is a modern, Philips fiefdom. Luckily, the Prinsenhof (governor's palace), Gothic cathedral and Munsterkerk have been well restored since 1945. But Roermond's greatest attraction is water: just outside the town are the **Maasplassen**, artificial lakes in former sand and gravel pits. Now, these landscaped shores are covered with sailors and windsurfers.

**Below Belgium and Germany:** Below Roermond, Limburg narrows, visibly crushed between the Belgian and German borders. Virtually on the Belgian border is **Thorn**, a self-conscious white village which barely escapes tweeness. Cobbled streets lead past former almshouses, converted abbey buildings and white-washed brick cottages. Thorn's saving grace is a quiet spirituality in keeping with its earlier incarnation as a religious centre.

The original religious community was centred on a 10th-century abbey run by an abbess and a chapter of noblewomen. The Romanesque crypt remains but the rest of the church now standing is Gothic with a baroque facelift. An overblown Rubens painting competes for attention with the mummified remains of past canons and canonesses.

South of Thorn, the river Maas traces the Belgian border and the rolling landscape of South Limburg ushers in wilder, less classically Dutch views. A cosmopolitan flavour is added by the presence of border castles and fortified farms. Just south of the Susteren lakes, two feudal castles, Wittem and Limbricht, survey the wooded scene. Just north of Heerlen is **Kasteel Hoensbroek**, the finest castle between the Maas and the Rhine. The 14th-century red-brick towers squat in a murky green lake. Inside the castle, 16th and 17th-century furnishings reflect the date of Hoensbroek's first major restoration. Views towards distant narrow river valleys and hills beyond shatter another Dutch stereotype.

Vacationers can stay in a 17th-century castle or an old farmhouse. Just outside Maastricht, and in Kerkrade and Bad Valkenburg, hotelier Camille Oostwegel has several unique properties. For further information contact: Restaurant Château Neer Canne, Cannerweg 800, 6213 ND Maastricht, tel: 043 325 1359; fax: 043 321 3406.

It is wise to skirt industrial Sittard and Geleen in favour of **Heerlen**, a diffuse but nevertheless rewarding town. At first glance, Heerlen is an overgrown shopping centre, Limburg's answer to Eindhoven. Historically, though, Heerlen has a richer past.

**Imaginative museum:** As a Roman trading post on the road from Cologne to Calais, Heerlen supplied glassware, earthenware and provisions to the troops. The remains of *Coriovallum*, the Roman centre, were excavated in the 1960s and a small museum later built to house the circular Roman baths, furnace room, shops and sports field. The result is the imaginative **Thermenmuseum**, a metal hangar painted in primary red, yellow and blue. Inside, the narrow steel walkway offers views over the baths below. The Romans went from the circular sauna to warm, luke warm, cold, and full immersion baths. In another room are the remains of a stone temple, a reconstruction of a potter's workshop and a collection of jewellery, coins and statuettes found during the excavation.

Roermond.

From the late 19th century until 1975, Heerlen was the centre of the Dutch coal-mining industry. However, the discovery of natural gas in Groningen in 1960 spelt the end of Heerlen's "black fairytale". Local people proved themselves adaptable; they donned white collars and persuaded government departments and new industries to relocate in Limburg's fastest growing city.

Now Heerlen is home to the headquarters of the Dutch State Mines, DSM chemicals, ABP pension funds and the Central Bureau of Statistics. As a result of this rapid expansion, Heerlen has reclaimed its identity. Resentment towards incoming Hollanders has faded, along with the local dialect. But, as if in protest, the city accent rejects the northern hard "g" in favour of a softer, more Flemish pronunciation.

**Southern Limburg:** Visually, southern Limburg is not at all Dutch and, for that very reason, attracts many Dutch tourists. The novelty is the undesigned natural landscape, an irregular patchwork of woods, meadows and hills with forbidding border castles and half-timbered farms set at all sorts of jaunty angles.

For many foreigners, however, the novelty lies in the historic caves and castles rather than in the landscape. In a different location, the "Dutch Alps" could easily pass for the Belgian Ardennes, the German Eifel or, in England, the rolling countryside of Hampshire and Dorset. Yet there is enough innate Dutchness to enjoy in the shallow valleys and freshly whitewashed farms.

**Casinos and spas: Valkenburg**, situated in the wooded Geul valley, is the most popular non-coastal destination for Dutch visitors. The spa-town atmosphere and casino provide stimulation when country walks pall. For a more history-oriented stay in the region, you can spend a weekend at Kasteel Erenstein (tel: 045 541 1333; fax: 045 546 0748) or the farmhouse hotel Winselerhof (tel: 045 546 4343; fax: 045 535 2711), each with a gourmet restaurant.

**Thermae 2000**, a spa centre in the hills, is an invigorating exercise in inter-

Thorn.

nationalism: treatments include Roman, Turkish and Swedish baths, as well as *Medizinisches Heilwaser*, German health cures. Housed under a glass pyramid, the mineral-rich springs are channelled so as to allow swimmers to glide easily from one exotic water experience to another. Reservations for a spa visit and accommodation nearby can be arranged by calling 043 601 9419; fax: 601 4815.

Following Grotestraat from the Spaans Leenhof (the tourist office) to the castle provides a snapshot of the town. At the lower end of the street is the **Streekmuseum**, a cluttered collection redeemed by the elegant marlstone building, decorated with stained-glass windows and a stone falcon. Unpromising lines of gift shops and tawdry bars are overshadowed by glimpses of the tumbledown castle. As the only elevated fortress in the Netherlands, the jagged ruins, towering over modern excrescences, still have a dramatic appeal.

At the foot of the castle, turn left into Berkelstraat and walk through the **Berkelpoort**, the medieval gateway, before visiting the castle. From the De la Ruine hotel, steep steps lead past a curious sandstone grotto hewn into the rock; at carnival time, a dummy of a witch is suspended over the entrance.

Still higher is the castle and fine views over the Geul valley. Built by the feudal lords of "Falcon castle" (Valkenburg), this 11th-century castle has attracted Flemish, Spanish and French hunters. It finally succumbed to Louis XIV after a siege and was partially demolished in 1672. The remains include a tower, chapel and arsenal, and a network of secret tunnels leading to the Fluwelengrot caves and former quarries.

**Replica of Lourdes:** Once fortified by eel on toast at the De la Ruine hotel, revisit Berkelstraat and turn left into Munstraat. After passing under Grendelpoort, the second medieval gate, glance back at the statue of a Virgin in a niche, a foretaste of the Lourdes grotto to come. The **Lourdesgrot**, situated on the Cauberg, was built as a replica of the French shrine and attracts sick pilgrims, par-

Thermae 2000 spa.

ticularly on the Feast of the Assumption. The Valkenburg hills are pitted with such caves, including reconstructions of modern coal mines and even of Roman catacombs.

The most incongruous caves, and hence the most typical of Valkenburg, are the **Gemeentegrot**, the city caves situated between the Grendelpoort and the Lourdes grotto. As with all Dutch caves, these are man-made but are exceptional in having been quarried since Roman times. The marlstone, a type of limestone, was worked here until recently. Now that it is prohibitively expensive, marlstone is restricted to restoration work and statuary.

The caves are vast, covering 275 acres (110 hectares) and 47 miles (75 km) of tunnels, of which about 3 miles (5 km) are open to the public. Given the constant temperature of 11°C (52°F), it is best to see the caves in cold weather when it feels warmer inside. This logic was followed by earlier visitors who amused themselves during the winter by carving and painting the caves. This winter pastime was made possible by the porous nature of the rock, filtering through oxygen, and by the softness of the underground marlstone. Once exposed to the air outside, the rock hardens rapidly. The oldest known sculptures and paintings inside the caves go back to the 15th century but the modern ones are no less intriguing.

While waiting for a guided tour by train or on foot, expect to be accosted by an enterprising sculptor who, working on the captive audience principle, is willing to carve anything on the spot. Typical commissions range from family crests for Belgian aristocrats to statuettes of beloved pets for homesick globe-trotting Canadians.

**History of art in stone:** The first section of the cave is covered with abstract art carved by students of Breda University. Many of these 1960s designs are primitive, even by prehistoric caveman standards. The 15th and 16th-century works of art include a sculpture of St George, an impressive lion rampant, and a painting of Knight Willem, a local hero. The best modern picture is of the Dutch royal family: different generations of royals attended sittings in this damp site between 1885 and 1950.

The strangest sculptures, however, are by a 19th-century blacksmith who, inspired by the prehistoric world, spent all his time underground, carving dinosaurs. One looks like the Loch Ness monster while another, a life-size megalosaurus, resembles a demented crocodile.

**Flying bomb factory:** The caves have played an important role in local history as well as local art. During World War II, 3,000 citizens hid inside, leaving their names, messages and occasionally paintings. The Germans eventually gained control of the caves and built a secret factory to produce flying bombs. Now largely ruined, the factory was dismantled by liberating American forces in September 1944.

As experienced cave-dwellers, it is hardly surprising that Valkenburgers applauded the government's decision to build a huge nuclear shelter here in 1979. In the event of an attack, this

Valkenburg caves.

network of galleries can house 15,000 people, the present population of Valkenburg. In theory, the mayor alone can press the button sealing the galleries, food stores, dormitories, 40 showers and 200 lavatories.

The chambers are dotted with black lamps, dusty crates, rusty generators and precise signs announcing "section for 78 people" or, more ominously, "lavatory for 75 people." The deepest section of the tunnel lies 235 ft (70 metres) below the hill; residents above occasionally complain of vibrations as a train passes underneath their home or garden. The train makes an oddly musical noise as it travels over the former sea bed: here and there lie animal fossils, proof of an earlier geological existence. In such porous caves, water collects in five eerie underground lakes. If the guide points to the luminous green waters where Julio Iglesias was filmed singing, expect to see Canadian and Belgian matrons swoon in ecstasy.

**To Maastricht:** From Valkenburg, a short route leads across the plains to **Maastricht,** the regional capital. Maastricht is the most Burgundian city in the Netherlands, a sophisticated, open-minded border town, far removed from the regimentation of the northern provinces. In his satirical novel, *In Nederland*, Cees Nooteboom decries the north as "an orderly human garden" but praises the south as a land of untamed cave-dwellers leading freer lives.

Of all the southern towns, Maastricht has the least trammelled spirit. As the oldest city in the Netherlands, Maastricht has been open to foreign influence from Roman traders, Charlemagne's soldiers and Burgundian merchants.

The result of such a cosmopolitan history is not, however, bland internationalism but a relaxed society, confident of its dialect and traditions. Unlike many parts of the Netherlands, Maastricht has retained its dialect, one so distinctive that locals half-jokingly claim not to speak Dutch. The city accepts three languages, three currencies and three cuisines, reflecting its position in the important economic triangle of

**2CV in the style of Mondriaan.**

Maastricht, Aachen and Liège. Germans regularly cross the border to visit art exhibitions, buy ceramics and enjoy the hearty French-Dutch cuisine; Belgian students appreciate the nightlife while the northern Dutch come for the hilly countryside and a chance to release their Calvinistic inhibitions.

Maastricht started out as a Roman garrison and trading post commanding an important river crossing. From there, all roads led to Cologne, London and Rome. The establishment of a 4th-century bishopric under St Servaas brought the town great prestige and wealth. However, its role as a frontier town resumed in 1204 when the Duke of Brabant shared power with the prince-bishops of Liège. For over 200 years, this dual authority was reflected in the city's geography: upstream from St Servaasbrug, the Bishop of Liège held sway while Brabant governed the area downstream of the bridge.

In the 15th century the city was absorbed by the Burgundian empire and became a great trading centre, matched by its flourishing reputation for *Maasland (Mosan)* art. At its apogee in the early 16th century, Maastricht rivalled Flemish Ghent and Antwerp. Thereafter, the city's fortunes fluctuated according to the effects of repeated Spanish and French invasions. From the successful Spanish siege in 1579 to the last French invasion in 1794, Maastrichters became used to adapting to foreign tastes.

**Rich heritage:** Architecturally, however, this foreign influence brought greater architectural diversity than in most Dutch cities. The city's Roman remains are still in evidence, as are its rings of medieval fortifications. The city also boasts Romanesque arches and murals, French Gothic churches, indigenous *Maasland* Renaissance architecture, onion towers imported from the East, and, in the 17th century, the Classical style favoured by northern Dutch Calvinists.

Under Louis XIV, the presence of an aristocratic French community encouraged the creation of Baroque residences.

**Maastricht, at the Vrijthof.**

Later in the 18th century, symmetry gave way to frenzied rococo lines. As for German influence, Maastricht's helm roofs are a direct copy of those in the Rhineland. The city's architecture continues to be inspired by the past, particularly in its saddle-back roofs. More imaginatively, the city's bold modern statues delight in holding a distorting mirror to the past. At best, as in Mari Andriessen's *Mestreechter Geis* (Spirit of Maastricht), there is both a past memory and the essence of the city today. Maastricht may be a result of dynastic bargaining but its spirit remains intact.

The centre of Maastricht is located on the west bank of the river Maas (Meuse) and stretches outwards towards the Belgian border. Most visitors, however, arrive in the Wijk district on the east bank so need to cross the river. Once in the historic heart, visitors can explore the city's three most appealing districts. The Centre, including the two major squares, churches and the town hall, is the civic and spiritual core. The Stok quarter, the Roman and medieval district, is bounded by St Servaasbrug to the north, the Maas to the east, the church of Onze Lieve Vrouwe to the south, and Wolvenstraat to the west. The Jeker quarter embraces the city's medieval fortifications, mills and almshouses. It lies just south of the Stok quarter and follows the course of the river Jeker to the south and Tongersestraat to the northwest.

**The Centre:** The heart of Maastricht is the **Vrijthof** but the first glimpse of so much space is a shock. Approached via the inward-looking alleys that typify old Maastricht, this light-filled square is apparently out of keeping with Maastricht's nature. The square's origins are disputed: built over the marshes of the river Jeker, the area was originally unsuitable for building but, by medieval times, was used as a military parade ground, an execution site and a pilgrims' meeting place. Every seven years, the Fair of the Holy Relics attracted pilgrims, craftsmen and traders to the lively square. Something of this chaotic

Left, Maas river, Maastricht. Right, the Vrijthof, heart of Maastricht.

spirit is recaptured in the Vrijthof at carnival time.

During carnival, festooned children, wizened old hags, costumed herring sellers and shivering harlequins congregate in the shadow of turreted St Servaaskerk. Top-hatted tuba-players join forces with a church band while the faint-hearted crawl into one of the cafés that line the square. The noise of the brass band is soon drowned by demands for beer, *jenever* and salted herrings, traditional carnival fare.

As ceremonial gunshots ring out over the Vrijthof, Maastrichters drown their neighbours in beer and generally cultivate their reputation for lunacy. Yet until the actual "season of lunacy" breaks forth on 11 November, Maastrichters must be content with memories of previous carnivals and with visits to **Momus**, the Carnival House on the Vrijthof, distinguished by the sculpted jester on the facade.

This, however, is just one side of the the *Stad aonde Maos*, the local expression for "the town on the Maas." On the far side of the square, two magnificent churches, **St Servaaskerk** and **St Janskerk** offer a counterbalance, or even a reproach, to café life. St Servaaskerk is one of the oldest churches in the Netherlands and a fitting tribute to its founder, the Armenian bishop who brought fame and fortune to Maastricht.

Although begun in the 11th century, the Romanesque church was enlarged and embellished over the next four centuries. The front facade has the grim impregnability of a fortified town but this forbidding impression is a feature of Romanesque *Maasland*, the style prevalent along the river Maas. The heavy apse is flanked by square, twin towers while, beyond, soars the Gothic spire of St Janskerk.

**Gothic fancy:** But St Servaas hides its lyrical side around the corner. The **Bergportaal**, a 13th-century sculpted doorway, is a *trompe-l'oeil* of inner arches. Each section is adorned with fabulous vegetation, mythological animals, Biblical scenes and hidden symbolism. Viewed from the sloping steps

**Apse of St Servaaskerk.**

beside this French High Gothic doorway, St Janskerk appears to offer a severe Protestant rebuke to the fanciful aspirations of St Servaas.

A side entrance leads to the interior of St Servaas which, once dark and mysterious, has been over-restored. The 10th-century crypt, the Gothic porch, chapels and cloisters are now more authentic than the clinical choir. Catholic Maastrichters ruefully say that the latter-day builders and restorers must have been Protestants.

The bright zig-zag patterns on the capitals are a preparation for the jewellery shop appearance of the **Schatkamer** (Treasury), housed in the former sacristy. This Aladdin's Cave glitters with silver, gold, copper and precious stones. Apart from a 12th-century cross encrusted with amethysts, treasures include a lovely statue of St Anne, a platter depicting St John's head on a plate, ivory reliquaries and illuminated manuscripts.

The undisputed masterpieces, however, are the 16th-century silver bust of St Servaas and a bejewelled 12th-century chest reliquary which is a high point of *Maasland* art. The craftsmanship shines through the richness of the decoration so that it is not the profusion of emeralds and sapphires that one admires but the workmanship itself.

Outside, in the dull daylight, awaits the faded 15th-century exterior of **St Janskerk**, a Protestant church since 1632. Surrounded by gabled houses and flower beds, the church is more remarkable for its location and exterior than for its stark interior. Apart from a Louis XVI pulpit, a few marble tombs and testaments to local notables, the church is a disappointment.

As the travel writer (and contributor to this guide) Derek Blyth has written: "The contrast between the rich, glittering interior of St Servaaskerk and the sparse, whitewashed interior of St Janskerk demonstrates the opposition of Catholicism and Protestantism."

Before leaving the Vrijthof in the direction of Dominikanerplein, notice the **Spanish Government House**, the 16th-century seat of the provincial governors. The exterior is adorned with Habsburg symbols, including the motto: *"Plus oultre"* (Still further). The interior contains an uninspired collection of French 18th-century furniture and indifferent paintings.

**Dominikanerplein**, the adjoining square, is a small, intimate affair, crowded with café tables. A sober Gothic church, the Dominikanerkerk, dominates the scene. The austerity and rigor of the exterior is a reminder that the Dominicans were renowned for their intellect – and for their unbending role in the Inquisition. The dark interior contains faded murals but the overall impression is sombre. Only at carnival does the church really come alive with children's displays of monsters and figures of fun. The Dominicans would not have approved.

**Italian Masters:** The stylish, modern **Bonnefanten Museum** at the ceramique site comprises a collection of works by Italian and Flemish Masters, and the country's finest collection of *Maasland* art. The Italian collection, covering work

Resting between the acts, Maastricht carnival.

between 1300 and 1550, includes some of the greatest Sienese, Florentine and Venetian artists, from Sano di Pietro to Filippo Lippi and Bellini. Domenico di Michelino's *Expulsion from Paradise* approaches the power of Masaccio's Florentine frescoes while Sano di Pietro's luminous *St Catherine* is envied by Sienese museum curators.

It is no accident that the Netherlands' ever-growing Italian collection is housed here: national museum policy confirms the view that, as the nation's most Latin city, both in spirit and in reality, Maastricht is the rightful home for such southern European works.

The same logic applies to the museum's collection of Flemish Masters, tactfully known as "South Netherlandish" painters.

Covering the period from 1480 to 1650, these paintings embrace the region of old Flanders, stretching from Bruges and Antwerp to Den Bosch and Maastricht. The collection includes Pieter Brueghel's animated *Wedding in front of a Farm* and the *Census at Beth-*

**In den ouden Vogelstruys café, Vrijthof.**

*lehem*, as well as local landscapes, still lifes and portraits. Although the Rijksmuseum's collection is far bigger, Maastricht's pre-17th-century works are comparable with those on display in the capital.

The pride of the collection is the *Maasland* art, created along the length of the river Maas from 1270 to 1550. Often known by its French term, *Mosan*, this important school is best represented in Maastricht and in Liège, just over the Belgian border.

*Maasland* art is rooted in craftsmanship, expressive details and is at its best in silver work and sculpture, especially wood carvings. Sadly, the School's frequent incorporation of jewels and precious metals means that many of the works have been stolen, dismantled or melted down, to realise their value, in former times.

However, enough precious works remain to confirm the thesis that "Maastricht doesn't feel part of the Dutch Golden Age – all that belongs to northerners – here, the Golden Age came

much earlier and had different influences." The highlights include a 15th-century wooden *Pietà*, a life-size 16th-century *Mary in Sorrow*, and a serene angel from the Liège School that looks graceful enough to fly away at any moment.

**Crowded markets:** From the Dominikanerplein, attractive alleys and shopping streets lead to the **Markt**, which vies with the Vrijthof as the city centre. On Wednesday and Friday mornings the Markt wins out because market days attract crowds of locals as well as day-trippers from Aachen and Liège. Even on other days, the bars are crowded, the herring stall is busy and cheery students cluster round *'t Mooswief*, a statue of a plump stallholder.

The centrepiece of the square is the **Stadhuis**, the severe 17th-century town hall built in Classical style by a pupil of Jacob van Campen. The interior is approached by two sets of stairs, a reminder of the time when the two city authorities literally went their own way. The entrance chamber radiates cool grav-

ity but the exuberant rococo ceiling adds a touch of fun. It is here that the Mayor hands over the keys of the city to the Carnival Prince. Once outside, you may be lucky enough to hear the carillon of 43 bells. In typical Maastrichter style, the 17th-century council decided to abandon solemn dirges in favour of spirited folk tunes; and happily the practice has continued.

**Local cooking:** From the Markt, **Grote Staat**, the main shopping street, leads to the Stok quarter, the heart of the medieval and Roman city. Grote Staat, like most other streets in this area, is well provided with bars, *pâtisseries* and cheese shops. There are frequent opportunities for local snacks, including a *Limburgse vlaai* (fruit flans) or *rommedou* cheese. Those who resist the aromas of asparagus omelette or trout often succumb to tempting displays of *pralines* and gingerbread delicacies. Any of these delights can be washed down with beer, which is the local drink, or with a bottle of rare Maastrichter wine. Although Napoleon closed down most **Maastricht restaurateurs.**

of the region's vineyards, three small ones still produce 25,000 bottles a year.

At the end of Grote Staat is the **Dinghuis**, a narrow Gothic building with a steep saddle-back roof. Although now the city's friendly tourist office, the building has barred ground-floor windows, a reminder of its Napoleonic past as a prison.

The compact Stok quarter is the oldest part of the city, dating back to Roman times. The northern boundary of the quarter is the Gothic **St Servaasbrug**, the oldest bridge in the Netherlands, built of grey Namur stone.

Alongside it, Mari Andriessen's *Mestreechter Geis* statue represents the spirit of Maastricht and guards the entrance to the old quarter.

**Fashionable quarter:** The buildings in the Stok quarter date from medieval times when the quarter was home to a series of markets. The street names still testify to the presence of grain, fish, meat and timber markets although **Stokstraat** itself acquired its name because of its proximity to the stocks and the city prison. In the 17th and 18th centuries the area became fashionable and a number of intricate facades and wandering gable stones remain from the period.

Number 26 is one of the finest, a masterpiece of *Maasland* Renaissance style, a jumbled vernacular which owes more to freely interpreted Gothic than to the symmetry of the Renaissance. Number 17, an ornate rococo facade decorated with scallop shells, was peeled off a town house on Grote Staat street: proof that wandering is not restricted to gable stones.

Leading off Stokstraat are a handful of charming medieval squares, including **Op de Thermen**, a chic square with a couple of boutiques and a half-timbered medieval tower. A statue of a decapitated *Amazon* gives a focus to the spot. The square lies on top of the old Roman baths, the outlines of which are traced on the pavement.

Just around the corner, in Plankstraat, is the **Derlon Museum**, housing a small Roman collection unearthed when the Derlon hotel was built. The remains, dating from the 2nd century, include a wall, gate, well, part of a temple to Jupiter and a section of a cobbled Roman road. Tired visitors can view the display from the comfort of the hotel's tea rooms.

In the 19th century, the fashionable centre moved to Markt and the Vrijthof, leaving Stokstraat to degenerate into a cholera-infested slum with open drains and equally open brothels. Since its sensitive restoration in the 1960s, however, the Stok quarter has become a perfect place for pottering. Apart from designer boutiques, the quarter rubs shoulders with friendly working-class bars and has more than its fair share of modern statues and gable stones. Swans, lions, cherubs, grapes, trees and even a sphinx are clues to the trades and professions of previous owners.

**Oldest church: Onze Lieve Vrouwe** (Church of Our Lady) grandly delimits the south-western end of the district. Placed on the site of a Roman temple, the Romanesque church is the oldest in the town. Built in the year 1000, this

**Maastricht's weekly market.**

fortified church, flanked by two circular turrets, is pierced by arrow slits for windows and topped by a squat helm roof. The forbidding western front owes more to German Rhineland architecture than to Flemish or Dutch styles.

Compared with St Servaas, the interior is infinitely more rewarding. The slight eeriness heightens the atmosphere created by the delicate sculpted capitals and an apse decorated with gauzy Romanesque frescoes. Christ is depicted against an azure backdrop with stars and angels beyond.

Onze Lieve Vrouwe's struggle for supremacy over St Servaas ended in failure: by the 15th century it was banned from displaying relics or selling indulgences. As a result, Onze Lieve Vrouwe today has a much smaller collection of treasure. Once back in the sunlight, call in at one of the many cafés on the shady square.

**Student quarter:** From the square, St Bernardusstraat leads south to the **Jeker quarter**, a gently tumbledown district of mill streams and ruined fortifica-
tions. This is also a popular area with Maastricht's large student population so bars and "alternative" shops are tucked into the side streets. Compared with the Stok quarter, this is a relatively large area, offering lesser known churches, mills and almshouses as well as quiet walks through parks or along the three tiers of ramparts.

**Helpoort** (Hell Gate), situated at the end of St Bernardusstraat, is a sinister steep-roofed gateway marking the medieval boundaries of the city. Beside it is a lone tower, the **Jekertoren**, once the territorial demarcation between Liège and Brabant. Beyond the Helpoort, a peaceful walk leads along the top of the city walls to Heksenstraat and the University quarter. The walk passes the city's main park, a mini zoo and various derelict towers.

The **river Jeker** lies on the far side of the Helpoort and is flanked by an old tower and a row of neat 17th-century cottages that once formed part of the city's enclosed Begijnhof. On the opposite bank of the river is the **Anker**, a

Restoration of Onze Lieve Vrouwe church.

water-driven paper mill that was built on the site of the former Pesthuis. This Plague House was designed to keep contagious plague victims safely out of harm's way – which meant outside the city walls.

Instead of tracing the city walls, however, visitors can follow the atmospheric alleys from the Helpoort to the Lange Gracht, a filled-in river enclosed by the high city walls. This leads to **Grote Looiersstraat**, which is one of the city's loveliest spots. Until the 16th century, it was a street of tanneries but later became a sought-after residential area. Although the canal is now filled in, many gracious 17th and 18th-century houses remain.

Several of these bear witness to the virtuous nature of 17th-century Dutch society: number 27 was once a Catholic almshouse while number 17 served as a Poor House. An admonitory motto remains over the door: "He who gives to the poor shall suffer no harm." En route, look out for the informal group of bronze figures sitting on a stone bench. The sculpture is dedicated to Fons Olterdissen, a local storyteller.

**Musical city:** Grote Looiersstraat leads to **De Bosquetplein** and the University quarter crushed between the arms of the Jeker. Steep Heksenstraat offers a mill and clear views over the fast-flowing river. On the wall is a stone carving of a witch – hence the name of the street.

Heksenstraat adjoins the Academy of Music so the air around here is often filled with conflicting snatches of classical music and jazz. Also on this stretch of the Jeker is the Huis op de Jeker, a perfectly preserved *Maasland* Renaissance house spanning the river. Nearby is the former Grey Sisters Convent, a poetic if dilapidated haunt now favoured by romantic couples in search of a little bit of privacy.

From here, most streets lead back to the centre via Platielstraat and **St Amorsplein**, a fashionable square overlooked by a reproving statue of the saint. On the square, the *Troubadour Chantant* is a lively student café which lives up to its name: bursting with performances of singing, dancing, cabaret and even poetic monologues. If this is too boisterous, walk back to the Vrijthof for open-air cafés, varied restaurants and summer bands.

**Choirs and organs:** Maastricht is a musical city, offering everything from classical music to cabaret, opera to musical puppet shows and, in October, a well-known jazz festival. Churches, including St Servaas, hold regular organ recitals. On Sunday mornings, the voices of the *Mestreechter Staar* male choir can be heard rehearsing in the *Staargebouw* concert hall.

Visitors with any energy left can visit the Casemates, the city's old fortifications, or explore the galleried St Pietersberg and Sonneberg caves just outside town. These are similar to the Valkenburg caves but had a more pronounced military function, used both in 17th-century sieges and during World War II. For those who have exhausted Maastricht, there are summer cruises down the river Maas to Liège in the neighbouring country of Belgium.

One of Maastricht's venerable bars.

# GELDERLAND

On a fine spring day, when the quiet river and fruit-growing area of Gelderland was looking its best, a small river boat moved slowly through the lush still countryside near the town of **Zaltbommel**. Suddenly the chimes of the town's carillon rang out, holding the boat's passengers transfixed.

One visitor, the composer Franz Liszt, found the high sweet tones particularly seductive, so much so that he asked to be put on land. He made his way to the town, met the carillon player and was introduced to his beautiful daughter, a gifted pianist. Liszt arranged for the girl to study in Paris and it was there she met the Impressionist painter Edouard Manet. The couple eventually went back to Zaltbommel to be married in the historic town hall.

Another visitor of note was Karl Marx, who, while staying with relatives, worked on his monumental *Das Kapital*. Then came the Philips brothers, who worked on the design for the first electric light bulbs, going on to found the famous Philips multinational company in Eindhoven. Zaltbommel seems to encourage the creative; it may have something to do with the pastoral beauty of the surrounding countryside and the heavy scent of fruit blossom. On the other hand, it could have been, and probably was, mere coincidence which drew so many famous names to the area.

The Province of Gelderland is a many-faceted area with much to do and see. It is the largest of the Netherlands' 12 provinces, and several hundred years ago was an independent duchy. Gelderland can be divided into three major areas. To the north of the Rhine is the area known as the Veluwe, with the **Hoge Veluwe National Park**, one of the country's most outstandingly beautiful nature conservation areas. Here you will also find the former royal hunting domain and miles of forests, rich in wildlife, including deer and boar. There are areas of wild heather, pines, heathland and vast sandy beaches along what was formerly the Zuiderzee.

At the centre of the Hoge Veluwe Park is the **Kröller Muller Museum**, one of the country's more attractive museums, with its glass-walled, light-filled rooms housing a magnificent collection of 278 of Vincent van Gogh's paintings and drawings. The collection also includes works by Mondrian, Van der Leck, Seurat, Redon, Braque, Picasso and Gris.

In the grounds of the museum is Europe's largest sculpture park. Try to pick a fine day and wander at will through beautifully kept gardens where you will come across the work of Rodin, Moore, Lupchitz, Tajiri, Volten, Visser, Paolozzi and Marini.

In a pond in the middle of this park you will find the beautiful white shape of Marta Pan's floating sculpture *Otterloo*. This just perceptively moving piece looks like a strange and silent copulation of two swans frozen in time – or, to be more mundane, like a meringue in an *île flottante*.

In this Rietveld-designed pantheon

you can stand under the sky and enjoy the work of Barbara Hepworth. Nature and Art is in peaceful harmony in this park, making you feel that life and the human race is worthwhile after all, especially when it brings forth artists who produce work like this.

A ticket to the Kröller Muller museum also entitles you to visit the gardens of the **St Hubertus hunting lodge**. The lodge, designed by Berlage, can be visited if you telephone first.

The second area of Gelderland is called the Achterhoek. This is the area between the river IJssel and the German border. It used to be a marshland area but land reclamation during the last few centuries has turned the landscape into fertile fields and meadows hemmed on all sides by woods. In the eastern section of the Achterhoek, and around the town of **Winterswijk**, you can still find marshland areas where rare plants and flowers flourish, including certain varieties of orchid.

To the north of Winterswijk there is another beautiful rural area with woodland streams and masses of wild flowers, perfect for long walks. This is also where you will find the famous "mosaic floor of the Netherlands", an area where ancient stones have risen to the surface. Geologists love this area and some of them have claimed to have found traces of dinosaurs.

The IJssel, which is a tributary of the river Rhine, forms the western border of the Achterhoek. This is a lovely meandering river with green banks and bays which are used for water sports such as windsurfing and swimming.

The old town of **Doesburg** in this area has a beautifully restored centre which is certainly well worth a visit. In addition, there is **Zutphen**, with its magnificent old city walls complete with lookout towers. Zutphen Church houses the "Librije", a medieval library which is unique in Europe.

The third main region of Gelderland is the river Area. This lies between the rivers Rhine and the Meuse. The river Waal, a wide tributary of the Rhine, cuts through to form the busiest shipping

**Zutphen.**

route in Western Europe, since the Waal is the most important link between the German Ruhr area and the North Sea. Along this route sail ships from Germany, Switzerland and Belgium.

This region is also watered by the delightful river Linge, which flows through the fruit vineyard district called the Betuwe. The Rhine and the Meuse are excellent areas for water sports, which the Dutch particularly enjoy. Some of the river meanders, now cut off from the main stream, have been turned into water sports resorts with marinas, beaches and camp sites.

A particularly attractive trip can be taken from **Zaltbommel**, either by bike or car, which runs along the top of the gently stepped dykes. Here you can enjoy wonderful views, with the river Linge on one side and orchards and picturesque houses actually built into the dykes on the other.

**The cities:** Gelderland has three main cities. One of them is **Arnhem,** the city which will always be associated with the Allied paratroopers who landed here in September 1944 in a brave attempt to invade Germany and end the war. The Battle of Arnhem actually took place around **Oosterbeek**, about 5 miles (8 km) west of Arnhem. Here, on the north bank of the Rhine, in the beautifully kept **Oosterbeek War Cemetery**, lie the bodies of the 1,748 Allied troops who tried to take the Arnhem Bridge.

The cemetery, located within shooting range of the battleplace, lies in a peaceful green clearing surrounded by trees, and is maintained by the staff of the War Graves Commission. Each year in September a touching memorial service is held, usually attended by about 3,000 people, including ex-servicemen and the widows, children and grandchildren of the dead. A special touch of poignancy is added by children from the local schools who place bunches of flowers on each grave during the ceremony.

**War museum:** The devastating story of the Battle of Arnhem can be traced at the **Airborne Museum**, in Oosterbeek, located in the former Hotel Hartenstein, which served as the former headquar-

**Gelderland orchard.**

# THE BATTLE OF ARNHEM

As the month of September 1944 began, the population of Nazi-occupied Holland waited in expectation and hope. The Allied armies of liberation were poised on the Dutch–German border and the German army was on the run. It seemed that the four-year nightmare of occupation was about to end.

But the Allied offensive from Normandy was beginning to run out of steam. The forward units had advanced so fast they had outstripped their supplies, and the soldiers were exhausted by three months of continuous fighting. German resistance on the Dutch border stiffened and the advance ground to a halt.

Something special was needed to break open the front and get things moving again. The strategy called Operation Market Garden was born.

British Field Marshal Montgomery's plan was simple in essence, but breathtakingly daring. Some 35,000 parachute and glider-borne troops of the 1st Allied Airborne Army would drop from the sky to capture each of the river, stream and canal bridges along a 60-mile (96-km) road running from the border through the cities of Eindhoven, Nijmegen and Arnhem.

Meanwhile, an armoured column would punch a hole in the German front then race along this road, over the captured bridges, and cross the Rhine at Arnhem, gateway to Hitler's Reich.

It was a high-stakes roll of the dice that could end the war by Christmas. The Airborne Commander, General Browning, thought the operation feasible, but told Montgomery: "We might be going a bridge too far."

Battle commenced on 17 September. Dutch civilians watched in amazement as thousands of parachutes blossomed in the daylight sky. Troops of the US 101st and 82nd Airborne Divisions quickly secured most of their objectives, but an important canal bridge near Eindhoven was blown up and the vital bridge over the river Waal at Nijmegen was strongly defended by the Germans. The ground assault, spearheaded by the Guards Armoured Division, and including the Dutch Princess Irene Brigade, was held up.

At the far end of what became known as "Hell's Highway", the British 1st Airborne Division, supported by the Polish 1st Parachute Brigade, ran into serious trouble right away. The British had played down Dutch Resistance reports that German armoured formations were in the Arnhem area, and the lightly equipped airborne troops came down virtually on top of the crack 2nd SS Panzer Corps and were shot even before hitting the ground.

The airborne force landed on heathland some 10 miles (16 km) west of Arnhem and from there the assault troops set out to walk to the bridge. Most of them never even got close to their target before they ran into SS tanks and artillery. The attack units were decimated and pushed out of the city. Only some 600 airborne troops, under Lt Colonel John Frost, fought their way to the Rhine bridge at Arnhem: This handful of "Red Devils" held the bridge for four days against overwhelming odds, when the entire 10,000-man force had been expected to hold it against light opposition for only two days. But eventually they were overcome.

Survivors held out at the nearby village of Oosterbeek for another week. The relief column from the south, which had faced heavy counter-attacks, arrived too late. Less than 2,000 men escaped back across the Rhine to Allied lines.

The Battle of Arnhem ended in defeat for the Allies. Much of Eindhoven, Nijmegen and Arnhem was destroyed in the fighting. Today, the cities are rebuilt and the only evidence of former conflict is in the peaceful military cemeteries that dot Hell's Highway. The Liberation Museum outside Nijmegen and the in 1994 completely renovated Airborne Museum at Oosterbeek contain mementoes of the fighting, and record the struggle of the soldiers who came from the sky.

They still come, those veterans, though fewer every year. At the rebuilt "bridge too far" in Arnhem, now called the John Frost Bridge, an occasional solitary figure wearing his red beret with pride can be seen looking down into the muddy water, remembering. ∎

ters of General Urquhart. From here he kept vigil during the harrowing days of the battle, and visitors can now follow the various stages of the bloody confrontation with the aid of large-scale dioramas, a spoken commentary and a slide and photographic display.

If you are visiting the original Arnhem Bridge, a detour to the **Historical Open Air Museum**, just on the outskirts of Arnhem, is also well worthwhile. The museum does not have any direct connection with the war years, but its reconstructed ancient farmhouses were used as temporary accommodation for the homeless after the plundering of Arnhem and Oosterbeek.

The Historical Open Air Museum is laid out in a pretty park where you can view the inside of authentic traditional Dutch farmhouses, some of them up to 300 years old and transported here stone by stone to prevent them being lost for ever. There are also some old watermills, traditional windmills and a collection of national costumes.

**Nijmegen** is the second city of Gelderland. Formerly called *Noviomagus*, it was granted city rights 1,900 years ago under the Roman emperor Trajan. Nijmegen is the oldest city in the Netherlands, and its Roman past is preserved at the **Nijmegen Museum**, where one can find hundreds of Roman artefacts. Nijmegen was a Frankish city in the early Middle Ages. Emperor Charlemagne built a palace on the Valkhof; this was later destroyed by the Normans but the city centre is still rich in imposing medieval buildings, relics of the city's former wealth and power.

Nijmegen is built on seven hills overlooking the river Waal. It is the main city of the Catholic south and many religious institutions are situated here, including the main Catholic University, with a student faculty of 15,000.

The third city of Gelderland is **Apeldoorn**, formerly a moorland village, now with a population of 140,000. Apeldoorn is known as the "Penpushers Paradise" because of its large population of civil servants; they arrived in the 1960s when many government offices

were relocated from Amsterdam and The Hague to Apeldoorn. The city has many lush green parks and, before the civil servants arrived, was a favourite retirement spot for wealthy pensioners who felt they would be in the best of company, near the Dutch royal family.

For one of the loveliest of the Dutch royal palaces, **Paleis Het Loo**, is located near Apeldoorn. Formerly much used by the Royal House of Orange Nassau, the last royal resident, Princess Margriet, sister of the present Queen Beatrix, moved out in 1975. Restoration work started the following year, and continued until 1984.

This beautiful 17th-century palace was first occupied by William III, Stadholder of the Netherlands and King of Great Britain, who built Het Loo between 1685 and 1692 as a country seat. In the 18th century William III's successors, the Stadholders William IV and V, used it frequently. In the 19th century Kings William I, II and III all lived there. For the Dutch, Het Loo is especially associated with Queen Wilhelmina, who retired to this country residence after her abdication in 1948 and lived here until her death in 1962.

Now the palace is a museum which traces the history of the House of Orange Nassau and its ties with the Netherlands, which have existed since 1403. The palace itself is the result of magnificent restoration work which entailed peeling off the white plaster facade to reveal the original brickwork, hidden since the 19th century when Napoleon I, installed by his brother Louis Napoleon as King of Holland in 1806, took over Het Loo and "renovated" it. Mercifully his idea of what constituted good taste proved reversible.

The gardens, too, have been restored to their former 17th-century glory, making them the best surviving example of the horticultural taste of the William and Mary period. The Royal Stables, built between 1906 and 1910, now house a collection of carriages, coaches, sledges and vintage cars which were used by members of the House of Orange Nassau and their household.

**Below**, Paleis Het Loo.
**Right**, Lelystad.

268

# FLEVOLAND

**M**uch of Flevoland consists of recently re claimed land and its modern towns are built on what was formerly the bottom of the Zuiderzee. The area is therefore the flattest part of the Netherlands, so if you are looking for gently hills and verdant valleys stay away from Flevoland. If you are after excellent water sports facilities, fresh green countryside and modern, well laid-out towns, then Flevoland is just the right place for you. And, if all this sounds too energetic, there are also miles of sandy beaches.

Reclamation of Flevoland began after World War II and was finally completed in 1986 when the newly created polders were officially declared the 12th province of the Netherlands. The area does not have historic towns but received a great deal of interest from archaeologists and historians during the reclamation process.

As the sea was gradually drained away, some fascinating and often gruesome secrets were revealed – the wrecks of wartime British Royal Air Force planes, sometimes with pathetic human remains still inside, and wrecks of Dutch 17th-century ships.

Almere was the province's fastest-growing new town, but although the ambitious town planners created a pleasing design, with modern

sculpture an integral part of the town's layout, it is not the success people had hoped it would be.

Almere's town hall is an interesting work from architect Cees Dam, built in 1984, with its round arena-like, marble-and-glass Councillors' Chamber. De Fantasie is a mixture of modern housing showing 10 different modern designs for the average family home. Bouw Rai is another modern housing area, with 225 homes built by 15 different architects.

Near Almere is the Oostvaardersplassen region, one of Europe's more important nature reserves, with its 15,000 acres (6,000 hectares) of wetlands – small lakes, reed marshland and woods. Half-wild horses and cattle have been imported to this area and there is an excellent protected natural bird sanctuary. There are even colonies of cormorants.

The town of Dronten is an excellent base for bicycle trips and walks in the surrounding nature areas and ideal for camping holidays, too.

Lelystad is the capital of the new province. The first inhabitants arrived, mainly from Amsterdam, in 1967, and since then the town has grown into an attractive place with many parks and – again – nearby nature areas.

Apart from some interesting housing developments, the main point of interest is the Informatie Centrum Nieuw Land, located in the west of the city, which explains the polder reclamation process using audio-visual presentations.

The province does have a few older areas, and Urk, formerly a small island, is an especially interesting place to visit. The 1,000-year-old fishing village is a very pretty, traditional place, where many of the older inhabitants still wear the local costume. The area is intensely Protestant, which means that everything stops on Sundays.

Nowadays the atmosphere has relaxed somewhat: once upon a time you would have had your craft stoned if you sailed into Urk harbour on Sunday. Urk remains a hard-working fishing village but has also become a yachting centre – it's the ideal centre for a waterways holiday.

The chain of lakes which separate the "old land" from the newly created polders are shallow and bordered by wide, reeded areas – excellent water for fish. The province has nine lakes and Flevoland fish are famous for their strength, making them a challenge to land for serious anglers, who take along special equipment according to the type of fish they hope to catch.

The Dutch take their fishing activities very seriously, and the fish are well looked after (until they reach the oven), the waters are clean and the lakes well stocked. Town lakes, in particular, are excellent for their sport: the Gooimeer is reached by crossing the Hollandse Brug and driving along the Gooimeerdijk towards the town of Almere. The Eemmeer is popular with eel fishermen who catch large specimens near the sluices that control the water level in the lake. ■

32 km/ 20 miles

FRISIAN ISLANDS

SCH

AMELAND

Nes

TERSCHELLING

Oosterend

Holwerd

West-Terschelling

North Sea

Oost-Vlieland

Waddenzee

St. Jacobiparochie

Stiens

VLIELAND

Leeuwarden

Harlingen

Franeker

De Cocksdorp

Dr

TEXEL

Sneek

Sneekermeer

Den Burg

Workum

Joure

Heegermeer

Heerenveen

Marsdiep

Den Helder

Balk

Tjeukemeer

De Kooi

Den Oever

Staveren

De Lemmer

Callantsoog

Middenmeer

IJsselmeer

Noordhollands Kanaal

Medemblik

Emmeloord

Blokzijl

Oude Niedorp

Enkhuizen

Bergen

Urk

Hoorn

Zwarte Meer

Egmond aan Zee

Alkmaar

Ketelmeer

Egmond a/d Hoef

De Rijp

Kampen

Egmond Binnen

Oosthuizen

Markerwaard

Dronten

Alkmaardermeer

Castricum

Purmerend

Lelystad

Beverwijk

Edam

OOSTELIJK

Zaandijk

Volendam

FLEVOLAND

Monickendam

IJmuiden

Zaandam

MARKEN

Broek-in-Waterland

Amsterdam

Nunspeet

Zandvoort

Haarlem

Durgerdam

ZUIDELIJK

Harderwijk

Muiden

Almere

FLEVOLAND

Naarden

NEDERLAND

Schiphol

Ouderkerk

(NETHERLANDS)

Aalsmeer

Abcoude

Bussum

Nordwijk aan Zee

HET GOOJ

Nijkerk

Vinkeveen

Baarn

Katwijk aan Zee

Nieuwkoopse

Loosdrechtse

Hilversum

plassen

plassen

Leiden

Amersfoort

Wassenaar

Alphen

a/d.Rijn

Utrecht

Scheveningen

Den Haag

(The Hague)

Ede

Delft

Amerongen

Gouda

Arnhem

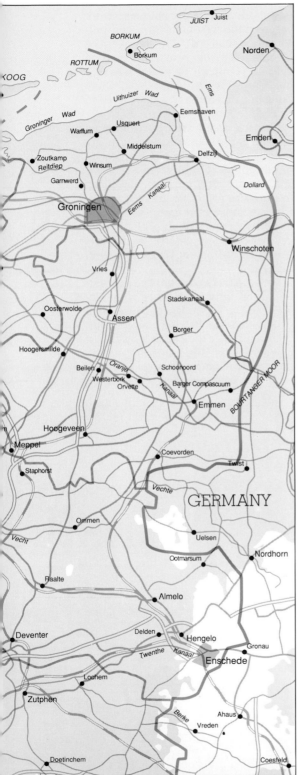

The IJsselmeer is a large inland lake to the north of Amsterdam created in 1932 by the enclosure of the Zuiderzee. This huge engineering project took five years to complete and involved the construction of the **Afsluitdijk**, a 20-mile (32-km) long dam. A road runs along the top of the dam to connect the village of Den Oever in Noord Holland province with the province of Friesland.

The Zuiderzee was gradually formed by flooding in the Middle Ages, eventually turning Lake Flevo into an inlet of the North Sea. From as early as the 13th century, the Dutch began to claw back the land that had been lost by constructing dykes and draining the enclosed areas to form polders. Large areas of Noord-Holland province have been reclaimed in this way. Polder is a very distinctive form of landscape which stands out clearly on the ANWB 1:100,000 maps. The outline of the drained lake is marked by an irregular canal (often called a *ringvaart*), which is lined with windmills used for pumping out the water. The reclaimed land has a distinctive grid pattern of roads and drainage ditches, and the towns built on it are laid out in straight streets.

Many of the old villages around the drained lakes were forced to transform themselves from fishing and whaling ports into inland market towns. In the landlocked town of **De Rijp**, it is surprising to come upon a local museum devoted to fishing and whaling. But in the Middle Ages De Rijp was a port on the western edge of a large lake called the Beemster. In 1612 this lake was drained by Jan Leeghwater to create a large polder, prompting the Italian ambassador, Trevisano, to observe: "It seems incredible, when one tells it, a land dry and ploughed that shortly before was a deep and large lake."

In financial terms this project was highly successful; Amsterdam merchants eagerly bought up the new land

**Preceding pages:** Hoorn harbour.

m country estates, while the remainder was turned into extremely fertile farmland. Encouraged by the profits realised, Leeghwater drained two other lakes to create the Wormer polder in 1622 and the Purmer polder in 1626. The economy of **Purmerend**, which lay between the three lakes, changed dramatically as a result. Like De Rijp, it had once been a fishing and whaling town, but in the 17th century it metamorphosed into a landlocked market town in the midst of fertile polders.

Most villages prospered immensely from the land reclamation schemes, and many celebrated their success by erecting imposing new town halls in the 17th century. Jan Leeghwater was kept busy designing new town halls for the communities of De Rijp, Graft and Jisp (one of the few towns in the area still standing on a lake).

The reclamation of the Zuiderzee was an even more ambitious project, drawn up in 1891 by Cornelis Lely (after whom the new town of Lelystad was named). After endless debate, the Afsluitdijk was finally built, and work began on the creation of three new polders in the southern part of the lake. The Noord-Oostpolder was reclaimed in 1937–42; Oostelijk Flevoland was won back from the sea in 1950–57, while Zuidelijk Flevoland was completed in 1959-68.

The reclamation of the IJsselmeer had enormous repercussions for the many fishing towns on its shores. A proposed fourth polder (the Markerwaard) was abandoned after strong local objections from Hoorn and other affected towns, which did not want to end up landlocked like Purmerend. The dyke that would have enclosed the Markerwaard now carries a road linking Enkhuizen with Lelystad.

**History on the waterfront:** The fascinating history of the Zuiderzee is vividly presented at the **Zuiderzee Museum** in **Enkhuizen**. Though the idea of a museum devoted to the Zuiderzee was first mooted in the 1930s, it was only in 1950 that the **Binnenmuseum** (indoor museum) was opened, and a further 33

**Enkhuizen harbour.**

years elapsed before a **Buitenmuseum** (open-air museum) was added. The Binnenmuseum is situated in a historic waterfront complex built in Dutch Renaissance style in 1625 as the combined home and warehouse of an Enkhuizen merchant. It was later acquired by the Enkhuizen Chamber of the United Dutch East Indies Company, and became known as the **Peperhuis** because of the lucrative trade in Indonesian pepper that was then carried on by the Company.

A large hall (Room 1) has been added to the museum to house an extensive collection of traditional Zuiderzee fishing boats and pleasure craft. It is interesting to see the different styles of boat building that developed in fishing towns only a short distance apart.

Local furniture (Rooms 4 and 7) also varied in style from one town to the next. But undoubtedly the greatest diversity is in local costume, as can be seen in the series of furnished rooms (13–15) illustrating the local styles of Terschelling Island, the industrial Zaanstreek, West-Friesland, Hinde-

loopen (famous for its hand-painted furniture), Marken Island, Urk Island (now incorporated into the Noord-Oost-polder), Spakenburg and Volendam.

The open-air museum stands nearby, but the only way to reach it is by boat, either from the pier near the railway station or from the car park at the beginning of the dyke road to Lelystad. The inconvenience of this arrangement is outweighed by the sheer excitement of arriving by boat, even though the style of the landing-craft boats built for the museum looks out of place alongside the traditional brown-sailed boats in Enkhuizen harbour.

The museum now has about 130 buildings rescued from numerous towns around the Zuiderzee. Some of the houses were shipped intact across the IJsselmeer, while a three-storey wooden cheese warehouse from Landsmeer (number LA1) was transported on two barges along the inland waterways of Noord-Holland. The layout of the museum is based on *buurtjes* (quarters) modelled on different towns. Interest-

**Jan Reid, specialist in restoration of old sailing ships.**

ingly, the town of origin of each building is indicated by the same system of letters as on fishing boats: MO for Monnickendam, MK for Marken, UK for Urk and ZK for Zoutkamp.

The first street of houses you come upon forms the Monnickendam quarter. You then turn a corner into the Zoutkamp *buurtje*, behind which is a cluster of houses forming the Urk quarter. The main canal divides the Edam quarter (with the museum shop) from the more rural Staveren quarter. The church and cemetery come from Den Oever, at the west end of the Afsluitdijk, and the street of houses beyond forms the Harderwijk *buurtje*. The harbour, modelled on that at Marken, has several old fishing boats moored on the quayside. There is even a small reconstructed corner of Amsterdam hidden behind the museum shop.

The labels attached to the houses tell some interesting details about the former occupants. Often families with numerous children inhabited the tiniest of houses, such as the couple with nine children who lived in the house from Venhuizen (number VH1).

Many houses are furnished in period style, and tea trays are set out in the front room as if the occupants might return at any moment. A grocery shop in the Harderwijk quarter sells delicious smoked sausage and boiled sweets, and the baker's shop on the main canal sells traditional cakes. Demonstrations of local trades are given in some of the buildings, such as the painter's shop and the steam laundry. The museum has three restaurants situated in historic buildings: one occupies the Landsmeer cheese warehouse, another has a tiled interior from a restaurant in Zandvoort, but perhaps the most attractive is the dyke house overlooking the harbour, with a gleaming tiled interior from Hindeloopen.

A whole day is needed to visit both parts of the Zuiderzee Museum, while ideally another day should be devoted to **Enkhuizen** itself. This modest, well-preserved town (population 15,700) was Holland's foremost herring port in the

**Fishing boats, Enkhuizen.**

17th century, hence the motif of three herrings on its coat of arms. The fishing industry is not quite dead yet, and a small fish auction still takes place on **Buitenhaven**.

**Dutch Mannerist style:** Many of the most striking buildings in Enkhuizen are designed in a jaunty Dutch Mannerist style, such as the **Munt** (Mint) of 1611 at Westerstraat No. 22, and the Weeshuis (Orphanage), built five years later, at Westerstraat No. 111. The most attractive spots are around the harbours, particularly the secluded promontory overlooking the backs of the houses on Bocht.

But there is another side to Enkhuizen which is often overlooked. To the north of Westerstraat is a peaceful, almost rural area known as the **Boerenhoek** (Farmers' Quarter), where you still come across a few large farmhouses overlooking urban canals.

In the summer months, a steam train runs from Hoorn railway station to the old port of Medemblik, 13 miles (21 km) northwest of Enkhuizen. The main attraction in this quiet town is the medieval **Kasteel Radboud**, named after the Frisian king who was defeated by the Franks in AD 689 at the Battle of Wijk bij Duurstede.

**Hoorn**, 12 miles (19 km) south, was one of the great seafaring towns of the Dutch Republic. Many famous mariners were born here, including Abel Tasman, who was the first European to reach Tasmania, and Jan Pietersz Coen, founder of the Dutch trading post of Batavia (now Jakarta). Another Hoornaar, Willem Schouten, named Cape Horn after his home town. Though the town is nowadays virtually a suburb of Amsterdam, many mementoes of its maritime history have survived.

The harbour quarter to the south of **Grote Oost** is particularly interesting to explore. The best view is from the promontory south of Binnenhaven looking towards the row of step-gabled merchants' houses on Veermanskade. A curious row of three 17th-century houses stands on nearby Slapershaven. Named the **Bossuhuizen** after a Spanish admiral, these are decorated with colourful

**Hoorn.**

friezes depicting a sea battle fought off the coast of Hoorn in 1573.

A magnificent Dutch Mannerist building overlooks the **Rode Steen**. Built in 1632 for the College of the States of West-Friesland (which comprised the seven towns of Alkmaar, Edam, Enkhuizen, Hoorn, Medemblik, Monnickendam and Purmerend), it now houses the **Westfries Museum**. This museum of local history is charged with the confidence of the Dutch Golden Age, and contains furniture, guild group portraits, ship models and period rooms.

Opposite, the **Waag** is a handsome weigh house in Dutch Classical style built in 1609. The streets to the north of Rode Steen contain other relics of Hoorn's glorious past, such as the **Statenpoort** at Nieuwstraat No. 23, the former lodgings of the representatives of States of West-Friesland built in Dutch Renaissance style in 1613. Opposite, in Muntstraat, is the Hoorn Chamber of the Dutch East Indies Company, completed in 1682.

**Monnickendam**, 10 miles (16 km)

northeast of Amsterdam, is an attractive little port with picturesque canals. The enticing smell of smoked eel wafts through the narrow lanes by the harbour, where several old smokehouses are situated. The best place for fish is the café-restaurant **Nieuw Stuttenburgh** on the harbour. The interior is filled with curiosities, including old mechanical musical instruments which are sometimes played to amuse the customers.

**Island bound:** From the harbour, boats ply in the summer months across the Gouwzee to **Marken**. Once an isolated and somewhat eccentric fishing community, Marken was first discovered by French tourists in the 19th century. The island lost some of its romantic appeal when a causeway was built linking it to the mainland in 1957. But the community has staunchly held on to its identity, and Marken's traditional black and green wooden houses on stilts still form a very attractive unity.

The island consists of several independent quarters built on mounds as a protection against flooding. The **Havenbuurt** (harbour quarter) and **Kerkbuurt** (church quarter) are quite crowded, but there are quiet corners to explore in the eastern part of the island. The lighthouse at the end of the island can be reached by a brisk walk along the old sea dyke. The café *De Taanderij* overlooking the harbour is a convivial place for lunch or coffee.

A boat service links Marken with the former fishing town of **Volendam**, a short distance north of Monnickendam. This town is unusual in these parts for its predominantly Catholic population. Unfortunately, the harbour front has been ruined by tourist shops, but there are still a few narrow canals behind the dyke worth exploring. In the 19th century, Romantic painters flocked to Volendam to paint the fisherfolk in traditional costumes. The Spaander Hotel where they stayed still stands, and on the walls of the café are paintings that were accepted by the owner as payment.

A few miles from Volendam in a pastoral setting is a charming hamlet, Broek-in-Waterland, with distinctive painted farmhouses.

**Left, traditional costume in Volendam. Right, Monnickendam.**

# OVERIJSSEL

Despite being a small, overpopulated country, there are still many provinces in the Netherlands where you can get away from it all. After all, the Dutch have to have somewhere to go when they want to get away from each other. One area with everything to offer is Overijssel – pronounce the "ij" in the middle to rhyme with "my" and you will be speaking like a native.

Overijssel lies between the German border and the IJsselmeer, and the province is divided into three regions. The **IJssel Delta**, in the west, is famous for its flora and fauna and is a popular area for water sports enthusiasts. In **Salland**, in the middle part of the province, you will find some of the very few hills to be found anywhere in the Netherlands. The third area, **Twente**, is the perfect spot for walking and exploring its many tiny and picturesque villages.

The West-Overijssel area, and the IJsselmeer (*meer* is Dutch for lake) is an ideal spot for water sports enthusiasts who also want to spend some time on land. The IJsselmeer offers sailing, swimming and windsurfing. The pretty, old waterways leading into the lake are ideal for canoeing or rowing.

One of the loveliest villages to visit in this area is **Giethoorn**. Not unexpectedly, it is called "the Venice of the North" because of its amazing network of waterways, and the punts that are used for transport. There the similarity ends. There is none of the terracotta-coloured, precariously beautiful lattice-work facades of the Venetians. Here you will find instead clean-lined and neat Dutch sugar-loaf houses, smooth thatched cottages and the occasional austerely elegant merchant's house.

If you enjoy looking at 17th and 18th-century patrician houses with a variety of gables, but do not necessarily want to swap the tranquillity of Overijssel for Amsterdam, then you should stop off at **Blokzijl**. This little fortified town was

**Left**, Giethoorn, the "Venice of the North".

founded in the 15th century by the merchants of the county of Holland. The town prospered in the 17th and 18th centuries thanks to shipping and commerce. The IJsselmeer was then the Zuiderzee and deep enough for large vessels to call in here, as well as doing business in Amsterdam.

On the Brouwersgracht is a 17th-century **Dutch Reformed Church**, in the form of a Greek cross and dating from 1609. The church, in the sober style of most Reformed churches in the Netherlands, is a little austere but worth a visit for the splendid pulpit dating from 1663 and magnificent chandeliers. A cleverly made model of a 17th-century merchantman, *The Seven Provinces*, is also on display. The nearby restaurant, called *Kaatje aan de Sluis* is one of the best in the Netherlands.

**Genemuiden**, which was awarded town status in 1245, is possibly the only town in the world with a street where pedestrians are forbidden to smoke. The small street is called the **Achterweg**, and smoking is forbidden because of the

fire risk to the old wooden buildings with their hay storage areas. The prohibition, and one of the signs telling you not to smoke, dates from 1899.

Most visitors like to stop off at the village of **Staphorst** to see the strict Reformed Church. The inhabitants visit the church every day and they wear traditional village costume, which is relentlessly black for men, but with a little intricately coloured relief for women and children. On Sundays, the inhabitants sit silently behind their lace curtains reading the Bible or glaring at passing tourists. They venture out of doors only to visit the church.

The town and environs has a strict religious culture of its own, which, to a modern observer, may seem highly oppressive. The inhabitants hardly ever smile and they keep themselves to themselves, often intermarrying to do so. One feels sorry for the children who look as if they could do with a trip to McDonald's, followed by a rampage through a toy shop.

The farmhouses in the village are

**Collecting reeds for thatching.**

certainly unique, adding a touch of colour to the place, but don't take a camera. Photography is frowned upon because Staphorsters see the camera as a dreaded symbol of modernity.

**Kampen** has the Netherlands' loveliest series of gables and facades. It reached its peak as an important trading town in the 16th century, when the most beautiful of the buildings were constructed. On the **Kroonmarkt** there is a graceful 15th-century Gothic Church of St Nicholas, and a 14th-century town hall. This building was partly devastated in 1543 but was rebuilt in the same decade. The town has a plethora of towers and gateways, rather like a Disneyland creation, making it well worth your while to take a leisurely stroll.

Dutch guide books will tell you that **Zwolle** is the economic and cultural centre of West-Overijssel, but they often omit to say that it is also a town of great architectural beauty. It is a fortified city with 17th-century bastions and a star-shaped moat. Most of the inner city's old buildings have been well restored and there are some beautiful old gateways, some dating from the 15th century. The city also has its supply of pleasing canals, and a pleasant way of seeing the city is by water-pedal boat.

In the Salland part of Overijssel, the delightful old town of **Deventer** has a 12th-century Berg church, again dedicated to St Nicholas. Deventer also has an interesting toy museum.

In Twente, near the German border, you will find the town of **Delden** and **Twickel Castle**. Both names sound like places in a children's storybook. The castle is not open to the public, but the gardens are (on Wednesdays and Saturdays). The castle is surrounded by a magnificent oak forest, the largest in Western Europe, and great for walkers.

Another very attractive town is **Ootmarsum**. Most of its 18th-century houses have now been restored and there is a magnificent 12th-century church. But prettiest of all is the surrounding countryside, with walks through quiet fields past wonderful 16th-century windmills.

**Kampen's town hall.**

# DRENTHE

Vincent van Gogh was perhaps Drenthe's greatest admirer. It was love at first sight for the artist, who spent his short life in pursuit of serenity and found it for a time in Drenthe.

More famous for his paintings of the sunflowers in the fields around Arles, Van Gogh was equally captivated by the peaceful bog and moorland countryside of this province, where he painted some of his best canvases. Once, while visiting Drenthe, he wrote: "What peace it would give me if I could settle permanently in this region." Instead of settling, he went to live in France where he died (1890) prematurely after a life of unrelenting poverty and misery.

A visit to the province will quickly reveal what appealed to Van Gogh. In an overpopulated, highly industrialised country Drenthe can still be described as sparsely populated. This very green province in the north-east of the Netherlands, bounded on the east by Germany, was once rather snootily regarded by the Dutch as being no more than a backward "Farmers' Republic".

Now its beautiful rustic villages, soft rolling green hills, quiet woodlands and maze of bicycle routes are jealously guarded from any encroaching industrial developer who may have designs on it. Land is at a premium in the Netherlands, which is approximately one-third the size of Ireland but with more than three times the population. The Dutch see Drenthe as their historical homeland, as indeed it is, for Drenthe existed before much of the Netherlands was reclaimed from the sea.

**The old country:** Drenthe was once an area of bog or fenland and archaeologists have managed to recover a vast number of amazingly well-preserved wooden artefacts and utensils from the peat bogs. The province also has all but one of the Netherlands' *hunebedden*; these prehistoric sepulchral mounds are built of boulders or megaliths and date to the 4th and 3rd centuries BC.

During more recent times Drenthe was bartered between various European conquerors. The Romans came first, and the province still has traces of their roadways; then came the Frankish kings and German emperors. Later, when all the southern and northern provinces were confederated in the Republic of Holland, Drenthe had no separate representation; it was seen as being a backwater not worth bothering about.

Local people did not mind much and continued to enjoy the serenity of their cosy rural life. When the area was officially declared a province in 1815 life continued exactly as before. Even today Drenthe has that peaceful forgotten-world quality that is increasingly difficult to find in more developed north European countries. Drenthe is where the Dutch now go when they really want to relax and get away from the crowds.

Many of the rural villages of the province still have their *brinken*, or village green, surrounded by beautiful traditional Dutch cottages, old-fashioned gardens and pristine cobbled streets, which echo to the clatter of clogs. While

**Left**, rural horse fair. **Right**, sheep graze safely in Drenthe.

not in Scandinavia, there is something about the villages of Drenthe which conjures up Hans Christian Andersen. You feel there could be inch worms measuring the marigolds, gingerbread houses in the woods and fairies at the bottom of every garden.

Not content with its collection of naturally preserved villages, Drenthe also has a "show" village called **Orvelte**, dubbed a "living monument of historically interesting rural architecture." Though this sounds pretty gruesome, it is quite unlike those so-called "native" villages in different parts of the world where the "natives" arrive in the morning, park their cars, and pretend to be honest-to-goodness villagers during the day while the cameras click. The nice thing is that people are actually born in Orvelte, go to school, marry and die there. Maybe if Van Gogh had stayed there, the Netherlands would have had to wait a little bit longer than 1990 to commemorate the 100th anniversary of his death.

Orvelte today is a largely thatched village of 17th- to 19th-century houses, farm buildings and craft workshops, with an informative visitor centre providing background on the development of the province as a whole.

Similar in concept are two other museums close by. The **Nationaal Veenpark**, near the town of Barger Compascuum to the east of Emmen, is a museum-village illustrating life in a mid-19th-century peat colony. Exhibitions explain the process of extracting peat, primarily for use as fuel, but also for the construction of turf-walled cottages. You can then take a trip on a peat barge to the nearby village.

The **Open Air Museum** (De Zeven Marken) at nearby Schoonoord brings the story of life in Drenthe forward by some 50 years, recalling, through its buildings and exhibitions, life at the turn of the 19th century.

Drenthe also has its sad reminder of World War II. The **Remembrance Centre**, at "Kamp Westerbork", is where thousands of Dutch Jews and others singled out by the Nazis spent their last

**Still waters.**

days on Dutch soil before being moved to death camps.

**Towns:** Drenthe has four main towns. The best known among speed fans would be **Assen**, where the famous TT Grand Prix Motorbike Race is held annually on the last Saturday in June.

But the town also has its antiquities; the most beautiful and historically interesting is the 13th-century convent of the Cistercian order of **Maria in Campis**. The convent was originally built on bogland in 1245 in an area called Coevorden near Assen. However, the nuns found the area too damp and the building was moved lock, stock, barrel and bricks to the town.

After the Reformation, in 1598, the convent was secularised and taken over by the district council. Today, in the grounds of the beautiful 13th-century abbey church, you will find the **Drents Museum**, which has a fine collection of Germanic, Roman and medieval artefacts, as well as several bodies of prehistoric bog people discovered well-preserved in their peat graves.

**Meppel** is one of the oldest towns in Drenthe with a 15th-century church and characterful houses. This pretty place with its 23,000 inhabitants is an important traffic junction for land and water transport. It has some of the area's best water sports facilities.

**Hoogeveen** used to be a busy inland harbour in the days when South Drenthe was the land of the peat colonies. Today it is an attractive place to shop. On Sunday mornings a drummer parades through the streets calling people to church. This custom dates back to the time when the inland waterway was the most important source of income for the town. The population wanted things to stay that way and so they followed the drummer to church every Sunday to enlist heavenly aid.

**Emmen** is the largest town in Drenthe. It has a lively market place where you can buy, amongst other things, comfortable wooden clogs for walking around the nearby **Noorder Dierenpark**, a zoo where animals roam freely in an open natural landscape.

*Drenthe's timeless byways.*

# GRONINGEN

The north of the Netherlands is where many visitors, perhaps disappointed by the crowded, ultra-modern south, finally find the Holland they've been looking for, the small villages and windmills and, yes, even the friendly locals who still wear their wooden shoes every day.

Groningen, like its neighbour Friesland, is *terp* country. These mounds – usually built on top of what was once a kind of communal rubbish heap – were used by the earliest inhabitants, the so-called "marsh Dutch", to raise their buildings above the floodplain.

Boating, biking or driving through the northern countryside, typically as flat as a billiard table and just as green, there are still many remaining terps that serve to elevate medieval churches and sometimes even whole villages. Eventually the northerners turned to dykes, in preference to mounds, building row after row of some of the biggest in the world as they painstakingly reclaimed the land from the sea – a process that is still going on and which can be witnessed today, especially in northern Groningen.

**Groningen** is the name of the capital as well as of the province. The city (population 170,000) is a busy commercial centre that regards itself as the Amsterdam of the North. One of the dominant aspects of Groningen is its youthful population – an estimated 20,000 students live in the city along with an equal number of other young people below the age of 30.

Aside from the university, the main industry is producing sugar from beet. The locals, with the typical northern Dutch wryness of humour, like to say Groningen's sugar production makes it "the sweetest town in Europe" – unless the wind from the factory is blowing the wrong way.

Groningen gets few foreign tourists, save for passing Scandinavians and Germans. Locals ruefully admit that many of those tourists are en route to Amsterdam, often to buy drugs, and the

drugs trade has now come to Groningen itself – another reason the city is called the Amsterdam of the North. But even for those not interested in drugs, Groningen's history and its lively pub scene are worth a visit.

The centre of Groningen, 1 mile (1.6 km) across, is encircled by a canal with further bisecting canals. One of the main landmarks is the **Martinikerk**, the imposing Gothic church that dominates the **Grote Markt**, one of the city's two main squares. The spire, 315-ft (95-metres) high, was destroyed and rebuilt several times, and is familiarly known as "The Old Grey Man." Late 16th-century wall paintings, discovered in 1924, decorate the interior.

Like most Dutch towns, Groningen was made for strolling, and there are plenty of interesting sights in almost every corner of the city. This was a rich town in the Golden Age, and there are several museums dedicated to shipping and the history of tobacco. The **Groninger Museum**, at its new waterfront location at Museumeiland 1, opposite the

train station, boasts one of Europe's finest collections of oriental ceramics, as well as a fine display of local paintings, including several works by Jan Wiegers and other members of the well-developed Groningen School of Expressionism. There are also interesting changing exhibitions throughout the year in this splendid contemporary museum building.

Groningen is a city that attracts many artists, because of its university and its vibrant intellectual life. Near the Groninger Museum, on the northwestern edge of the circle, a couple of small streets make up Groningen's red light district with the same type of carnal window displays as in the much larger red light district of Amsterdam.

Visitors walking through Groningen should keep an eye out for the many surviving *gasthuizen* and *hofjes*, almshouses built around pretty little courtyards providing accommodation for travellers, the elderly and the poor. It is permissible to peer in through the gates, but visitors should get permission be-

fore entering the courtyards to look around. Good examples can be found on Munnekeholm, Kerkstraat, Nieuwe Kerkhof and Visserstraat.

One of the locals' favourites is the **Pepergasthuis**, on Peperstraat, dating from the 15th century. It has been renovated but still provides low-rent homes for the elderly and poor. Also, keep an eye out for aptly named streets, such as Oude Kijk in 't Jatstraat ("I'm Just Looking into the Street" Street), named after the evil-eyed statue that has been staring down for centuries from high up on a building wall.

Alongside the "official" events and curricula of the university, Groningen's cultural scene centres on the bars, pubs and brown cafés. They are ubiquitous, especially around the central squares and on Peperstraat and Poelestraat. Pubs are generally open most of the day, and seem to serve as much coffee as alcohol. People set themselves up at the big wooden tables with newspapers, books, note pads and sketch books, leisurely sip their coffee and wait for friends – **Groningen city.**

new or old – to arrive so that the conversation can begin.

A good example is **Café Mulder**, Grote Kromme Elleboog No. 22. Like many other pubs in this artistic outpost, *Café Mulder* is decorated with local paintings, and it is not unusual to find the artist taking his or her ease beneath one. In fact, one of the best ways to get into conversation with the locals – and Groningers, as they call themselves, love to talk even in a country full of talkers – is to ask them about the paintings. Likely as not, they'll have an anecdote about the painter, the subject (some, like the fat blonde lady with the huge breasts, are as well known in Groningen as the artists) and how the painting came to hang where it does. The whole scene has a vaguely beatnik feel, and most visitors find it entirely comfortable.

The villages north of Groningen can be explored easily by car, but the quiet, flat roads and many picturesque canals are a magnet for many Dutch, especially southerners, with the time and energy to spend a few days biking, hiking or boating. Indeed, most of the weeklong or fortnight holidays taken by the Dutch involve some combination of all three – whether making their way by bike or canoe between camp sites, or travelling on a houseboat or covered pontoon and making daily jaunts out away from the canal into the countryside. Camp sites are plentiful, but many people prefer to knock on a farmer's door and ask for permission to pitch a tent. Sometimes they'll get breakfast into the bargain.

Several attractive villages, including **Oostum**, lie barely 2 miles (3 km) from central Groningen and are easily reached by bicycle, boat (which can be rented in Groningen) or on foot by lunchtime. Nearly every village has a little café that serves passable food in what looks like, and probably is, someone's sitting room. An especially popular stop for tea, coffee or a meal is *Café Hummingh*, a quaint little red-brick house in the even quainter village of **Garnwerd**, a mere 7 miles (11 km) from central Groningen.

Canoeists may want to start in **Winsum**, the "canoe village", where canoes

**Water and wheels.**

can be rented and the locals are eager to give their recommendations on where to go and what to see. Another village, **Warffum**, is a mecca for folk dancers, especially around the annual folkdancing festival in June.

In **Middelstum**, the village elders drink *jenever* (gin) in the local café at 10 a.m. and pick up their daily conversations – actually, it's probably the same conversation that's been going on for 20 years – without even saying hello to each other. Middelstum is also recommended for its restored bakery, where visitors can taste great bread straight from the oven.

Many village names rival those in rural England for originality: **Doodstil** means "Dead Quiet." Many locals say it's still as quiet – some say as boring – as when it earned its name.

Groningen has a number of "castles" and big old feudal houses, but perhaps the most interesting is **Menkamaborg**. This fortified manor house dates to the 15th century, was rebuilt in the late 17th century and has been restored and refurbished to the casual, functional elegance of the 18th century.

Six rooms are open to the public, including the ladies' drawing room (walls covered in damask silk), the state apartment (a pipe organ in a fake cabinet), the library (several good paintings and an ornate desk) and – always the most interesting in any restored landmark home – the kitchen, with its big black pots and huge open fireplace, flanked by all manner of antique cooking tools and utensils.

Groningen's swamps and mud flats lack the attraction of Friesland's natural sand beaches and cosy coves, but at the top of Groningen the **Lauwersmeer**, a huge man-enclosed lake, is another popular area for boating and it features some man-made bathing beaches. **Lauwersoog**, the port on the lake, is the place to catch the ferry for Schiermonnikoog, the wildest and most isolated of the Frisian Islands. Naturalists should not miss the famous environmental centre at Pieterburen not far away.

292

# FRIESLAND

Like their neighbours in Groningen, the other northernmost province of the Netherlands, the Frisians enjoy a lifestyle that is far removed in every way except miles – this is, after all, a very small country – from the sophistication and bustle of the southern parts of the Netherlands. This northern section of the country is where many of the Dutch go for their own holidays, and offers an attractive array of outdoor and cultural activities for holiday-makers, especially those with families.

Friesland was actually one of the earliest areas of human settlement in the Netherlands, and Iron Age remains have been found dating back to around 400 BC. Over the centuries the Frisians have won and lost battles with many different invaders. The Romans had a fairly typical experience. They found the Frisians much tougher to beat in battle than they had anticipated and, even after the Frisians were subdued, they refused to pay the taxes demanded by the Romans. In the end, the Romans left Friesland alone; it just wasn't worth the trouble involved.

**Distinct from the rest:** The overriding characteristic of the Frisians is their provincial chauvinism; they make it clear that they are a distinct people from the rest of the Dutch – the "Scotland" of the Netherlands, some call it. Their own language, Frisian, is spoken regularly by about half the province's 600,000 residents and used in many schools. Frisian is an odd language, with the same Germanic roots as Dutch but more similar to English. Many Frisians speak Frisian at home and Dutch at work or out in the shops, but the language most heard on the streets is "town Frisian", a corruption of both languages where the speaker might switch from Frisian to Dutch from sentence to sentence or even word to word, depending on which language offers a more vivid expression.

Frisians are proud that they are apparently descended from a different race to the rest of the Dutch. Instead of developing from people who emigrated from central Europe, their ethnic heritage is Scandinavian or possibly Celtic. Hitler was particularly keen on recruiting people from Friesland into his bureaucracy and army because the Frisians, with their height, strong features and blond hair, matched his concept of Aryan genetic supremacy.

Within the Netherlands, Frisians are sometimes the butt of jokes because of their supposed backwardness, their rural ways and their lack of modern sophistication. The people of neighbouring Groningen, perhaps to compensate for their own sense of inferiority at being so far – by Dutch standards – from the urban south, are particularly fond of telling Frisian jokes. The Frisians retaliate with the same jokes about their neighbours from Groningen.

It is easy to see why the jokes paint the northerners as country bumpkins, as hillbillies without hills. They do not speak with the same speed or use the same city slang as southerners. The north has more than its share of windmills that

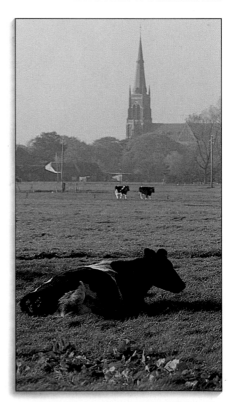

**Left**, bringing home the flock. **Right**, dreaming spire.

still work, including at least one that is actually used as a mill, to make flour. And while two million pairs of wooden shoes manufactured in the Netherlands each year are sold to tourists, most of the other one million are sold to people in Friesland (and Groningen) who wear them as everyday shoes, particularly in the wet. These aren't, of course, the big, sharp-pointed clodhoppers sold at the souvenir shops; instead, they are light and strong, made out of poplar, usually painted black, with some leather trim – and they last for years. Visitors seldom notice that the man riding by on a bike or the woman shopping with her children is wearing wooden shoes unless it's pointed out.

One thing visitors, even other Dutch, are careful not to joke about is the issue of Frisian independence. There is a strong, long-time movement in the province to declare independence and secede from the rest of the Netherlands, and it would be unwise to mock the movement in the presence of its most ardent supporters, most of whom refuse to speak anything except Frisian but nonetheless understand both Dutch and English perfectly.

Most Frisians, of course, realise that secession is a political and economic unreality and have no interest in its actual realisation, but that, perhaps, helps them lend their casual support to the notion of Frisian independence. The VVV has entered into the spirit to the extent of issuing visitors a "Friesland Passport" which serves as a primer on provincial culture in several languages and offers discounts for a number of tourist attractions ranging from museums to restaurants to bowling alleys.

**Sports fans:** Perhaps even more than other Dutch, the northerners love sports. Cycling, camping, canoeing, sailing and hiking are all typical weekend pursuits. In winter, even the smallest villages have a field, especially flooded so that the locals can skate with each other after work. In the summer, many communities enjoy that form of pole vaulting peculiar to the Dutch – the vaulters plant their pole in the middle of a canal and

**The moated village of Sloten.**

leap to the other side, with the possibility of a hilarious mid-canal landing.

In the coldest winters, when the canals all freeze solid (it happens, on average, once every five or six years), Friesland has its Elfstedentocht, or "11-cities race", so named because skaters must traverse a 125-mile loop of frozen canals between the 11 cities of the province. Twenty thousand people or more, some wearing the traditional wooden skates still popular in the north, may be gathered at the early-morning starting line for this punishing race – but only a fraction of them will finish it hours later, in darkness, sore and tired and sometimes frostbitten. When Crown Prince Willem-Alexander skated under an assumed name in 1985 and managed to finish the race (though well behind the winner), his public popularity soared.

**First stop:** The ancient fishing village of **Harlingen**, on the Waddenzee (variously translated as "mud sea" or "salt flat sea"), is the first stop for many who enter Friesland after driving up from Amsterdam across the Afsluitdijk, the 20-mile (32-km) long, 100-yard (90-metre) wide dyke built to enclose the Zuiderzee, now the IJsselmeer. With a population of 16,000, nearly all of central Harlingen – the part along the docks – is a national conservation area because of the exquisitely gabled 16th, 17th and 18th-century homes and buildings, including a number of old East Indies Company warehouses.

In the dock area is the near-obligatory statute of the little Dutch boy who allegedly stuck his finger in the dyke to save the sea wall from collapsing. In the interests of civic pride and tourism, many Dutch seafront communities today claim the legendary boy as their own little hero.

Leading away from the harbour, the main street, **Voorstraat**, has many pleasant little shops. It is especially attractive on Saturday market days, when colourful stalls and booths are run by people in local costume.

Harlingen is still a working seaport, and in strolling along the harbour you can watch a variety of boats coming and going or look over the dockside to the

The Elfstedentocht (11-cities race).

fishing trawlers and small shipping steamers that carry cargoes to Germany and other Dutch ports. Harlingen harbour is also the place to get ferries that run up to four times a day, in season, to two of the most popular Wadden Islands, Vlieland and Terschelling.

The ships that always draw the most attention, however, are the antique sailboats, many of them a century or more old. Many of them were designed specifically for sailing the peculiar waters of the Waddenzee, the shallow, and often wild, corner of the North Sea that stretches from Friesland to Germany and Denmark.

The Waddenzee is no more than 3 ft (1 metre) deep in many places, and rarely more than 10 ft (3 metres) deep in any one place, even at high tide. Consequently, when the tides go out, the salt flats and mud that gave the sea its name are revealed. The Fries, who seem to be able to make a sport out of almost any activity, subsequently invented *wadlopen*, or "mudwalking".

The first organised walk on the sea-bed was held in 1963. Since then, hundreds of thousands of people – always led by registered guides – have joined walks from the mainland to one of the outlying inhabited Wadden Islands a few miles away, or to one of the larger uninhabited salt flats. Some mudwalkers compare it to mountain climbing, given the amount of exertion required to make your way through the mud.

The walks are particularly popular among birdwatchers because of the many species, some quite rare outside Friesland, that feed on the exposed seabed. Besides the bird life, the Waddenzee serves as something of a nursery for many different types of fish that are spawned in the North Sea and then seek out the slightly warmer waters of the shallow Waddenzee until they mature and head back out to the bigger sea.

*Wadlopen* trips, usually undertaken only in the summer months, became very popular in the late 1960s and early 1970s, but Friesland officials have since severely restricted the number of walks for two reasons: to reduce the number of

**Friesland harbour.**

drownings among mudwalkers who set off on their own, without guides, and in order to avoid damaging the delicate Waddenzee environment.

Because of the restrictions and the limited number of groups licensed to sponsor *wadlopen* outings, visitors who are interested should try to make arrangements in advance. Various groups offer walks according to variable schedules from different seaside towns, so it is best to find the contacts through local vvv offices in Friesland.

The depth of the Waddenzee, or rather the lack of depth, makes navigation tricky, even for the antique sailboats with their remarkably shallow draft. The boats are all but flat-bottomed and, instead of keels, they have large wooden "swords" amidships to both port and starboard; the swords are lowered and raised by means of back-breaking cranks on the deck.

Antique sailboats are especially popular among Dutch and German school organisations or groups of families that hire them, along with a captain and mate, for a week or a weekend. With full galley facilities on board and berths for up to three dozen, the ships ply the Waddenzee, hopping from island to island, beach to beach, all the way to Germany, mooring in the tiny island villages or simply dropping anchor on an inviting sandbar.

One of the attractions of such a trip is that, while the captain and mate can sail their boats themselves in any weather, the passengers are encouraged to learn and take up as much of the running of the boat as they want. Various individuals and groups offer sailing packages on antique vessels, but one of the largest and best (open all year round) is a 32-boat co-operative supervised by an economics teacher, Adrian Bakker, and his wife, Therese. (For information, write to: Rederij Vooruit Holland, Geeuwkade 9, 8651 AA IJlst, or tel: 0515-53 14 85.)

**Water sports capital:** There are many small villages in Friesland, and visitors who wander by car, bicycle, canal boat or on foot are rarely disappointed. For those interested in water sports, **Sneek** (pronounced *snake*) is a must; this town is the water sports capital of Friesland, a province whose numerous seaports and lakes make it the water sports playground of the Netherlands.

Some non-boating places are appealing, too. **Franeker**, 6 miles (10 km) inland from Harlingen, was an influential university and market centre in the Middle Ages. It is little more than a pleasant small town today, though its elaborately decorated 1594 Dutch Renaissance town hall and several museums still draw many tourists.

Across from the town hall, one of the most popular museums – a home-made planetarium – is truly unique. It was built by Eise Eisenga, a wool-comber and amateur scientist, in the sitting room of his family home between 1774 and 1781 in an attempt to quell local fears that a collision among the planets would lead to the Earth's destruction. To help convince the local burghers that devastation was not imminent, Eisenga made sure to put Franeker at the centre of the universe.

Now the oldest planetarium in the world, Eisenga invited local people in to

Wadlopen outing.

# THE ISLANDS OF FRIESLAND

The Wadden Islands, separating off the Waddenzee from the North Sea, are a natural wonder treasured by people who look for a certain kind of holiday: somewhere definitely out-of-the-way, a bit hard to get to, with plenty of outdoor activities and lots of opportunity for comfortable cosiness.

The islands represent the remains of an arching natural dyke that lay between the North Sea and a huge ancient marshland. That marshland is now the Waddenzee, flooded by the gradual raising of the sea level that took place when the Ice Age glaciers melted. Because of their unique physical history, and the shallowness of the Waddenzee, all the islands are renowned as havens for feeding and migratory birds – and consequently for birdwatchers.

The largest and southernmost island, Texel, is the most accessible because it is reached by a short ferry ride, not from Friesland but from Den Helder, on the other side of the IJsselmeer. Texel is the most developed island, and is consequently quite crowded in summer – especially with cars, which are either rare or legally banned from the other Wadden islands.

The next island, Vlieland, is accessible by ferry (90 minutes, depending on the weather) from Harlingen, the busy little port where chartered antique sailboats and commercial ships nestle up to the foot of the historic town centre. Vlieland (population 1,100) is quieter and less popular year-round than Texel – partly because visitors complain that there is relatively little to see or do. Except, that is, for birdwatchers and naturists: Vlieland claims to have 96 species of birds, along with the longest nudist beach in Europe.

The two northernmost islands, Ameland (population 3,000) and Schiermonnikoog (population 925), are too quiet for all but the most world-weary, privacy-seeking Dutch. Ameland's ferry is from Holwerd, a village about 25 miles (40 km) up the coast from Harlingen. The VVV tourist office lists, as one of Ameland's top entertainments, watching

the horses that are used to pull the lifeboat into the sea being trained.

Schiermonnikoog, the most isolated island, is accessible only from the tiny port of Laeuwersoog in northern Groningen, but travellers who can use the words "bleak" and "beauty" in the same breath often find it worth the effort to get there. For those who appreciate wild flowers and plant life, this island boasts 50 percent of the species of flora native to Europe, including some very rare varieties of orchids that are otherwise extinct in the wild.

The second-largest of the five main Wadden islands, Terschelling (population 3,000), the one in the middle, is a good compromise between crowds and desolation. Terschelling was important as a port in the 16th to 18th centuries, and was a centre of the Dutch whaling industry.

The harbour of the main town, West-Terschelling, is guarded by the 16th-century Brandaris lighthouse, the largest in the Netherlands. The town itself is known for its little 17th-century gabled houses. There is a small cultural museum on Commandeurstraat and a number of unpretentious family restaurants both in West-Terschelling and in nearby villages. Cranberries and their by-products, from wine to tarts, are a local speciality.

Terschelling offers exhilarating cycling on paved or dirt-packed paths through spectacular scenery, ranging from grassy dunes to mature forests whose tall trees block out the sun, emit a sweet scent and obligingly scatter pine cones for children to collect (bikes with child seats can be hired on the harbour front).

The vast North Sea beaches of Terschelling are backed by dunes that are constantly being formed and re-formed by the wind and currents. Considerable areas have been planted with grass and breakwaters have been constructed to hold the dunes in place, keeping them from shifting eastward under the constant battering of wind and waves from the west. Terschelling, like the other Wadden islands, is in effect a laboratory of wind and sea and land. For anyone who travels as far north as Friesland, it is a crime against the ethics of good travelling not to take a ferry out to one of these beautifully wild islands. ∎

his house to show them how the solar system worked – even though Uranus is missing because it hadn't been discovered then. In over 200 years, the timing of the planetarium's movements – hours, days, weeks, months, seasons and years – has been readjusted only once, and was off by only two degrees.

Visitors can explore the whole house – not just the sitting room but also the attic which houses the mechanism, made of oak hoops and 10,000 hand-forged nails, that Eisenga used to create his model on a scale of one millimetre to one million kilometres. It is an inspiration to anyone who has ever tinkered with an invention in a workshop, and fascinating to everyone else. The house features other globes, maps, models and timepieces, and is refurbished to show how a tradesman in 18th-century Friesland might have lived.

**Last resort:** A few more miles inland is **Leeuwarden** (population 85,000), the capital of Friesland. The city is pleasant enough and the people are charmingly self-deprecating, despite their pride in their province and its independent history. People will say, for example, that yes, of course, Leeuwarden gets tourists – when it's raining and all the people sailing from Harlingen or biking or camping elsewhere in Friesland head for the town to dry out.

In truth, there are several museums, a number of decent restaurants and an active pub scene. For example, on the **Oude Doelesteeg**, a small alley off the main shopping street, Nieuwestad, are several different inviting bars and brown cafés, ranging from one that draws a billiards crowd to another that pulses with heavy-metal rock music to yet another (*Bar de Wipsluip*) that is small, has candles on the tables, red roses on the bar and quiet jazz.

The VVV office adjacent to Leeuwarden station offers a free pink brochure setting out a recommended walk through the town that points out the buildings and provides interesting background on the town. Of particular interest is the childhood **home of Mata Hari** (Margaretha Geertruida Zelle), the re-

**Left, mudwalking, official guide. Below, Franeker planetarium.**

nowned dancer, supposed temptress and purported World War I spy who was born in Leeuwarden. She has been adopted as a heroine of modern tourism despite a shadowy career that ended when she was shot by the French. Her former home now houses the Frisian Literary Museum.

Also noteworthy in Leeuwarden are the small statues scattered on various corners, and two of the museums: the **Frisian Museum**, which displays antiquities and costumes and provides a comprehensive history of Friesland; and the **Resistance Museum**, comprising a series of walk-through exhibits dedicated to the Dutch role in World War II. At the Resistance Museum, for a small fee, visitors get a headset and a 25-minute cassette that relates the hardships of Friesland under German occupation, when there were 30,000 deaths and a famine in the final winter of the war that forced people to eat anything they could find, including tulip bulbs, just to survive.

Leeuwarden has a bare handful of cheap hotels. For those who can afford it, the VVV usually recommends the 80-room, modern Oranje Hotel across from the station. There are many more family-style restaurants, however, and a few places for the Leeuwarden trendy set, many of whom make a living as artists and designers.

One of the most popular eating places in the town is **Het Leven** (The Life) situated on Druifstreek. This is a large restaurant, by Frisian standards, with plain wooden tables that easily accommodate the noisy group meals so loved by the Dutch in general and Frisians in particular. People who enter alone usually end up dining together. The main courses are typically Dutch: hearty meat or vegetarian main courses with herring or baked cheese to start and plenty of cold beer or French table wine, all at reasonable prices. Another place in Leeuwarden, that serves the same type of food and draws the same sort of lively crowd, is *Café Silberman*, next door to Het Leven.

**Right**, out fishing. **Overpage**, windmill keeper.

# INSIGHT GUIDES

# TRAVEL TIPS

# The World of Insight Guides

**400 books in three complementary series cover every major destination in every continent.**

### Insight Guides

Alaska
Alsace
Amazon Wildlife
American Southwest
Amsterdam
Argentina
Atlanta
Athens
Australia
Austria
Bahamas
Bali
Baltic States
Bangkok
Barbados
Barcelona
Bay of Naples
Beijing
Belgium
Belize
Berlin
Bermuda
Boston
Brazil
Brittany
Brussels
Budapest
Buenos Aires
Burgundy
Burma (Myanmar)
Cairo
Calcutta
California
Canada
Caribbean
Catalonia
Channel Islands
Chicago
Chile
China
Cologne
Continental Europe
Corsica
Costa Rica
Crete
Crossing America
Cuba
Cyprus
Czech & Slovak Republics
Delhi, Jaipur, Agra
Denmark
Dresden
Dublin
Düsseldorf
East African Wildlife
East Asia
Eastern Europe
Ecuador
Edinburgh
Egypt
Finland
Florence
Florida
France
Frankfurt
French Riviera
Gambia & Senegal
Germany
Glasgow

Gran Canaria
Great Barrier Reef
Great Britain
Greece
Greek Islands
Hamburg
Hawaii
Hong Kong
Hungary
Iceland
India
India's Western Himalaya
Indian Wildlife
Indonesia
Ireland
Israel
Istanbul
Italy
Jamaica
Japan
Java
Jerusalem
Jordan
Kathmandu
Kenya
Korea
Lisbon
Loire Valley
London
Los Angeles
Madeira
Madrid
Malaysia
Mallorca & Ibiza
Malta
Marine Life in the South China Sea
Melbourne
Mexico
Mexico City
Miami
Montreal
Morocco
Moscow
Munich
Namibia
Native America
Nepal
Netherlands
New England
New Orleans
New York City
New York State
New Zealand
Nile
Normandy
Northern California
Northern Spain
Norway
Oman & the UAE
Oxford
Old South
Pacific Northwest
Pakistan
Paris
Peru
Philadelphia
Philippines
Poland
Portugal
Prague

Provence
Puerto Rico
Rajasthan
Rhine
Rio de Janeiro
Rockies
Rome
Russia
St Petersburg
San Francisco
Sardinia
Scotland
Seattle
Sicily
Singapore
South Africa
South America
South Asia
South India
South Tyrol
Southeast Asia
Southeast Asia Wildlife
Southern California
Southern Spain
Spain
Sri Lanka
Sweden
Switzerland
Sydney
Taiwan
Tenerife
Texas
Thailand
Tokyo
Trinidad & Tobago
Tunisia
Turkey
Turkish Coast
Tuscany
Umbria
US National Parks East
US National Parks West
Vancouver
Venezuela
Venice
Vienna
Vietnam
Wales
Washington DC
Waterways of Europe
Wild West
Yemen

### Insight Pocket Guides

Aegean Islands★
Algarve★
Alsace
Amsterdam★
Athens★
Atlanta★
Bahamas★
Baja Peninsula★
Bali★
Bali Bird Walks
Bangkok★
Barbados★
Barcelona★
Bavaria★
Beijing★
Berlin★

Bermuda★
Bhutan★
Boston★
British Columbia★
Brittany★
Brussels★
Budapest & Surroundings★
Canton★
Chiang Mai★
Chicago★
Corsica★
Costa Blanca★
Costa Brava★
Costa del Sol/Marbella★
Costa Rica★
Crete★
Denmark★
Fiji★
Florence★
Florida★
Florida Keys★
French Riviera★
Gran Canaria★
Hawaii★
Hong Kong★
Hungary
Ibiza★
Ireland★
Ireland's Southwest★
Israel★
Istanbul★
Jakarta★
Jamaica★
Kathmandu Bikes & Hikes★
Kenya★
Kuala Lumpur★
Lisbon★
Loire Valley★
London★
Macau★
Madrid★
Malacca
Maldives
Mallorca★
Malta★
Mexico City★
Miami★
Milan★
Montreal★
Morocco★
Moscow
Munich★
Nepal★
New Delhi
New Orleans★
New York City★
New Zealand★
Northern California★
Oslo/Bergen★
Paris★
Penang★
Phuket★
Prague★
Provence★
Puerto Rico★
Quebec★
Rhodes★
Rome★
Sabah★

St Petersburg★
San Francisco★
Sardinia
Scotland★
Seville★
Seychelles★
Sicily★
Sikkim
Singapore★
Southeast England
Southern California★
Southern Spain★
Sri Lanka★
Sydney★
Tenerife★
Thailand★
Tibet★
Toronto★
Tunisia★
Turkish Coast★
Tuscany★
Venice★
Vienna★
Vietnam★
Yogyakarta
Yucatan Peninsula★

**★ = Insight Pocket Guides with Pull out Maps**

### Insight Compact Guides

Algarve
Amsterdam
Bahamas
Bali
Bangkok
Barbados
Barcelona
Beijing
Belgium
Berlin
Brittany
Brussels
Budapest
Burgundy
Copenhagen
Costa Brava
Costa Rica
Crete
Cyprus
Czech Republic
Denmark
Dominican Republic
Dublin
Egypt
Finland
Florence
Gran Canaria
Greece
Holland
Hong Kong
Ireland
Israel
Italian Lakes
Italian Riviera
Jamaica
Jerusalem
Lisbon
Madeira
Mallorca
Malta

Milan
Moscow
Munich
Normandy
Norway
Paris
Poland
Portugal
Prague
Provence
Rhodes
Rome
St Petersburg
Salzburg
Singapore
Switzerland
Sydney
Tenerife
Thailand
Turkey
Turkish Coast
Tuscany
UK regional titles:
  Bath & Surroundings
  Cambridge & East Anglia
  Cornwall
  Cotswolds
  Devon & Exmoor
  Edinburgh
  Lake District
  London
  New Forest
  North York Moors
  Northumbria
  Oxford
  Peak District
  Scotland
  Scottish Highlands
  Shakespeare Country
  Snowdonia
  South Downs
  York
  Yorkshire Dales
USA regional titles:
  Boston
  Cape Cod
  Chicago
  Florida
  Florida Keys
  Hawaii: Maui
  Hawaii: Oahu
  Las Vegas
  Los Angeles
  Martha's Vineyard & Nantucket
  New York
  San Francisco
  Washington D.C.
Venice
Vienna
West of Ireland

# CONTENTS

# Getting Acquainted

## The Place

**Area:** 33,950 sq km (13,000 sq miles)
**Area Below Sea Level:** one-fifth
**Population:** 16,000,000
**Capital:** Amsterdam
**Seat of Government:** The Hague
**Time Zone:** GMT + 1 hour in winter, + 2 hours in summer (last weekend in March to last weekend in September)
**Language:** Dutch
**Religion:** Roman Catholic (40 percent), Protestant (30 percent)
**Currency:** guilder (gulden), written NLG, sometimes called florin (f), made up of 100 cents. There are about 2.5 guilders to £1, 1.7 to $1.
**Weights and Measures:** Metric
**Electricity:** 220 volts AC, round two-pin plugs
**National Airline:** KLM Royal Dutch Airlines
**International Dialling Code:** 31 + 20 (Amsterdam), 70 (The Hague), 10 (Rotterdam)

## Government & Economy

The provinces of The Netherlands were united as an independent state in 1648, and the constitution was approved in 1848. The Head of State, Queen Beatrix, lives with her husband, Prince Claus and their three sons outside The Hague.

From its position on the North Sea at the estuaries of three major rivers – the Rhine, the Meuse and the Schelde – The Netherlands is, and has been for centuries, a maritime trading nation. Although a small country, it has increased its size by reclaiming land from the sea. The windmills, dykes, dams and locks are all witnesses to the success achieved by a hard working people.

The country rose to greatness in the 17th century when explorers and merchants roamed the world. From the enterprising spirit of the Dutch, prosperity and spiritual wealth manifested themselves in treasures of crafted silver and gold, the unique architecture of canal houses and artistic masterpieces.

The Dutch have a highly organised economy and although the country has suffered from unemployment as new technology replaced labour-intensive industry, it remains cushioned against the worst effects of recession. The European Union imports more than 75 percent of Dutch goods and 30 percent of all trade to European countries passes through the world's largest port, Rotterdam.

## Climate

Amsterdam has a mild, maritime climate with much the same temperatures as the UK but is wetter and marginally cooler in winter. Summers are generally warm but you can expect rain at any time of year. Spring is the driest time of year and a favourite time for tulip enthusiasts. The advantages of a visit in winter are the cut-price package deals and the fact that museums and galleries are pleasantly uncrowded.

The Netherlands is the world's largest exporter of plants, flowers and bulbs and the second largest exporter of farm produce. Electronics, publishing and the processing of oil to produce petroleum products are major industrial sectors. The Netherlands has produced several multinationals, including Heineken, Shell, Philips and Unilever.

## The Provinces

The Netherlands is made up of 12 provinces, each administered by an elected Provincial Council and each with its own characteristics. There are also many beautiful towns in the provinces, of which 150 have a total of over 42,000 "protected" buildings, such as historic farmhouses, windmills and castles.

**Friesland**, in the north, has an historic capital, Leeuwarden. There are daily ferry connections to four of the Friesian Islands. Frieslanders have an independent spirit and continue to speak their own language.

**Drenthe** has ancient Saxon villages scattered among woods and heathland. Perfect for cyclists to explore, there is no shortage of museums, castles and churches.

**Groningen**, in the northeast, with its capital of the same name, has 33 museums, 80 windmills and 100 medieval churches.

**Overijssel**, to the southeast, embraces the picturesque town of Giet-hoorn where you can travel by boat through canal "streets". The two Hanseatic towns of Zwolle and Kampen delight with their historic buildings and the villages of Urk and Staphorst still follow ancient customs and traditions.

**Gelderland** is the largest province, stretching from the great southern rivers to the northern sand dunes. It contains the country's largest open-air museum; the Hoge Veluwe National Park has deer, wild boar and sheep plus the treasures of the Kröller-Müller art gallery.

**Flevoland** is The Netherlands' newest province, reclaimed from the IJssel-meer. The principal towns are Lelystad and Almere.

**Utrecht**, in the centre, is like The Netherlands in miniature. There are historic towns, countryside, woods, lakes and polders; castles and country houses.

**Noord-Brabant**, in the lively south has 's-Hertogenbosch as its capital with the largest cathedral in the country: St Jan, built in the 14th century. Social occasions have undisguised zest – from the Carnival in February to jazz festivals held in Breda.

**Limburg** too enjoys life. The capital, Maastricht, is one of The

Netherlands' oldest towns and a centre for haute cuisine, tradition and natural beauty.

**Noord-Holland**, in the influential west – not in the north, as its name suggests – is particularly rich in folklore. Traditional dress is common in old towns such as Volendam, Marken, Edam and Monnickendam. Haarlem has influenced painters and the Frans Hals Museum is one of The Netherlands' principal attractions. Alkmaar is famous for its weekly cheese market.

**Zuid-Holland** contains the seat of government, in The Hague, and other well-preserved cities such as Leiden, Delft and Gouda. It holds the nickname of the "vegetable garden of Europe" because tomatoes, cucumbers and peppers are grown here. Bulbfields also cover the north of the province in a riot of colour in spring.

**Zeeland** is the delta of The Netherlands – a little kingdom of peninsulas, inland seas and lakes. The most ambitious engineering project in the world, the Delta Works uses high technology to keep the sea in check. Seafood is its lifeblood. The old capital, Middelburg, has a wealth of Flemish-Renaissance architecture.

## Business Hours

Normal shopping hours are 9am–6pm. Late-night shopping is usually Thursday. Food stores close at 4pm on Saturdays. All shops close for one half-day a week, always on Monday morning. Banks are open: Monday–Friday 9am–4pm; Thursday 9am–7pm.

## Public Holidays

Banks and most shops close on the following days:
New Year's Day
Good Friday
Easter Sunday and Monday
30 April (Queen's Day)
Ascension Day
Whit Monday
Christmas Day
26 December

# Planning the Trip

## Entry Regulations

Visitors from the European Union, the US, Canada, Australia, New Zealand and most other European and Commonwealth countries require a passport only. Citizens of most other countries must obtain a visa in advance from Dutch embassies or consulates.

Personal possessions are not liable to duty and tax provided you are staying for less than six months and you intend to take them out again. There is no restriction on the amount of currency that you can bring into The Netherlands. Among prohibited or restricted goods are plants, flowers, weapons and narcotic drugs.

## Animal Quarantine

An official certificate of vaccination is required for cats and dogs brought into The Netherlands from any country other than Belgium and Luxemburg.

Duty-free allowances vary according to where you bought the goods, as follows.

Goods obtained duty and tax-paid within the European Union: 300 cigarettes or 150 cigarillos or 75 cigars or 400g of tobacco; 1.5 litres of alcoholic drinks over 22 percent volume or 3 litres of alcoholic drinks under 22 percent volume plus 4 litres of still wine; 75g (3fl oz or 90cc) of perfume and 375cc (13fl oz) of toilet water; 1,000g of coffee and 200g of tea.

Goods bought duty-free or in non-EU countries: 200 cigarettes or 100 cigarillos or 50 cigars or 250g of tobacco; 1 litre of alcoholic drinks over 22 percent volume or 2 litres of alcoholic drinks under 22 percent volume plus 2 litres of still wine; 50g (2fl oz or 60cc) of perfume and 250cc (9fl oz) of toilet water; 500g of coffee and 100g of tea.

## Health

No health certificates or vaccinations are required for European Union citizens. EU citizens who have obtained an E111 form from their local social security office before departure are entitled to free treatment by a doctor and free prescribed medicines. This insurance is not comprehensive and won't cover you, for example, for holiday cancellation or the cost of repatriation. If you want full cover, you should take out separate medical insurance.

## Money Matters

The Dutch monetary unit is the guilder (gulden), sometimes called a florin (for NLG). One guilder is equivalent to 100 cents. The euro will come into circulation in 2002, when it will replace the guilder.

Coins in current circulation are the *stuiver* (5 cents), *dubbeltje* (10 cents), *kwartje* (25 cents), *guilder* (100 cents), *rijksdaalder* (250 cents), and *five guilder* coin (500 cents).

Existing bank notes are 10, 25, 50, 100, 250 and 1,000 guilders.

### Changing Money

GWK (Grenswis-selkantoren NV) is a national financial institution where you can exchange any currency and also use credit cards, travellers' cheques and Eurocheques. There are GWK offices located at 35 main railway stations in The Netherlands and at the country's borders. They are open Monday–Saturday 8am–8pm, Sunday 10am–4pm and sometimes in the evening for longer hours at main stations and airports. The Amsterdam Centraal Station GWK exchange office is open 24 hours a day.

Change is also available at post offices (at a good rate of exchange) and banks. There can be a considerable difference in commission charged between the various institutions and at the different times of night or day.

### Credit Cards
Credit cards are accepted at hotels, restaurants, shops, car rental companies and airlines. Access, American Express, Diners Club, Eurocard, Visacard, Master-Card and JCB card are all recognised, plus many more.

## What to Bring

The unpredictability of the weather calls for a raincoat and/or umbrella at all times of the year. Light clothing should be sufficient in summer, but take a jacket or light coat for the evenings. Very warm clothing is advisable for winter. Comfortable footwear is essential for sightseeing and walking on the cobbled streets. Casual dress is the norm, though a very few of the smarter hotels and restaurants require men to wear jacket and tie.

## Getting there

### BY AIR
Most visitors, whether from America or other parts of Europe, fly into Schiphol Airport, 9 miles (14km) southwest of Amsterdam. The airport has connections to 196 cities in 90 countries. With its huge range of duty-free goods, reputation for efficiency and easy access to all parts of The Netherlands, it is one of Europe's most popular international airport. Taken together, British Airways (tel: 0181-897 4000), KLM Royal Dutch Airlines (tel: 0181-750 9000) and British Midland (tel: 0181 745 7321) operate an almost hourly service during the day from London Heathrow and from East Midland airport (tel: 01345-554 554). (All telephone numbers are in the UK)

Best value of the lot for British visitors is the Amsterdam Air Express from Gatwick, departing on

## Tourist Offices

The Netherlands Board of Tourism (NBT) provides a number of useful publications, including *Holland's Seaside, Cycling in Holland, Watersports in Holland* and *Rail Holidays in Holland*, plus addresses of hotels and restaurants. For copies and information, visit or write to your nearest office:

● **Canada:** 25 Adelaide Street East, Suite 710, Toronto, Ontario M5C 1Y2.
● **Great Britain:** 18 Buckingham Gate, London SW1E 6LB.
**Switzerland:** 12 Rautistrasse 8047, Zurich.
● **United States:** 355 Lexington Avenue (21st Floor), New York, NY 10017; 225 North Michigan Avenue, Suite 1854, Chicago, Ill 60601; 9841 Airport Blvd, Suite 710, Los Angeles, California 90045.

Friday afternoons only and returning on Monday evenings. Services from major regional airports are covered by various British and Dutch airlines.

Several airlines offer cut-price fares which work out to little more than the cost of a standard rail ticket. These cheaper flights usually mean that you have to spend a Saturday night in The Netherlands.

Very regular flights link Schiphol with all major European airports, and there are several flights a week from North America, Canada and Australia.

### BY TRAIN
There are good rail connections to all parts of The Netherlands from Brussels, Paris, Antwerp, Cologne and Hanover and London, and the North Sea ports.

The Eurostar Channel Tunnel train goes direct from London (Waterloo) to Amsterdam via Brussels in neighbouring Belgium and takes about eight hours (tel: 0345 881 881 or, from abroad 44-1233 617575).

Day and night services operate from London (Liverpool Street) to The Netherlands via the Hook of Holland – journey time is around 12 hours by ferry, 10 hours by jetfoil. A further option is London (Victoria) to Ostend via Dover, but there are several transfers involved. You can also go via the Sheerness to Vlissingen rail ferry. British Rail European Enquiries, tel: 0171-834 2345.

### BY SEA
From the UK, Sealink (tel: 01223-647 047) operates two sailings a day from Harwich to the Hook of Holland: crossing time 7 hours by day, 8 hours at night. North Sea Ferries (tel: 01482-77177) has a daily sailing from Hull to Rotterdam, taking 14 hours. Sheerness Travel Agency (tel: 01795-666 666) is one of the main east coast agents dealing with this route.

The fastest sea route from the UK is the Jetfoil from Dover to Ostend (tel: 01843-595 522), which takes 1 hour 45 minutes.

### BY BUS
From the UK the cheapest deal is the Hoverspeed City Sprint (tel: 01304-240 241), departing daily from Victoria. Journey time is roughly 9 hours.

### BY CAR
To drive in Holland, you must carry a current driving licence (an international licence is not necessary), vehicle registration document, Green Card insurance policy and a warning triangle for use in the event of an accident or breakdown. Holland has an excellent network of roads and signposting is good. But once you're in the cities, a car is often more of a hindrance than a help.

From the UK, the Channel Tunnel's Le Shuttle provides a 35-minute drive-on service between Folkestone and Calais, France, from where there is a straightforward motorway connection up through Belgium.

Except for the Jetfoil service, all the companies mentioned in the *By*

*Sea* section above offer a car ferry service. Advance bookings are advisable in summer.

From the Hook of Holland to Amsterdam, travel time is roughly 2 hours 30 minutes. If you don't mind a longer drive on the Continent you can, of course, take the shorter cross-Channel ferry routes: Ramsgate/Dunkirk (Sally Line, tel: 01843-595 522, 2 hours 30 minutes) or Dover/Calais (Sealink and P&O, 1 hour 15 minutes to 1 hour 30 minutes). P&O's service from Felixstowe to Zeebrugge in Belgium includes an 8-hour overnight sailing (tel: 01304-203 388).

## Package Tours

Numerous companies offer two to seven-day packages, principally to Amsterdam. These often (but not always) work out cheaper than fixing your own travel and accommodation. To qualify for the air packages, you have to spend a Saturday night away.

The packages range from all-inclusive (meals, excursions, welcome parties included) to basic travel and accommodation.

# Practical Tips

## Media

The main national newspapers are *NRC Handelsblad*, the most respected paper, the more left-wing *De Volkskrant* and *De Telegraaf*, on the political right. English newspapers arrive on the same day they are published and are widely available. The weekly English-language *What's on in Amsterdam* gives listings and reviews of what's on in the city (f.3.50 from vvv). Brown café notice-boards are another good source of information on local events.

On cable TV you can watch Britain's BBC1 and BBC2 plus Sky, CNN Fox and Super Channel. English-language films are frequently shown on Dutch TV channels, undubbed. On the radio, you can tune into the BBC World Service and BBC Radio 4.

## Postal Services

Main post offices are usually open Monday–Friday 8.30am–6pm; 8pm on Thursday; Saturday 9am–12pm. Stamps are available from post offices, tobacconists, news-stands and stamp machines attached to the red and grey letter boxes. *Poste restante* facilities are available at main post offices – you need a passport to collect your mail.

## Telephones

Telephone boxes are green and most take phonecards and/or 25c, f.1 and f.2.50 coins. You find them in post offices, large stores, cafés and in some streets. Larger post offices have booths where you can make international calls which work out cheaper than using a hotel phone where rates may be double or even treble those of the post office or telephone boxes.

## Tourist Information

Tourist information offices are clearly marked vvv and are usually located just outside the railway station in every main town and city. They are a mine of useful information and services but there is a charge for most of them. It is useful to carry passport-sized photographs for various identity cards you may purchase.

The registered address of the head office is:
**vvv Amsterdam Tourist Office**
P.O. Box 3901
1001 AS Amsterdam
The Netherlands
Tel: 06-3403 4066 or 0900-400 4040 (f.1 per minute)
Fax: (3120) 625286

For the purposes of personal visits, it is situated at 10 Stationsplein (white building across the road to the left outside the Centraal Station). Open: daily 9am–5pm. Also inside Centraal Station, open 8am–8pm Monday–Saturday, 8am–5pm Sunday.
**vvv Information Office**: 1 Leidseplein, Amsterdam. Daily 9am–5pm. (Tram: 1, 2, 5.)

If you wish to write to a town tourist office, address the letter with vvv and the name of the town.

## Embassies

**Australia**: 4 Carnegielaan Koninginnegracht, The Hague, tel: 070–310 8200
**Canada**: 7 Sophialaan, The Hague, tel: 070–311 1600
**Great Britain**: 44 Koningslaan, Amsterdam, tel: 020-676 4343
**United States**: 19 Museumplein, Amsterdam, tel: 020-575 5309

## Doing Business

The Netherlands has always been a trading nation; lacking its own raw materials, it has survived by means of *entrepôt* trade and distribution, one reason why Schiphol airport and the Port of Rotterdam are so important to the country's economy. Most of this trade is with EU countries, principally Germany, the UK and Belgium.

Doing business with the Dutch is usually a pleasure: they are informal, honest and excellent linguists. They are also efficient and expect their trading counterparts to be the same.

## Travelling with Children

Children are treated with respect and affection. The notion that they should be seen and not heard is alien, and children are involved in adult life from an early age – one reason why Dutch children can seem unusually well-behaved and mature.

Children are welcome in restaurants and cafés, many of which serve a *kindermenu* (children's menu). It is easy to hire bicycles fitted with children's seats for getting about town or for excursions into the country.

Ask at the vvv for details of special activities for children. Several cities now have *kinderboerderijen*, or children's farms; in Amsterdam for example, there are city farms within the zoo complex and another at the Amstelpark (located near the rai Exhibition Centre in the southern suburbs).

Top children's attractions include Madame Tussaud's and the Tropenmuseum in Amsterdam; the Zuiderzee Museum in Enkhuisen; the Omniversum Space Museum and the Madurodam miniature town in The Hague; the zoo in Rotterdam and Utrecht's railway museum (Nederlands Spoorwegmuseum). For details of all of these, see *Culture: Museums.*

This is, of course, far from being an exhaustive list; in fact the towns of The Netherlands, with their harbours, bridges, canals, parks and windmills, seem almost deliberately designed to appeal to children.

## Disabled Travellers

"Holland for the Handicapped", available free from The Netherlands Board of Tourism (see pages 308 and 309) lists hotels, restaurants, museums and other places of interest with special facilities.

Many older city-centre hotels have very steep staircases; check before booking whether your hotel has wheelchair access and a lift.

## Students

"Use It", available free from vvv tourist information centres and youth hostels, is packed with practical advice on living cheaply in The Netherlands, and the range of discounts available to young people. Don't forget, too, that university campus restaurants (called Mensas) are open to anyone, and a good source of cheap, filling food, though they are only open for lunch Monday–Friday during termtime.

## Service Charges & Tips

Service charges and VAT are included in restaurant and bar bills. An extra tip can be left for extra attention or service but this is by no means compulsory. Taxi meters also include the service charge, though it is customary to give an extra tip. A lavatory attendant is usually given 50 cents.

## Emergency Numbers

● **Amsterdam (code 020)**
Police/ambulance:   112
SOS doctor/
dentist/chemist:   592 3434
Lost property
(noon–3.30pm daily):559 3005
● **The Hague (code 070)**
Police/ambulance:   112
SOS doctor/dentist: 345 5300
            (night) 346 9669
Lost property:    310 4911
● **Rotterdam (code 010)**
Police/ambulance:   112
Doctor:        420 1100
Dentist:        455 2155

## Medical Services

The standard of medical and dental services in The Netherlands is very high, and most major cities have an emergency doctor and dental service; enquire at your hotel or consult the introductory pages to local telephone directories.

## Security & Crime

Amsterdam and Rotterdam are major European centres for drugs, and much crime here is drug-related. As a visitor, you are unlikely to be affected directly by the drugs trade, but you should take sensible precautions against becoming a victim of petty crime. Keep a careful watch on wallets, bags and other valuables, especially on public transport. Leave large amounts of cash and jewellery at your hotel. Deserted areas should be avoided after dark.

### LOST PROPERTY

You should report loss or theft of valuables to the local police immediately, as most insurance policies insist on a police report. Loss of passport should be reported immediately to the police and your embassy or consulate.

Most large cities have a police lost property office and there is usually a separate office for items lost on public transport.

## Etiquette

The Netherlands has a reputation for tolerance. Foreigners, including minorities, are always welcome and, as a visitor, you are likely to find local people pleasant, polite and civilised. They may not be very demonstrative or vivacious, but they are rarely inhospitable or unfriendly.

You may be surprised at the leniency towards drugs and prostitution, especially in cities like Amsterdam. There has been a crackdown on hard drugs, but you can still buy soft drugs in many city cafés. Many locals argue that the drugs problem is no worse than in other major cities – just more open.

# Getting Around

Exploring The Netherlands is made easy by the excellent and inexpensive public transport system. All towns of any size have a railway station, which usually also acts as the main terminus for the bus, coach, tram and metro services.

Tourist information centres (Vereniging voor Vreemdelingen-verkeer – or vvv for short) are usually located within, or very nearby, the station complex. Here the multilingual staff will answer all your questions, provide maps and brochures, handle your accommodation bookings and reserve tickets for the theatre, etc. Bicycles can also be hired at most stations.

Tickets are sold in the form of Nationale Strippenkaart to be used on buses, trams, metro and the train between certain stations anywhere in Holland. The easiest place to buy the cards is at a vvv office (or tel: 0900-4004040, fax: 3120-625286), though they are also sold at railway stations and many newsagents and tobacconists. You can buy tickets from the bus or tram driver, but they cost more than tickets purchased in advance.

Transport routes are divided into zones; you must cancel one strip for your journey and one strip for each zone you travel through (i.e. cancel two strips for one zone, three for two zones, and so on). The stamp on your *stripenkaart* is valid for one hour. Within that time you can change from one route to another, or from one form of transport to another without cancelling more strips. Two strips cost f.3.75 and 15 strips cost f.11.50. An alternative is an unlimited travel ticket (called a *dagkaart*), valid for one, two or three days.

Tram 20 is a new circle tram with two different routes which take you across the city to most of the museums and tourist attractions. The trams run daily from 9am–7pm every 10 minutes. One ticket entitles you to unlimited use of the tram for one day.

## Maps

The vvv issues a useful road map of The Netherlands, updated each year, for f.2. For anyone who requires more detailed maps for walking or cycling, the ANWB 1:100,000 series is sold in many vvv offices and bookshops.

Most vvv offices sell street plans of towns and cities in their locality; when using them it helps if you remember that *straat* means street, *plein* means square and *gracht* means canal.

## BY AIR

Schiphol, near **Amsterdam** is The Netherlands' principal airport. Amsterdam Schiphol railway station is located below the arrivals hall. Trains leave for the principal Dutch cities every 15 minutes or so between 5.25am and 0.15am, and every 60 minutes or so during the remaining period.

**Rotterdam** has a small airport served by flights from Amsterdam, London and Paris, located 15 minutes from the city centre. A regular local bus service runs between the airport and the city.

**Eindhoven** and **Maastricht** both have airports, principally for domestic flights.

Domestic flights within The Netherlands are operated by KLM City Hopper. For information: tel: 020-474 7747.

### Sightseeing by Air

Flights over south Limburg, neighbouring Germany and Belgium from Maastricht airport are organised by Air Service Limburg, tel: 043-3645 030. One-hour flights cost f.150 per person, with a maximum of three passengers.

## BY TRAIN

Netherlands Railways (Nederlandse Spoorwegen) has a national inter-city network of express trains linking major cities. There is a fast direct train link every 15 minutes between the airport Schiphol and Amsterdam. There is also an hourly night service between Utrecht, Amsterdam, Schiphol, The Hague, Rotterdam and vice versa. Stopping trains provide connections to smaller places. There are at least half-hourly services on most lines with anything from four to eight an hour on busier routes. It is not possible to reserve seats on national train services.

### Tickets

It is invariably cheaper to buy a day return than pay for two singles. There are a number of special tickets available from any main station. Staff are helpful in calculating the cheapest tickets if given full details of your requirements. Some of the available tickets (with approximate prices) are:

**Day Rover:** Cost: about f.65 or f.100 (first class) to travel throughout Holland.

**Seven-Day Rover:** Cost: about f.160 standard and f.230 first class.

**Multi Rovers:** One day's unlimited travel for 2–6 people. Valid all day Saturday and Sunday and after 9am weekdays. In June, July and August you can also travel before 9am. Cost about f.100 for 2; f.170 for 6.

**Eurodomino:** This card entitles you to unlimited rail travel on any 3, 5 or 10 days within a one-month period. Prices start at about f.85 for 3 days. Children under 4 travel free, those between 4 and 11 can travel on a much cheaper Railrunner if accompanied by fare-paying adults – up to 3 children on Railrunners per adult.

**Tour Time:** Available in June, July and August to passengers under 19 years of age. Allows unlimited train travel on any 4 days within a specified consecutive 10-day period. Cost: about f.70.

**Benelux Tour Rail Card:** Valid for any 5 days within a specified period of 17 consecutive days. Holders may travel through Holland, Belgium and Luxembourg. Cost: about f.150 (over 26); f.100 (aged 4–25).

**Day Trips:** More than 75 day trips by rail are timetabled to a wide choice of tourist attractions, mostly between May and September. A combined ticket, Dagtochtkaartjes, covers the train, boat or bus trip and admission fee from most railway stations in Holland. More information is in the free booklet, published in English, *Rail Travel in Holland* and the fares are among the lowest in Europe.

### Information

For further information about public transport information and tickets:
**Amsterdam GVB:** 1 Stationsplein, Centraal Station, tel: 06-9292 (Monday–Friday 8am–10pm, Saturday and Sunday 9am–10pm).
**Nationwide:** tel: 06-9292 (f.1 per minute).

## Vehicle Rental

Here are the Amsterdam addresses of some rental firms:

### ● Car Rental

The main car rental firms have offices at Schiphol airport. These are their Amsterdam addresses:
**Avis:** 380 Nassaukade, 1054 AD, tel: 020-683 6061
**Ansa International:** 6–7 Hobbemakade, 1017 XK, tel: 020-664 8252
**Budget Rent a Car:** 121 Overtoom, 1054 HE, tel: 020-612 6066
**Diks Autohuur:** 278–280 van Ostadestraat, 1073 TW, tel: 020-662 3366
**Europcar:** 51–53 Overtoom, 1054 HB, tel: 020-683 2123
**Hertz:** 333 Overtoom, 1054 JM, tel: 020-612 2441; Schiphol Airport, tel: 020-601 5416

**Kuperus:** Van der Madeweg 1/5, 1098 AM, tel: 020-668 3311

### ● Camper Van Rental

Vans must be booked in advance. Deposit is often 50 percent of the rental. Hire charges from f.950 per week. The following rental offices are located in Amsterdam:
**ACC:** 4 Akersluisweg, 1069 MB, tel: 020-610 1819
**A-Point:** 11 Kollenbergweg, 1101 AR, Tel: 020-430 1647
**Braitman & Woudenberg:** 4/A Droogbak, 1013 GE, tel: 020-622 1168

### ● Bicycle Rental

**Damstraat Rent-a-bike:** Damstraat 20, tel: 020-625 5029
**MacBike:** Mr. Visserplein 2, tel: 020-620 0985
See also under *Cycling*.

## Taxis

Taxis will not stop if hailed in the street. It is customary in Holland to book a taxi by phone, although they can always be found at taxi ranks near hotels, stations and busy road junctions. The taxi meter price includes service charge. A fare starts at f.5 then increases about f.5 per kilometre. A 3-mile (5-km) journey in town would cost approximately f.15.

## Driving

### Highway Code

Stay on the right and overtake on the left. All road users should allow free passage to approaching police cars, fire engines and ambulances that are using their sound and light signals. A tram may not be held up on its course. Seatbelts must be worn in the front seats of vehicles.

### Speed Limits

Within a built-up zone the maximum speed is 50kph (30mph). In residential areas, indicated by signs of a white house on a blue background, vehicles may only be driven at walking pace. Outside the built-up area the speed limit is 80kph (50mph). A speed limit of 120kph (75mph) applies on motorways and a speed limit of 100kph (62mph) on most major roads in The Netherlands.

### Fuel

Petrol stations situated on national highways are open 24 hours. Most major petrol stations sell LPG (car gas). Unleaded petrol is readily available.

### National Highways

**A.1:** Amsterdam–Hoevelaken–Apeldoorn–Holten–Borne
**A.2:** Amsterdam–'s-Hertogenbosch/Eindhoven–Maastricht–Eijsden
**A.4:** Amsterdam–Burgerveen–Leiderdorp–Den Haag
**A.5:** Amsterdam–Haarlem
**A.6:** Muiderberg–Flevopolder–N.E. Polder–Emmeloord
**A.7:** Amsterdam–Hoorn/Lambertsschaag–Den Oever–Zurich–Joure–Drachten–Groningen–Hoogezand
**A.8:** Amsterdam–Westzaan
**A.9:** Alkmaar–Haarlem–Schiphol–Ouderkerk
**A.12:** Den Haag–Utrecht–Arnhem–Bergh (German border)
**A.13:** Den Haag–Rotterdam
**A.16:** Rotterdam–Breda–Hazeldonk (Belgian border)

## Cycling

Bicycles are ubiquitous. The 11 million bicycles in The Netherlands are used extensively by people of all ages for commuting, shopping, walking the dog, transporting young children, towing windsurf boards and sometimes even to move house (using an old-fashioned *bakfiets* – baker's bicycle). Even on the coldest winter days, you will see hardy cyclists. The Dutch favour old-fashioned heavy-framed bicycles for town use, without gears or hand-brakes (you stop by back pedalling).

By hiring a bicycle, you join in the life of the nation. Though bicycles are discouraged on crowded Dutch trains, they can be rented cheaply for a day or longer at most railway stations (with a small reduction on production of a train ticket). Parents with young children can also hire a small seat which is fixed on the back of the bicycle. Most railway stations provide secure lock-ups especially for bicycles.

Principal railway stations with bikes for hire are:
**The Hague:** tel: 070-385 3235
**Delft:** tel: 015-2143 033
**Leiden:** tel: 071-5120 068
**Rotterdam:** tel: 010-412 6220
**Gouda:** tel: 0182-519 751
**Dordrecht:** tel: 078-6146 642
**Utrecht:** tel: 030-2311 159

Otherwise, vvv offices can supply a list of hire companies. There is usually a deposit of between f.50 and f.200, depending on the sophistication of the bike, and rental costs are about f.10 a day or f.40 a week.

**Be warned:** The Netherlands may be Europe's cycling mecca, but it is also a nation where theft is all too common, especially in the larger cities. Always lock your bike and, wherever possible, secure it to an unmovable object.

## CYCLE ROUTES

A network of almost 6,250 miles (10,000km) of cycle lanes has been created in The Netherlands, complete with separate traffic lights for bikes at road intersections. Though cycling is safer than in many other countries, it is worth familiarising yourself with the bicycle and the rules of the road before setting off into the traffic. Bear in mind that cars entering a road from your right usually have priority.

The best maps to use are the ANWB 1:100,000 series, on which cycle lanes (*fietspaden*) are indicated by a dotted black line. Cycle routes are well signposted and signs at important junctions are often numbered so you can pinpoint your location on the map.

In planning a route through the country try to avoid large cities and busy intersections. Cycling across the flat Dutch polders or along long straight canals or roads can be bleak, especially in bad weather. Though The Netherlands is dotted with attractive camp sites, hotels

are often difficult to find, particularly in rural areas. It is also worth bearing in mind that restaurants outside Amsterdam tend to close early in the evening.

### River Routes

By far the most attractive routes in the north of the country are those that follow the rivers. The Lek (which changes its name to the Neder Rijn east of Wijk bij Duurstede) provides an attractive route between Rotterdam and Arnhem, passing through pleasant river towns such as Schoonhoven, Culemborg, Wijk bij Duurstede and Rhenen. There are hardly any bridges across the Lek; numerous small ferries link the two banks.

### National Park

From Arnhem, the most interesting cycling country is to the north through the rolling hills and moors of the Nationaal Park De Hoge Veluwe. A unique feature of this park is the free white bicycles which can be used anywhere within the park boundaries (a similar scheme foundered in Amsterdam when all the white bicycles were immediately stolen and repainted). Beyond the park, you can continue through moorland to Zwolle, north of which is an extensive area of lakes stretching to the attractive Frisian town of Sneek.

### The IJsselmeer

It may seem tempting to head west across the IJsselmeer by the 20-mile (32-km) Afsluitdijk, but this tends to be an ordeal, particularly in high winds. A far better way to cross the IJsselmeer is by the small ferries that ply between Stavoren and Enkhuizen in the summer.

### Between the Towns

In the densely populated Randstad, safe cycle routes are often difficult to find. To cycle from Rotterdam to The Hague, the best route is to follow the River Schie to Delft, then the Vliet to the outskirts of The Hague. The meandering Oude Rijn is a good route to take from Leiden to Utrecht, keeping always to the

quiet side of the river. Cycling from Leiden to Amsterdam, you can follow a string of lakes north to Uithoorn, then enter the city by the beautiful Amstel route.

To cycle from Amsterdam to Utrecht, follow the Amstel to Ouderkerk, turn down the Holendrecht to reach Abcoude, then take the Angstel to Loenersloot. Here, you cross the Amsterdam-Rijnkanaal to reach the aristocratic River Vecht, which then flows into the heart of Utrecht.

### Among the Dunes

The dunes offer an alternative route along the west coast, linking Hoek van Holland, The Hague and Haarlem. Once across the Noordzee Kanaal at Ijmuiden, you can continue along the coast north to Den Helder, where the ferry departs for the quiet island of Texel.

## Water Transport

A popular way to get to know Amsterdam is by taking a canal tour; numerous companies operate from the canal basin opposite Centraal Station and tickets can be booked in advance from the nearby vvv office. Tours take an hour or more; candle-lit dinner cruises are also available. Fuller information is given in the *Excursions* section.

While canal tours are geared essentially to visitors, you can also use Amsterdam's canal bus system. Modern glass-topped launches (equivalent to the Parisian *bâteaux mouches*) will pick you up at various points of the city and take you through some of the loveliest parts of Amsterdam. Day tickets with unlimited mileage are available. Be prepared to queue in summer.

The Museum Boat service stops at nine major museums at 75-minute intervals – well worth considering if you intend doing a lot of sightseeing. You can buy a day ticket from the vvv office opposite Centraal Station, where the boats leave. There is now also a canal bus offering a regular service through the canals between the Rijksmuseum and Centraal Station,

# Where to Stay

## Reservations

Wherever you plan to stay, it is wise to book in advance during the summer and holiday seasons and (in the case of North Holland) during the bulb season (April–May). This is especially true of Amsterdam, where the central hotels are usually booked up during June, July and August. Having said that, it is worth telephoning hotels if you visit Amsterdam at short notice, to check for cancellations.

You can book directly with the hotel; invariably the person who answers the phone will speak English. Alternatively, book in advance through: The Netherlands Reservation Centre, P.O. Box 404, 2260 AK Leidschendam, tel: 070-419 5500, fax: 070-419 5519.

The services of The Netherlands Reservation Centre are free and cover the whole country. Tell them where you want to stay, the dates, the price you are prepared to pay, and the number of rooms, with or without private bathrooms. Booking forms are stocked by branches of The Netherlands Board of Tourism.

Alternatively, you can book in person by going to vvv offices in major towns (those that offer the service display the i-Nederland sign). You will be expected to pay for the accommodation on the spot, plus a small booking charge, and you will be issued with a voucher confirming your booking. These offices will make reservations for any hotel in The Netherlands.

## Hotels

All hotels are graded according to their facilities. The Netherlands Board of Tourism issues a free annual Hotels brochure listing every hotel in the country, its star rating and facilities. As a general rule, the quality of accommodation in The Netherlands is high – but you do get what you pay for. Prices vary according to the season; winter prices are commonly 30–50 percent lower than the published rates. But you need to ask for a discount – it will not be offered automatically.

The following is a selective list of hotels in the major cities and towns covered by this guide.

## AMSTERDAM

**Acro** ££
Jan Luykenstraat 40–44
1071 CR
Tel: 020-662 0526
Fax: 020-675 0811
One of the better value budget hotels close to the art museums and the Vondelpark. Pleasant modern furnishings, in good condition.

**Ambassade** £££
Herengracht 341
1016 AZ
Tel: 020-626 2333
Fax: 020-624 5321
Highly popular, very friendly B&B converted from a series of 17th- and 18th-century canal-side houses. Lots of antiques, paintings, steep steps and spiral staircases. Book well in advance for this one.

**American** ££££
Leidsekade 97
1017 PN
Tel: 020-624 5322
Fax: 020-623 2375
Outstanding Art Nouveau building on the lively Leidseplein. Comfortable well-equipped bedrooms, popular café famous for Tiffany-style decor and colourful clientele, Night Watch cocktail bar with converted terrace.

**Amstel Inter-Continental** ££££
Professor Tulpplein 1
1018 GX
Tel: 020-622 6060
Fax: 020-6225808
Lavishly furnished 19th-century hotel, on the banks of the River Amstel (20 minutes' walk from the centre). Popular among visiting celebrities and royalty. High-class cuisine in 2-star Michelin La Rive restaurant.

**Canal House** £££
Keizersgracht 148
1015 CX
Tel: 020-622 5182
Fax: 020-624 1317
American-owned hotel, expertly converted from merchant houses on a quiet canal. Lots of antiques and a charming breakfast room.

**Concert Inn Hotel** £–££
11 De Lairessestraat
1071 NR
Tel: 020-305 7272
Fax: 020-305 7271
A family-operated B&B near the Concertgebouw and museum quarter.

**Die Port van Cleve** £££
176 Nieuwe Zijdsvoorburgwal.
Tel: 020-6244860
Fax: 020-6220240
Well located behind the Royal Palace and Dam Square. An old traditional hotel.

**Estherea** £££
Singel 305
1012 WH
Tel: 020-624 5146
Fax: 020-623 9001
17th-century canal house, 2 minutes from Dam Square. Steep stairs but there is a lift.

**Golden Tulip Barbizon Palace** ££££
Prins Hendrikkade 59–72
1012 AD
Tel: 020-556 4564
Fax: 020-624 3353
Nineteen old houses converted into a new luxury hotel overlooking Centraal Station. Interior is a combination of the old Dutch, French and post-Modern styles. Facilities include sauna and fitness room.

**Grand Hotel Krasnapolsky** ££££
Dam 9, 1012 JS
Tel: 020-554 9111
Fax: 020-626 1570
Deluxe. Spacious comfortable rooms on main Dam square facing the Royal Palace. Breakfast served in a glass-roofed winter garden.

**Grand Westin Demeure** ££££
Oudezijds Voorburgwal 197
1012 EX
Tel: 020-555 3111
Fax: 020-626 6286

This elegant hostelry in the heart of the city was once the city hall and a royal residence. Café Roux is a poular dining spot for locals as well as guests.

**Hotel de Europe ££££**
Nieuwe Doelenstraat 2–8
1012 CP
Tel: 020-531 1777
Fax: 020-531 1778
Grand late 19th-century hotel overlooking the River Amstel and the Mint Tower. Facilities include swimming pool, open-air terrace, meeting rooms, fitness centre and two restaurants.

**Hotel Fita ££**
37 Jan Luykensstraat
1071 CL
Tel: 020 679 0976
Fax: 020-664 3969
In the museum quarter between PC Hoofstraat shops and the Van Gogh and Stedelijk museums. Small, cosy and eccentric.

**Jan Luyken Residence ££££**

## Hotel Price Guide

Approximate prices for a double room with bathroom, usually including breakfast, are:

| | |
|---|---|
| ££££ | f.280–500 |
| £££ | f.200–275 |
| ££ | f.85–195 |
| £ | Under f.85 |

Jan Luykenstraat 58
1071 CS
Tel: 020-573 0730
Fax: 020-676 3841
Late 19th-century building close to major art museums and the Concertgebouw. Quiet rooms and bar/lounge with adjacent patio.

**Keizershof £–££**
618 Keizersgracht
1017 ER
Tel: 020-622 2855
Fax: 020-624 8412
Cosy family-run B&B offering rooms with canal or garden views.

**Le Méridien ££££**
Apollolaan 2
1077 BA
Tel: 020-673 5922
Fax: 020-570 5744

Formerly the Apollo. Modern luxury hotel on the waterside, 2 miles (3km) south of the centre; two restaurants with waterside terraces.

**Okura Amsterdam ££££**
Ferdinand Bolstraat 333
1072 LH
Tel: 020-678 7111
Fax: 020-671-2344
Essentially a hotel for business travellers, not far from the RAI building and with car parking space. Twenty-three floors with top-floor bar and restaurant. A good choice for gourmets – see *Where to Eat* for the Yamazato Japanese restaurant.

**Prinsen ££**
Vondelstraat 38
1054 GE
Tel: 020-616 2323
Fax: 020-616 6112
Converted 19th-century houses in quiet street, 2 minutes from Leidseplein.

**Pulitzer ££££**
Prinsengracht 315–331
1016 GZ
Tel: 020-523 5235
Fax: 020-627 6753
Terrace of 17th- and 18th-century canal-side residences and warehouses, converted into a charming luxury hotel. Exposed brick, old beams, antiques and beautiful furnishings.

**Wijnnobel £**
Vossiusstraat 9
1071 AB
Tel: 020-662 2298
Cheap, clean and cheerful, with views of the Vondelpark. No private bathrooms.

## NOORD-HOLLAND

### Bergen
**Zee Bergen £££**
Wilhelminalaan 11
1861 LR Bergen
Tel: 072-5897241
Fax: 072-5817260.

### Enkhuizen
**Die Port van Cleve ££££**
Dyk 74–78
1601 GK Enkhuizen
Tel: 0228-312510.
Fax: 0228-318765.
**Het Wapen van Enkhuizen ££**

Breedstraat 59
1601 KB Enkhuizen
Tel: 0228-313434
Fax: 0228-320 020.

### Haarlem
**Golden Tulip Lion d'Or ££££**
Kruisweg 34–36
2011 LC Haarlem
Tel: 023-5321 750
Fax: 023-532 9543.

**Carillon ££**
Grote Markt 27
2011 RC Haarlem
Tel: 023-5310 591
Fax: 023-5314909.

## ZUID-HOLLAND

### Delft
**Best Western Museum Hotel £££**
Oude Delft 189
2611 HD Delft
Tel: 015-2140 930.
Fax: 015-2140935
Located in the picturesque old quarter along the canal.

**Juliana £££**
Maerten Trompstraat 33
2628 RC, Delft
Tel: 015-256 7612
Fax: 015 256 5707
A cosy, family-run hotel with a garden, located just outside the city centre.

### The Hague
**Corona ££££**
Buitenhof 39–42
2513 AH Den Haag
Tel: 070-363 7930
Fax: 070-3615785
Luxurious hotel on a quiet central square, with a highly regarded restaurant.

**Esquire £££**
van Aerssenstraat 65
2582 JG Den Haag
Tel: 070-352 2341
Fax: 070 352-0195
Small and comfortable with a good restaurant.

**Inter-Continental Des Indes ££££**
Lange Voorhout 54–56
2514 EG Den Haag
Tel: 070-363 2932
Fax: 070 345-1721
Former palace built in the 1850s, once the haunt of Mata Hari and Pavlova, now used by diplomats and

well-heeled travellers.

**Steigenberger Kurhaus** ££££
Gev. Deynootplein 30
2586 CK Scheveningen
Tel: 070-352 0052
Fax: 070-416 2646
Architecturally splendid with
seafront views and located in the
resort of Scheveningen, in the
suburbs of The Hague.

**Vreugd & Rust** ££££
14 Oosteinde Voorburg
Tel: 070-387 2081
fax: 070-387 7715
In a small village, 15 minutes from
The Hague city centre by car. Early
18th-century villa with 14 rooms in
a park environment and a top
restaurant frequented by
government heads and other
movers and shakers.

*Leiden*

**Golden Tulip Leiden** ££
Schipholweg 3
2316 XB Leiden
Tel: 071-522 1121
Fax: 071-522 6675
Just opposite the train station in
the heart of the city.

**Nieuw Minerva** ££
Boommarkt 23
2311 EA Leiden
Tel: 071-5126 358
Fax: 071-514 2674
Homely hotel furnished with
antiques, located in a group of
historic buildings on a quiet
tributary of the River Rhine.

*Rotterdam*

**Bilderberg Park Hotel** ££££
Westersingel 70
3015 Rotterdam
Tel: 010-436 3611
Fax: 010-436 4212
Characterful hotel with garden,
recommended Empress restaurant
and fitness centre.

**Golden Tulip Rotterdam** ££££
Aert von Nesstraat 4
3012 CA Rotterdam
Tel: 010-206 7800
Fax: 010-413 5320
Formerly the Atlanta. Central,
friendly and with Art Deco touches.
An extensive renovation has added
60 more rooms.

**Hilton Rotterdam** ££££

Weena 10
3012 CM Rotterdam
Tel: 010-424 9249
Fax: 010-424 9200
Deluxe. The centre of Rotterdam's
business life by day and of its
social life by night.

**Hotel New York** ££££
Koninginnenhoofd 1
3072 AD
Tel: 010-439 0500
Fax: 010-484 2701
A splendid, very popular hotel with
uniquely furnished rooms and
waterfront views. Also has a good
restaurant.

# NOORD-BRABANT

*Den Bosch*

**Eurohotel** £££
Hinthamerstraat 63–65
5211 MG Den Bosch
Tel: 073-6137 777.

**Golden Tulip Central** ££££
Mr Loeffplein 98
5211 RX Den Bosch
Tel: 073-6125 151.

## Hotel Price Guide

Approximate prices for a double
room with bathroom, usually
including breakfast, are:

| | |
|---|---|
| ££££ | f.280–500 |
| £££ | f.200–275 |
| ££ | f.85–195 |
| £ | Under f.85 |

# LIMBURG

*Kerkrade*

**Kasteel Erenstein** ££££
Oud Erensteinerweg 6
6468 PC Kerkrade
Tel: 045-546 1333
Fax: 045-546 0748
Romantic 13th-century moated
castle, part of the Camille
Oosterwegel group (see *page 246*),
where you can lodge and dine in an
elegant setting. Two minutes away
is an alternative, Hotel Berghof, in
an 18th-century farmhouse.

*Landgraaf*

**Hotel Winselerhof** ££££
Tunnelweg 99
6372 XH Landgraaf

Tel: 045 546 4343
Fax: 045-535 2711
Majestic 16th-century farmhouse
with lodging around an historic
courtyard. Authentic Italian cuisine
in the Restaurant Pirandello.

*Maastricht*

**De La Bourse** ££
Markt 37
6211 CK Maastricht
Tel: 043-321 8112
Fax: 043-321 7706
Friendly and central.

**Golden Tulip Derlon** ££££
O.L. Vrouweplein 6
6211 HD Maastricht
Tel: 043-321 6770
Fax: 043-352 1933
Charming hotel in old quarter built
on Roman foundations (relics in the
basement).

**Holiday Inn Crown Plaza** £££–££££
Ruiterij 1
6221 EW Maastricht
Tel: 043-350 9191
Fax: 043-350 9192
On the Maas river near the Bonifant
Museum. Ask for a room with a view.

**Hotel Bergère** ££££
Stationsstraat 40
6221 BR Maastricht
Tel: 043-325 1651
Fax: 043-325 5498.
An elegant hotel in an intimate
setting opposite the train station.
Has special arrangements with
Thermae 2000 (see *page 247*).

*Valkenburg*

**Hotel Château St. Gerlach** ££££
Joseph Corneli Allée 1
6301 KK Bad Valkenburg
Tel: 043-608 8888
Recently restored to its former
glory, this spectacular complex
dates from the 18th century.
Gourmet restaurant and modern
facilities, including an indoor
swimming pool and spa.

**Thermaetel** £££–££££
Couberg 25
6301 BT Bad Valkenburg
Tel: 043-601 6050
Fax: 043-601 4777
Futuristic hotel, with 60 rooms and
suites and a restaurant, attached to
the Thermae 2000 health resort
(see *page 247*).

## Bed & Breakfast

vvv tourist offices in major towns keep lists of *pensions* (rooms in private houses) where you can stay the night inexpensively. Prices are usually quoted per person, rather than per room, and breakfast is usually extra.

The standard of accommodation in *pensions* does depend on the attitude of the owner – varying from spotless to appalling. It is best to check the room on offer first, before parting with your money.

### UTRECHT
**Holiday Inn £££showing**
Jaarbeursplein 24
3521 AR Utrecht
Tel: 030-297 7977
Fax: 030-297 7999
Caters for business visitors to the next-door Exhibition Centre, with a panoramic restaurant and a bar on the 20th floor.
**Tulip Inn ££–£££**
Janskerkhof 10
3512 BL Utrecht
Tel: 030-231 3169
Fax: 030-231 0148
Charming hotel and restaurant in the heart of the old quarter.

### OVERIJSSEL
*Zwolle*
**Bilderberg Grand Hotel Wientjes ££££**
Stationsweg
8011 CZ Zwolle
Tel: 038-425 4254
Fax: 038-425 4260
Characterful hotel with a good restaurant.

### FRIESLAND
*Harlingen*
**Anna Caspari £££**
Noorderhaven 67–71
8861 AL Harlingen
Tel: 0517-412065
Fax: 0517-414540.

*Leeuwarden*
**Leeuwarder Eurohotel £££**
Europaplein 20
8915 CL Leeuwarden
Tel: 058-213 1113
Fax: 058-212 5927.

### GRONINGEN
**De Doelen £££**
Grote Markt 36
9711 LV Groningen
Tel: 050-3127 041
Fax: 050-314 6112.

## Youth Hostels

There are 45 official Youth Hostels in The Netherlands, including two in Amsterdam (in Vondelpark and on the Kloveniersburgwal canal). If you do not already belong to the YHA, membership can usually be taken out on the spot. Most offer dormitory accommodation but some have private rooms. For full details, contact the Nedelandse Jeugdherberg Central, Professor Tulpstraat 2, 1018 GX Amsterdam, tel: 020-551 3155.

In several cities, especially in Amsterdam, you will find numerous so-called "Youth Hostels", and you may well be approached at the station by touts looking for likely customers. Some of these hostels are well-run establishments offering clean, basic accommodation – though you should expect to have to share rooms and bathrooms. Others are fleapits and may be located over a noisy all-night bar.

Do not pay until you are satisfied with the room on offer, and never leave valuables unattended.

## Camping

Dutch campsites are numerous and well equipped. Some sites offer *trekkershutten* – cabin accommodation with basic furniture – for up to four people, for around f.50 a night. The Netherlands Board of Tourism (see *Planning the Trip: Tourist Offices*) publishes a free list of sites and facilities. Cabins are best booked in advance through The Netherlands Reservation Centre (see *Reservations* at the start of this section).

# Where to Eat

## What to Eat

Although the heavy, calorie-loaded typical Dutch dishes have gradually given way to the demands of diet-conscious Dutch, you can still find plenty of vegetable hotchpotches, thick pea soups, wholesome stews, apple pies and pancakes with lashings of cream. Dutch food may not be very exciting, but usually it is good and is sure to fill you up.

Typical Dutch breakfasts – consisting of a variety of cheeses, cold meats, smoked sausages, breads and rolls, with coffee, tea or chocolate – are more than adequate.

The Dutch excel in delicious snacks: salted or pickled herrings served from street stalls (and traditionally swallowed whole on the spot), smoked eel, meat croquettes, sausages, french fries with mayonnaise, sweet and savoury pancakes, waffles and *poffertjes* (mini-pancakes coated with icing sugar). Even the *automatieken*, the food-dispensing machines, provide some surprisingly appetizing snacks such as meat and cheese croquettes, saté and egg-roll.

The local equivalent to sandwiches are *broodjes*, soft rolls loaded with fish, smoked sausage, spiced ground beef, roast beef, ham, cheese and an infinite variety of other savoury fillings.

A lunch in a café might comprise a *Koffietafel* ("coffee table"), similar to a Dutch breakfast, plus fruit and perhaps a hot dish in winter; *Uitsmijter*, an open sandwich, with roast beef, meat balls, ham or cheese on bread topped with fried egg; or *Erwtensoep*, a thick soup with peas and pork.

Dinner is the main meal of the day, usually taken early at 6pm or 6.30pm. If you are on a tight budget, look out for the "Tourist Menu" sign, indicating a three-course main meal for an all-inclusive price. Restaurants displaying the sign "Neerland Dis" serve regional specialities.

You can find every type of cuisine in Amsterdam, from Argentinian to Thai, but, as far as most visitors are concerned, the city's gastronomic forte is Indonesian cuisine, a legacy of Dutch colonialism. The *pièce de résistance* is the *rijsttafel*, an exotic variety of meat, fish and vegetable dishes such as saté, spicy meatballs and *loempia* (a kind of egg roll), all served with steamed rice.

Bear in mind that 15 percent service charge and VAT are invariably included in bills, both for restaurants and bars, and there is no compulsion to tip in addition.

## Restaurants

See also hotel listings for recommended hotel restaurants open to non-guests.

### AMSTERDAM
**Bojo** £
Lange Leidsedwarsstraat 51
Tel: 020-622 7434
Good value Indonesian food just off Leidseplein. Open all night.
**Christophe** £££
46 Leliegracht
Tel: 020-625 0807
Christophe Royer, a Toulouse chef, earned his Michelin star deservedly for this extremely chic, upmarket restaurant.
**D' Theeboom** ££
210 Singel
Tel: 020-623 8420
A charming French bistro with imaginitive, delicious cooking.
**De Blauwe Hollander** £
Leidsekruisstraat 28
Tel: 020-623 3014
Straightforward wholesome Dutch food in cosy setting.
**Golden Temple Vegetarian Restaurant** £
126 Utrechtsestraat

Tel: 020-626 8560
Some people come just for the salad buffet, but the main courses feature Indian, Mexican and vegetarian cuisine.
**Halvemaan** £££
320 Van Leijenberghlaan
Tel: 020-644 0348
John Halvemaan, formerly of the Amstel Hotel, opened his own restaurant in a southern suburb a few years ago and it's worth the 25-minute taxi ride from the centre. Asian and Mediterranean influences.

## Price Guide

Price for a three-course meal for two, including two glasses of wine and service:

| | |
|---|---|
| £££ | More than f.250 |
| ££ | f.150–250 |
| £ | Less than f.100 |

**La Rive** £££
Amstel Hotel
Professor Tulpplein 1
Tel: 020-622 6060
Closed: lunch Saturday and Sunday. French cuisine in intimate and elegant hotel restaurant. Faultless service. Robert Kranenbourg was the first chef in Holland to earn two Michelin stars.
**Lucius Seafood Restaurant** ££
247 Spuisstraat
Tel: 020-624 1831
Fresh shellfish platters and a diverse selection of what's at the market that day.
**The Pancake Bakery** £
191 Prisengracht
Tel: 020-625 1333
This is the place to try oversized Dutch pancakes, savoury or sweet. A wonderful atmosphere in a 17th-century warehouse cellar on a canal.
**Poentjak Pas** £
366 Nassaukade
Tel: 020-618 0906
Like dining in the home of your Indonesian aunt. Delicious, reasonable, and a good atmosphere.
**Speciaal** £
Nieuwe Leliestraat 142

Tel: 020-624 9706
Unspecial street in the Jordaan district, but good Indonesian food, including *rijsttatel*, in a semi-tropical setting.
**Umeno** ££
Agamemnonstraat 27
Tel: 020-767 6089
Closed: Monday. Good Japanese restaurant patronised by businessmen, fairly close to RAI exhibition centre.
**Witteveen** £
256 Ceintuurbaan
Tel: 020-662 4368
This elegant old world restaurant takes you back in time. A simple menu of classics like filet of sole and *entrecôte* is offered.
**Yamazato** £££
Okura Hotel
Ferdinand Bolstraat 333
Tel: 020-678 8351
Best Japanese food in Holland. Afterwards go up to the 23rd floor for a drink with a view.

### THE HAGUE
Note: there are also many good, lower priced restaurants in the city.
**Corona** £££
Corona Hotel
Buitenhof 39–42
Tel: 070-363 7930
Fax: 070-361 5785
Sophisticated French cuisine.
**Djawa** £
12a Mallemolen
Tel: 070-363 5763
Djawa is considered one of the best restaurants in The Hague.
**It Rains Fishes** ££
123 Noordeinde
Tel: 070-365 2598
Thai-French cuisine in this restaurant with a stylish ambience.
**Kandinsky** £££
Kurhaus Hotel
Gevers Deynootplein 30,
Scheveningen
Tel: 070-416 2636
Fax: 070-416 2646
Innovative classic cuisine.
**Le Bistroquet** ££
98 Lange Voorhout
Tel: 070-360 1170
Diplomats and the theatre-going crowd love to dine at this cosy bistro.

## Drinking Notes

The most popular drinks are fresh coffee and lager. Holland is the world's number one producer of beer and the local lager is served in cafés and restaurants throughout the country, usually in 25cl measures. Heineken is the most popular. Foreign brands are available at much higher prices. The native gin is *jenever*, drunk neat (and traditionally knocked back in one) or with a beer chaser. Various varieties include *oude* (old), which is the sweeter, and *jonge* (young), the more powerful. The place to try out the local spirits and liqueurs is a *proeflokaal* or tasting house, the best known being De Drie Fleschjes in Amsterdam (see *Nightlife*).

**Le Haricot Vert** ££
9a Molenstraat
Tel: 070-365 2278
Family-run French bistro with "old Paree" atmosphere.
**Mero** ££
50 Schokkerweg
Tel: 070-352 3600
This seafood *shock* attracts an upmarket crowd for its fresh assortment from calamari to caviar.

### ROTTERDAM
**Blauwe Vis** ££
Weena-zuid 33
Tel: 010-213 4243
A late night dinner and dancing spot in a former pedestrian tunnel – one of Amsterdam's most unique nightspots.
**Brasserie Boompjes** ££
Boompjes 701
Tel: 010-413 6070
Built overlooking the Meuse river with wonderful views and a lively bistro ambience.
**Cafe Restaurant Loos** ££
1 Westplein
Tel: 010-411 7723
In the maritime quarter, this restaurant attracts an artistic crowd. Dine simply or extravagantly in a post-modern ambience.
**Chalet Suisse** ££

Kievitslaan 31
Tel: 010-436 5062
Located in the park in the maritime quarter, by the Euromast. Swiss/Dutch kitchen.
**Dewi Sri** ££
Westerkade 20
Tel: 010-436 0263
Colonial atmosphere and regal *rijsttafels* (and prices).
**Estaminet Het Gelagh** ££
40B Witte de Withstraat
Tel: 010-240 0333
Charming *eetcafé* with Belgian influence. Try some mussels and beer from the tap.
**Old Dutch** £££
Rochussenstraat 20
Tel: 010-436 0344
Heavy beams and traditional Dutch food in a stylish setting.
**Parkheuvel** £££
Heuvellaan 21,
Tel: 010-436 0530
Bauhaus-style building in the park overlooking the port, with terrace dining in the summer.

## Cafés

Every Dutch town has a choice of cafés, invariably serving good coffee – often with apple tart or spicy biscuits. A typical brown café is an intimate, semi-bohemian bar with nicotine-stained walls (hence the name), rugs on tables, sawdust on the floor and newspapers to peruse. These are usually frequented by the locals (as well as tourists) and are places where you can often get good quality food at reasonable prices or linger over a drink and a book on a rainy afternoon.

Cafés displaying a marijuana plant sign sell soft drugs as well as coffee.

See the *Nightlife* section for café and bar listings.

# Culture

## Museums

There are more than 600 museums in Holland, with 440 of them listed in the Attractions booklet (f.1) from vvv offices. The entry price varies; some museums are free. A Museum Year Card gives free admission to all of them – see the box overleaf.

Most museums are open from Tuesday–Sunday 10am–5pm. On public holidays they normally open Sunday hours.

Listed below are some of The Netherlands' most important museums and public art galleries.

### ALKMAAR
**Kaasmuseum** (Cheese Museum)
2 Waagplein
Tel: 072-511 4284
Antique cheese-making implements. Open: April–October, Monday–Thursday and Saturday 10am–4pm, Friday 9am–4pm.

### AMERSFOORT
**Museum Flehite**
Westsingel 50
Tel: 033-4619 987
Archaeology and history of the town. Open: Tuesday–Friday 10am–5pm, Saturday and Sunday 1–5pm.

### AMSTERDAM
**Ajax Museum**
Arena Stadium, 3 Arena Boulevard
Tel: 020-311 1333
New museum at the stadium in the southeast of the city. History of the football team. Video installations and multimedia. Open: daily 9am–6pm. Closed: match days. (Metro: Centraal Station to Strandvliet.)
**Allard Pierson**
127 Oude Turfmarkt
Tel: 020-525 2556

The University of Amsterdam's archaeological collection. Open: Tuesday–Friday 10am–5pm, Saturday, Sunday and public holidays 1–5pm. (Tram: 4, 9, 16, 24, 25.)

**Amstelkring Museum**
40 Oudezijds Voorburgwal
Tel: 020-624 6604
Golden Age merchant's house with clandestine Catholic church in the attic (renovation of which will be completed in autumn 1999). Open: Monday–Saturday 10am–5pm, Sunday and public holidays 1–5pm.

**Amsterdam Historical Museum**
92 Kalverstraat or
359 Nieuwezijds Voorburgwal
Tel: 020-523 1822
Paintings, prints and objects relating to the history of the city. Open: Monday–Friday 10am–5pm, Saturday and Sunday 11am–5pm. (Tram: 1, 2, 4, 5, 9, 16, 24, 25.)

**Anne Frank House**
263 Prinsengracht
Tel: 020-556 7100
Hiding place of the Frank family 1942–44. Photos and text of the history of World War II.An extensive addition in the adjacent building, with café, bookshop and new exhibition space, opens in autumn 1999. Open daily 9am– 7pm; 1 April–31 August 9am–9pm. Closed day of Atonement (Yom Kippur 29/9). (Tram 13, 14, 17, 20; Bus 21, 170, 171, 172).

**Artis 23**
38–40 Plantage Kerklaan
Tel: 020-523 3400
Comprises a zoo, planetarium, aquarium, and geographical and zoological museums. Open: Monday–Sunday and public holidays 9am–5pm; 1 January 10am–5pm. (Tram: 9.)

**Bijbels Museum**
366 Herengracht
Tel: 020-624 2436
Museum of biblical antiquities. Open: Monday–Saturday 10am–5pm, Sunday and public holidays 1–5pm. Closed: 30 April and 1 May. (Tram: 1, 2, 5.)

**The Holland Experience**
Waterlooplein 17
Tel: 020-422 2233
A 25-minute trip through The

The **Museum Year Card** allows free entry to all museums in The Netherlands. The card costs f.55 for people aged 19 to 64; those aged 18 or under pay f.25, and those aged 65 or more pay f.45. It is valid for one calendar year.

The Museum Card can be obtained at vvv Tourist Information offices and many museums. A passport photo is required when purchasing the card. Special exhibitions with a separate admission charge may not be covered by the Museum Card.

Netherlands with the help of multi-dimensional film. Open: late March to end September, 9.30am–7pm; winter 9.30am–6pm. Admission fee includes entry to Rembranthuis.

**Joods Historisch Museum**
2–4 Jonas Daniel Meijerplein
Tel: 020-626 9945
Paintings, objects and documents relating to the history of the Jewish people in Amsterdam and Holland. Open: Monday–Sunday and public holidays 11am–5pm. Closed: 1 January and Day of Atonement (Yom Kippur 29/9).

**Koninklijk Paleis**
Dam Square
Tel: 020-6204060
Former Town Hall converted into a Royal Palace by Louis Napoleon in 1808. Open: Tuesday–Thursday 1–4pm; Easter, Summer and Autumn school holidays daily 12.30–5pm. Call to confirm times.

**Madame Tussaud's Waxworks**
Dam 20
Tel: 020-622 9949
National and international figures; various themes including Rembrandt. Open: Monday–Sunday 10am–5.30pm. (Tram: 1, 2, 4, 5, 9, 16, 24, 25.)

**Nederlands Scheepvaart Museum**
(Maritime Museum)
Kattenburgerplein 1
Tel: 020-523 2222
Excellent museum of maritime history. Features a replica of the VOC sailing ship *The Amsterdam*

along with a golden sloop once used by the Queen. Open: Tuesday–Saturday 10am–5pm, Sunday and public holidays 1–5pm. (Bus: 22, 28.)

**Rembrandthuis Museum**
4 Jodenbreestraat
Tel: 020-520 0400
Rembrandt's home is appropriately furnished with original etchings and has been recently renovated. Open: Monday–Saturday 10am–5pm, Sunday and public holidays 1–5pm. Admission fee includes entry to The Holland Experience. (Tram: 9; Metro.)

**Schiphol Aviodome Museum**
201 Westelijke Randweg (Schiphol airport)
Tel: 020-604 1521
Aviation and space travel, past and present, with a glimpse into the future. Open: 1 April–30 September daily 10am–5pm; 1 October–31 March Tuesday–Friday 10am–5pm, Saturday and Sunday 12–5pm. (Train.)

**'t Kromhout Werf Museum**
(Dockyard Museum)
147 Hoogte Kadijk
Tel: 020-627 6777
Working shipyard, dedicated to restoring historic vessels. Open: Monday–Friday 10am–4pm. Closed: public holidays. (Tram: 7, 9, 20; Bus: 22, 32.)

**Theatre Museum**
168 Herengracht
Tel: 020-551 3300
Lavishly decorated house used for changing displays of everything from costumes to TV and video. Has a charming café with garden. Open: Tuesday–Sunday and public holidays 11am–5pm. Closed: 30 April. (Tram: 13, 14, 17, 20.)

**Tropenmuseum**
2 Linnaeusstraat
Tel; 020-568 8200
Great for rainy days. Walk through typical streets from India to China, with authentic smells. "World" music concerts. Open: Monday–Friday 10am–5pm, Saturday, Sunday and public holidays 12 5pm. Closed: 30 April, 5 May and 25 December. (Tram: 6, 9, 10, 14.)

**Verzetsmuseum** (Dutch Resistance Museum)
61 Plantage Middenlaan

Tel: 020-620 2535
Now in a new location opposite
Artis 200. Sobering and fascinating
account of the Dutch Resistance
during World War II. Open:
Tuesday–Friday 10am–5pm,
Saturday, Sunday and public
holidays 12–5pm. Closed: 1 May.
(Tram: 7, 9, 14, 20.)

**Willet Holthuysen Museum**
605 Herengracht
Fine 18th-century house with formal
garden. Open: Monday–Friday
10am–5pm; Saturday and Sunday
11–5pm. (Tram: 4, 9, 14, 20.)

## DELFT
**De Porceleyne Fles**
Rotterdamseweg 196
Tel: 015-256 0234
Shop and Delftware exhibition.
Open: Monday–Saturday 9am–5pm,
Sunday 10am–5pm.

**Koninklijk Nederlands
Legermuseum** (Royal Netherlands
Military and Weapons Museum)
"Generaal Hoefer" 1 Korte Geer
Tel: 015-215 0500.
Dutch military history. Open:
Monday–Friday 10am–5pm,
Saturday, Sunday and public
holidays 12–5pm.

**Lambert van Meerten Museum**
Oude Delft 199
Tel: 015-212 1858
Collection of Netherlands tiles and
Delftware. Open: Tuesday–Saturday
10am–5pm, Sunday from 1pm.

**Stedelijk Museum Het Prinsenhof**
St Agathaplein 1
Tel: 015-260 2397
Open: Tuesday–Saturday
10am–5pm, Sunday from 1pm.

## DORDRECHT
**Dordrechts Museum**:
Museumstraat 40
Tel: 078-648 2148. Open:
Tuesday–Sunday 11am–5pm.

**Grote Kerk**
Grote Kerksplein
Open: November–March, Tuesday–
Saturday 10.30am–4.30pm,
Sunday 12–4pm.

**Gemeente Museum Mr Simon van
Gijn**
Nieuwe Haven 29
Tel: 078-6133 793
The charming house of a serious

toy collector. Open: Tuesday–
Sunday 11am–5pm. *Speelgoedhuis*
(toy house) closed Tuesday,
Thursday and Friday.

## ENKHUIZEN
**Rijksmuseum Zuiderzeemuseum**
Wierdijk 1222
Tel: 0228-351111
Outdoor museum with 135 houses
and places of work, many with
authentic interiors, from all over The
Netherlands, surrounded by
reconstructed streets and gardens.
Also indoor museum with displays
on the Zuiderzee area. Open:
Monday–Sunday 10am–5pm (until
7pm in summer). Closed: 1 January.

## GOES
**Museum of South and North
Beveland**
Singelstraat 13
Tel: 0113-228883
Collection of 17th-century paintings,
silver and assorted objects typical
of the region. Open: Tuesday–Friday
10am–5pm, Saturday 1–4pm.
Closed: Sunday and Monday.

## GOUDA
**Stedelijk Museum "De Moriaan"**
Westhaven 29
Tel: 0182-588444
Tobacco pipes, tiles and ceramics.
Open: Monday–Friday 10am–5pm,
Saturday 10am–12.30pm,
1.30–5pm, Sunday 12–5pm.

**Stedelijk Musuem Het Catharina
Gasthuis**
9 Oosthaven
Tel: 0182-588440
Open: Monday–Saturday
10am–5pm, Sunday from noon.

**St Janskerk**
Achter de Kerk 16
Tel: 0182-512684
Open: Monday–Saturday 9am–5pm.
Closed: Sunday and public holidays.

## BURGH HAAMSTEDE
**Delta Expo**
Neeltje Jans Island
Tel: 0111-652702
Exploration of the workings of the
massive Delta Plan storm-surge
barrier. Open: April–October daily
10am–5.30pm; November–March,
Wednesday–Sunday 10am–5pm.

## HAARLEM
**Frans Hals Museum**
62 Groot Heiligland
Tel: 023-516 4200
Works by Frans Hals and Haarlem
masters, old pharmacy, doll's
houses. Open: Monday– Saturday
11am–5pm, Sunday and public
holidays 1–5pm. Closed: 1 January
and 25 December.

**Teylers Museum**
16 Spaarne
Tel: 023-531 9010
The oldest museum in Holland,
housed within an 18th-century
building. Collections include prints,
drawings, paintings, coins, fossils
and minerals. Open:
Tuesday–Saturday 10am–5pm,
Sunday and public holidays
12–5pm.

## THE HAGUE
**Clingendael**
Wassenaarseweg
Japanese Garden. Open: early May
to mid-June, daily 9am–8pm.

**Haags Gemeentemuseum**
Stadhouderslaan 41
Tel: 070-338 1111
Costume museum, paintings and
applied art. Open: daily 11am–5pm.

**Haags Historisch Museum**
Korte Vijverberg 7
Tel: 070-364 6940
Open: Tuesday–Friday 11am–5pm,
Saturday and Sunday 12–5pm.
Open Monday in winter.

**Madurodam**
1 George Maduroplein
Tel: 070-355 3900
The Netherlands in miniature. Fully
and beautifully renovated. Open:
Tuesday–Saturday 10am–5pm,
Sunday 11am–5pm.

**Museon**
Stadhouderslaan 41
Tel: 070-338 1338
Popular scientific exhibits – great
for kids. Open: Tuesday–Friday
10am–5pm, Saturday and Sunday
from 12pm.

**Omniversum**
President Kennedylaan 5
Tel: 070-354 7479
Space theatre and planetarium.
Open: daily 10am–5pm (may
change according to season).

**Panorama Mesdag**
Zeestraat 65
Tel: 070-310 6665
One of the few remaining panorama paintings, on a huge circular canvas, which shows the beach at Scheveningen in 1881. Well worth a visit. Open: Monday–Saturday 10am–5pm, Sunday from 12pm.
**Ridderzaal**
Binnenhof 8a
Part of Dutch Houses of Parliament. Open: Monday–Saturday 10am–4pm.
**Rijksmuseum Meermanno-Westreenianum**
Prinsessegracht 30
Tel: 070-346 2700
Open: Tuesday–Friday 11am–5pm, Saturday and Sunday 12–5pm.
**Vredespaleis** (Peace Palace)
Carnegieplein 2
Tel: 070-302 4242
Guided tours hourly from

10am–3pm Monday–Friday. Reservation recommended.

---

### KERKRADE
**Industrion Museum of Industry**
Museumplein 2
Tel: 045-567 0809
Dynamic exhibitions about man and machine in the past, present and future. Open: Tuesday–Saturday 10am–5pm.

---

### LEIDEN
**Academisch Historisch Museum**
73 Rapenburg
Tel: 0715-277242
Wide collection of objects and documentation of university history and student life. Open: Wednesday–Friday 1–5pm. Admission free. Conducted tours on request.
**Gemeentearchief Leiden**
2a Boi-sotkade
Tel: 0715-120191

Records of the city from about 1300. Library has a collection of drawings and photographs of Leiden and the surrounding area. Open: Monday–Friday 9.30am–5pm, Saturday 9am–12.15pm.
**Leiden American Pilgrim Collection**
Beschuitsteeg 9
Tel: 0715-122413
Based around the group of English Pilgrims who settled in Leiden in 1609 and left on the *Mayflower* in 1620 for America. This novel exhibition contains records such as letters and certificates and interesting prints of Leiden in the 16th century. Open: Wednesday–Saturday 1–5pm.
**Molenmuseum "De Valk"**
1 Tweede Binnenvestgracht
Tel: 0715-165353
Windmill and furnished miller's house plus exhibitions on the role and workings of windmills generally.

## The Top Art Galleries

● **Amsterdam:**
**Rijksmuseum**
42 Stadhouderskade
Tel: 020-6732121
The National Gallery of The Netherlands. Stupendous collection ranging from old Dutch Masters (Rembrandt's *Night Watch*) to Asiatic art and doll's houses. Open: daily 10am–5pm. Closed 1 January. (Tram: 1, 2, 5, 6, 7, 10, 16, 24, 25.)
**Stedelijk Museum of Modern Art**
13 Paulus Potterstraat
Tel: 020-573 2737
Continually changing displays of modern art. Open: Monday–Sunday 11am–5pm. (Tram: 2, 5, 20.)
**Van Gogh Museum**
7 Paulus Potterstraat
Tel: 020-570 5200
After a complete renovation the museum will reopen June 1999 with a new wing for exhibition space designed by Kisho Kurokawa. Outstanding collection of paintings and drawings of Vincent van Gogh and his contemporaries. Open: Tuesday–Saturday 10am–5pm, Sunday and public holidays 1–5pm. (Tram: 2, 5, 16.)

● **The Hague:**
**Mauritshuis**
8 Korte Vijverberg
Tel: 070-302 3456
A Dutch Renaissance mansion which houses paintings by Rubens, Vermeer, Rembrandt and more – the Royal Collection of Old Masters. Open: Tuesday–Saturday 10am–5pm, Sunday from 11am.
**Museum Mesdag**
Laan van Meerdervoort 7f
Tel: 070-362 1434
Hague and Barbizon school art, including Delacroix, Mauve and Breitner. Open: Tuesday–Sunday 12–5pm.
**Schilderijengalerie Prins Willem V**
Buitenhof 35
Tel: 070-318 2486
The country's first ever art gallery. Open: Tuesday–Sunday 11am–4pm.

● **Leiden:**
**Stedelijk Museum De Lakenhal** (Municipal Museum)
28–32 Oude Singel
Tel: 0715-165360
Paintings by Rembrandt, Jan Steen, Lucas van Leyden and Gerard Dou. Sculptures, decorative glass and

silver from the 17th century; rooms in the styles of the 17th to 19th century. Open: Tuesday–Friday 10am–5pm, Saturday, Sunday and public holidays 12–5pm.

● **Otterlo (near Arnhem):**
**Kröller-Müller Museum**
Hoge Veluwe National Park
Tel: 0318-591041.
One of Europe's finest art museums. 276 Van Gogh paintings and others by Seurat, Mondrian, Braque, Gris. Modern sculptures in the garden include works by Moore and Maillol and Jean Dubuffet's *Jardin d'Email*. Open: Tuesday–Sunday 10am–5pm. (Bus 12 from Arnhem station.)

● **Rotterdam:**
**Boijmans van Beuningen Museum:**
Museum Park 18–20
Tel: 010-441 9400
From Old Masters to Surrealism and modern art. They will be renovating extensively in 1999, and some of the galleries will be closed during this time. Open: Tuesday–Saturday 10am–5pm, Sunday from 11am.

Open Tuesday–Saturday 10am–5pm, Sunday from 1pm.

**Rijksmuseum het Koninklijk Penningkabinet**
28 Rapenburg
Tel: 0715-120748
The national collection of coins, paper money, medals, engraved gems and seals. Open: Tuesday–Friday 10am–5pm, Saturday, Sunday and public holidays 12–5pm.

**Rijksmuseum van Geologie en Mineralogie**
17 Hooglandse Kerkgracht
Tel: 0715-143844
Minerals, meteorites, textiles and gems; geology and biology of The Netherlands. Open: Monday–Friday 10am–5pm, Sunday 2–5pm.

**Rijksmuseum van Oudheden**
28 Rapenburg
Tel: 0715-163163
Archaeological treasures from Egypt, Greece, Italy, the Roman Empire and The Netherlands. Open Tuesday–Friday 10am–5pm, Saturday, Sunday and public holidays 12–5pm. Closed: 1 January, 3 October and 25 December.

**Rijksmuseum voor Volkenkunde**
(Museum of Ethnology)
1 Steenstraat
Tel: 0715-168800
Artefacts from all territories outside Europe. Open: Tuesday–Friday 10am–5pm, Saturday, Sunday and public holidays 12–5pm. Closed: 1 January and 3 October.

## MAASTRICHT

**Bonnefanten Museum**
Avenue Ceramique 250
Tel: 043-329 0190
Archaeology, old and contemporary art. Distinctive building with a silver dome. Summertime terrace with views over the River Maas. Open: Tuesday–Sunday 11am–5pm.

## MIDDELBURG

**Zeeuws Museum**
Abdij 3
Tel: 0118-626655
Regional archaeology, industry and rural life. Open Tuesday–Saturday 11am–5pm, Sundays and public holidays 12–5pm.

## OUDEWATER

**Heksenwaag**
Leeuweringerstraat 2
Tel: 0348-563 400
Witchcraft. Open: April–October, Tuesday–Saturday 10am–5pm, Sunday from 12pm.

## ROTTERDAM

**Diergaarde Blijdorp**
Van Aerssenlaan 49
Tel: 010-465 4333
Rotterdam's zoo with animal houses designed according to De Stÿl principles. Open: daily 9am–5pm.

**De Dubbelde Palmboom**
Voorhaven 10–12
Tel: 010-217 6767
Life and work in the Maas river region. Open: Tuesday–Friday 10am–5pm, Saturday and Sunday from 11am.

**Euromast**
Parkhaven 20
Tel: 010-436 4811
Open daily 9am–6pm (from mid-March to mid-October until 9pm).

**Kijk Kubus**
Overblaak 70
Tel: 010-414 2285
Open: mid-March–December, Monday–Friday 10am–5pm, Saturday and Sunday 11am–5pm.

**Kunsthal**
West Zeedijk 341
Tel: 010-440 0301
In Rem Koolhaas' modern building is a permanent collection and changing contemporary art shows. Open Tuesday–Saturday 10am–5pm, Sunday 11am–5pm.

**Maritiem Museum Prins Hendrik**
Leuvehaven
Tel: 010-413 2680
Maritime museum. Open: Tuesday–Saturday 10am–5pm, Sunday from 11am.

**Museum voor Volkenkunde**
Willemskade 25
Tel: 010-411 1055
Ethnology. Open: Tuesday–Friday 10am–5pm, Saturday and Sunday 11am–5pm.

**Nederlands Architecture Institute (NAI)**
Museumpark 25
Tel: 010-440 1200
Exhibitions on architecture. Open:

Tuesday–Saturday 10am–5pm, Sunday 12–5pm. Closed: Monday.

**Schielandshuis Historisch Museum**
Korte Hoogstraat 31
Tel: 010-2176767
Paintings and prints on historical themes. Open: Tuesday–Friday 10am–5pm, Saturday and Sunday from 11am.

## UTRECHT

**Centraal Museum**
Agnietenstraat 1
Tel: 030-236 2362
Archaeology and history of Utrecht. Open: Tuesday–Saturday 10am–5pm, Sunday from 1pm.

**Domtoren**
Domplein
Tel: 030-291 9540
Highest church tower in The Netherlands. Open Monday–Friday 10am–5pm (except mid-October to March), Saturday and Sunday from 12pm all year round.

**Museum het Catharijneconvent**
Nieuwe Gracht 63
Tel: 030-231 7296
Superb museum of religious art. Open: Tuesday–Friday 10am–5pm, Saturday and Sunday from 1pm.

**Museum van Hedendaagse Kunst**
Achter de Dom 12–14
Tel: 030-231 4185
Contemporary art. Open: Tuesday–Sunday 12–5pm.

**Nationaal Museum van Speelklok tot Pierement**
Buurkerkhof 10
Tel: 030-231 2789.
Mechanical musical instruments. Open: Tuesday–Saturday, excellent guided tours on the hour from 10am–5pm, Sunday from 12pm.

**Nederlands Spoorwegmuseum**
(Dutch Railway Museum)
Maliebaan Station
Tel: 030-230 6206
Trains, trams, rolling stock and memorabilia. Open: Tuesday–Friday 10am–5pm, Saturday and Sunday 11.30am–5pm.

**Rietveld-Schröder House**
50 Prins Hendriklaan
Tel: 030-236 2310
A contemporary house designed in 1924 by acclaimed architect Gerrit Rietveld. Tours are held throughout the day, but it is advisable to book,

especially for English speakers.
Open: Wednesday–Saturday
11.30am–3.30pm, Sunday
12.30–3.30pm.
**Zuylen Slot**
Oud Zuilen, Tournooiveld 4
Tel: 030-244 0255
Attractive moated castle and
museum. Open: mid-March–
October, Tuesday–Saturday. Guided
tours are available – phone first.

## VLISSINGEN
**Vlissingen Municipal Museum**
Bellamypark 19
Tel: 0118-412498
Open: Monday–Friday 10am–5pm,
Saturday and Sunday 1–5pm.
Closed 1 January.

## ZAANDAM
**Zaans Historisch Museum**
Lagedijk 80
Tel: 075-616 2862
Reopens in September 1999 as a
furnished period house of the
1830s. Open Tuesday–Saturday
10am–5pm, Sunday noon–5pm.
(Train: Centraal Station to Zaan,
then bus 88.)
**Zaans Museum**
Schansend 7
Tel: 075-616 8218
New museum focusing on themes
of the Zaan region – wind, water
and industry, etc. (headset
commentary in English). Changing
local art exhibitions. Open:
Tuesday–Saturday 10am–5pm,
Sunday noon–5pm. (Train: Centraal
Station to Zaan, then bus 88.)

## ZIERIKZEE
**Maritiem Museum Zierikzee**
(Martime Museum)
Mol 25
Tel: 0111-452000
Open: 1 April–31 October and in
school holidays, Monday–Saturday
10am–5pm, Sunday 12–5pm.

## Performing Arts

The number of cultural centres in
The Netherlands has recently been
swelled by two new complexes: Het
Muziektheater on Waterlooplein,
Amsterdam, and Anton Philips Zaal
in The Hague. The national opera,

## Ticket Offices

● **Amsterdam:**
For most of the annual 12,000
concerts, theatre, ballet and
opera performances in
Amsterdam, seats can be
booked in advance at one of the
**vvv theatre booking offices**
situated in the information
offices at Stationsplein,
Leidseplein and inside Centraal
Station. Open: Monday–Saturday,
10am–4pm. No bookings by
telephone. The monthly
programme is available in
"What's on in Amsterdam,"
f.3.50 from the vvv.
   Tickets can also be booked at
the **Amsterdam Uit Buro (AUB)** at
26 Leidseplein/corner.
Marnixstraat, 1017 PT
Amsterdam, tel: 020-621 1211.
Open daily 10am–6pm.

● Reservations can be made
from abroad via the **National
Reservations Centre (NRC)**, P.O.
Box 404, 2260 AK
Leidschendam, tel: 070-419
5500, fax: 070-419 5519.


ballet and theatre companies are all
based in Amsterdam.
   In Amsterdam, over the last
weekend in August, theatre, dance
and music companies from all over
The Netherlands perform extracts
from their year's forthcoming
programme in the streets and
squares of the city (the Uitmarkt). In
June the country presents an
ambitious month-long arts
programme called "Holland Festival",
which takes place in cultural
centres across the nation, featuring
national and international artists.
   Most performances are in Dutch
but during the Holland Festival
foreign companies also perform in
different languages. For details
contact: Holland Festival, Kleine
Gastmanplantsoen 21, 1017 RP
Amsterdam.
   See *Festivals* for details of other
special events in the arts.

*Music*
The Netherlands has several
symphony orchestras of international
repute. The Amsterdam
Concertgebouw Orchestra achieved
world-wide fame under the baton of
Bernard Haitink. The Rotterdam
Philharmonic and the Residentie
Orchestra of The Hague are also
well known. Small ensembles
including the Eighteenth-Century
Orchestra, the Amsterdam Baroque
Orchestra and the Schonberg
Ensemble are very successful.
   There is a wide range of jazz and
improvised music; Willem Breuker
and Misha Mengelberg have an
international reputation.

*Opera and Musicals*
The main opera companies are: The
Netherlands Opera Company, which
stages about 10 productions a year,
mainly in Amsterdam and The
Hague; and the Forum Opera
Company, which performs mostly in
the east and south. Visiting
companies often perform at the RAI
congress centre.
   Musicals are popular in The
Netherlands. Several companies
tour the country with Dutch
productions and adaptations from
foreign musicals, which are
presented mainly at the elegant
century-old Carré on the Amstel.

*Ballet*
The Amsterdam-based National
Ballet Company performs
traditional, classical and romantic
ballets. The Netherlands Dance
Theatre in The Hague specialises in
modern dance. The Scapino Ballet
performs narrative ballets mainly
for young people.

## Cinema

The Netherlands not only shows
imported films in the original
language with Dutch subtitles, but
is also acquiring an international
reputation for its own home-
produced films. The Rotterdam Film
Festival (January/February) and the
Utrecht Film Festival (September)
provide a chance to see the past
year's production of Dutch films.

# Nightlife

## Amsterdam

After dark in Amsterdam, entertainment focuses on three main areas: Leidseplein, for lively discos and nightclubs; Rembrandtplein for clubs, cabarets and strip shows pandering to older tastes; and the Red Light District, notorious for scantily dressed females sitting in windows and notice-boards saying "room to hire".

Strip shows, porn videos and sex shops centre on the main canals of Oude Zijds Voorburgwal and Oude Zijds Achterburgwal. The smaller, sleazier streets leading off these two canals are best avoided, and you are advised never to take photographs.

On an entirely different note, you could spend the evening on a candle-lit canal cruiser, with wine and cheese or full dinner provided.

In any case, try out one of the numerous brown cafés (see *Where to Eat: Cafés*), or alternatively one of the new-wave bars, with cool, whitewashed and mirrored walls, an abundance of greenery and a long list of cocktails. Some cafés and bars have live music, often jazz or blues.

Here is a selection of recommended nightspots, including cafés, bars, clubs and music/dance venues:

**Americain**
American Hotel
Leidseplein 28
Splendid Art Nouveau café overlooking Leidseplein, very popular amongst fashionable locals. Mata Hari had her wedding reception here.

**Bamboo Bar**
Lange Leidsedwarsstraat 66
Live jazz and blues in an exotic setting.

**BIMhuis**
Oudeschans 73
The "in place" for jazz, especially modern and improvisational.

**Boom Chicago**
Leidseplein
Tel: 020-423 0101
An improvisational comedy club which performs in English at a renovated theatre.

**De Drie Fleschjes**
Gravenstraat 18
Traditional *proeflokaal* just off the Dam where you can sample local spirits and liqueurs.

**Escape**
11 Rembrandtplein
A cavernous disco with a variety of music, and a lively, mixed crowd.

**Eylders**
Korte Leidsedwarsstraat
Former haunt of the literati, just by Leidseplein. Occasional modern art exhibitions.

**Havana**
Reguliersdwarsstraat 17–19
Up-market gay bar with yuppie clientele and super-cool atmosphere – starting bar for later drinking and dancing at the Exit disco at No 42.

**Het Hok**
Lange Leidsedwarsstraat 134 Café specialising in chess, backgammon and draughts.

**Hoppe**
Spui 20
Smoke-filled and crowded bar, unremarkable except for the fact that the locals all love it. Crowds usually spill out on to the street.

**It**
Amstelstraat 24
Music is a mix of all the new sounds, something for everyone, and special theme evenings make this one of the city's top discos.

**Melkweg**
Lijnbaansgracht 234a
Off-beat arts centre-cum-club near Leidseplein, with concert hall, disco, experimental plays (some in English) and art exhibitions. Dope and space cakes for sale.

**Odeon**
Singel 460
Elegant 17th-century house, converted into disco and café, with suitably smart clientele.

**Paradiso**
Weteringschans 6–8
Jjust off Leidseplein. The hot spot for rock, reggae and live pop concerts.

**Roxy**
Singel 465
House-style disco, but with eclectic theme nights for a rather older audience.

**Schiller**
Rembrandtplein 26
This café is worth visiting for the splendid Art Deco interior and interesting after-theatre crowd.

**Sinners in Heaven**
Wagenstraat 3
The hip, "upmarket" crowd comes here to dance and mingle.

**Soul Kitchen**
Amstelstraat 32
The name says it all – good dance venue.

## The Hague

Look for the free listings magazine, *Den Haag Day by Day* at hotels and the vvv.

Nightlife revolves around the music bars and late-night cafés, such as **Jazz Café Le Musicien**, Van Bylandtstraat 191 (live bands Wednesdays and Fridays), and **La Valetts**, Nieuwe Schoolstraat 13a. The casino at the **Kurhaus**, Scheveningen, is open daily 2pm–2am.

## Rotterdam

Look for the local listings magazine *Rotterdam This Month*, free from hotels and the vvv.

A popular jazz venue is the Jazzcafé Dizzy, s'Gravendijkwal 129. **Rotown**, 19 Nieuve Binnenweg, hosts local and well-known bands during the week, or visit Holland Casino's **The Gambler** at 624 Weena for another kind of action. At the **Hilton Hotel**, Weena 10, the disco attracts a cosmopolitan crowd and the hotel's casino is open 2pm–2am. **De Après Skihut**, 29 Stadhuisplein, is a lively spot modelled on a skihut, with dancing and entertainment.

# Festivals

## January

**Leiden**, 14–21 January: a lively jazz week in this university town.
**Rotterdam**, 25 January–4 February: International Film Festival.

## February

Big pre-Lent carnivals take place all over the country, especially in the southern provinces of Noord Brabant and Limburg, but with parades in Amsterdam and The Hague as well. Forget about Rio; temperatures are low here in February, so don't expect scanty costumes. Floats are wittily decorated, and there is always lots of beer.
**Rotterdam**, 26 February–4 March: The Dutch ABN Bank hosts its International Tennis Tournament which brings world-class stars to Rotterdam.

## March

**Amsterdam**, 1–3 March: the Antiquarian Book Fair; Good Friday: the dramatic and emotional St Matthews Passion is performed by the Concertgebouw Orchestra.
**Amsterdam, Maastricht**, 9–17 March: the European Fine Art Fair brings hundreds of antique and fine art dealers together and attracts thousands of visitors.
**Lisse**: 29 March–24 May: this is the month the world-famous tulip park, De Keukenhof, opens for the bulb season.

## April

**Amsterdam**, 1 April–31 October: the city switches on its illuminations, turning the canals into a fairyland.
**Alkmaar**, 13 April–14 September: the traditional cheese market opens with porters wearing their historic guild uniforms. There are usually demonstrations of old crafts during the very colourful market that is held every Friday.
**The Hague**, 15 April–21 October: the International Rose Exhibition featuring 20,000 roses and some 350 varieties, opens in Westbroekpark.

## May

**Amsterdam**, every Sunday, May–October: Antique Markets on the Waterlooplein.
**The Hague**, May and June: the beautiful Japanese Gardens at Clingendael Park are open; 3 May–30 September: the city's Antique Market, along the elegant Lange Voorhout, opens every Thursday (until 9pm) and Sunday (until 6pm).
**Scheveningen**: the wonderfully colourful Vlaggetjesdag at Scheveningen Harbour marks the opening of the herring season. All the fishing boats are decorated with flags, there is a traditional market and, of course, lots of fish to eat.

The Dutch have a way of eating herring which will either delight or repel you. They first dip the raw, salted fish into a dish of chopped onion, raise it by the tail above their tilted head and then slowly lower the fish into open mouths. At this point you either swallow or gag.

## June

This is Holland Festival month, with various events taking place around the country.
**Amsterdam**: International rowing competition, the Bosbaan; 3 June–2 September: the summer-long Open-Air Theatre season begins in Vondelpark, where it has all been happening since the 1960s.
**Scheveningen**, 2 June: a wonderfully exhilarating Air Show with stunt flying demonstrations;

16–24 June: fly your kite, it's great fun, at the International Fokker Kite Festival, with kite fliers from as far as Japan coming to fly their often strange-looking but always wonderfully colourful kites on the beaches of Scheveningen.
**The Hague**, 9 and 10 June: horse-lovers flock for the grand equestrian event, called Paardendag. Two days of events, again on the lovely Lange Voorhout.
**Rotterdam**, 16–23 June: Poetry International. Draws poets and poetry lovers from around the world.
**Assen**: the big, and very noisy, International Netherlands Motorcycling T.T. Grand Prix. Big bikes, newest in fashion leathers, lots of fun, bring your own earplugs.

## July

**Amsterdam**: International Chess Tournament, with many well-known Masters. International Ballet Festival at the Muziektheater.
**The Hague**, 13–15 July: the North Sea Jazz Festival with all the big names in jazz at the Congress Centre. A must for jazz lovers.
**Zandvoort**, 26–29 July: the KLM Golf Open Championship.
**Scheveningen**: street parades, with jazz and dixieland concerts, take place along the main boulevard.

## August

**Rotterdam**, 15–19 August: the year's major horse show.
**Leersum**, 18 August: a wonderfully colourful Flower Parade.
**Yerseke**, 18 August: this is the month to eat mussels and the fishing village of Yerseke is the place to eat them, especially on Mussel Day, the first of the new season.
**Amsterdam**, last weekend in August: Uitmarkt Festival, when previews of the next year's artistic events are performed in the city streets and squares.
**Scheveningen**, last weekend in August: major fireworks display for the International Firework Festival.
**Zandvoort**, 26 August: the International Motor Races start,

with Formula 1 drivers competing for the Zandvoort Grand Prix.

## September

Taking place countrywide (date varies each year) is the Monument Preservation Day, when listed buildings around the country are opened to the public.
**Amsterdam**, 3–9 September: the famous Gaudeamus Music Week.
**The Hague**, third Tuesday in September: the State Opening of Parliament by Her Majesty Queen Beatrix. Colourful parade along Lange Voorhout to the Binnenhof (Parliament Square), with the Queen sitting in the traditional Golden Coach.

## October

**Delft**, 11–25 October: the major Art and Antiques Fair.
**Scheveningen**, 19–21 October: Pall Mall Export's International Windsurfing Event. The event that launched a thousand cigarette ads; 28 October: International Beach Motorcycle Races.

## November

**Amsterdam**, 1–4 November: "Jumping Amsterdam", the international horse show at the RAI complex.
Countrywide, 17 November (or nearest weekend): this is the time for children, when St Nicholas arrives in the country from his home in Spain. At all major harbours a traditional steam boat pulls in, complete with St Nicholas, riding on his white stallion and accompanied by his Moorish assistant known as Black Pete.

## December

**Gouda**, 15–25 December: beautiful scenes in this old town where the historical town square is lit by candles. The lighting of the Christmas Tree, accompanied by singing and a carillon concert, is a major crowd-puller.

# Excursions

**Note:** For suggested cycle tours, see the *Getting Around* section.

## Boat Trips & Charter

Water is everywhere in Holland and there are always boats for hire and local tours. Most trips have multilingual guides. Some of the main tourist attractions are listed below.

### NOORD-HOLLAND
#### Amsterdam
Viewing Amsterdam's canal-side mansions from a glass-topped canal cruiser gives you a different perspective on the city. There are several cruise companies and a detailed leaflet may be obtained from the vvv, which will also handle bookings. All cruisers have toilets. Arrangements may be made for groups; there may be dining facilities and music on board.

Most cruises run every 15 minutes in summer and every 30 minutes in winter. The different trips take 60, 75 or 90 minutes. Seeing the city by night on the candlelight and wine cruise, which

## The Museum Boat

Many Amsterdam museums lie on or near the canals. Two boats run every 45 minutes from jetties all over town. On each boat a guide gives details about the different museums. A day ticket costs f.12 and entitles you to discounts on museum entrance charges. A combi-ticket gives free entrance to three museums of your own choice. Tickets may be bought from the vvv tourist office.

runs daily in summer at 9.30pm, except 2 May, will take 120 minutes.

**Departure points:**
**Rederij Amsterdam:** opposite Heineken Brouwerij, 21 Nicolaas Witsenkade, 1017 ZS, tel: 020-626 5636 (75 mins/f.15).
**Holland International:** opposite Central Station, Prins Hendrikkade 1012 TK, tel: 020-622 7788 (60 mins/f.15).
**Rederij P Kooy BV:** near Spui, Rokin t/o No 125, 1012 KK, tel: 020-623 3810 (60 mins/f.13).
**Rederij Lovers BV:** Prins Hendrikkade opposite No 25, 1000 AV, tel: 020-622 2181/3 (facilities for disabled/60 mins/f.15).
**Meyers Rondvaarten:** Damrak, jetty 4–5, 1012 LG, tel: 020-623 4208 (60 mins/f.12).
**Algemene A-Dam Rederij Noord-Zuid:** Stadhouderskade 25, opposite Parkhotel, 1071 ZD, tel: 020-679 1370 (75 mins/f.17.50).
**Rederij Plas CV:** Damrak, Jetty 1–3, 1012 LG, tel: 020-624 5406 or 622 6096 (60 mins/f.13).

#### Outside the City
For excursions along the picturesque river Vecht or the Loosdrechtse waterway (in Het 'Gooiland') from May to September, contact Wolfrat Rondvaarten, Oud Loosdrechtsedijk 165, 1231 LV, Loosdrecht, tel: 035-5823309.

### ZUID-HOLLAND
A *leede* is a watercourse, so the name of **Leiden** may be interpreted as "a town on the watercourses". During the summer season there are boat trips on the Leiden canals. Departures from Beestenmarkt and Hoogstraat. In the afternoons and evenings there are boat trips to the Kagerplassen lakes (windmill cruise). Information: Rederij Rembrandt, tel: 071-513 4938. Rowing boats are for hire in the summer at the bridge, Rembrandtburg, tel: 071-514 9790.

### ZEELAND
This area is popular with those who enjoy boating. Sailing schools and boat hire companies abound, with

one in virtually every harbour. A special attraction lies in the traditional old sailing vessels of Zeeland. These can be hired, with skipper, from Zeilvloot "De Zeeuwse Stromen",Nieuwe Bogerdstraat 7 4301 CV, Zierikzee, tel: 0111-415 830.

## NOORD-BRABANT
At **Lage Zwaluwe**, Biesboschtours, 7 Biesboschweg, offer boat trips in magnificent scenery. Easter Sunday–June and September, Sundays and public holidays; July and August daily.

## LIMBURG
In **Maastricht**, contact Rederij Stiphout Bordertour, 27 Maaspromenade, tel: 043-3254 151. Several boat trips on the Maas. January–March 2pm and 4pm; 15 April–29 September daily on the hour 10am–5pm. Trips take 1–3 hours (including caves); adults f.8–13.50, children f.4.75–7.75.

## GRONINGEN & FRIESLAND
Around the **IJsselmeer** and in the northern provinces of Groningen and Friesland, boat rental agencies offer a range of craft, some of which have living accommodation.

Especially recommended are the week-long or weekend trips aboard the many antique sailing ships moored in **Harlingen**. For more information, write to: Rederij Vooruit Holland, Geeuwkade 9, 8651 AA IJlst, tel: 0515-531 485. Day boat trips and sailing boat (with skipper) rentals can also be arranged through Zeilvloot Harlingen, Noorderhaven 17, 8861 AJ, tel: 0517-417 101.

## Coach Tours

These may be booked through any vvv office. All depart from Amsterdam.

**City Sightseeing:** Duration 2½/3 hours. Summer, 10am daily. Winter, 2.30pm daily. A drive through Amsterdam which takes in an open-air market, a windmill, the Royal

Palace and a visit to a diamond-cutting workshop. Plus, in winter, a ticket for a canal ride.

**Marken and Volendam:** Summer, 10am and 2.30pm daily. Winter, 10am daily and 2.30pm Sunday only. Duration approx 3½ hours. A chance to see the traditional costumes still worn by many residents in these old fishing villages. Also included is a visit to "De Jacobs Hoeve" cheese farm at Volendam or to the cheesemaker "De Catharina Hoeve" at the Zaanse Schans, plus windmills.

**Grand Holland Tour:** Summer 10am daily. Winter 10am Tuesday, Thursday and Sunday. Duration 8 hours. Lunch not included. First to the flower market at Aalsmeer (or to a clog factory on Saturday and Sunday), on to a porcelain factory in Delft, Rotterdam and then The Hague, including, in summer, the miniature village of Madurodam.

**Tulip fields and Keukenhof flower exhibition:** 10am and 2.30pm daily. 25 March–14 May. Duration 3½ hours. A drive through the colourful flower-growing region with a visit to a bulbgrower and the Keukenhof flower exhibition.

**Alkmaar Cheese Market and Windmills:** 9am departures every Friday from 21 April–15 September. Duration 4½ hours. Alkmaar on Fridays shows the traditional market life of old Holland. Porters in ancient dress carry cradles heaped with yellow cheeses. Then to de Zaanse Schans to visit a windmill.

## Steam Trains

● **Hoorn-Medemblik** (Noord-Holland): historic steam train ride through characteristic landscape and attractive villages. Open: May to beginning of September (except Monday).
● **Goes-Oudelande** (Zeeland): steam train ride through the typical South Beveland landscape with fields divided by hedges. Open: mid-May to beginning September and Christmas holiday.

# Shopping

## Opening Times

Shops are generally open from 9am–6pm or 6.30pm Tuesday–Friday, 1–6pm or 6.30pm Monday (closed am), and 9am–5pm Saturday. On Sunday it is almost impossible to shop, although you may find some grocery stores open in the larger cities. All shops must close for one half-day a week by law, but all of them display their opening times in the door or window. Shops open late (until 9pm) one day a week in big cities: Thursday in Amsterdam and The Hague; Friday in Rotterdam and Delft.

## Amsterdam

Bargains are a rarity but browsing is fun, particularly in the markets and the small specialist shops. For general shopping the main streets are Kalverstraat and Nieuwendijk, for exclusive boutiques try P.C. Hooftstraat and for the more off-beat shops, head to the Jordaan northwest of centre where many of the local artists live. Two unusual shopping centres are worth a visit: Magna Plaza opposite the Royal Palace and Kalvetoren on Kalverstraat.

The vvv Tourist Office produces brochures on shopping for antiques and diamonds. These give maps, route descriptions, places of interest and a list of addresses and shop specialities.

## ANTIQUES
Nieuwe Spiegelstraat (starting opposite the Rijksmuseum) is lined with small and immaculate antique shops. Look out for old Dutch tiles, copper and brass, glass, pewter, snuff boxes, clocks and dolls; and

look for the names of respected dealers like Frides Lameris, Ines Stodel, Frans Leidelmeijer and Jaap Polak. In markets, beware of imitation antique copper and brass, made in Tunisia.

## ART & PRINTS

The major museums and art galleries have excellent reproductions of paintings in their collections, particularly the Rijksmuseum and the Stedelijk. There are numerous small commercial galleries selling original oil paintings, watercolours, drawings, engravings and sculpture. For old prints and engravings, try Antiek-markt de Looier, Elandsgracht 109.

## BOOKS

The city has an exceptionally large choice of books, both new and second-hand. For second-hand English-language books, try Book Traffic, Leliegracht 50 (near the Anne Frank House). Allert de Lange, Damrak 62, is strong on literature, travel and art; the Athenaeum Boekhandel & Nieuwscentrum, Spui 14–16, has a superb selection of literature and academic books and very helpful staff.

## CLOTHES

The major department stores are concentrated along Kalverstraat and Nieuwendijk, but the biggest and most prestigious is De Bijenkorf, Dam 1. For designer labels, try P.C. Hooftstraat, Rokin, Van Baerlestraat and Beethovenstraat; for less conventional boutiques, the Jordaan or the side streets between the canals are the places to go. Also visit Magna Plaza shopping complex opposite the Royal Palace or Kalvertoren on the Kalverstraat by the Muntplein.

## JEWELLERY

Jewellery shops all over town have eyecatching displays of modern and traditional pieces, some original and designed on the spot. Note: the fact that Amsterdam is a major diamond-cutting centre doesn't mean you'll get them cheap.

## PORCELAIN

Cheap imitations of the familiar blue Delftware are sold all over town. The genuine article, always with a capital "D", is sold at Royal Delft's official retail branch, De Porceleyne Fles, Muntplein 12. You can watch painting demonstrations in their showrooms.

Focke & Meltzer, with branches at P.C. Hooftstraat 65–69 and the Okura Hotel, have a good choice of porcelain and glass, and some attractive reproduction Delft tiles. For a huge range of antique tiles, try Eduard Kramer, Nieuwe Spiegelstraat 64.

## OTHER GIFTS

**Tulips and bulbs** are always popular. If you fail to get them at the flower market (see below) you can buy them at higher prices at Schiphol Airport. Other things typically Dutch are **cigars** (the best known shop is Hajenius, Rokin 92), **chocolates** (made by Van Houten, Verkade and Droste; Pompadour at Huidensstraat 12 has a superb selection), Edam and Gouda **cheeses** and **clogs**. Excursions to Volendam and Marken usually take in a cheese farm and a visit to a craftsman making clogs – one pair can take as little as five minutes to make.

## SCHIPHOL AIRPORT

If there are any guilders left you will no doubt be tempted by the enormous range of goods at Schiphol Airport. Apart from duty-free goods, there is an excellent food section, selling smoked Dutch eel and cheeses, and shops specialising in bulbs and seeds, flowers, Delftware, clothes and souvenirs. The shops are pricey, but you can find some unusual and affordable gifts.

## MARKETS

Amsterdam's street markets are a source of amusement and interest.

**Flower market:** Singel. Monday–Friday 9am–6pm, Saturday 9am–5pm. Probably Amsterdam's

Tourists from non-European Union countries are entitled to claim back the 20 percent local Value Added Tax (BTW) on any goods purchased with a value of over f.300. Upon purchasing the item the shopkeeper has to fill in a certificate of export (form OB90). When leaving The Netherlands the form is handed to Dutch customs. The returned certificates of export are sent back to the shops and the BTW will then be forwarded by cheque or postal order.

Some shops are affiliated to "Holland Tax Free" shopping which caters for the repayment of this tax, but administration and service charges are deducted from the amount of tax refunded. For further details, obtain the leaflet, "Tax Free for Tourists" from Schiphol airport or vvv offices.

most famous market, housed in boats and bright with colours and perfumes even in the depths of winter. Prices are reasonable and quality is excellent.

**Flea market:** Waterlooplein. Monday–Saturday 10am–5pm. Lively and fun.

**Farm produce:** Noordermarkt or Oudemanhuispoort. Saturday 10am–4pm.

**Book market:** Oudemanhuispoort. Monday–Saturday 10am–4pm. Unusual books and prints. Also Friday 10am–6pm at the Spuiplein and during the summer one Sunday each month at Dam Square or next to the Muzeiktheater.

**Stamp market:** NZ Voorburgwal. Wednesday and Saturday 1–4pm. Stamps and coins.

**Open-air antique market:** Nieuwmarkt. Daily 9am–5pm May–September.

**Antiques, curiosities and junk:** "De Looier", 109 Elandsgracht. Saturday–Thursday 11am–5pm Indoor market.

**Textile market:** Noordermarkt/ Westerstraat. Monday 9am–1pm.

**Bird market:** Noordermarkt. Saturday 8am–1pm.
**Art market:** Thorbeckeplein. April–October, Sunday 10.30am–6pm. Artists sell their own drawings and paintings.
**General markets:** Albert Cuypstraat: Monday–Saturday 9.30am–5pm; Westerstraat: Monday 9am–1pm.

## The Hague

The main shopping street is Grote Marktstraat. Here you will find the department store De Bijenkorf, notable for its fine architecture and interiors. Behind is a network of covered arcades lined with small and characterful shops. For art, antiques and cafés, go to Noordeinde.

## Rotterdam

In Rotterdam the better shops are concentrated around Lijnbaan and Binnenweigplein. Antiques, art and crafts can be found in the market on Mariniersweg, in the old port, on Tuesday and Saturday 9am–5pm and also in the museum quarter on side streets.

# Sport

## Participant Sports

### CANOEING
For all information contact The Netherlands Canoe Association, Postbus 1160, 3800 BD, Amersfoort, tel: 033-4622341, fax: 033-4612714.

### CYCLING
The leaflet *Cycling in Holland*, available from The Netherlands Board of Tourism (see *Planning the Trip: Tourist Offices*) contains information on long-distance routes and special holidays. See also *Getting Around: Cycling*.

### FISHING
*Holland – The Ideal Angling Country* contains information on licences, angling centres, fishing excursions and the hire of equipment and can be had from The Netherlands Board of Tourism (see *Planning the Trip: Tourist Offices*) or contact the NNVS, Postbus 288, 3800 AG Amersfoort, tel: 033-463 4924.

### GOLF
For information on courses open to non-members, contact the Dutch Golf Federation, Postbus 221, 3454 ZL, De Meern, tel: 030-662188, fax: 030-662 1177.

### HORSE RIDING
For details of facilities ask The Netherlands Tourist Board for its *Horseriding* brochure or contact the NHS, Postbus 456, 3740 AL Baarn, tel: 035-548 3600, fax: 035-541 1563.

### SAILING
For an introduction to the multitude of options, with practical advice and suggested itineraries, ask for the brochure *Holland: Watersports Paradise*, which is available from The Netherlands Board of Tourism . The NBT also has brochures on *Traditional Sailing, Boat Hire* and *Sailing Schools*. See also *Excursions: Boat Trips & Charter*.

### WATERSPORTS
Apart from the brochure mentioned above, information on windsurfing, skiing, motor-boating, etc can be obtained from Koninklijk Nederlands Watersport Verbond, Postbus 53034, 1007 RA Amsterdam.

## Spectator Sports

### FOOTBALL
Amsterdam's Ajax is one of the top European clubs and tickets for games, played at the Ajax Stadium, 3 Arena Boulevard, in southeast Amsterdam, can be booked in advance through the vvv or travel agents, or bought at the gate.

Many cities in The Netherlands have clubs of world class (e.g. Rotterdam's Feyenoord FC; The Hague's FC Den Haag; PSV Eindhoven). The local vvv can supply details.

### GOLF
The Open Dutch Championship Golf Tournament is held in Hilversum every July.

### MOTOR RACING
National and international events are held at the Circuit Park Zandvoort329. The big event of the year is the Zandvoort Grand Prix, which is held at the end of August. Assen is the place to be in June for the International Netherlands Motorcycling T.T. Grand Prix.

### TENNIS
The International Tennis Tournament, held in Rotterdam in late February/early March, brings world-class players to The Netherlands. The Dutch Open Championships are held in Amsterdam every July.

# Language

## Useful Words

Almost every Dutch person speaks English, but it is useful to recognise some words and phrases in timetables and menus and you will gain more respect if you try to speak the language, however hesitantly.

**Monday** *Maandag*
**Tuesday** *Dinsdag*
**Wednesday** *Woensdag*
**Thursday** *Donderdag*
**Friday** *Vrijdag*
**Saturday** *Zaterdag*
**Sunday** *Zondag*

**Hello/Goodbye** *Dag* (pronounced "Dach")
**Good morning** *Goedenmorgen*
**Good afternoon** *Goedenmiddag*
**Good evening***Goedenavond*
**Goodbye** *Tot ziens*

## Numbers

**One** *Een*
**Two** *Twee*
**Three** *Drie*
**Four** *Vier*
**Five** *Vijf*
**Six** *Zes*
**Seven** *Zeven*
**Eight** *Acht*
**Nine** *Negen*
**Ten** *Tien*
**Twenty** *Twintig*
**Thirty** *Dertig*
**Forty** *Veertig*
**Fifty** *Vijftig*
**Sixty** *Zestig*
**Seventy** *Zeventig*
**Eighty** *Tachtig*
**Ninety** *Negentig*
**Hundred** *Honderd*

**See you later** *Tot straks*
**Thank you very much** *Dank u wel*
**Please** *Als't u blieft*
**I am sorry, pardon** *Neemt u mij niet kwalijk*
**How much does it cost?** *Wat kost dit?*
**Open** *Open*
**Closed** *Gesloten*
**Entrance** *Ingang*
**Exit** *Uitgang*
**Admission free** *Vrije toegang*
**Yes** *Ja*
**No** *Nee*
**Left** *Links*
**Right** *Rechts*
**No smoking** *Verboden te roken*

**Church** *Kerk*
**Theatre** *Theater*
**Cinema** *Bioscoop*

**No entry** *Verboden toegang*
**Through traffic** *Doorgaand verkeer*
**No parking** *Niet parkeren*
**Hospital** *Ziekenhuis*
**Police** *Politie*
**Fire brigade** *Brandweer*

**Bottle** *Fles*
**Glass** *Glas*
**Cup** *Kop*
**Lager***Bier*
**Dutch gin** *Jenever*
**Coffee, wine, liqueur** *Koffie, wijn, likeur*
**Newspaper** *Krant*
**Magazines** *Tijdschriften*

**Airmail** *Luchtpost*
**Ordinary mail** *Gewone post*
**Registered** *Aangetekend*
**Stamp** *Postzegel*

# Further Reading

## General

***Of Dutch Ways*** by Helen Colijn, Dillon Press Inc, Minneapolis, Minnesota (1980).
A personal look at Holland by the granddaughter of a Dutch Prime Minister who now lives in the USA but returns each year.
***The British and the Dutch*** by K.H.D. Haley, George Philip, London (1988).
Political and cultural relations through the ages. A clear and exciting study of the love-hate relationship between the countries.
***The Dutch Revolt*** by Geoffrey Parker, Peregrine Books (Penguin Group), London (1988).
A brilliant picture of the character of the Dutch in their revolt against the Spanish overlords during the Eighty Years War (1568–1648).
***Dutch Art and Architecture 1600–1800*** by Jakob Rosenberg et al., Penguin, London (1988).
A standard work, first published in 1966, rewritten by popular demand, with new insights especially into the works of Frans Hals and Rembrandt. Richly illustrated but in monochrome.
***The Story of Amsterdam*** by Anthony Vanderheiden, Rootveldt Boeken, Amsterdam (1987).
All the clichés about the Dutch capital in one volume of colour photographs and colourful prose.
***The Embarrassment of Riches*** by Simon Schama, University of California Press (1988).
An academic but very readable insight into Golden Age culture.
***The Low Sky: Understanding the Dutch*** by Han Vander Horst, Scriptum/Nuffic Books, The Hague (1996).
This thoughtful book investigates below the surface, into the dilemmas and taboos of modern Holland.

## Other Insight Guides

The *Insight Guides* series, with 200 titles, plus more than 100 *Insight Pocket Guides* and over 80 *Insight Compact Guides*, covers every major travel destination in the world.

*Compact Guide: Holland* is in essence a mini-encyclopedia designed for handy on-the-spot reference and, as such, is the ideal companion to this Insight Guide. For maximum convenience, a mine of information is closely cross-referenced with pictures and maps.

A companion to the present volume is *Insight Guide: Amsterdam.* Combining incisive text and incomparable photography, it is a stimulating companion on any trip to the capital of The Netherlands.

*Compact Guide: Amsterdam* distils the essence of this absorbing capital into this unbeatably portable format, integrating text, pictures and maps to guide the visitor on the ground.

*Insight Pocket Guide: Brussels* is written by local hosts who have designed specific itineraries and made personal recommendations to help you make the most of your stay. The book comes with a full-size fold-out map.

# ART & PHOTO CREDITS

*Cartographic Editor* **Zoë Goodwin**
*Production* **Stuart A Everitt**
*Design Consultants*
**Carlotta Junger, Graham Mitchener**
*Picture Research* **Hilary Genin**

# Index